Southern Baptist Preaching Today

SOUTHERN BAPTIST PREACHING TODAY

R. Earl Allen and Joel Gregory
Compilers

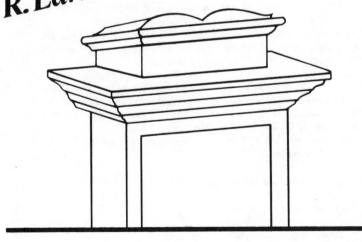

BROADMAN PRESS
Nashville, Tennessee

© Copyright 1987 • Broadman Press
All rights reserved
4257-14
ISBN: 0-8054-5714-3

Dewey Decimal Classification: 252
Subject Heading: SERMONS—COLLECTED WORKS // PREACHING
Printed in the United States of America

Library of Congress Cataloging-in-Publication Data

Southern Baptist preaching today.

1. Southern Baptist Convention—Sermons.
2. Baptists—Sermons. 3. Sermons, American.
I. Allen, R. Earl. II. Gregory, Joel, 1948–
BX6333.A1S68   1987   252'.06132   87-6335
ISBN: 0-8054-5714-3

Dedication

From Joel C. Gregory . . .
to Linda
and to Garrett and Grant

From R. Earl Allen . . .
to Norma Joyce
to James Todd, Dee, Christina,
   and James Clinton Allen
to Joy Earline, Stephen Gordon,
   Justin Allen, and Joshua Gordon
     Newcom
and in memory of Norma Alline Allen

Preface

Not since H. C. Brown's two-volume compilation, *Southern Baptist Preaching,* over a quarter-century ago has Broadman dared attempt such a vast undertaking. This book, *Southern Baptist Preaching Today,* compiled by R. Earl Allen and Joel C. Gregory, contains sermons from forty-nine pastors from across the Southern Baptist Convention.

At least a decade ago Dr. Allen, himself a widely published author-pastor, envisioned a new work of this nature. Five years ago he first discussed the matter with his Broadman editor. He invited Dr. Gregory, then a professor of preaching at Southwestern Baptist Theological Seminary, to collaborate on the compilation.

It was tentatively decided to include not only pastors but also preachers who were involved in denominational work with Southern Baptist Convention agencies, state Conventions, colleges and universities, seminaries, and other Southern Baptist institutions.

Through considerable discussion and prayer, however, it was decided to include only representations of Southern Baptist *pastoral* preaching. The process of inviting pastors to contribute has been fraught with soul-searching. Southern Baptists by reputation have many effective, dynamic pastoral preachers, not merely forty-nine but perhaps thousands of pastors who proclaim the Word of God with the anointing of the Holy Spirit, none of whose "words fall to the ground" (1 Sam. 3:19).

Broadman and Drs. Allen and Gregory recognize that many preachers may be disappointed they were not included, but for this volume the number had to be narrowed down. Fifty-five were finally invited. For various reasons six were not able to contribute a sermon. All were requested to submit a sermon, a biographical sketch, and an article on "How I Prepare to Preach," somewhat similar to the makeup of Brown's earlier works. Some sent only a sermon without a biographical sketch or an article on their preparation methodology. Forty-two of these preachers—some in two or three short paragraphs, others in several pages— share with you how they prepare. Only in a few instances do they touch upon their actual delivery in the pulpit.

There is no substitute for a powerful pulpit. Years ago a young pastor was on the horns of a dilemma in a church business meeting. He was caught in the crossfire (many of our readers will identify with that seemingly hopeless frustration). Two of the men stormed out of the church building. One was heard to exclaim, "That preacher shore is a mess!" To which the other man replied, "Yep, but he shore can preach!"

It is no wonder Southern Baptists have grown. These sermons represent a cross-section of Southern Baptists, some who gladly wear theological labels and others who eschew them. They pastor in all parts of the nation—from the East to the West, from the North to the South. As in the song, they are "red and yellow, black and white—they are precious in His sight." By affiliation and support all of them are genuine Southern Baptists. Some readers may exclaim, "Aha, you've just included the 'Super Church' pastors." Not so. A few of their churches would be considered "small." Yes, at least two of them number more than twenty thousand members.

As you read, study, and treasure these sermons, you'll see one overriding similarity. They are filled with the Holy Scriptures, the Bible, the authoritative written Word of God. In many resources you will sense that the Bible is somehow being rationed, as though it were still being chained in some sanctuary or monastery. Not in *Southern*

Baptist Preaching Today. The Word of God is used copiously, lavishly, extravagantly in these pages.

Laying all theological debate aside, these pastors have something else in common: they all believe the Bible is the "sword of the Spirit," the inspired, written Word of God.

Here they have preached "the whole counsel of God" from Genesis to Revelation. Only a few books of the Bible have been left unquoted. The content is as varied as the preachers themselves. There are sermons on the attributes of God, the second coming of the Lord Jesus, the Bible, discipline in the church, evangelism, missions, soul-winning, hell, prayer, Christian giving, the essence of the Gospel, loving one another, living in fellowship with Christ, victory over depression, citizenship, God's help, the power of the Holy Spirit, the personhood of Christ, the moral climate, spiritual growth, religious liberty and Christian citizenship, Christian characteristics, only one sermon (would you believe it?) on the prodigal son, and more!

We pray that this volume will be well-received and will be a blessing to preachers, Sunday School teachers, evangelists, missionaries—in fact, every Christian who loves the preaching of the glorious Gospel of the Son of God.

R. Earl Allen and Joel Gregory
and The Broadman Staff

Contents

The Sermons

R. Earl Allen

What God Is Like
Luke 15:1-32

A book entitled *What Is God Like?* was written by Eugenia Price about ten years after her conversion. She devoted a whole chapter to the story of the prodigal son, with whom she strongly identified. "Is God really like this?" she wrote. "Does the mere fact of our coming to Him, even in our disgusting condition, bring joy to His heart? According to Jesus Christ, yes! And according to anyone who has dragged his wasted life home to the Father, yes."

In the fifteenth chapter of Luke, Jesus gave us a clear picture of the heart of God. "And he [the prodigal son] arose, and came to his father. But when he was yet a great way off, his father saw him, and had compassion, and ran, and fell on his neck, and kissed him" (Luke 15:20).

Jesus' purpose in coming to earth was to reveal God the Father, as well as to die for mankind's sin. He particularly displayed the Father's boundless love that desired to gather in all of lost mankind. The Bible says, "No man hath seen God at any time; the only begotten Son, which is in the bosom of the Father, he hath declared him" (John 1:18). But even yet, and even as Christians, the concepts we have of God are very inadequate: they are far too small.

The truth of the matter is that many people do not understand the very nature of God, the heart of God, and the mind of God. The Father sent Jesus into the world that we might better know what God is like. What *is* God like?

Job acknowledged what all of us feel when he exclaimed, "Oh, that I knew where I might find him" (Job 23:3). He felt that if he could find God and share with Him the emotions of his own heart, surely God would not only know more about Job, but Job would know more about God.

The idea of God is foreign to many people, and the concept of God is inadequate in all of us. Some feel they must have a God they can see and identify with—"a God with a face." Some want a God they can manipulate. It is often "the God we want" versus "the God we need."

Others have strange ideas about what God is like. Is He a giant policeman, an absentee landlord, or a ranch foreman riding herd on all of us? Some have coined such expressions as "The Man Upstairs" and "Somebody up there likes me." Many feel they have outgrown God, while some even claim that God is dead.

But God is not dead; God is very much alive and would be alive in you, if you would let Him speak to your heart. How real is God to you?

We will not have a genuine spiritual revival in our land until first we have among our people far more respect for the awesome majesty of Almighty God. There is a tremendous difference between *informality* in our services and *familiarity* toward the sacred things of God.

The Pharisees and Sadducees of Jesus' day hugged to their bosoms the laws of the God of the Old Testament and those rituals with which they worshiped Him. They tried to counteract the effectiveness of Jesus' ministry by confining Him to their forms and rituals. Jesus knew they completely misunderstood God. So He spoke to them, using stories, as He did many times in His teaching.

If we look at this chapter as a whole, we realize that the first two verses might be called an introduction. Here there is more than an introduction—it is an *interrogation* (vv. 1-2). The leaders of the Jews were challenging Jesus to account for His choice of companions.

The Pharisees could not understand why Jesus associated with sinners. They kept themselves strictly apart from the "common people"; they had no time to spend with those who were lowlier than they.

Years ago I was asked to moderate a meeting where a

church was to renew an annual call to their pastor. The first person who stood to speak said, "I live across the road from the parsonage, and I've watched the preacher. Why, he spends a lot more time visiting people who never come to church than he does those who are members."

What a shock! Could this actually be a New Testament church, where the people were supposed to be interested first in winning others to Christ?

This was the attitude of the Pharisees. They were proud of their status as religious leaders; if Jesus wanted to discuss religion, He should join their private club. They understood what the sabbath meant, but they did not know the meaning of salvation. They memorized the laws of Moses, but they paid no mind to the love of God.

In Matthew 9:12-13 we find that Jesus told the Pharisees plainly, when they had made the same accusation: "They that be whole need not a physician, but they that are sick. . . . I am not come to call the righteous, but sinners to repentance." In contrast to the religious leaders, who overemphasized the details of the Law, Jesus declared that "the Son of man is come to seek and to save that which was lost" (Luke 19:10).

That is what the fifteenth chapter of Luke is all about: lost things—and more precisely: *lost things found.* Jesus came to bring the light of God's love into the world so people might be reconciled to the Heavenly Father.

Philip asked, "Lord, shew us the Father, and it sufficeth us." Jesus answered. "Have I been so long time with you, and yet thou hast not known me, Philip? he that hath seen me hath seen the Father" (John 14:8-9).

Dr. Jack MacGorman many years ago told a very beautiful story. A little girl had shown him a picture of Jesus. As she was moving away, she turned her head and added, "Jesus is the best picture of God that's ever been took." And that's the truth!

We have no actual picture of God, but we have Jesus Christ as His likeness. Jesus most perfectly revealed to us the Father, for He stated, "I and my Father are one" (John

10:30). In Jesus Christ we find everything we need to know about the Father: everything about His sacrificial love, everything about His deep compassion, everything about His holy character, and everything about His immense forgiveness.

God's people knew something about God from their religious rituals and the words of Moses and the prophets, but they had lost sight of His true character. Jesus came to give them a new vision of what the Father was like.

Jesus recognized that the interrogation of the Pharisees stemmed from the fact that they refused to accept Him as the Son of God. They gave Him place only as a teacher among other teachers, rather than *the* Teacher, *the* Immanuel, *the* Messiah. Jesus said, "I, if I be lifted up from the earth, will draw all men unto me" (John 12:32). Jesus Christ is the One who must be accepted!

Jesus responded to the murmuring of the Pharisees by giving three distinct *illustrations* (vv. 3-24) of the love of God. Many feel these pictures are the most beautiful that ever fell from the lips of Jesus. He told the Pharisees three parables: *the seeking shepherd, the searching woman,* and *the suffering father.*

We call the third illustration "the parable of the prodigal son"—but the word *prodigal* is not mentioned. We've focused so much attention on the hog pen that we have left the impression the prodigal son is the hero. God is the hero of this story! He is the One we see in each of these pictures. The thrust of the passage is how much God loves us and not merely the devastation of sin.

We often consider one separate picture without realizing the whole—the truth these three parables, taken together, imply about the Godhead. They emphasize the one overwhelming verity: God loves us and seeks us out! The shepherd exulted, "Rejoice with me; for I have found my sheep which was lost" (Luke 15:8*b*).

First of all, we see God as *The Seeking Shepherd.* Jesus the Son identified Himself as a shepherd: "I am the good shepherd: the good shepherd giveth his life for the sheep"

(John 10:11). Isaiah preached, "All we like sheep have gone astray: we have turned every one to his own way: and the Lord hath laid on him [Jesus] the iniquity of us all" (53:6). We have no hope outside the fold of the Good and Great Shepherd.

When I traveled to the Holy Land the first time, we came to a place in the Judean hills where there were many sheep. We watched as the shepherds masterfully separated their flocks, watering them and taking each flock inside its own fold, which was a pen made of rocks.

I noticed there were no gates, only an opening. Through the interpreter I asked the shepherd, an Arab lad, "Son, where are the gates?"

He beat himself on the chest and answered, "I am the gate. None of my sheep go in and out without me knowing about it." He went on with great detail to explain that he slept in the gateway. Nobody could touch his sheep without his being conscious of it. No animal could come in and destroy them. He himself was the gate.

I ought to have known my Bible well enough to understand that without being told. That is exactly what Jesus taught: "I am the door: by me if any man enter in, he shall be saved, and shall go in and out and find pasture" (John 10:8). Sometimes the sheep go astray. Some of them become lost ignorantly.

In the parable, the shepherd emphasizes the value of the one lost sheep by his diligent search until he finds it. It was an all-absorbing and inconvenient search.

One knotty problem I find in churches is that they spend nearly all of their time and priority on the people in the church and very little on the lost and dying outside the flock of the church. This parable reveals the mind and heart of God, the purpose and compassion of God, that the lost must be found. God is pictured as "The Hound of Heaven" in His search for lost humanity. Ever since Eden, man has been searching for possessions, while God has been searching for persons.

Much of our time as shepherds, I admit, is spent on the

ninety and nine and not on the one that is lost. If we are going to get our priorities right, we must go back and submit to the character of God, which is to search after those who are lost.

Next, we look at *The Searching Woman*. Luke 15:8 reads, "Either what woman having ten pieces of silver, if she lose one piece, doth not light a candle, and sweep the house, and seek diligently till she finds it?" Something precious was lost, and the woman searched urgently all over her house. Coins cannot lose themselves—they are lost by someone.

The coin could represent those in our area who are lost. What about the precious lost souls in our neighborhood? How many unsaved people have slipped through our fingers and away from Sunday School and us?

Some think this coin was of monetary value; perhaps it went beyond that. Many times women in that culture used coins as a necklace or bracelet. Perhaps the coin she had lost had been a gift: it was something very precious.

We all have keepsakes we have put away—beyond monetary value. You cannot insure them but you would not sell them. Her coin may have been such a keepsake.

She lit a lamp and searched all over the house. Light is a symbol of the Holy Spirit, and with His light we must search for lost souls. They are ... infinitely precious to God. This woman searched—how long? Until she found it! The shepherd searched—how long? Until he found it!

Unfortunately, we too often become judgmental around our churches; we judge who is worth seeking out. We hear words that ought to be foreign to a New Testament Church, such as "selective visitation."

Who, then, ought to be selected? Who is worthy to be saved and added to our churches? Jesus selected everyone of us; He didn't leave any person out. It is not ours to judge the world, for God loves us all, in spite of our waywardness. How dare we decide whom we will visit and whom we will ignore? How many of the people Jesus sought would we have left unnoticed and untouched?

When people come to church, one of two things will happen. They will either get in or they will get out! They will hear the Gospel and be saved under the convicting power of the Spirit of God, or they will get out where they will not have to hear the Gospel and will not be convicted of sin.

If you had been living in the depths of the Depression, would someone have thought you were a good prospect for their church because you were able to carry the burden and finances of the church? I suspect that several of us would have been passed by.

We're not in God's army until we become tired; we are in this battle until the end, and we are to search until we *find them*—wherever they are and whoever they are!

Then Jesus told a third story, about *The Suffering Father*. The father had two sons, the younger and the elder. We usually focus on the prodigal son, but the father is the hero of the story. He sat on the porch and looked for his wayward boy.

During a revival meeting long ago, I was staying in a home. There was no motel in the little town. As my elderly host ushered me into the bedroom, there were pictures all around—many poses, over many years, of one boy growing up. "My son," the man pointed out. "He's married and gone now."

He asked me if I had any children, and I told him about my family. He confided, "Preacher, I want to tell you something: there's no joy like the joy your children bring you, and there's no hurt like the hurt the children can bring you."

The father in the parable knew this. The younger son demanded, "I want what's coming to me, and I want it right now!"

Then, being already distant from his father's attitudes and principles, the son traveled to a far country. There he wasted not only his money but his life. This son portrays the individual that is lost deliberately.

In the far country, the younger son had some acquaintances for a while—as long as he had plenty of money. But when he was starving, no one gave him food. Jesus continued, "And he would fain have filled his belly with the husks that the swine did eat" (Luke 15:16).

The Jews were most attentive to Jesus at this point. As far as they were concerned, this was total depravity—it was as low-down as a Jewish boy could go. Their law had declared, "Cursed is he that feeds the swine."

When we hear the word "husks," we think first of that which covers an ear of corn, but in Bible times, what they referred to was a pod, somewhat like a small, dried melon. They were very low in nutrition—filling but with no substance. So many of our people have filled themselves on the pods of this world—and there is no substance in them, nothing satisfying, nothing healing. May God help us to hear His voice and give us an appetite for the matters that count!

The younger son willfully rebelled against his father and lost himself in a far country. But the wonderful fact is that "he came to himself." He mused, "How many hired servants of my father's have bread enough and to spare, and I perish with hunger? I will arise and go to my father" (Luke 15:17-18*a*).

These words, "I will arise" and "when he came to himself," are some of the greatest in the Bible. We *can* come to ourselves. We can come to ourselves and return to God.

So the boy started home, and his father saw him coming a long way off. The boy had his speech ready. He was going to confess he had sinned against his father, giving evidence against himself.

This father had been anxious, gazing down the road with a broken heart. Finally he saw his boy coming home—and then he waited for him? No, he ran to meet him. This pictures the only time we see God in a hurry.

The young man began the speech he had rehearsed. He got as far as, "Father, I am not worthy . . ." when his father hushed him. This son had come home, and the father would hear nothing against him.

I hope we have reached the place in our spiritual journeys where we recognize our unworthiness. Paul came to that place; the closer he approached God, the less he bragged about being an apostle. He confessed to being the chief of sinners.

Much to the young man's surprise, his father took the signet ring off his own finger and put it on the son's hand. It bore his seal and bestowed the authority of sonship: "He's my son!" Then the father commanded the servants to bring a splendid robe and put it on him and shoes on his feet. In those days, servants went barefooted, but the children of the house wore sandals. As the old spiritual goes, "All God's Children Got Shoes!" God does take care of His own!

En route to Ridgecrest, you go through Asheville, North Carolina. There the house Thomas Wolfe grew up in has been made into a museum. They have preserved the chair and desk where he wrote his famous novel, *You Can't Go Home Again*. When I visited that place, I thought, *He was dead wrong!*

You and I have had to go home again and again, like Jacob did when he returned to Bethel and asked God for His forgiveness. When you and I have the Father to whom we can go home, we *can* indeed go home again. That makes all the difference in the world.

Then we need to look at *why* Jesus spoke these parables. There was an *interrogation;* there were three *illustrations.* Now we come to the heart of the matter—the *implication* (vv. 25-32).

Most people focus their attention on the younger son. He had wasted his substance with riotous living, but the elder son was fully as guilty. He misunderstood his father; he rebelled against his father's decisions; he had no love for his brother.

The elder son was in the field: that is, he was busy doing the chores of the place. When he heard the noise and came to the house, he was informed, "Your brother has returned, and your father has killed for him the fatted calf."

"And he was angry, and would not go in: therefore

came his father out, and entreated him" (Luke 15:28). The father ran to one and entreated the other. The father did for the elder son exactly what he had done for the younger one. He treated both of them according to their needs, but the elder son would not go in.

To these Jewish leaders, Jesus was teaching, in effect, "You are like the elder son." He was implying, "You have no idea what My Father is like; you have no realization of why I've come."

The elder son answered his father, "Lo, these many years do I serve thee. . . . and yet thou never gavest me a kid, that I might make merry with my friends: But as soon as this thy son was come, which hath devoured thy living with harlots, thou hast killed for him the fatted calf" (Luke 15:29-30).

You see, the older brother had a bad attitude. He said, "*Your son . . .* devoured his living with harlots!" The father had never used this word—evidently it arose from the jealous mind of the elder son.

Often we have in our churches elder brothers who have no love for a lost world. Sometimes the spirit the unconverted find in our churches isn't conducive to their receiving the Lord. We must be careful how we treat new converts, new Christians—how they see us, the spirit in which we welcome them. Perhaps the greatest sin of the church is an unforgiving spirit.

The father killed the "fatted calf" for his prodigal son. There were no deep freezers. When you wanted to fatten an animal for slaughter, you put it in a small pen and gave it nothing but food and water. It became "the fatted calf," the next one to be served up for company.

The elder brother complained accusingly, in the language of today, "You killed for him the fattest and best calf that we had, and you haven't even given me a billy goat! You haven't given *me* a party!" Obviously, he served his father out of a sense of duty rather than a sense of delight. Have you known people like that?

The father replied to his elder son, "Oh, how much you

misunderstand my heart! All that I have is yours!" If we miss the spirit of service, we bypass the spirit of the father.

In Old Testament times, when the father died, the eldest son had the responsibility of carrying on for the family, and he therefore received the larger part of the estate. This elder brother was determined to stand up for his own rights: "He has gotten his third, and he isn't going to get my two-thirds!" He had doled out his service and said to his father, "I want full payment for doing my duty."

In our churches today, we often see people with a grim sense of duty and a judgmental attitude, like the Pharisees. They count their good deeds and think God owes them something. Don't you believe it!

We must pity the basic emptiness of the elder son. His father did everything he could—except violate the elder's free will. The elder son refused to come in and enjoy the festivities. He only hurt himself. And his refusal did not stop the music and jollity inside, only within his own heart. The father did everything he could for the younger son—except violate his free will; the boy chose for himself to come home.

"It was meet that we should make merry, and be glad: for this thy brother was dead, and is alive again; and was lost, and is found" (Luke 15:32). This final comment reflects God's boundless joy in all who respond to His love.

"All that I have is thine!" Do we claim what our Father promised? James wrote, "Ye have not because ye ask not." Will you come in? And will you ask Jesus to enter your heart?

John R. Bisagno

Into All the World
Matthew 28:18-20

The Great Commission is the magnificent obsession of the Church. It is the heartbeat of our beloved Convention and the very lifeblood of Christendom itself. When we cease to dream, we cease to live. The step from risktaker to caretaker is but a short step to undertaker. In a day in which millions are plunging into eternity without Christ, if we are standing still we are backing up. An automobile company has as its slogan: "We are driven!" As believers, we too are driven. We are driven to the ends of the earth by the Great Commission, to the end of time by the coming of Christ, and to the end of ourselves by love for our Lord.

So profound were the pronouncements and experiences in the life of our Lord Jesus that it was impossible for one man to completely comprehend and record the full magnitude of His ministry. Thus the Holy Spirit assigned not one but four reporters to follow Him. Only in examining the unique contribution of each can one gain insight into the fullness of our Lord's earthly ministry. Nowhere is this more true than in the various accounts of the Great Commission. While Luke records two, one in his Gospel and one in his letter to Theophilus, which we call the book of Acts, and John recorded none, it is still true there are four accounts of the Great Commission. Each account gives a different perspective which, taken together, comprise the whole.

First, the account in Matthew says "Go everywhere."

> And Jesus came and spake unto them, saying, All power is given unto me in heaven and in earth.

> Go ye therefore, and teach all nations, baptizing
> them in the name of the Father, and of the Son, and of
> the Holy Ghost:
> Teaching them to observe all things whatsoever I
> have commanded you: and, lo, I am with you alway,
> even unto the end of the world. Amen.

In verse 18—"in earth," verse 19—"all nations," and in
verse 20—"end of the world." It is quite clear, from Matthew's perspective, that Jesus was emphasizing world penetration.

Each of the evangelists were "coming from somewhere." Their unique backgrounds gave a particular perspective to the divine commission. Matthew was a tax collector, a scribe, a bookkeeper, a statistician, an accountant, a chronicler of events. Matthew took note that Jesus absolutely insisted on "line-upon-line, precept-upon-precept" evangelism. The gospel must penetrate *all* the world. No strata of society was to be excluded, no fortress of hell unpenetrated, no bastion of darkness unimpregnated with the light of the gospel. Every religion must be confronted, every tribe invaded, every error exposed, every language translated, every city and hamlet, every country and continent assaulted with the battering ram of the gospel until, at last, the foundations of hell tremble and Satan's walls crumble to the ground.

> For the darkness shall turn to dawning
> And the dawning to noonday bright!
> And Christ's great Kingdom shall
>   come on earth,
> The Kingdom of love and light!

That means all nations, all cultures, all religions, all ethnic groups, all tribes of the earth—"to the end of the world." Matthew makes it clear that Jesus said "GO EVERYWHERE."

Second, the account in Mark says "Go with Me."

> And he said unto them, Go ye into all the world,
> and preach the gospel to every creature. He that be-

> lieveth and is baptized shall be saved; but he that be-
> lieveth not shall be damned. And these signs shall
> follow them that believe; In my name shall they cast
> out devils; they shall speak with new tongues; They
> shall take up serpents; and if they drink any deadly
> things, it shall not hurt them; they shall lay hands on
> the sick, and they shall recover. So then after the Lord
> had spoken unto them, he was received up into
> heaven, and sat on the right hand of God. And they
> went forth, and preached everywhere, the Lord work-
> ing with them, and confirming the word with signs
> following. Amen (Mark 16:15-20).

Going everywhere into all the world is a thought
frightening beyond words. Mark's perspective is different.
Mark's account of the Great Commission is different because Mark is different. Far from the Roman official that
was Matthew before his conversion, Mark was a nobody.
Some have suggested him to be an older teenager or, at
best, a young man in his early 20s. He had no great wealth
or reputation. He was no great scholar; he held no government position. He was only a servant, and as such, he was
accustomed to being cared for, provided for; greatly secure
under the umbrella of a master who assumed full responsibility for his servant. The exposure of the problems of world
evangelism were staggering to Mark, and he was careful to
record things important to him.

What are the greatest fears of a missionary? There are
four:

First, Satanic opposition. To leave the confines of a
country such as America and march headlong into the satanic strongholds of this earth, the kingdoms of darkness
as yet unopened by the light of the gospel, is a frightening
thought. But Mark hears Jesus say, "In My name, in My
authority, by My personal presence and power, demonic
forces will fall before you. In My name, you shall cast out
devils. Fear not, timid servant, you go not alone to foreign
lands." Jesus says, "When you go, you go with Me, for I will
go with you and before you."

Second, a strange language. Jesus said "Fear not—when we go together, I will empower you to speak with new tongues." No New Testament reference is ever made to garbled gibberish. Tongues are a known language. Not only does Jesus promise to help missionaries to learn the language, but the promise can even include the miraculous capacity, when necessary, to speak a language one does not know.

Third, a hostile environment. Nothing is more devastating to the missionary than culture shock. Everything is different. Everything is difficult: schools, water, food, money. Misunderstanding and suspicion abound. But the promise of Jesus is that, when necessary, He will even provide "miraculous protection" for the missionaries' need to adjust and survive. His reference to surviving deadly serpents and poison potions may well symbolize an all-inclusive umbrella of protection over any and every need in a hostile environment, even to the point of the miraculous when circumstances dictate.

Fourth, rampant disease. What greater fear could a young missionary couple have than for the health of themselves and their children? Jesus' promise to recover from sickness could include not only healing those to whom the missionaries minister, but also themselves and their families. But perhaps the greatest wonder of Mark's entire account is that Jesus would use all this not only to meet the needs of the missionaries, but to authenticate His message to the unbeliever as well. Early on in Exodus, God laid down the principles that He would authenticate His word to those who did not believe by the miraculous; i.e., the shepherd's rod before Pharaoh, not to mention the plagues.

The Pharisees demanded of Jesus, "Show us signs and wonders, and we will believe." Paul added, in essence, "The signs of an apostle characterized his ministry." Jesus' statement in verse 17, "These signs shall *follow* those who believe," means to "engulf" or "create an atmosphere." The presence of the divine, and even the miraculous, touch of God upon a missionary will not only protect him/her, but authenticate his message to such a degree that in that atmosphere men will believe. Young servant Mark makes it clear in verse 20 that this is precisely what happened. "They preached everywhere, the Lord working with them, and *CONFIRMING THE WORD* with signs following" (caps mine).

Luke's account says "Go together." His person-centered account of the Great Commission emphasizes what people one by one can do when they join together. Notice his use of the word "ye" or "you." It is a collective you, an "all of you" to which he refers. He emphasizes it four times, and "they" and "them" five times.

> And said unto THEM, Thus it is written, and thus it behooved Christ to suffer, and to rise from the dead the third day: And that repentance and remission of sins should be preached in HIS name among all nations, beginning at Jerusalem. And YE are witnesses of these things. And, behold, I send the promise of my Father upon YOU: but tarry YE in the city of Jerusalem, until YE be endued with power from on high. And he led THEM out as far as to Bethany, and he lifted up his hands, and blessed THEM. And it came to pass, while he blessed THEM, he was parted from THEM, and carried up into heaven. And THEY worshipped him, and returned to Jerusalem with great joy: And were continually in the temple, praising and blessing God. Amen (Luke 24:46-53, caps mine).

As Southern Baptists, we practice cooperative missions, not only through education and prayer, but through finances and personnel as well. The New Testament church survived against impossible odds and even penetrated the world with the gospel because whatever happened to ALL of them was more important to EACH of them than what happened to ANY of them. The CAUSE was worth any sacrifice for the benefit of the common good. This may be clearly seen in the Book of Acts, where, for the sake of missions and evangelism, houses and lands were sold, and the proceeds laid at the feet of the apostles. The Southern Baptist Cooperative Program makes possible four factors that are essential in world evangelism:

First, penetration. Campus ministries, rescue missions, hospitals, television, radio, theological education, tent evangelism, church planting, medical missions—every strata of life and society is permeated as 3,600 home missionaries penetrate all fifty states, Canada, the Virgin Islands, Puerto Rico, and Samoa, and over 3,700 foreign missionaries bring the gospel light to penetrate the dark corners of 108 world countries.

Second, mutuality. In the 1950s, Wichita, Kansas, had a serious financial recession. Many missionaries supported by independent churches had to be called home. But Southern Baptist missionaries stayed on the field, as the rest of the country picked up the slack for Wichita. In the mid-1980s, Houston was hit by a recession, but no Southern Baptist missionary was ever called home from the field for lack of funds. While Houston suffers, other cities prosper and make up the difference.

Third, presence. Missionaries from many sending agencies spend nearly half their time in the States raising funds, and only half their time on the mission field. Southern Baptist missionaries maintain a perpetual presence in countries to which they are assigned and never spend a minute raising their own support.

Fourth, accountability. A popular television evangelist raises a hundred million dollars a year for his ministry. He is president of the board of his association, his wife is the vice-president, and his son is secretary-treasurer—and there is no accountability. I believe him to be a man of integrity, but a man lacking in wisdom at that point.

Southern Baptists have penetration, mutuality, presence, and accountability.

The account in Acts says "GO FROM HERE."

> But ye shall receive power after that the Holy Ghost
> is come upon you: and ye shall be witnesses unto me

> both in Jerusalem and in all Judaea, and in Samaria,
> and unto the uttermost part of the earth (Acts 1:8).

In Acts, Luke changes his emphasis. He is looking beyond his earthly human experience with Jesus to a strategy of world evangelism. He is now Luke, the missionary, the traveling companion of the world-class evangelist, the Apostle Paul. He is Luke, the mission strategist, and it is he who records Jesus' strategy for the progressive evangelism of the world, beginning at Jerusalem.

Imagine the reticence of the apostles to attempt the Great Commission. It was more than a world mission; it was in many ways a "mission impossible."

1. *It was geographically impossible.* The world had not even been discovered yet. They believed the earth was flat and that to sail the seas was inevitably to drop off into oblivion.

2. *It was physically impossible.* There was no way to go—no boats, planes, radios—nothing.

3. *It was numerically impossible.* There were far too few. At most, no more than 500 followers of Christ could possibly be rallied—and how many of those would "surrender for foreign missions"?

4. *It was financially impossible.* Historians suggest that the wealth of the early church at this juncture of world history was less than the equivalent of $10,000 American dollars. What percentage of your congregation's wealth can you get at any given time? Ten percent? Twenty percent? Suppose it were 50 percent. Can you put on a program of world evangelism for $5,000?

5. *It was legally impossible.* It was against the law to speak or teach in the name of Jesus. Followers of "The Way" were being persecuted, imprisoned, and martyred.

6. *It was socially impossible.* They were the discards and rejects, Paul reminds us in 1 Corinthians 1:26. "For ye see your calling, brethren, how that not many wise men after the flesh, not many mighty, not many noble, are called."

Influence flows uphill, not down. Who would listen to them? Who would believe?

But then they remembered Jesus' admonition to pray. Perhaps someone suggested that rather than fret over what they could not do, *they should do the one thing they could do: pray.* So off to the upper room they went. And in ten days, miracle of miracles, wonder of wonders, the Lord—Who knew all along they could not go to all the world—brought the world to them because they had done what they COULD with what they HAD. At Pentecost, devout men from every nation under heaven heard the gospel in their own language and believed. Miraculously, the simultaneous evangelism of the world began, beginning at Jerusalem. Two years ago, we realized that over one hundred thousand persons from other countries of the world lived within five miles of our church. As at Pentecost, God had literally brought the world to our doorstep. Anxious to seize this marvelous opportunity for our Lord, we began building missions. In just over two years, ten thriving missions under our church's sponsorship flourish in the very shadow of our building.

It is the epitome of hypocrisy to send money to India to witness to a Hindu while we ignore the one who lives next door. World missions "BEGIN AT JERUSALEM." Evangelism begins at home. Missions start at our front door. Luke, the physician, has become Luke the mission strategist and is quick to record Jesus' plan for spiritual conquest of the earth. Begin at home—GO FROM HERE.

In 1967, the coldest day on which a professional football game has ever been played was recorded. In a 67-degree-below-zero chill factor, the Green Bay Packers entertained the Dallas Cowboys for the division championship. With less than a minute to play, the Packers—trailing by just two points—pushed the ball to Dallas' two-yard line. As one, the tens of thousands of Green Bay fans stood and began to cheer: "GO! GO! GO!"

Sportscasters reported it be the most electrifying, pulsating crowd noise they had ever heard, reverberat-

ing, throbbing through the stands, charging the souls of
the players, pumping their adrenaline level to the skies.
The quarterback called the signal, and the center hiked the
ball. As one man, the indomitable Packers, driven by the
cheers of their fans, pushed the ball across the goal line for
the winning touchdown.

History has recorded the familiar sayings of her sons.
Who can forget Patrick Henry's "Give me liberty or give
me death" or MacArthur's "I shall return." But nothing in
or out of sacred literature can compare with the last commandment of our Lord: "Go ye into all the world and preach
the gospel to every creature."

We stand today at our greatest hour of opportunity. We
are at the final juncture of world history. Kingdoms crumble, and men's hearts fail them for fear as the possibility of
the nuclear annihilation of the human race casts its fright-
ful shadow across the path of mankind.

But what an hour for the church! What an hour for
missions and evangelism! With knees knelt in prayer, with
hands filled with more than adequate resources, talent,
funds, and personnel, may Southern Baptists lock arms.
May this be our finest hour as we seize what may be the
best opportunity to bring our world, as a precious gem, to
the feet of our blessed Savior. Surely the Father, the Son,
and the Holy Spirit, the redeemed of the ages, the saints of
the Old and New Testament, are straining at the precipice
of Heaven and saying as one to Southern Baptists:

GO! GO INTO ALL THE WORLD! GO TO EVERY
CREATURE! GO EVERYWHERE! GO WITH ME!
GO TOGETHER! GO FROM HERE! GO! GO! GO!

Morris H. Chapman

When the Trumpet Sounds
1 Thessalonians 4:13-18

When the trumpet sounds, the Lord Jesus is coming. Jesus said, "I will come again" (John 14:3). His promise is the promise of promises!

In 1 Thessalonians 4 Paul describes the first phase of the second coming of Jesus, and he claims a word from God as his authority. Paul said, "For this we say unto you by the word of the Lord" (v. 15). When you have divine revelation you don't need human speculation. We have God's word that Jesus is coming again. And that word is written down in glory. The Psalmist declared, "Forever, O Lord, thy word is settled in heaven" (Psalm 119:89). When God's Word says it, it is settled in heaven, and it ought to be settled on earth.

In Revelation 20, Jesus settled the millennial question. He said we shall reign with Him on earth for a thousand years. Now that's what Jesus says, and I just believe what Jesus says. That's all the sense I've got. Some people say my perspective is too narrow. I simply want to be as broadminded as Jesus.

When I was a boy growing up in a Mississippi Baptist church, I heard a view of the second coming preached which I abandoned as a young ministerial student. For five years as a pastor, I tried to preach amillennialism. I want to tell you something. It won't preach. I don't have one drop of amillennial blood left in my veins. If I did I would go to the hospital and ask for a transfusion! Sometimes I go to the doctor with a sore throat. When he says, "Say, 'ah,'" I say, "I'll not do it!"

Let me give you the names of some of the premillennialists of history. I frankly believe Jesus was one. The second name is *Paul*. The third name is *John*. Then Martin Luther, John Wycliffe, Melancthon, Savonarola, William Tyndale, R. A. Torrey, Alexander Maclaren, Robert Murray McCheyne, Matthew Henry, C. H. Spurgeon, D. L. Moody, Billy Sunday, Gipsy Smith, Adoniram Judson, William Carey, F. B. Meyer, G. Campbell Morgan, J. Hudson Taylor, George Müeller, J. B. Gambrell, Jeff D. Ray, Polycarp, Ignatius, Irenaeus, Tertullian, Justin Martyr, J. R. Graves, Mordecai Hamm, John Wesley, Charles Wesley, John Bunyan, John Milton, George Whitefield, John Knox, A. J. Gordon, H. A. Ironside, R. G. Lee, Leo Eddleman, J. D. Grey, W. A. Criswell, and Billy Graham.

Some call premillennialism fanaticism. Some call it foolishness. Some call it heresy. The Bible calls it the "blessed hope" (Titus 2:13). When Jesus comes He is coming visibly, and He is coming victoriously.

Visibly

Look at the *return* of the Lord Jesus. The Bible says, "For the Lord himself shall descend from heaven" (1 Thess. 4:16). The Lord Himself . . . not somebody else. There will be no substitute. The Lord Himself is coming visibly, bodily, actually, personally, and gloriously!

In Acts 1:10-11, we read, "And while they looked stedfastly toward heaven as he went up, behold two men stood by them in white apparel; which also said, Ye men of Galilee, why stand ye gazing up into heaven? this same Jesus, which is taken up from you into heaven, shall so come in like manner as ye have seen him go into heaven."

This same Jesus who was born of a virgin is coming back. This same Jesus who stilled the raging storm is coming back. This same Jesus who fed the 5,000 is coming back. This same Jesus who was nailed to the cross is coming back. This same Jesus who conquered the grave is coming back.

Jesus went away *visibly* with the scars of the cross upon His body. He's coming back with those same scars. An old infidel once said to Fanny Crosby, "How are you, an old blind woman, going to know Jesus when you come into His presence should He come back?" Fanny Crosby went to her room and wrote that beautiful hymn "I Shall Know Him."

> I shall know Him,
> I shall know Him,
> And redeemed by His side I shall stand.
> I shall know Him
> I shall know Him
> By the print of the nails in His hand.

Paul speaks not only of the *return* of Jesus, he calls our attention to the *rapture* of the saints. When the trumpet sounds, Paul said, "the dead in Christ shall rise first: Then we which are alive and remain shall be caught up together with them in the clouds, to meet the Lord in the air" (1 Thess. 4:16-17). Can God say it any plainer?

The word "rapture" comes from the Latin verb *rapere* which means "to seize, to snatch, to rescue." The word does not appear in the Bible, but the Greek word *harpazō* has the same meaning and is translated "caught up." Whether you say it in Latin, Greek, or English, the Bible declares that when the trumpt sounds, every believer will be raptured.

Jesus will come *suddenly*. The events of His coming will happen in rapid succession. Jesus said, "Behold, I come quickly" (Rev. 3:11). It will be a cataclysmic coming!

Jesus will come *secretly*. Paul said, "The day of the Lord so cometh as a thief in the night" (1 Thess. 5:2). When Jesus comes in the air, He will go unnoticed by the unsaved of the world. Only the saved shall hear the shout of the Savior, the voice of the archangel, and the trump of God. All over the world people will be missing, but they won't be lost. The frantic people who will be sending missing-person bulletins around the world will be the lost ones. The saved dead and the living believers will be "caught up" to meet the Lord in the air.

The Bible says, "In a moment, in the twinkling of an

eye . . . we shall be changed" (1 Cor. 15:52). Now the "blink-ing of an eye" is a long time compared to the "twinkling of an eye." The "twinkling of an eye" is that little sparkle which flashes in your eye when you recognize someone whom you haven't seen in a long while or for whom you have a special feeling. Just that quickly all believers will be drawn to Christ in the air like metal shavings to a magnet.

Oh, to be standing in a cemetery when Jesus comes! As the dead in Christ begin to rise, I'd shout, "Come on, brother! Come on, sister! Let's go!" At the rapture Jesus is coming *for* His saints. Those who are living when He comes will be caught up in the clouds, along with the saved dead whose bodies and spirits will be reunited. These old bodies of the saved, living and dead, will be transformed by the power of Jesus into glorified bodies. They will be "fashioned like unto his glorious body" (Phil. 3:21).

We'll spend seven glorious years with Him in heaven. Those who are left behind will face the tribulation, a time of unprecedented misery and untold sorrow on the earth. All hell will break loose on earth. "For then there shall be great tribulation such as was not since the beginning of the world to this time, no, nor ever shall be" (Matt. 24:21).

Some who have heard the gospel, but have failed to place their trust in Jesus, might say, "if the rapture comes, then I will be saved." Don't you believe it! The Bible says, "For this cause God shall send them strong delusion, that they shall believe a lie" (2 Thess. 2:11).

During the terrible days of the tribulation on earth, those who have believed in Jesus Christ as personal Savior will be rejoicing in heaven. All believers shall appear be-fore the judgment seat of Christ, and He "shall reward every man according to his works" (Matt. 16:27). Then the Lord Jesus Christ will receive the church unto Himself. All believers will become one with our Lord Jesus in a union so intimate that the Bible describes it as the consummation of a marriage. On earth all attention is given to the Bride. She comes down the aisle accompanied by "Here Comes the Bride." But in the heavenly wedding all eyes will be riveted upon Jesus, and the music which fills the corridors of eternity will be "Here Comes the Groom!"

Following the wedding there will be a great celebration, the Marriage Supper of the Lamb. Then the gates of heaven will burst open and Jesus will come with "ten thousands of his saints" (Jude 14). The King is coming and when He comes, the saints of glory are coming with Him. Jesus is coming victoriously. He is going to intervene in the awesome, catastrophic holocaust of the tribulation.

Revelation 1:7 says, "Behold he cometh with clouds; and every eye shall see him." At the *rapture* Jesus will come in secret *for* His saints. At the *revelation* Jesus will come *with* His saints and every eye shall see Him. The rapture is the *first phase* of Jesus' coming. The *revelation* is the *second phase* of Jesus' coming. At the rapture the Lord will remain in the air. At the revelation Jesus will once again actually set foot upon the earth.

When He comes at the revelation Jesus is going to face the armies of the antichrist which have gathered from all over the globe on the fertile fields of the Valley of Esdraelon (Rev. 19:19). The Bible calls this conflict the Battle of Armageddon. The rising sea of blood from the slain and the wounded will splash against horses' bridles over a distance of 200 miles (Rev. 14:20).

The war will be won with a word from the lips of Jesus (Rev. 19:15). The Bible describes the weapon as "the sword that goes out of the mouth of Jesus" (Rev. 19:15). In Hebrews 11:3, we read, "the worlds were framed by the word of God." The same Jesus who spoke man into existence will speak man into oblivion. For a thousand years, there will be peace on earth. Jesus shall *reign.*

The word millennium is not a Scriptural word, but it is a Scriptural fact. The word comes from two Latin words "mille," meaning a thousand, and "annum," meaning year. The kingdoms of this world will become the kingdom of our Lord and of our Christ. When Jesus comes He is going to redeem this old world!

"Thy kingdom come, thy will be done in earth as it is

in heaven" shall come to pass. In the beginning God gave man dominion over the earth, but man forfeited that dominion, and the devil has had his day. But when Jesus comes back to the earth, Satan will be bound for a thousand years in a bottomless pit. At the end of the millennium, Satan will be released, only to be cast into hell for all eternity. Today the devil is not in hell. He is the "prince of the power of the air" (Eph. 2:2). He has been allowed to roam this earth "as a roaring lion . . . seeking whom he may devour" (1 Pet. 5:8). But when he goes to hell, it will be on a one-way ticket! And when he arrives, he will not be in charge. He will be tormented day and night just as those who live by his standards (Rev. 20:10). Satan will not rule. Jesus is the ruler of three worlds. He rules heaven above, earth beneath, and hell below (Phil. 2:10). Jesus is Lord over all. "Every knee should bow . . . and every tongue confess that Jesus Christ is Lord, to the glory of God the Father" (Phil. 2:11).

Years ago I heard Dr. R. G. Lee tell this story: "Mother and I were very close. We lived on a poor farm . . . so poor that you could hardly raise an umbrella on the place, much less a mortgage. One day the family was in town, except for Mother and me. She was sitting in a rocker on the old porch, knitting. I was lying on the floor, my face in my hands and my heels sticking up in the air. I looked at my Mother's hands. They were hard and toil worn. I asked her, 'Mother, tell me about the happiest hour in all your life.' She told me, but not what I expected.

"I thought she might tell me about the day my Dad, a tall six-footer with dark eyes, spoke the love of his heart to her. But that's not what she told me. I thought she might tell me about that night when the moon spread over the little old farm and how at the fence gate he asked her to be his bride. But that's not what she told me. I thought she might tell me about that hour in the little house on the corner of the farm where she and Dad stood to speak their wedding vows which they kept for fifty years, until his death. But that's not what she told me either.

"Rather she said, 'Son, you've asked a hard question. The war between the North and the South brought days of heartache and separation. Our salt came from the smokehouse floor, our tea from sassafrass leaves and our coffee from grains of corn. The men were all away. My mother, your grandmother, worked alongside all the women.

"The news came that my father, your grandfather Bennett, had been killed in the war. That was the only information we had. Mother didn't cry at first or much in the day, but at night I could hear her sobbing into her pillow.

"One day we were sitting on the porch of the old river house looking down the long river road. Mother had a lap full of beans, stringing and snapping them. Suddenly a man appeared way down the road. My mother said, 'Elizabeth, honey, don't you think me foolish, but that man way down yonder reminds me of your father.' The man came on. She said, 'Elizabeth, honey, that man walks like your father.' 'Oh Mother,' I said, 'don't be so sad. We wish he could come back, but they told us he was dead.' The man came on and started across a little cotton patch. My mother sprang to her feet, spilled the beans, jumped from the porch, and cried, 'Elizabeth, honey, it's your father. It's your father!'

"And she ran! She ran down by the roadside where my father stood with an empty sleeve at one side. He wrapped his other arm around my mother, and they hugged and kissed. They laughed and cried.

"Mother said, 'I ran as fast as my little legs would carry me, and I ran my little girlish hand up that empty sleeve and felt that funny little arm. I think that is the happiest hour I ever knew!'"

Dr. Lee concluded by saying, "My mother's happiest hour is but a small joy compared to seeing the face of Jesus and His pierced hands which opened the gates of grace 'til we shall stand at the gates of Glory."

Even so, come quickly, Lord Jesus!

W. A. Criswell

The Preservation of the Word of God

Heaven and earth shall pass away, but my words shall not pass away (Matt. 24:35).

Is the Bible we hold in our hands the Word of God as God delivered it through the prophets and the apostles? How can we know? How can we be sure? Hundreds of years before the invention of the modern printing press the holy books were copied by hand. Did the scribes mutilate the text? Did they add to it and take away from it?

The assured results of scholarly inquiry say that the ending of Mark is lost, that the Gospel of Mark stops in the middle of the story of the resurrection at verse 8 in chapter 16. They also say that the story of an angel coming down at stated intervals to stir up the water at the pool of Bethesda, recorded in John 5:4, is certainly spurious; that a copyist wrote the explanation on the margin of the book he was copying, and the next scribe placed the note in the text itself. The passage about the Trinity in 1 John 5:7 is also an interpolation, they say.

If these passages are glosses, what about other passages? If some are false, how shall I be able to pick out the true? I must have an answer to these questions, or else I have no foundation upon which to build faith in the revealed Word of God. I must know that the Word is God's Word and not man's interpolation.

We have a sure and certain answer. The same Lord God who inspired the holy prophets and apostles to write the Word also was careful through infinite and multiplied ways to preserve the true Word. That we possess the true text is demonstrable fact.

The scientific study of the preservation of the true text

of the Holy Scriptures is called textual criticism. It is one of the most blessed and rewarding fields of inquiry in the theological world. Nothing could be more interesting or more pertinent to the student of the Bible.

One of the early presidents of the Southern Baptist Theological Seminary in Louisville, Kentucky, and one of the great Greek scholars of all time, was Dr. John A. Broadus. The son-in-law of Dr. Broadus, Dr. A. T. Robertson, himself a world-famous Greek scholar, said that Broadus loved textual criticism. He said that in Broadus's last illness, in his fever and delirium, he would dictate long passages of New Testament criticism; and each word that he spoke and each observation that he made was wonderfully correct, even though he was delirious and speaking out of his mind.

The first New Testament in Greek was published by Erasmus in 1516 and for two hundred years his edition, the Textus Receptus, was supreme in the world. In the year 1611 the English King James Version was made from that text. It is not a bad text; it is substantially correct; but it was based on later manuscripts and left much to be wanted. Among the scholars of the theological world there arose an intense desire to find those manuscripts that went back many hundreds of years to the very beginning of the Christian era. Surely, somewhere, the Bible texts used by the early Fathers were preserved and in existence. Where were they? Thus began the long and patient search for the ancient manuscripts of the Scriptures. Its story is one of the most romantic among the chapters of textual criticism.

At first each New Testament book was a roll in itself and was circulated separately in the place to which it was inscribed and for whom it was written. For example, there are some scholars who think that Matthew was written for the Palestinian and Syrian Christians and was circulated especially by the Christians at Antioch. They say that Mark was written for the Christians at Rome and was circulated by the church at Rome. They say that Luke was written for the churches of Greece and was circulated by the churches of Macedonia. They say that John was written in Ephesus and was circulated especially in Asia. And thus it was that, as the years passed and the churches began to exchange Gospels and Epistles, our New Testament was finally gathered together.

The change from a book roll to a codex, that is, a leaf book, was brought to pass about 300 AD. The Christians needed to find a passage quickly; consequently the roll was cut up, and the leaves were put together at the back so they could be easily turned one after another. It was only after the codex supplanted the roll that we began to have a complete New Testament.

The codex was written in large, even, capital letters called uncials. With the beginning of the seventh century another kind of Greek manuscript began to appear. It is called the minuscule, or cursive—running hand written in much smaller letters. By the ninth century there were no more uncials. In our search for ancient manuscripts, therefore, we are seeking the codex written in large, capital letters.

Into this search great Greek scholars through the last several hundred years have poured their very lives. They have paid untold prices in toil and suffering in order to learn the true and original Word of God. Some of them have been like Tregelles, a scholar who lived in poverty, whom England allowed almost to starve to death, and who went blind deciphering the ancient documents. Other scholars have been like Count Tischendorf, who was sponsored by the German and Russian governments. He was a professor at Leipzig University and regarded himself as an instrument in the hands of God for the discovery and publication of ancient manuscripts of the New Testament.

God has signally blessed these and many other scholars in their search for the ancient writings. Possibly one of the most romantic and interesting stories of all time is the discovery of ALEPH, the alphabetical designation for CODEX SINAITICUS which was discovered by Tischendorf in a monastery at the base of Mt. Sinai in the desert beyond the Red Sea. For centuries this prized Greek manuscript lay beneath the books and rubbish of the old monastery and was accidentally brought to light by Tischendorf.

Tischendorf had been traveling throughout the East and searching all of the old libraries for texts of the Scriptures. In 1844 he came to the monastery of St. Catherine located at the foot of Mt. Sinai. In the hall of the convent was a basket full of parchments used for starting fires. He was told that two similar basketfuls had already been used for burning. Tischendorf looked at the parchment leaves and recognized them immediately. They came from a copy of the Old Testament Greek Septuagint (a translation of the Hebrew into Greek), and they appeared to be from the most ancient manuscript he had ever seen. Being unable to conceal his joy, he aroused the suspicions of the monks and, though the lot was destined for the fire, the monks refused to let him have the codex, thinking it might have value of which they had been unaware. They finally gave him forty-three sheets of the codex but refused to give him more.

In the year 1859, this time sponsored by the Russian government (and therefore having an easier entrance into the Greek Orthodox Monastery of St. Catherine), Tischendorf came back with a commission from the Russian Emperor to secure the rest of the leaves. His second visit promised to be a complete failure. The codex had simply disappeared. In despair and disappointment the faithful scholar was again turning away empty-handed.

On the evening before he had arranged to depart he was walking on the grounds with the steward of the monastery, a gracious person who asked him into his cell to share some refreshments. As they conversed, the monk produced a bundle wrapped in red cloth. To Tischendorf's unutterable and indescribable delight, he found in the bundle not only the leaves he had seen before in the wastebasket but other parts of the Old Testament and the complete New Testament, the only such ancient Greek manuscript containing all the New Testament that had ever been found. Tischendorf said that when the monk placed that precious volume in his hands, he knew that he held in his hand "the most precious biblical treasure in existence." It was made in about 350 AD, about the time the codex came into being.

Tischendorf brought the manuscript to the Imperial Library at St. Petersburg and gave it the name of ALEPH, the first letter in the Hebrew alphabet. On December 24, 1933, ALEPH was purchased by the British government from Russia for five hundred thousand dollars and was placed in the British Museum. Upon my visit to London it was my great and inexpressible joy to look upon the pages of this sacred manuscript. I was reminded as I looked at it that on the same day that the British government paid one-half million dollars for this copy of the Bible, one of my friends bought a first edition of Voltaire for eleven cents!

But by no means is ALEPH the only ancient codex that has been discovered. Codex A, ALEXANDRINUS, is almost as old. It was also my joy to look upon its pages in the British Museum. It is called ALEXANDRINUS because it once formed a part of the library at Alexandria. It was presented to Charles I, in 1628, by Cyril, the patriarch of Constantinople.

Another and equally ancient Greek manuscript is Codex B, also called CODEX VATICANUS because it is in the Vatican Library at Rome. It was written about the same time as ALEPH.

Still another and most interesting manuscript is Codex C, named also Codex Ephraem. It was brought from the East to Florence, Italy, in the sixteenth century and a few years later was deposited in Paris where it has remained ever since. This Codex is a palimpsest, which means that the parchment was used twice. Under the top, cursive Greek script, someone noticed there were traces of writing in the uncial style. In the olden days, to save parchment which was most costly, some of the scribes just scraped off the top writing and used the parchment again. About the twelfth century someone worked this process on Codex C. They took the parchment, scraped and rubbed it to clean off the old writing in order to make it fit for use again. When this was done the skins were used to write down the discourses of Ephraem, a Syrian Father of the fourth century. What he had to say was not one one-thousandth part as valuable as the ancient writing, because the first writing was that of the New Testament. Since impressions of the old uncial script, however, still were to be seen, the parchment was sacredly and earnestly kept. About seventy-five years ago chemicals were discovered which, when applied to the old manuscripts, would revive their ancient form. It was thus that fragments of each book of the New Testament were brought to light in the palimpsest Codex C.

In our search for the verification of the true, exact Word of God, we not only have these ancient Greek codices, but we also have the many, many quotations from the sacred Scriptures by the Fathers of the early Church.

Years ago a group of scholarly men met around a dinner table in England. During the conversation someone in the party put a question no one present was able to answer. It was this: Suppose the New Testament had been destroyed and every copy lost at the end of the third century; could it be collected together again from the writings of the Fathers of the second and third centuries? Two months afterward, one of the company called upon Sir David Dalrymple, who also had been present at the dinner. Pointing to a table covered with books, Sir David said: "Look at these books. Do you remember the question about the New Testament and the Fathers of the Church? As I possessed all the existing works of the Fathers of the second and third centuries, I commenced to search, and I have found the entire New Testament except eleven verses."

The early Fathers of the Church, such as Polycarp of Smyrna, Papias of Hierapolis, Clement of Rome, Irenaeus of Lyons, Tertullian of Carthage, Clement of Alexandria, Origen and Eusebius of Caesarea, were marvelous expositors of the written Word. They quote long and extensively and accurately from all the books of the Bible. Through their eyes we look upon the pages of the Scriptures as they were in their original form and text.

Likewise the many, ancient versions of the holy books translated into other tongues bear witness to the exact word of the original text. There are thousands of ancient manuscripts of the Bible in the Latin, Syrian, Coptic, and other languages. Every one of them helps to verify the true and exact Word of God.

No more startling evidence of the true text of the Scriptures has ever been found than that unearthed by the spade of the archaeologist. The ancient cities of Egypt, with their grand palaces and dismal rubbish heaps, were buried and hermetically sealed by the drifting sands of the desert. Digging beneath the sands, into the graves and cemeteries and ash heaps and streets of long-perished civilizations, the scholars unearthed contemporary records of the daily life of the people. Among other things they found that people wrote of their affairs on thin, flimsy sheets called papyri, made from the stalk of the papyrus plant which grows profusely along the banks of the Nile. Elsewhere in the world these papyri sheets decayed and were destroyed, but in Egypt, under the sands, protected from the ravages of the elements, they were perfectly preserved.

Reading these bits and fragments from the pens of those ancient peoples, the scholars made an astounding discovery. It was once thought that the language of the Greek New Testament was a special, holy, different kind of language, used just in the Bible, not to be found in any other literature of the world. The papyri changed all that. To the joy and delight of the archaeologist it was discovered that the common, ordinary, everyday language of the people was the language of the Greek New Testament now called Koine Greek. The discovery served to explain many idioms of the Bible. But it did far more. As the scholars continued to unearth these ancient papyri manuscripts from the waste and rubbish heaps of the cities of Egypt, they found many parts of the sacred Scriptures and many verifications that the Greek words used in the Gospels and the Epistles were current in everyday life. The Bible became even more a loving, pulsating book.

It is thus that from every part of the ancient world,

from the tombs, from the rubbish heaps, from the libraries, from the writings of the Fathers, from the versions, there comes evidence piled on top of evidence for the authenticity of the text of the Word of God. The multiplication of these ancient manuscripts is unbelievable. They come from every part of the ancient world, and they cover every portion of the New Testament and of the whole Bible. For example, one scholar estimates there are 4,105 ancient Greek manuscripts of the New Testament. It has also been variously estimated that there are as many as 15,000-30,000 Latin versions of the Holy Scriptures. Beside these, there are at least 1,000 other early versions of the Sacred Word. When all those thousands of documents are checked, compared, combined, grouped, and studied, we have a certain and final answer regarding the text.

When we remember that there is but a single manuscript that preserves the annals of Tacitus; when we remember that there is but a single manuscript that preserves the Greek Anthology; when we remember that the manuscripts of Sophocles, of Thucydides, of Euripides, of Virgil, of Cicero, are most rare and the very few in existence are, for the most part, very late; then we can see with what profusion of evidence God supported the truth of the transcription of His Sacred Word.

With complete and perfect assurance I can pick up my Bible and know that I read the revealed Word of God. The God who inspired it also took faithful care that it be exactly preserved through the fire and the blood of the centuries. When Jesus went away He said to His disciples: "These things have I spoken unto you, being yet present with you. But the Comforter, which is the Holy Ghost, whom the Father will send in my name, he shall teach you all things, and bring all things to your remembrance, whatsoever I have said unto you" (John 14:25-26). The same blessed Paraclete, the Holy Spirit of God, who brought to the remembrance of the disciples the spoken Word of Jesus that it might become indelible in the written Word, also preserved the sacred writing from mutilation and destruction.

John sealed the last page of the Sacred Scriptures with

these awesome sentences: "For I testify unto every man that heareth the word of the prophecy of this book, If any man shall add unto these things, God shall add unto him the plagues that are written in this book: and if any man shall take away from the words of the book of this prophecy, God shall take away his part out of the book of life, and out of the holy city, and from the things which are written in this book" (Rev. 22:18-19).

The Ancient of Days, through the centuries since, has kept the holy books as they were written. Where there have been the slightest additions or deletions or changes we know it and can easily separate the glosses from the true and inspired text. Each line, each letter, each syllable, has been kept for us even as the holy men of God spoke and wrote, "moved by the Holy Spirit" (2 Pet. 1:21).

Earl C. Davis

Behold the Lamb

Genesis 22:7-8; Exodus 12:26-27; John 1:29; Revelation 5:5-7

In a church in Belgium you may see one of the wonders of the world of painting, the "Adoration of the Holy Lamb." Painted early in the fifteenth century by two brothers, Jan and Hubert Van Eyck, it is a meditation on one of my favorite Scripture passages, the seventh chapter of Revelation, which describes the great multitude of the redeemed in heaven.

Considered by many to be the pinnacle of all the skills of hand and eye attainable by a painter, it has endured the ravages of time and the horrors of war (spirited off by Nazi art collectors and hidden in an Austrian cave during World War II). The scene is that of a paradise, with a great multitude worshiping the central figure, the Lamb of God.

The lamb is a dominating theme of the Bible, second only to the symbol of the cross. As I have studied its sweep from Genesis to Revelation, I have been blessed and refreshed and challenged. A survey of our hymns shows how this theme has echoed in our praise to God, too. We begin our worship by singing morning hymns to the Lamb:

> Crown him with many crowns, The Lamb upon
> his throne;
> Hark! how the heav'nly anthem drowns All
> music but its own . . .
>
> Son Eternal, we adore thee! Lamb upon the
> throne on high!
> Lamb of God, we bow before thee, Thou hast
> bro't thy people nigh!

And as we offer our praise to God through our gospel songs we again sing of the Lamb:

> Would you be free from the burden of sin?
>> There's pow'r in the blood, pow'r in the
>> blood . . .
> There is pow'r, wonder-working pow'r in the
> blood of the Lamb.
>
> Oh, that old rugged cross so despised by the
> world,
> Has a wondrous attraction for me;
> For the dear Lamb of God left His glory above,
> To bear it to dark Calvary.
>
> Near the cross! O Lamb of God, Bring its scenes
> before me;
> Help me walk from day to day With its shadow
> o'er me.

And when we come to the hymn of invitation, none is more popular than the old favorite, "Just As I Am":

> Just as I am, without one plea,
> But that Thy blood was shed for me,
> And that Thou bidd'st me come to thee,
> O Lamb of God, I come! I come!

Come with me; let me show you the lamb! It will speak to your head, speak to your heart, speak to your sins!

At the start I must point out two things about the lamb in Scripture. First, the lamb is the symbol of *sacrifice*—more so than any other animal. Why? Perhaps because of its meekness, its trustfulness, its seeming purity, and its harmlessness. We can never really know why God chose the lamb as the symbol of sacrifice, and yet we can never get away from the fact that it is so. Second, the lamb in Scripture is the symbol of our *Lord Jesus*. Seldom do we see a lamb in the Bible without seeing behind it, in the shadows, the life and death of Jesus portrayed.

Now come with me to the biblical gallery of art. Let us look at *four pictures of the lamb*—all either pointing forward to Jesus or looking back to Him. The first picture is found in Genesis 22:7, and the caption above this scene is: "Where is the lamb?" The second picture is found in Exodus 12:13, and the emblazoned title is: "When I see the blood, I will pass over you!" The third scene is found in the first chapter of John's Gospel, verse 29, and has the title: "Behold the Lamb of God!" The fourth and last of our selected portraits of the lamb is seen in Revelation 5:6-14, and the caption above it reads: "Worthy is the Lamb!"

Almost the first mention of a lamb in Scripture is found in Genesis 22:7. The background story is one of the most emotional scenes in Scripture. Abraham feels that God has called for the sacrifice of his son Isaac as a sign of Abraham's commitment and obedience. It must have been a terrible struggle for Abraham, for it seemed to destroy either the root or the fruit of the covenant God had made with him. If he disobeyed God's command to offer up Isaac, that would mean the destruction of the grounds of the covenant itself—Abraham's obedience and trust of God. Yet if he obeyed God, it would mean the destruction of the fruit of the covenant—Isaac, the promised heir!

How God spoke to Abraham we do not know; perhaps in a dream. Maybe it was that same night, just before dawn, that Abraham quietly arose, roused the servants, and told them to pack provisions for a journey, and then woke Isaac. Leaving a note for Sarah, unable to face her before the deed was done, Abraham and the lad and the servants took their journey to the land of Moriah.

With every axe blow as he chopped the wood for the fire; with every ringing of the donkeys' hooves; in every night breeze as they camped along the way—Abraham kept hearing the unmistakable call of God: "Abraham!" "Here am I." "Take your son . . . your only son . . . whom you love . . . and offer him as a burnt offering . . ." They have left the servants behind now, and together they walk toward the looming mountain. Something is wrong—even little Isaac feels it—and he raises the heartbreaking question: "Behold, the fire and the wood; but where is the lamb for a burnt offering?" And the brokenhearted father's answer seems yet to hang in the air above the Dome of the Rock: "God will provide himself the lamb . . . And so they went . . . both of them together."

What a powerful statement: "God will provide!" And God will provide what is needed and best, even when it comes to our sacrifices to Him. But certain things are clear in this episode: First, we see that God has a right to demand—and certainly expects—our best to be offered to Him if we, like Abraham, have entered into covenant with Him.

Second, we see that God doesn't have to destroy us in order to bless us; the child is not killed. Third, we see how much we forfeit by not obeying and trusting God—suppose Abraham had refused to make this supreme sacrifice? And, fourth, we see that God will even place in our hands the sacrifice that He wants us to give back to Him.

In such light, what a lack of faith not to serve God with all our hearts and lives! What a lack of faith not to serve Him with a tenth of our possessions! And all this is in regard to a sacrifice of commitment and obedience—we see sacrifices for sin appearing only after the giving of the Law at Sinai. Still, back in the shadows, we see that when it comes to the giving of an adequate sacrifice for our sins, God will provide! And God must, for only He can do that. Pagan religions are crimson with the slaughter of children for parents' sins—yet not even the purest of the fruit of our body can take away our sin. But God will provide that lamb, too, as we see in the second picture.

Look now upon a second portrait of the lamb in the Bible. In the background of this picture we can see a basket among the bulrushes and a burning bush. A stubborn pharaoh and ten plagues make the canvas dark. And now in this portrait of the lamb we see God's instructions to His people to escape the avenging angel of the tenth plague. He tells them to select, on the tenth day of the month, an unblemished lamb out of the flock. No doubt that meant setting this lamb apart, maybe bringing it into the humble home, letting the children play with it and grow fond of it.

Then, on the fourteenth day, kill this lamb in the evening! Smear the blood on the doorposts and the lintel, and "when I see the blood, I will pass over you" (Ex. 12:13).

And so they obeyed. At midnight the avenging angel passed through all the land of Egypt. And the cold chill of death lay on every house save those of the Israelites. The deep of midnight was broken by the sharp cries of fathers who lifted lamps over the beds of their firstborn and saw the mark of death; broken by the wails of mothers who felt the babe at their breast grow still in death, and laid that precious bundle down to scream.

Look carefully at that story, for even as in the first picture the Bible tells us that the lamb is the *appointed sacrifice,* so now we see that the lamb is God's *chosen means for deliverance* from our sins.

For 3,500 years men have slain the lamb and looked back to their deliverance from slavery in Egypt. I have seen a sight not witnessed by many Westerners—the ancient ceremony of the Samaritan's Passover. I have heard their prayers, felt the heat of the fires on which they would roast the lamb, and seen the sacrificial lambs themselves. So men killed and still kill the Passover lamb each year, still looking back to the physical deliverance from their Egyptian slavery and the passing over of the death angel.

Yet there must have been, deep in men's hearts from the very first, a realization of a great need for a lamb—perfect and unblemished—whose blood can set us free from our continual slavery to sin, and cover us once and for all from the wrath of God at the judgment day.

As long as the Temple stood, for a thousand years, a lamb was slain as a sacrifice every morning and every evening . . . as perfect a lamb as men could find. At the first of every month seven lambs were slain, and a vital part of every great religious occasion was the sacrificial ceremony. Yet the need for the perfect lamb remained—must man forever seek that lamb?

No, for when God says, "When I see the blood I will pass over you," it is not the blood of ordinary lambs we need over us. The bad news is that every lamb we possess is blemished! We have no perfect lamb to give God for our sins—no deeds good enough, no wealth great enough, no life dear enough. Yet the good news—the gospel—is that all those lambs pale before the perfect Lamb God provides for the sin of each one of us!

Turn now to see the third picture of the lamb, found in John's Gospel: *Jesus as the perfect Lamb of God.* Early in this Gospel we see John the Baptist pointing out Jesus to those standing with him with the words, "Behold the lamb of God, which taketh away the sin of the world!" (1:29). The writer of this Fourth Gospel sees Jesus as the eternal Lamb, the sin-bearer, the divine contrast to the lambs men had killed for all those years. And this good news of Jesus as God's Lamb for our sins continues through this Gospel. When Jesus is arrested and brought before Pilate, the Jewish leaders refuse to enter his court lest they become unclean and unfit to *eat the Passover* (18:28). John further says that when Jesus was crucified, it was "the preparation of the Passover," about noontime.

That is important, because John is saying that *at the same time the Passover lambs were being slain, Jesus was crucified.* From noon until about three o'clock in the afternoon each family brought the lamb they had selected as their Passover lamb to the Temple. There the priests cut its throat, caught the blood in a silver bowl, and threw it upon the altar. The lamb was then returned to the family to prepare for the Passover meal. John says that on another hill, another lamb was being slain that day—the Lamb of God who would take away the world's sins!

Not just another lamb—but one "slain before the foundation of the world." The lamb of whom the prophet Isaiah (chapter 53) spoke when he said, "like a lamb that is led to the slaughter . . . he was wounded for our transgressions, bruised for our iniquities; upon him was the chastisement that made us whole, and with his stripes we are healed." Not upon the thousands of lambs killed that day at the Temple did God lay our sins—but upon the spotless lamb of

God who died on that other hill on the old rugged cross! And His blood is on our doorpost!

Now walk on, walk on with me past Abraham's lamb of sacrifice, past Moses' lamb of deliverance, past Isaiah's lamb of substitution, past the pointing finger of John the Baptist, past Peter's lamb by whose blood, more precious than silver and gold, we are redeemed—walk on with me to see in the last book of the Bible our fourth portrait of the lamb: the *Lamb Victorious!*

The beloved name for Jesus in the Book of Revelation is the "Lamb," by which term He is called twenty-nine times. Notice the setting of this picture. In chapters 4 and 5 of Revelation is a beautiful picture of heaven, filled with the glory and presence of God the Father on His throne. And then we see the Lamb (5:6*ff.*) standing by the throne. He is still the Lamb of *sacrifice,* for His throat is cut; yet He lives.

In chapter 7 we see that He is the Lamb of *deliverance,* for the elder explains to the writer John as they gaze upon the great multitude gathered from every nation, tongue, and people and clothed in white robes: "These are they who have come out of the great tribulation; they have washed their robes and made them white in the blood of the lamb" (7:14). Only by the blood of *this* lamb is there true deliverance from the sins and trials and tribulations of this world.

But above all He is the Lamb *victorious,* who has *redeemed* His people out of every kindred, tongue, people, and nation. The Lamb victorious who gives *victory* to His people. In the twelfth chapter is a beautiful and terrible vision of the birth of Jesus, John's Christmas story, and the mighty struggle which ensued at His birth and continues even until this very day. In the midst of the cosmic struggle between the dragon and Christ are the followers of the Lamb, and it is said of them that "they have conquered him [Satan] by the blood of the Lamb and by the word of their testimony . . ." (12:11). He is the Lamb victorious who *guides the future* of His people, as the Lamb before the throne takes the book of the future (5:7). He is the Lamb victorious who will be the *light* of heaven: "And the city has no need of sun or moon to shine upon it, for the glory of God is its light, and its lamp is the Lamb" (21:23).

What lamb is this? The lamb God provided in Abraham's day—and ours. The lamb who held back the avenging sword of the death angel in Moses' day—and ours. The lamb who was offered once-for-all on "a green hill far away," upon an "old rugged cross." Call the name of this lamb "Jesus, for He shall save his people from their sins."

A minister visited a dying man who had never looked to Jesus, the Lamb of God, for the salvation of his soul and the lordship of his life. Even in this extreme hour, he would not accept Jesus. God, he said, was merciful and he would simply trust God. "Well, what will you do when you get to heaven?" asked the old minister. "What everybody else does," said the dying man. "Will you sing?" asked the minister. "Yes." Then the minister read to him that beautiful scene of Revelation 14 in which the multitude of those who follow the Lamb wherever He goes sing a new song of praise and glory to the Lamb. And nobody can learn that song except the redeemed. "No," said the old minister, "you cannot sing up there that new song, for it must be *learned* down here." Only those who follow the Lamb here can learn that new song which will ring through the halls of heaven. Can you sing the new song of the Lamb?

> None other lamb, none other name,
> None other Hope in heaven,
>   or earth or sea,
> None other Hiding-Place from guilt
>   or shame,
> None besides Thee.[1]

NOTE

1. Christina Rossetti, "None Other Lamb," in *The Oxford Book of Christian Poems,* Lord Cecil, editor (Oxford: The Oxford University Press, 1965), p. 304.

Cristobal Doña

The Discipline in the Church
Matthew 18:15-18

I had difficult cases throughout my ministry which today do not really cause my soul to be disturbed or troubled. At first I was engaged in a sort of quixotic battle. "How many of you know what I am talking about when I say quixotic battle?" It simply means a useless battle or a lost battle. You know, the greatest Spanish writer of all, Don Miguel de Cervantes Saavedra, wrote Don Quixote, which is a novel about a man who is an idealist, and he goes out to straighten out the world—who can do that?

As expected, most people took him for an insane person, one who was crazy. Who can straighten out the world? All right, that is the idea of Don Quixote. And I was sort of fighting a quixotic battle. Every time this certain situation was brought to my attention concerning my church, I was troubled; but again, this is probably the last time I am going to say it: it does not bother me anymore.

What kind of case is that? It is the case of Christians who were not converted, who did not become Christians, in a church; they became Christians outside of a church. It may have been in a revival, maybe on the street, but the start of their birth, their spiritual birth, had no commitment whatsoever to anybody. And this has been true, regardless of the parachurch organization through which the person was saved.

This is apparently a common syndrome in all the Christians who are spiritually born under those circumstances. What is the problem? Rather, what is the symptom (or symptoms)? One of these symptoms is that they have tremendous difficulty adjusting to the authority of the church. Tremendous difficulty. And most of them feel so uncomfortable that they leave. And they go, maybe to another church. Having no commitment whatsoever, their subconscious or unconscious attitude is: "Leave me alone."

Also they have a little flag they wave all the time, "If the Lord leads me I will do and work for the Lord in whatever He wants me to do." And with that they mean, "Don't bother me." But they still use the pious expression, "As the Lord leads me." And it looks as if the Lord never leads them to commit themselves to a church. Now, I remember I used to have a little difficulty with our associate pastor; you ask him. He will tell you. He came to know the Lord with one of those parachurch groups.

One day he even threatened me with leaving the church; as we were coming back from visiting Golden Gate Seminary. You know, I was very enthused and very happy with him when I went to show him our Southern Baptist Seminary: the man was not impressed with it. (Of course, later on he went to study there. All of this was about fifteen years ago.) Instead, he was charging me: "Pastor, I want to see you more deeply involved with the Word; I want to see you pouring yourself into the Word."

I asked him, "What do you mean?" He replied, "Yeah, I want to see that you are in the Word." And I said, "But, brother, I don't understand you." He said, "Oh, you don't understand me? I simply mean that I want to see you more into the Word." Then, later on I discovered: that particular organization is really disciplined concerning the Bible. But that is all they do.

They educate themselves through memorizing Scripture and reading the Bible; they have meditation every day. But they don't know anything about bringing families together or educating the children; they don't know anything about social concerns. They don't care about any of those things. They are not a church; they do not know what it is to have church obligations. They don't have a church, they are not a church.

Well, I said, "Brother, don't you realize, haven't you observed, that when I preach (in those days we didn't have but one service, and I had to preach back and forth in English and Spanish) in that service where you are sitting, we have people from Mexico or Texas, and some do not know how to read or write? And that in the same crowd is Dr. Wilshire, who has been professor of geology in the University of Australia, and in Tulsa, Oklahoma, and is here with a team of scientists to train the astronauts who are going to the moon?"

"And that man is there in every service, Sunday morning, Sunday night, and Wednesday night; he is there without fail. And that man expects to take something from what I preach. How would you do it? You have that man sitting alongside with someone who never went to school." And I said, "Be patient with me."

He was patient. I believe the Lord had counted him. He was one of His elect to work for Him because finally, we succeeded; we sent him to Glorieta, and while there in training, he responded to the call. God called him to the ministry. Immediately I sent him to pastor our mission in Redwood City, and from there (he had already graduated from college), I sent him to the seminary, and it was quite a struggle.

I really had to invest time, lots of time in him, to keep him in the seminary. I would tell him, "Just hold on, just hang in there, baby. Don't be disappointed, don't be discouraged, you're coming to an end, you're almost there, just one more year." Finally, he graduated! Whew! It was a battle. Do you know why? Because he had been in a parachurch group. No, I'm not talking behind his back. You can go and ask him to give you his testimony. He became a pastor in Redwood City and still had not solved that difficulty, that problem. He hadn't!

One day, he realized why the mission he was pastoring had the problem of stagnation and paralysis; why it wouldn't move but had come to a sudden stop. He prayed, and he really loved the Lord. And I was always in touch

with him. He finally came to me and said, "Brother, I can't
make it. You will have to help me." And I said, "Mike, you
know I'm for you. And I've been waiting for the opportunity
when I would be able to sit down and share with you. I
might not know more than you do, but I have more experience than you."

He prayed, and the Lord finally made him see, he says,
the situation so clearly that he not only called me on the
phone, but he came to my office; not only that, but before he
came to see me he told his congregation at the mission,
"Folks, I want you to know something. The Lord has directly dealt with me in my heart. And I believe I have been
ungrateful with our pastor at White Road Baptist, and I
want you to know that from this day on I'll consult with
him on every single thing. I realize I really don't know anything. He will train me; I want to be a pastor. And I admire
my pastor, and I want to be submissive to him."

And from that day on, he started to come here for training. He told me in my office: "Brother Doña, first of all,
before we continue, I want your forgiveness, I've been a
rebel. I really have been hard to deal with; I have been trying to go my way, and the Lord has dealt with me. Now I
realize that you have been right all along. I've been wrong,
but I promise you that the mission in Redwood City will go
a different route this time. I'll go as you direct me; you will
teach me how to do it."

He has been a totally different man from that day to
this. But he had to be converted from a "rebel" to a
church man. He has been open, frank, sincere, and honest
about what was the difficulty.

If you do not commit yourself to a church, you might as
well forget it. You are going to do whatever is "your thing"
in the name of the Lord. Do you remember what I said
about that? It used to trouble me. It does not trouble me
anymore. This is why I am not carried away when someone
who has been saved in another place comes to our church;
of course I'm happy to see people being saved not only in

the church but outside of it too. But why am I not impressed? Because of the experience. The Lord has called our church to go out and find those who are not saved and bring them into the fold, to see that they are saved, and then teach them, baptize them, incorporate them into the church; then to train them and send them again into the mission that Jesus has left for the church.

Now, we've come finally to the main point; this was in the preparation for the message. Jesus left his church on the earth with some authority. And no one can dictate anything to the church except the Lord Jesus Christ.

Number one is autonomy; no one can decide for the church who should be a member and whom we should refuse to receive as a member of the church. We have to decide ourselves. No one else will do it. It is our responsibility to decide whom we will receive and whom we will reject. Some churches have the philosophy or the theology or the custom of having an upper circle, an upper grouping, or an upper organization, like a mother organization which imposes on them those who are going to be members; they'd send a candidate with a letter saying, "So and so can be a member of that church." And that person is received into the church.

And that without any regard for salvation or testimony or age or any condition of any kind! I hope I'll train my church, so whether I am here or absent forever, they will know that no one has any authority to impose anything on our church. We are going to decide whom we will receive as a member and whom we will not receive as a member.

There may be several reasons why we would not receive persons as members. Number one has to do with salvation. Ours should be a regenerate church; that means whenever anyone says, "I'm a member of White Road," that should be enough to know this person is saved. You cannot say that about every church, but that should be the understanding when you say, "I'm a member of White Road," because if you're not saved, then you should not be a member of this church. You had better be saved today. You might be a member of another church but not of White Road.

Number two, it means that you have obeyed the Lord Jesus Christ in baptism, scripturally, biblically, by immersion in the name of the Father, the Son, and the Holy Spirit; if you have not been baptized the way Jesus Christ was baptized, you still may be saved, but you cannot be received into the fellowship of this church.

Number three, the church should have a say so in whom is received as a member of the church. It's not the pastor who will determine that. The pastor is not the owner of the church. Don't let any man come to this pulpit to be your pastor who is going to dictate who will and will not be a member of the church. You, the church, should be the ones to decide and determine who is going to be a member, not the pastor. You are competent; Jesus gave you the authority.

Number four, we should not receive, or have in our midst, members who do not respond ethically and morally to the high standards of Christian living. In fact, should we have someone like this, the church has the responsibility to call a meeting and dismiss such a member. To oust him, to cut his membership, to sever his relationship with us as a member of the church. If we don't do it, we are in violation of God's Word. We have an obligation to be loyal to God's Word, first of all.

For too long, churches have been led by sentiment; they have seen the gathering, the functioning, the organization, and the life of the church from a sentimental point of view. That should not be the rule in this church. We should be led by what the Scriptures say, not by what sentiments dictate. Read again what it says in chapter 18 of Matthew. Jesus says: "Whatever you shall bind on earth shall have been bound in heaven; and whatever you loose on earth shall have been loosed in heaven."

So, if you have dismissed someone here on earth, God has dismissed him in heaven too for you. And, He says, if

you have trouble with someone in the church for some reason, go and try to make up with him. And if the brother
does not want to make up, why don't you come to the
church and get one or two and go back with your brother or
sister and try to make up with him, "so that by the mouth
of two or three witnesses every fact may be confirmed"?

And if that person will not respond, but becomes stubborn, hard to reach, set in his opinions, believes he is right
in his own mind, and doesn't want to come in communion
again with his brother or his sister, then you have no recourse but to bring it to the church and let the church know
what is going on.

Do you know what the Bible says the church should
do? When the church hears that several ways have been
tried to bring the brother into the fold and he refuses, then
Jesus says outright, the church should declare that person
as if he had never been saved. Oust him. Now, in the New
Testament Paul writes two letters to a church that had
been playing with sins of different kinds, and in his first
letter to the Corinthians, chapter 5, we read of some conditions under which churches should act in that regard.

We read in 1 Corinthians 5:9: "I wrote you in my letter
not to associate with immoral people; I did not at all mean
with immoral people of this world, or the covetous, or slan-
derers, or with idolaters, for then you would have to go out
of the world," and go to the moon, "but actually I wrote to
you not to associate with any so-called brother if he should
be an immoral person, or coveteous, or an idolater, or a re-
viler, or a drunkard, or a swindler, not even to eat with such
a one, don't even invite him to your house." Cast him aside.
Cut his membership, he is no longer a member of your
church.

I know of many churches that are declining. They have
declined in their standards. They don't keep high standards anymore. These may be simple things, and yet these
simple things are testimonies.

I heard of a mother who was watching her two little
boys playing behind the kitchen in the backyard. They

were rolling a little piece of paper and putting it into their mouths, and when the mother caught them she asked, "Hey, you guys, what are you doing?" And they answered, "Nothing, we're just playing church."

The mother said, "Come on, explain it to me." Then one of the children with shyness began to explain: "Well, we are the deacons, and we were taking a smoke break outside the church." Churches like that have lowered their standards. Some of you have reported to me, that in the place where you work you have some people who even claim to be deacons in their church, and they cuss, they are revilers, they have a foul mouth, they smoke, drink; so what makes them different from anyone else?

Is it enough to believe with your mind in the Lord Jesus Christ? Who rules your life anyway? If you are like one of these people, Jesus Christ is not your Lord, and if He is not Lord, He is not your Savior. You may have no problem whatsoever accepting everything God says about Jesus His Son. But that is not the condition for being saved; the condition for being saved is to invite and receive Jesus Christ into your life, into your heart as Lord, so He will rule over your life, He will govern, He will run your life.

And if He has not changed your life, He is not there. Somebody else is. But now let us see how we might be disregarding the authority of the church in the little details. That is my subject here. And we have had the painful experience of suspending the membership of four of our dear people. We had no recourse but to dismiss them. I'd rather cry over their going away than having them in our church with such behavior because I'd find myself in contempt of the Scriptures. I don't want to do that. I love them, we all love them. God knows how we love them.

But I'd rather say to my church, "We must dismiss these people, if we want to continue to keep the high standards in our church." I don't want to deal with such members from a sentimental point of view but from a holy point of view. What does God say? But again, this was an extreme situation. Now let us go to the other extreme. What would be an innocuous, almost harmless way, in which we would violate the authority of the church? What do we do with the decisions we pass in our business meetings? We have some regulations, we have some agreements, we have voted sometimes on such matters. What do we do about those things?

Let's remember that the authority of our church comes from Jesus Who said he had all authority in heaven and on earth. Our convention and our association have some authority because they are legal entities, formed by individuals, organized legally as non-profit corporations, and their authority is derived from the people, but our church has no authority from the people but from Jesus, the Creator of the universe. The authority of the church is not man-given but God-given.

A church may or may not be a corporation, may or may not have real property, may or may not have any property at all, and yet the church has the authority given by its Founder and Proprietor, Jesus Christ. He said "My church," and if He said "My church," then it is His church.

Our authority, then, is not dependent upon people but upon God. And our church has received authority from its Master to command discipline, order, and obedience. If we do not, the convention will not bring us to accountability, nor the association, but Jesus Himself, the Lord of the church. And we must be found faithful in all areas of our responsibilities, the salvation of sinners, the training of believers, the holiness of life of its members, and the compassion for the ruinous state of the world. Let's be mindful of the authority over us.

What about our punctuality, our performance on the positions we have been elected for? We must respect, and we must recommit our lives to the holiness of our church, to the solidification, to the firmness, to the establishment, to the strong foundations. We have only 300 members today, but we will have 500, 750, 1000; we are planting the seeds of stability, order, efficiency, holiness, commitment, loyalty, faithfulness, and consistency right now, with the few that we have.

Those who come in the morning witness the great number of people making it to the English service. Most of you are not in the Spanish service. But if you were in the Spanish service, you would have seen that for the first time the balcony was completely filled, all the pews on the bottom were packed tight; we have to put more chairs in the center aisle; the back of the auditorium was full of chairs, and people were sitting on the stairs; there was almost no more room for people. And then I asked them, "We should have some of you folks come to our first service early in the morning at 9. How many of you would like to come to that service at 9 o'clock? How many of you would love to come to that first service?" Nobody responded. I asked, "Did you hear me?" They replied, "Yes, we did." Almost in a cynical way they were saying, "No, we don't want to come to the 9 o'clock service." Then I said, pointing to a lady: "You, sister, you used to go to 9 o'clock mass, huh?" "No," she said, "I went to the 12 o'clock mass."

We're growing, but now is the time when we should teach the new ones respect for the authority of our church, the authority of our leaders, the authority of our decisions, the authority of the Scriptures. Let us always recognize, let us always remember that you play an important part, that you can contribute. You can cooperate to see your church strong, holy, friendly, respectful, mindful of the Scriptures. Folks, that is the church Jesus Christ wants for us, after all, this is His church. Praise his holy name!

James T. Draper, Jr.

God's World and God's Word
Psalm 19

Throughout the Bible, God reveals Himself to us. In the prophets God speaks to the people through the prophet. "Thus saith the Lord" is the prophet's declaration. But, in the Psalms we find man in the midst of all sorts of problems reaching out to God.

The Psalmist is often discouraged, depressed, disappointed, oppressed, and the like. He reaches out to God in the midst of his frustrations, illnesses, and problems, and God is there. Rather than this being a prophetic "Thus saith the Lord," it is more of our identifying with the Psalmist in all the difficulties and problems and realizing that God has a word for every situation. Nothing we face surprises God. In the Psalms we find help for our everyday lives.

Before we look at the psalm itself, let me suggest a contrast in this psalm. "The heavens declare the glory of God; and the firmament sheweth his handywork" (v. 1). The first six verses are about natural revelation. We can look into the created world and see God. Only a fool does not see God in nature. Two times in Psalms, the psalmist says, "The fool hath said in his heart there is no God" (14:1, 53:1). Only the fool looks at this world and thinks it merely happened by some cosmic explosion, or that something came out of nothing. The first portion of the psalm reminds us of the great revelation of God we find in natural creation.

Then in verse 7 we have an interesting contrast. "The law of the Lord is perfect. . . ." The natural revelation of God in the world is great, but the special revelation of God in

His Word is perfect. Simon Peter declared, "For we have not followed cunningly devised fables, when we made known unto you the power and coming of our Lord Jesus Christ, but we were eyewitnesses of his majesty" (2 Pet. 1:16).

What could be more sure than personal experience? What could be more sure than what we see with our own eyes? "We have also a more sure word of prophecy . . ." (2 Pet. 1:19). Peter is speaking of the Word of God. It is more accurate, more to be trusted, more perfect than even our experience. We must measure our experiences by the Word of God. We measure truth by the Word of God, not by what we perceive truth to be. The more perfect, more sure word is the Word of God. Here we have the contrast. We have a beautiful witness to the testimony of this world, of the natural creation, to the glory of God. But the law of God is perfect.

The phrase, "law of God," refers to the revealed Word of God. Dr. Kyle Yates wrote it simply, "The word 'law' as found in this psalm denotes more than the first five books of Moses and includes all of God's sayings and God's messages to men. It certainly includes all of the books of the Bible that were then in his hands and would include today all of the books of the New Testament."[1]

In the first six verses, we have the greatness of God's creation; then we have the great God of creation giving us something absolutely perfect.

God's World Examined

There are three things to notice in these first six verses as we examine God's world. First, *THE PLACE* examined is the heavens.

The heavens declare the glory of God; and the firmament sheweth his handywork. Day unto day uttereth speech, and night unto night sheweth knowledge. There is no speech nor language, where their voice is not heard. Their line is gone out through all the earth and their words to the end of the world. In them hath he set a tabernacle for the sun, Which is as a bridegroom coming out of his chamber, and rejoiceth as a strong man to run a race. His going forth is from the end of the heaven, and his circuit unto the ends of it: and there is nothing hid from the heat thereof (vv. 1-6).

The glory of God is written across the heavens. This reminds us of Paul's declaration, "But the invisible things of him are clearly seen from the creation of the world" (Rom. 1:20).

When we look at this universe, we see the glory of God written over all the heavens. This is a vast, vast world. Our solar system, the system that basically revolves around the sun, is 7 billion, 300 million miles across. That is .001 light year. That is just our solar system, our sun, our earth. If you spanned all of it, it is only .001 of a light year. It is in a galaxy we call the Milky Way.

In the Milky Way there are 100 billion stars. From one side of the Milky Way to the other is 100,000 light years. Our Milky Way is also in what is called a Supercluster of galaxies. The Supercluster has 2,500 galaxies, everyone of them about the size or bigger than the Milky Way; from the center of that Supercluster, where our Milky Way is located, to the outside is 40 million light years. Then, looking beyond the Supercluster to the universe that we have been able to observe to the outer limit, is 10 billion light years!

Think about that a minute; then read Isaiah 40:12 concerning God: "Who hath measured the waters in the hollow of his hand, and meted out heaven with the span, and comprehended the dust of the earth in a measure, and weighed the mountains in scales, and the hills in a balance." Everything just described to you, 10 billion light years, one half the distance across the universe, God measures with the span of his hand. No wonder the psalmist says, "The heavens declare the glory of God; and the firmament sheweth his handywork." No wonder that is the place he began when he talked about the greatness of God. Think about the observable universe and all that we know. Did you know that 90 percent of all astronomers believe in God?

That is a higher percentage than any other profession. Those who study the universe believe in God. Do you know why? "The heavens declare the glory of God." What a beautiful, wonderful testimony. *THE PLACE:* the heavens.

Note now *THE PATTERN* of this world. "Day unto day uttereth speech, and night unto night sheweth knowledge. There is no speech nor language, where their voice is not heard. Their line is gone out through all the earth, and their words to the end of the world" (vv. 2-4*a*). In other words, the pattern is one of precision. "Uttereth" means to "pour forth." It means that every facet of this universe declares, speaks, reveals, bubbles forth with the glory of God. We cannot find disorder in this universe. It is a universe run in intricate precision with absolute principles, by specific laws. There is no perplexity, no chance. It all operates just as God planned. There is a universal consistency; thus all the heavens declare with one voice the glory of God. Think of all those billions and billions of stars moving precisely in their orbits at the exact speed that God tells them to move.

If our world were not tilted on its axis at precisely the angle it is, we could not live. If it were a fraction of a percent off one way or the other, life would not be possible on this earth. We are surrounded by a protective covering without which the sun would destroy us almost immediately. If the moon were not at the precise distance from the earth that it is, there would either be extremely low tides or tides would be so high the water would cover the earth. And if the moon were to be taken away completely, there would be no gravity or tides and our oceans would become one giant cesspool. But because God put the moon at the precise place He did, there is gravity that causes the oceans to ebb and flow in a way that continually cleans and keeps alive.

If we were a little closer to the sun, we would be burned to a crisp. If we were a little further away, we would freeze to death. Life would not be possible. There are a thousand reasons that tell us we are not here by accident or by chance. Everything is precisely worked out. We are able to function and enjoy what we do because God made it that way. Everything in this universe declares the glory of God.

The *PRINCIPLE* that is used to illustrate this message is the sun. The sun is personified as a character in this cosmic drama. "In them hath he set a tabernacle for the sun, Which is as a bridegroom coming out of his chamber, and rejoiceth as a strong man to run a race. His going forth is from the end of the heaven, and his circuit unto the ends of it; and there is nothing hid from the heat thereof" (vv. 4*b-6*). He uses the sun as an illustration that in this world God has put together there is continual glory given to God.

God's Word Exalted

"The law of the Lord is perfect, converting the soul: the testimony of the Lord is sure, making wise the simple. The statutes of the Lord are right, rejoicing the heart: the commandment of the Lord is pure enlightening the eyes. The fear of the Lord is clean, enduring for ever: the judgments of the Lord are true and righteous altogether" (vv. 7-9). Notice the synonyms for the Word of God. We have law, testimony, statutes, commandment, fear, the judgments. These exalt God's Word. Now that we have looked at this universe, we are going to look even higher. The world is magnificent, but there is something more glorious, more wonderful, more consistent, more solid, more sure. The day will come when this earth will be burnt up with fervent heat, but the Word of the Lord shall endure forever. Everything we observe in this world that so loudly declares the glory of God will one day be destroyed. But the Word of God will be forever. What a higher plane he goes to now as he points us to the Word of God!

There are two things in these verses we want to see about the Word of God. First, notice *THE ATTRIBUTES*. The law of the Lord is "perfect." It is a perfect Word from God. There are no errors. It is accurate and covers all of life. The law of the Lord is perfect! God meant what He said and said what He meant. Understanding it is not necessary to knowing that it is truth. We often want to understand things in the Word of God so we can decide if we accept them as true or if we are going to be obedient. But when we come to Him with an open heart and in faith, His Word becomes very clear. When you come with skepticism and doubt, wanting God to prove Himself, He rarely responds.

Then the testimony is "sure." The word "sure" is a foundational word. It means we can build our lives on it, we can count on it.

Then the statutes of the Lord are "right." The word "right" means to make a straight path. It will not lead us astray or into error. When we study, apply and appropriate the Word of God, we can be sure we will not be led into error. The Word of God will never lead us down a dead-end street to a disaster. It will always lead us in the right way.

The commandments are "pure." That means God's Word is unadulterated. There is no mixture of evil. There are no unwholesome elements in the Word of God. If we study and obey the Word of God, we will never bring that which is evil, unpleasant, or unwholesome into our lives.

The fear of the Lord is "clean." Again, here is the idea of no mixture of evil. And notice that it endures forever. The physical universe will one day pass away, but the Word of God endures forever.

The judgments of the Lord are "true" and "righteous." That means they are utterly dependable. I may let you down. I may not tell you that which is true. I may not do what I say I will do, but you can always count on the Word of God. Every bit of God's Word is true. It is my guide, my authority. It will not lead me astray.

These are the attributes of the Word of God: perfect, sure, right, pure, clean, true and righteous.

Notice now *THE ATTRACTIVENESS* of the Word of God. "More to be desired are they than gold, yea, than much fine gold: sweeter also than honey and the honeycomb. Moreover by them is thy servant warned: and in keeping of them there is great reward" (vv. 10-11).

Here are four things that make the Word of God attractive. First, "it is more desirable than gold." We spend our lives trying to buy a treasure we cannot keep and ignore the greatest treasure in all of the world—the Word of God. We think if we just had gold, we would be happy. If we had *fine* gold, we would really be happy. But the psalmist says that the Word of God is more to be desired than fine gold. The words of God are more attractive than anything this world can give you.

Second, it is "sweeter than honey." That was the sweetest thing he could think of. But he says that the Word of God is sweeter than honey or the honeycomb. In our day, it might be a hot fudge sundae or gourmet ice cream. Think of the sweetest thing in the world, and the psalmist says the words of God are sweeter. It is more precious than gold, sweeter than honey.

Third, it warns us of sin. Do we want to know how to live? How to keep from making mistakes? How to live our lives to their fullest? Then stay with the Word of God because by the words of God, our lives will be warned when we go astray. The reason we sin is because we get away from God and God's Word. We do things we should not do because we are not listening to God. His Word warns us of evil.

Finally, notice that it rewards obedience. The reward is that there is wholeness, happiness, meaning, and purpose. The very thing we strive for, the very thing we want in life, we have in keeping the Word of God.

God's Work Expressed

Who can understand his errors? cleanse thou me from secret faults? Keep back thy servant also from presumptuous sins; let them not have dominion over me: then shall I be upright, and I shall be innocent from the great transgression. Let the words of my mouth and the meditation of my heart be acceptable in thy sight, O Lord, my strength, and my redeemer (12-14).

Here is how God's Word works. *THE PURPOSE* of

God's Word is to help us know ourselves. "Who can understand his errors?" Who of us really understands himself?
Who of us really understands why we do what we do? Who
of us really comprehends what we are like inside? Who of
us has done things and not wondered why he did them?
Who of us has not discovered secret faults in his life?

The work of God through His Word is to detect and to
remove error in our lives. If we do not have protection from
the secret faults, those things we do almost automatically
through carelessness and casualness, then we will be led
into presumptuous sin. Most of our sins are things we did
not intend to do. We just do them. The purpose of the Word
of God is to so work in our lives that we see where our needs
are and are led away from error and sin in our lives. In
other words, the Word of God works in us to help us know
ourselves better.

Secondly, there is *THE PROTECTION* of the Word.
"Keep back thy servant also from presumptuous sins." Now
we are faced with sin of a different nature. In the Old Testament Levitical system, there was no sacrifice for presumptuous sins. There were sacrifices for the people that sinned
each year but no sacrifice for a deliberate, premeditated,
presumptuous sin. A presumptuous sin is a deliberate attack upon God. It is saying to God, "I will not do it!" It is
presumptuous for many reasons. One is that God could
deal with us severely if He chose to do so. When God gives
me a standard, and I refuse to abide by it, I am committing
a presumptuous, arrogant sin. The Word of God protects us
from that. I am referring to murder, adultery, stealing,
slander, gossip, brutality, abuse, and a thousand other
things. I am speaking of those things that are so clearly
inhuman as well as ungodly. The Word of God protects us
from these sins.

We may think we would not do anything like that. Yes,
we would. There is no sin we will not commit. In our hearts,
apart from the grace and strength of God there is the seed
of sin. We are sinners by nature, by character, by choice,
and by conduct. Away from the protective custody of God

there is nothing we will not do. We are all capable of presumptuous sins. But the Word of God works in our lives to
protect us from presumptuous sin.

Thirdly, there is *THE PRAISE* of the Word. All of this
leads us to the desire to praise God. When we consider the
God of all creation, when we understand the wonderful natural revelation of God in this world, when we understand
the perfect treasure of truth that God has given to us, and
when we understand how He protects us, we want to praise
the Lord.

The last verse is a beautiful acclamation of praise. Notice he calls God, "O Lord, my strength, my redeemer."
"Strength" could be translated "rock," and "redeemer"
could be translated "salvation." "O Lord, my rock and my
salvation." That is what God is. God in His essence, in His
basic being is *THE* God, our Strength and our Redeemer.
How much we ought to want to please Him!

This psalm is a call to our hearts to see God in the
created universe. Every wonder in this beautiful world is a
reminder of the glory and majesty of God. Beyond the clear
revelation of God's world is the perfect revelation of God's
Word. This ought to cause us to love God's Word and to seek
to plant it in our hearts and lives. As we do that, God's work
will be made manifest in our lives, and our hearts will
burst forth in His praise.

Paul D. Duke

Spared
Luke 13:1-9

Pick up any day's newspaper, and it will read the same. Here an accident, there a murder, everywhere a cry. Column after column, page after page dirges out the news of human blood and tears. If any of it were happening to you, or if you knew and dearly loved any of the victims, you'd be wondering why. You'd be scrambling to find some hint of meaning lurking in the shadows of all this pain. Why tragedy? Even when it's not our tragedy, we want to know.

I

So one day some people came to Jesus, newspaper in hand, asking about tragedy. Their governor had massacred some Galileans while they were praying. Pontius Pilate had them slaughtered while they worshiped, so that on the floor of the house of God human blood made a dark common puddle with the blood of pigeons and lambs offered to beseech the Lord's help. It's a gruesome story. You'd think God might have delivered them from that. Unless, of course, they were secretly wicked people, hypocrites in praying. Is it possible in any way they deserved what they got? With that kind of question perplexing them, those people wanted to know what Jesus thought. So do we.

Here's his answer: "Do you think that these Galileans were worse sinners than all the other Galileans, because they suffered thus? I tell you, No" (v. 2, RSV). Christ is as clear as He can be on this question. He didn't have much to say on the problem of evil, but He did say this: Tragedy is not reserved for the worst people. You can draw no equation

80

between disaster and deserving. To hammer down the point, Jesus does them one better. They had spoken of human evil. Now he pulled from the newspaper a natural evil. "What of those eighteen who were crushed when the Siloam tower fell? Do you think they were worse than the rest of the people in Jerusalem? I tell you, No!" It's a truth Jesus had to repeat again and again.

We who believe there's a God Who is both mighty and just are perennially tempted to feel human tragedy as a carrying out of sentence. It's how the friends of Job felt his tragedy. It's how Jesus' disciples felt the tragedy of a man born blind: "Lord, who sinned?" It's how too many of us have responded to the contemporary tragedy of AIDS. "Lord, who sinned?—*We* know!"

And, lest you and I assume we're above this kind of thing, remember for a moment how it feels when someone you love is suffering, or when you are suddenly out of your mind with your own pain, and the gall that rises up in your soul cries out, "This isn't fair!" As if you expected what comes to carry a fairness of punishment or reward. But Jesus said of the man born blind, "No one sinned." Jesus said, "It rains on the just and the unjust." He knew. For even as He talked with these people about massacred Galileans, He was Himself on His way to Jerusalem to become another Galilean massacred by Pilate while He prayed.

Tyrants kill, towers fall, cancer comes. These disasters take no particular aim at wickedness; they take no particular detours around righteousness. They simply come as part of the broken, random rhythm of a world out of sync. So when tragedy comes, and ancient terror rises in us again, and we feel it as the sinister hand of God, and the heart breaks its deepest on the terrible sense that even God has angrily abandoned us, let the word of Jesus break through: "I tell you no." Let it be clear correction of our pointing at others' pain. Let it be the calming of fear within our own pain. We have asked, is tragedy God's avenging answer to human wickedness? Jesus has answered, "I tell you no."

II

But having said this, Jesus says something else that's a little surprising. Having told us tragedy is not vengeance on particular wickedness, He does not go on to offer explanation of tragedy, nor does He go on to put his arms around us and give us comfort. Instead, with darkness on his face and fire in his eyes, He thunders these words: "But unless you repent you will all likewise perish. Do you think these people were victims of tragedy because they were the worst offenders? I tell you no. But unless you turn your life, tragedy is coming to you." So much for the pastoral approach!

What's He doing? He's plainly turning a truth to its other side. If it's true that tragedy is not the sign of sinfulness, then it's also true that the absence of tragedy says nothing about how we're doing. We're speaking now of ordinary life—with stress of course and conflict of course, and here and there some doubt or depression of course—ordinary life that isn't especially easy but that clearly isn't threatened by life-crushing crises. In such essentially uneventful, untragic living, isn't it sweet to assume that we are being blessed, that we're basically sound, solid people receiving the pleasant dividends that people like us can expect to receive?

Jesus says, "I tell you no." Your present comfort is no index of God's favor. The absence of crisis in your life or mine cannot be construed as God's approval of how we live. We want to set ourselves at a distance from the victims of tragedy and tut-tut "How terrible for them!" But Jesus holds up these pictures of tragedy and says, "Look to your own life. Let the fact of death and danger shock you into self-examination." He wants us to know we're the ones in need of changing. And He wants us to know, in a world where crisis can fall at anytime, we must do our changing soon.

III

And he tells a story to help us understand. "A man had a fig tree planted in his vineyard, and he came looking for fruit on it and he found none." Time-out for our first lesson on Palestinian Horticulture 101. A fig tree in Palestine is supposed to be enormously fruitful, bearing three different crops per year. But this tree, having gone figless for three years, has yawned through nine whole harvests, and the man is understandably out of patience. He says, "Why should this tree use up the ground? Cut it down." Now if this fig tree is somehow representative of people like us, would you notice something? The failure of the tree is not in doing anything wrong. It's not a nasty, hateful tree; it hasn't broken one of the commandments. It's not a heretic tree. Its failing is that it stands in the sun on a choice piece of ground drinking up nourishment and never fulfills its purpose. We are ever-eager to trivialize sin to mean the little misdeeds we do.

But here is our sin: it is the raw, unthinkable violation of our *purpose* here. The great evil of our living is the refusal to realize the possibility that God planted in us, the stubborn resistance to make something of it and bear the fruit of our promise. Like the fig tree, we've been set down on a sunny slope of the garden, and we absorb so many rich resources as we hold on to our privileged place. But when does that privilege ever find expression in an increase of obedience in us?

When does it ever burst into fragrant sweet witness of God's love? When does it ripen into deeds of compassion and justice? Are we waving leaves at the world? Are we shaking leafy branches at one another? Or is anybody actually getting fed by our common life? That is our purpose and our great promise. In Jesus' story the tree that will not answer with its purpose does not deserve its place in the garden. The owner reaches for his ax.

IV

But then a strange thing happens. The hired man leaps up and tells the owner—"Wait!" And he goes into a chorus of "Woodman, spare that tree!" "Give it one more year," he says, "let me work the ground and fertilize it and give this tree every conceivable advantage. If it doesn't bear fruit by next year, then cut it down."

Time-out for lesson #2 in Palestinian Horticulture. What's happening here is absolutely extraordinary. A fig tree isn't supposed to take any attention at all. Its root system is incredibly equipped to gather nourishment and produce fruit. It thrives upon neglect. But for this flop of a tree a gardener is ready to bend over backwards and do everything imaginable to make it right.

Here is an astonishing patience! It's not at all like the ending of another story about a tree that was well-known in Jesus' day. It was the fable of a palm tree that didn't produce. Its owner finally came to chop it down, and the tree hollered, "Don't cut me down! Transplant me to a better place, and I'll bear fruit." To which the owner said, "If you haven't borne fruit yet, you never will"; and he chopped it down. When Jesus told His story, people must have been surprised. The owner of this tree was unthinkably patient—amazingly willing to love a little tree toward its purpose.

Just how willing, the people listening to Jesus could never guess, but we can. This Gardener is gracious enough to lay down His life, to be Himself hanged on the shameful tree of our barrenness, watering the ground around us with His own outpoured Life—not just for our forgiveness, but for our bursting into bloom at last with Him and our bearing fruit with Him to free the world and fulfill our purpose at last. What more could be done? It is why in the story the gardener can say, "If the tree then will not bear fruit, cut it down."

Now do you see what Jesus meant about our lives these days? We began by asking: What does it mean when tragedy comes? But Jesus reverses the question: Have you thought about what it might mean when tragedy hasn't come? Have you stopped to ask why these ordinary days are given to you? These are not ordinary days at all. Do not receive them lightly as a string of expected benefits. Receive them with open-eyed gratitude as unexpected mercies. These ordinary days are not uneventful days; they are the days of crisis and decision. For these are the last days we have been given to take hold of God's abundant patience, to avail ourselves of the extravagance that God has poured upon us, and to fulfill our promise as God's sons and daughters.

A few times in my life, especially out in the country, I've heard an elderly saint or two pray a prayer something like this: "Thank you, O Lord, for sparing us another day." I was always troubled by this prayer because it seemed to me to presuppose a God always poised to strike and begrudgingly sparing us one more day before finally finishing us off. To this menacing figure, the generous God of Jesus bears no resemblance. And yet in the deepest sense Jesus invites us to see our days as a sparing. Today our lives are graciously spared. The life of our church has been spared. A nation, for now, has been spared—and a world. Our days are a sparing. There has long been repentance to do, a turning, a seizing of our promise. In the grace that God has given so far, there has been unimaginable patience, and at the heart of that patience a suffering beyond words. Not to respond with our lives to that grace is an unthinkable waste and invites upon us a terrible judgment.

The good and urgent news is that we've been granted a time—no one knows how short—to turn ourselves Godward and to answer the lavished love of the Gardener with the sweeter fruit that will feed the world. When shall we choose this, if not today? So let's thank the Lord for sparing us another day, and let's offer now the best fruit which these lives under grace can grow.

Peter James Flamming

On Letting Go and Trusting God
Genesis 22:1-14

An old German Bible story book of mine, published in 1713, has a woodcut of Abraham offering Isaac on the altar at Mt. Moriah. The woodcut shows a finely designed altar. Abraham stands above it with a knife in his right hand, looking up into heaven. Isaac, more the size of a teenager than a child, rests on the altar with wood stacked around. The ram looks at the whole scene from the background. What a strange sight!

What a strange story! It troubles us. What do we make of a God who would demand that a father offer up his son on a sacrificial altar? And Isaac was no ordinary son. He was the son of promise, the miracle that blessed the lives of Abraham and Sarah when they were past the age when they could have children. Isaac was God's answer to His covenant with Abraham that He would make his seed like the sand of the sea and the stars of the heavens. Isaac was a miracle. Isaac was an answer to prayer. Isaac embodied hope. Now God tells Abraham to offer up his miracle child whom he loves more than anything in the world. Strange story.

Abraham's response is even more incredible. He obeys. He obeys! As the father of three sons I say to you, Abraham's obedience is beyond comprehension. As he trudges brokenheartedly toward Mount Moriah his soul must have been groaning under a massive contradiction. On the one hand he knows that the God he worships is not a destroyer. Yet he knows also the God he worships demands obedience. So Abraham obeys. With Isaac he stumbles towards Mount

Moriah, chanting under his breath those immense words of trust, "God will provide."

What is going on here? What is the hidden agenda? Much is happening. Manifold are the agendas. I mention only one of them. It is this. *For Abraham to become who Abraham is supposed to be, and for Isaac to become who Isaac is supposed to be, neither can be god to each other.* Only God can be God to Abraham. Only God can be God to Isaac.

The Tug of War of Faith

Faith braces itself in a continual tug-of-war with the good things we make into gods. There is, you know, only one letter's difference between god and good. A small difference in spelling—a vast difference in life. Isaac was to be loved as Isaac, not like God.

Do you see the relationship between idolatry and stress? When the center of life has been displaced it is like life is suddenly out of balance. The result is the same as if both front tires of your car are terribly out of balance. Does it add stress to the journey? Indeed.

Stress and Idolatry

Many of the stresses, even the traumas we live under, we bring on ourselves. How do we do it? By making someone or something god, or by trying to play god. Isaac, you see, cannot be god for Abraham. Abraham cannot play god for Isaac. When either of those happen, being god or playing god, a bumper crop of traumas are reaped.

What God is about has nothing to do with human sacrifice. He is doing surgery, spiritual surgery, which will keep Abraham from destroying his relationship with his son. When God is replaced as center, nothing good results. Human love, without divine love as center and source, can bring great chaos. God is trying to protect Abraham from himself.

She sat in my office at the request of the dean at the College. She was depressed and had quit attending classes.

She would have gone home, but it was from home that the intense pressure stemmed. She felt trapped. Like Isaac she was an only child, and in her own way, a child of promise. Her parents had invested their whole lives in her. She was for them center, future, meaning, and hope. Their dreams for her were dreams of greatness.

Yet she was not coordinated enough to be a great dancer; musical enough to excel in music; bright enough to be a great scholar; mathematical enough to be a great scientist. *Greatness.* That is what her parents expected of her. She was above average, but greatness would never be her playground. She was neither beauty queen nor genius nor leader. She was expected to be what she could not become. The singular love of her parents for her had turned out to be a curse, not a blessing. She felt trapped on every side. What do you do when you've become god to your parents, and they don't know it?

Notice how the parents have begun to play god. Having made their daughter into a god, they now begin to play god for her. It is a paradox. When we start making a god of someone or something else, we start playing god at the same time. The two seem to go together. Oh, the stress and trauma that develop.

Human love, without divine love at the center, has the great potential to produce havoc. Those well-meaning parents lacked one thing, one absolutely crucial item. They had no divine love at the center of their wishes for their daughter. The center was the daughter, a spot she could not bear. They were playing god, a role they could not fulfill. Satan never had it so good. It didn't take drugs or alcohol or laziness. All it took was a good old-fashioned case of idolatry.

How Do Idolatries Happen?

Almost anything can be made into a false god. How does it happen? Usually quite innocently. May I speak of the work I know best, that of being a minister? A young man completes his seminary training and eagerly begins among the people to whom he has been called to serve. He finds gifts he didn't know he had. The demands are so many. He discovers to his amazement that God uses him. The more gifts he uses, the more he is called upon to use them. The better job he does, the more he expects of himself.

His reputation spreads. People are helped. More energy is invested and more time. Soon he begins to see his family like ships passing in the dark. He is so busy tending God's flock he hardly has time for his prayers. Finally, he is so busy being a minister to God's people he has no time for God! The stress level increases, the demands continue to accelerate until finally his body and emotions rebel, and he winds up in the hospital. The doctor talks to him about stress and slowing down. Rightly so. Who else is going to talk to him about it? But that is not his real problem. His real problem is center. His church has become his god, his ministry his master, and his calling his Christ. Is there any idolatry quite so subtle as religious idolatry?

But the ministry isn't the only calling open to this temptation. A bank president once said to me. "I have reached all of the goals I set out for myself in my earlier years. My main conclusion is, it wasn't worth it." There wasn't anything wrong with his goals, his job, his bank, his ambition. What was wrong was his god, his center.

The only way to keep our ambition from destroying us is to put God at the center of our lives and keep Him there. The only source to restore the soul is the Good Shepherd Himself. What is at stake here is our own destruction. Our petty idolatries do not threaten God. They destroy us.

A Severe Mercy

God's mercy has a tough task here. He must somehow perform some spiritual surgery on the selfish ego while still leaving the positive ego that makes faith possible. God's mercy is sometimes a "severe mercy," as C. S. Lewis once noted. One of the dimensions of God's love is like surgery. It is healing but is healing that hurts. Abraham experiences a healing, a restoring, but it is a healing that calls for the greatest risk of all, that of letting go of something or someone he has come to cherish with all of his heart, his son Isaac.

There are times in faith's journey when God confronts us with the demand to be prepared to part with something very dear to us. We are called upon to walk forward into uncertain territory and trust Him. The old map makers in earlier centuries believed the world was flat. They would draw their maps until that place they believed the world dropped off. Then they drew dragons. Sometimes God forces us to walk off of our own maps of security and control. Those maps we know well. They are for us comfort zones. We come to believe they are identical with God's maps for our lives. We hardly notice it when our priorities began to change, when our cherishing begins to change focus. Sometimes security and control turn out to be the basic items to give up. Perhaps we fear losing our security and our control more than anything else. We have forgotten that the basic control of our lives is in the hands of God. He and He alone embodies our security. He alone knows the maps of our lives from beginning to end.

A Spiritual Principle

We can see this issue fleshed out before us when we parents watch our children leave for college. We have invested much. Letting them go, relinquishing control, relinquishing control of the security we think we have provided, can be difficult. But it is a strange paradox. Parents who are willing to let their sons and daughters go find them coming back and learning to relate as adult to adult. Parents who continue to exercise control just wish their children would come home once in awhile.

What God is helping Abraham to do is to prepare to give up that which he most cherishes, his son Isaac who has become the center of his life. Mark this spiritual principle well: *what we want to keep, we must be willing to give up to the care and keeping of God."*

The pivotal point of the story to me is Abraham's dogged faith that God would provide. He trudges toward that mountain of surrender, muttering to himself, "God will provide. I just know it. Somehow, some way, God will provide." God did. And He does. Abraham gives to God his son. Abraham lets him go. God gives him back. It is a spiritual principle. Whatever you want to keep, you have to be willing to give away. Jesus said, "Whoever would save his life shall lose it, but whoever will lose his life for my sake and the gospel's shall find it." But that is only possible if you really believe "God will provide."

God's provision did not stop with Abraham. Abraham, the offering, the altar, the ram in place of . . . ; all are but a picture of God's provision for all of us at Calvary. Abraham and the altar on Moriah are but a type of a greater provision God will provide in Jesus Christ our Lord.

On another stone hill, in Christ, on a cross, "God will provide" took on new meaning. Look, like Abraham, our Lord trudges up Golgotha's hill carrying a cross, ready to make His own sacrifice. At stake is our salvation. Is He willing to let go of his life, to give it up in our behalf, to offer it as provision for our sins and for our forgiveness?

One of the earliest pictures of the crucifixion is a Byzantine wall-painting. The picture shows the stony hill and the rough-hewn cross. But instead of Christ hanging there, there is a huge nailed Lamb on that crossbar. "Behold the Lamb of God," said John the Baptist, "who takes away the sin of the world." Even the sin of our idolatries. Even the chaos of our misplaced values. Even the sins of our cherishing gone awry. Even the priorities we have placed on pedestals and begun to worship. Even the stresses all of these bring on ourselves and others. All of these are covered in God's provision for our idolatries and stresses.

What, my friends, do we do with our realized idolatries if we cannot present them to the foot of the cross? What we mostly do is pretend the idolatry doesn't exist, thus to continue the stress and havoc produced. Or we take out our stresses on ourselves or someone close to us. The truth of the cross is that God has covered our sins with His provision of forgiveness in Jesus Christ our Savior and Lord. Those who will not accept Christ's gift on the cross usually wind up making one for themselves or someone else.

In Genoa, Italy, after World War II they commissioned an artist to do an eight-ton statue of Christ. Unlike other statues of Christ throughout the world, this one was not put on a high hill overlooking the city. Instead, it was lowered into the depths of the bay where the great battle had taken place. Lowered into the depths, the depths where the sunken ships lay silent, where forgotten heroism rests in quiet memory. They called the statue "The Christ of the Deep." It is a beautiful picture of the ministry of Christ reaching into the depths of the human heart to provide for us new levels of spirit and stability.

And what is our part? David Buttrick of Vanderbilt Divinity School tells of a minister he knows who put some specially designed wallpaper on the wall fronting from her desk. The wallpaper repeats the words, line after line, all over the wall: Let go, trust God. Let go, trust God. When we have become enslaved by opportunities turned sour, our letting go and His healing touch may be our only rescue.

God's message to us is: Let go. Let go. God will provide. He has. In Christ He has. Are we willing to let go and trust our Lord? There is such great risk in letting go, we think, as if we were capable of running the universe as God does. But there is even more ruin in stress and chaos if we don't. Let go. Let go! God will provide.

Alfonso Flores

The Mind of Christ
Philippians 2:5-8

The portion we are going to consider today contains one of the best known Christological passages in the New Testament. It is also one of the most impressive and revealing concerning the incomparable price of our redemption by the Son of God. It is a passage that throughout the centuries has been considered, analyzed, studied, and restudied over and over again by some of the ablest of theologians, preachers, teachers, and laymen as well. And from those countless studies have come the concepts, theories, and doctrines which the church has today regarding the Person of the Son of God.

However, if you consider the context of the passage you will find that Paul, the writer of the letter in which this beautiful passage is found, did not really set out to pen a great theological treatise on the Person of Christ. His purpose in writing it was to reinforce his impassioned appeal for unity and harmony in a church that he loved very dearly, and in which problems of conflict, discord, and disharmony were beginning to surface. To show them the kind of attitude and spirit that leads to unity, accord, and harmony he places before them the example not of another man, nor even his own, but the impressive example of the Lord Jesus Christ Himself.

If you notice carefully you will see that what he says in verses 5-8 of that second chapter of the letter is directly connected and related with what he says in the first four verses. It is only after he has written these words:

> Doing nothing out of selfishness or conceit, but
> with humility regarding others superior to your-
> selves. Neither must each be looking out only for his
> own interests but also for those of others . . .

that he concludes his appeal with the words of the passage
that we are considering here:

> Let this mind be in you which was also in Christ
> Jesus who, though existing in the form of God, did not
> consider His equality with God something to cling to,
> but emptied Himself as He took on the form of a slave
> and become like human beings. So, recognized in ap-
> pearance as a human being, He humbled Himself
> and became obedient to death; yes death by the cross
> (NEB).

As you can see, the central theme is unity and harmony by having and living with the mind of Christ. What a
vital subject that is for us as Southern Baptists. Isn't it true
that one of the threats to our success in the fulfillment of
our Great Commission is our lack of unity and harmony.
Indeed, one of the tragic results of our conflicts is that in
some instances it has taken our eyes off our great and noble
goal of evangelizing the world with the Gospel of our Lord.
What we need individually and collectively as Christians and Baptists is to live with the mind of the Lord not
only for the sake of unity and harmony among ourselves,
but to be pleasing in the Presence of God.
Well, what does it mean to have the mind of Christ?
How can we possibly have the mind of the Lord? It is evident that when Paul writes of having the mind of Christ, he
was not referring literally to the Lord's genius as a thinker.
The Lord Jesus Christ was undoubtedly the greatest and
most original thinker the world has ever known.
Years ago, Dr. N. D. Hills wrote an interesting book
titled *The Influence of Christ In Modern Life*. In the book
there's a chapter titled, "Jesus Christ the Supreme Exam-

ple in the Kingdom of the Intellect," in which the author demonstrates some of the incomparable intellectual resources of Christ revealed in His teachings and His influence on law, literature, and life as a whole. He concludes that while there have been men whose intellectual genius was of the highest magnitude, none could ever compare with Christ. True.

What, then, did Paul mean when he wrote to those believers, exhorting them to let the mind which was in Jesus Christ be in them? Considering other passages where the same word "mind" is used, I believe the expression, "the mind of Christ," refers to the Lord's basic thoughts and attitudes, to His motives and fundamental principles and purposes; it refers to the way He thought about God, man, life, and eternity. In that sense we are to have the mind of our Lord.

I think that the passage we are considering sheds some light on that great subject. I want to show you three characteristics of the mind of Christ illustrated in this passage. Those are submission, servanthood, and sacrifice. In other words the mind of Christ was a submissive mind, it was the mind of a servant, and finally it was a sacrificial mind.

Notice:

I. The Mind of Christ Was Submissive . . .

Listen to the words of the text: "Let this mind be in you which was also in Christ Jesus, who, though existing in the form of God, did not consider His equality with God something to cling to . . ."

According to the dictionary, the word submission means: "the action and effect of submitting oneself." It is a synonym for the word surrender. Applying that to Christ, Paul was saying that Jesus did not consider His prerogatives and celestial privileges, His exalted position as God as something to cling to, but out of love was willing to surrender and submit them to the Father's redemptive will.

But that submission of Christ to the Father was made manifest not only in taking that giant step downward, coming to this world, but in His life and ministry and in His death. The truth of the matter is that He lived a life of total, complete, and perfect submission to the Father.

How different the conditions of the world would be if that spirit of submission could prevail in the world! Wouldn't you agree that many of the problems that prevail in the world today are due directly or indirectly to the fact that people are not willing to submit themselves to others? The great majority of us are more willing to fight if necessary, demanding and defending our rights.

One of the most controversial problems we are facing today as a nation is abortion. Last year, we are told, there were more than a million abortions performed in our nation. And they tell us the number is increasing dramatically each year. One of the arguments put forth by those who favor abortion at will is that a woman has the right to decide what she does with her own body. But what about the rights of the child in that woman's body? Don't the rights of the child count?

How many evils, injustices, and even crimes are committed by men and women demanding their rights? I remember a man who was about to destroy his home by leaving his wife and children who idolized him, to go with another woman. And the only reasons he could give for what he was about to do was that he had a right to be happy. To be happy? At the expense of others? That is nothing but cruel, naked selfishness.

"Let not that be the case with you," Paul says to those believers. You are not to have that mind or those thoughts. "Do nothing out of selfishness or conceit . . ." In other words, be willing to surrender your rights and to submit yourself to others for Christ's sake. To demand our rights when it will cause others to suffer, or when it will be a detriment to the cause of Christ, is not having or living with the mind of the Master.

The mind of Christ is a submissive mind. That mind is

needed in the home. How many homes and families are destroyed because either the husband or the wife, or both of them, were unwilling to submit themselves to each other? Many times the wife does not want to submit to her husband, and the husband finds it unthinkable to submit to his wife. I have heard many husbands quote Ephesians 5:22 to their wives. That is the verse where Paul says: "Wives, be subject to your husbands as to the Lord." But in many cases the previous verse 21 is completely overlooked. In that verse Paul says to both the husband and the wife: "Be submissive to one another out of reverence for Christ."

To be sure it is not easy to be submissive to each other within the home. I heard of the couple that came from Japan. After they had been here for several years the wife made an application for citizenship and several months later got it. As you know, in Japan the woman is very submissive to her husband. Well, on the day when she finally obtained her prized possession, the husband came home from work, picked up the newspaper, went to his favorite chair, and called his wife. "Wife," he called, "bring me my slippers." But the wife, with a new spark in her eyes, replied: "Husband, free country, me American citizen, get the slippers yourself!"

That same submissive mind is greatly needed in the church as well. How much the mind of Christ is needed with the church today. We need to remember that it was to a church that Paul was writing and exhorting them to have the mind of Christ. There were two women, sisters in the Lord named Euodias and Syntyche who were having a conflict that was upsetting the whole church. Paul was thus exhorting them to resolve their problem with the mind of Christ. And, brethren, if we have trouble surrendering our rights, let us think of what Christ surrendered for us. Can there be anything that we may have to surrender in an attitude of submission to each other that could possibly compare with what the Lord surrendered? Yes, the mind of Christ was a submissive mind.

Secondly, let us notice that,

II. The Mind of Christ Was the
Mind of a Servant . . .

Paul continues: "but emptied Himself as He took on the form of a servant and became like human beings . . ." Jesus Christ had the mind of a servant. He was a servant. Do you remember the words which we could correctly say expressed His life's motto? "For the Son of man," He said, "came not to be served, but to serve and to give His life a ransom for many" (Mark 10:45).

And serve He did. He preached, taught, healed, fed the hungry, served. His whole life was a long, extended act of service to man. He understood from the beginning that the purpose of His coming into the world was to serve. Furthermore, His life of service was a fulfillment of what the prophet had written about Him hundreds of years before He took the form of a man at Bethlehem.

Turn with me and see what was written about Him in the Book of Isaiah (52:13) hundreds of years before His coming: "Behold! My Servant shall work wisely. He shall arise, be exalted, and shall stand exceedingly high . . ." And although that verse, as well as the entire passage including chapter 53, is frequently applied to Israel, the consensus of opinion is that the primary application is to the Lord Jesus Christ.

He is the Lord's servant. More then that He is the Lord's Suffering Servant Who became our substitute on the cross. In other words, His service was costly. It cost Him His life on the tree. I believe that is the true meaning of the verse we have already quoted: "For the Son of man came not to be served, but to serve and to give His life as a ransom for many." What that means is that His faithful life would be culminated by one great and glorious act of service which would be His death on the cross. But that life of service, along with His great climactic death on the cross, began in His mind, which was in fact the mind of a servant.

That was the lesson He tried so hard to teach His disciples. They, like He, were to be servants. They were not to try to emulate the men of this world who think that the greatest is the one who receives the greatest service. In His Kingdom the greatest would be the servant of all. Tragically, however, of all the lessons He tried to teach them, that was the one they had the most trouble in understanding and accepting. Even to the end of His ministry among them they were constantly disputing among themselves as to who was the greatest and who would occupy the highest place. Perhaps for that reason one of the most impressive lessons He gave them was the night He was betrayed and as they celebrated the Passover feast.

There existed in those times the custom that when one entered the house of another as a guest, one of the servants in that household would take some water in a basin and wash the dust from his feet. Well, when the Lord and the disciples entered that upper room for the celebration of the Passover feast, not one of them had taken the initiative to assume the part of a servant to wash the feet of the Lord and the other disciples. Can you imagine their surprise when the Lord got up from the table, laid aside His robe, and, taking water in a basin, began to wash their feet? They were astonished. Peter even became defensive, refusing to let the Lord wash his feet, until the Lord told him that if he did not allow it, he would have no part in His kingdom. What a reproach to them!

After washing their feet and taking His garments, He sat at the table again and said to them: "Do you understand what I have done to you? You call me Teacher and Lord, and rightly so, because I am. Then if I, your Lord and Teacher, have washed your feet, you surely ought to wash one another's feet. For I have set you an example so that you might do just as I did to you" (John 13:12-15). See how difficult it was to them to serve one another? They didn't have the mind of Christ. They didn't have the mind of a servant.

But what about us today? Do we have the mind of Christ in that respect? We must remember that we, too, have been called to be servants. What Christ said to His disciples applies as well to us today. Tragically, we seem to have the same problem being servants as His first disciples.

How much that mind of service is needed in the church today! Surely, one of our great needs is to be sensitive to one another, and to be willing in the Spirit of the Lord to serve one another as He commanded us. All too often we sit in our comfortable pews, completely oblivious to those sitting around us who may be agonizing with a serious problem and waiting for someone to reach out to them. I believe that our service begins with the brethren in the church. Listen to what Paul says in that respect: "So then, while we have opportunity, let us do good to all men, and especially to those who are of the household of the faith" (Gal. 6:10).

Yes, the mind of Christ was the mind of a servant, and so should ours be. Finally notice that,

III. The Mind of Christ Was Sacrificial . . .

Listen again to the text: "He humbled Himself and became obedient to death, yes, even death by the cross." As we have already noted, it is evident that from the beginning the Lord recognized that He had come into the world to be a servant. And it is also very clear that He also realized that the price of His redemptive service would be His death or sacrifice on the cross. That's not to say it was easy for Him to face the cross and die upon it. All we have to do to see how difficult it was for Him to face that awful cross or to drink the cup, as He expressed it, is to read once again the account of His experience at Gethsemane. Luke says His agony of spirit was so intense that His sweat became as great drops of blood that fell to the ground.

The writer of the Letter to the Hebrews, referring to that same experience in the garden, says that He offered prayers and petitions with strong crying and with tears to Him who could save Him from death, and He was heard because of His humble devotion. Evidently, it was far from easy for Him to face the cross and His death upon it. But in spite of the pain, suffering, and shame that He saw in that cross, He never wavered from that path of sacrifice. "Nevertheless," He prayed, "not my will, but thine be done." "If I came into the world for this purpose," He told His disciples, "how can I ask to be spared now?" His mind was set upon that sacrifice.

But what about us? Isn't there a cross for us? The writer of that well-known hymn answers that for us:

> Must Jesus bear the cross alone, and all the
>   world go free?
> No, there's a cross for everyone, and there's a
>   cross for me.

Yes, there is a cross for us; there is a sacrifice to be made. Jesus made that very clear when He said: "Whosoever will come after me, let him deny himself and take up his cross and follow me" (Mark 8:34). The Christian life in the true sense of the word is a life of sacrifice. To be sure it is a living sacrifice, as Paul says in His letter to the Romans: "I beseech you, therefore, brethren, by the mercies of God, that ye present your bodies a living sacrifice, holy, acceptable unto God, which is your reasonable service."

Peter in his First Epistle says that we as believers as: ". . . living stones are built up a spiritual house, an holy priesthood, to offer spiritual sacrifices acceptable to God by Jesus Christ" (1 Pet. 2:5). In other words, we are to be continually laying our lives on God's altar as sacrifices that may be pleasing and acceptable unto Him. But that life of sacrifice begins in the mind. Ours are to be like the mind of the Lord, a sacrificial mind. That is what the church and the world as a whole needs today. That is the kind of heroism that is lacking and so sorely missed. However, there are still some of those heroes. Let me tell you of one of the youngest.

His name is Scott McKenzie, and he lives with his parents in a suburb of St. Louis, Missouri. Some time ago, one morning seven-year-old Scott, his three-year-old sister Carrie, and a four-year-old playmate were in the backyard of their house playing on the jungle gym. Across the fence in the neighbor's yard was a 100-pound German Shepherd, half-wolf, barking ferociously and pulling on the chain with which it was tied.

Suddenly, the huge dog broke the chain, jumped the fence running towards the children. Scott saw the dog coming and didn't hesitate for a moment. He helped his sister and playmate climb the jungle gym, which was large enough for only two, and then started running for help with the dog in pursuit.

But it was no contest, no race between Scott and the dog. The ferocious animal overtook him, clamped its huge jaws around the little boy's body, and dragged him about seventy feet, biting and mauling him. Meanwhile, his sister Carrie climbed down and ran screaming for her parents. A police officer who lived nearby heard the screams, ran outside with his .357 Magnum pistol, and killed the dog.

They picked up the bruised, bitten, mauled, almost dead boy's body. His mother said the doctor stopped counting the stitches in his face at 1,000, and added, "We're grateful that he's alive." Scott still faces three to five years of operations and psychological counseling. Scott McKenzie is a hero. He has a sacrificial mind. He laid down his life for his sister and their playmate.

Such was the mind of Christ. He is our Savior, Redeemer, and Hero par excellence. All the hounds of hell were unleashed upon Him there on the cross. When it was over they took His body down from the cross, beaten, crushed, and mauled, and even worse, dead. He had laid down His life for us. He had sacrificed Himself to save us.

Such was the mind of Christ. It was submissive, it was the mind of a servant, and it was sacrificial. God help us to grow in the likeness of His mind! Amen.

Charles G. Fuller

Barren Branches
Isaiah 17:1-11

The burden of Damascus. Behold, Damascus is taken away from being a city, and it shall be a ruinous heap.

The cities of Aroer are forsaken: They shall be for flocks, which shall lie down, and none shall make them afraid.

The fortress also shall cease from Ephraim, and the kingdom from Damascus, and the remnant of Syria: they shall be as the glory of the children of Israel, saith the Lord of hosts.

And in that day it shall come to pass, that the glory of Jacob shall be made thin, and the fatness of his flesh shall wax lean.

And it shall be as when the harvestman gathereth the corn, and reapeth the ears with his arm; and it shall be as he that gathereth ears in the valley of Rephaim.

Yet gleaning grapes shall be left in it, as the shaking of an olive tree, two or three berries in the top of the uppermost bough, four or five in the outmost fruitful branches thereof, saith the Lord God of Israel.

At that day shall a man look to his Maker, and his eyes shall have respect to the Holy One of Israel.

And he shall not look to the altars, the work of his hands, neither shall respect that which his fingers have made, either the groves, or the images.

In that day shall his strong cities be as a forsaken bough, and an uppermost branch, which they left because of the children of Israel: and there shall be desolation.

> Because thou hast forgotten the God of thy sal-
> vation, and hast not been mindful of the rock of thy
> strength, therefore shalt thou plant pleasant plants,
> and shalt set it with strange slips:
> In the day shalt thou make thy plant to grow,
> and in the morning shalt thou make thy seed to flour-
> ish: but the harvest shall be a heap in the day of grief
> and of desperate sorrow (Isa. 17:1-11).

At times, the Bible is like an album of word-pictures.
With the quickness of a photographer, the accuracy of an
eyewitness, the creativity of an artist, and the candor belonging only to the Holy Spirit, the Scriptures graphically
display persons, conditions, and lessons for our instruction.

Three such verbal sketches are found in the first few
verses of Isaiah's seventeenth chapter. The prophet is warning the people of his day about the consequences which
await those who persist in their disobedience to God. Having leveled his sights upon several of those nations nearby
his own, Isaiah then focuses the burden of his prophecy
upon the Hebrew people.

If the nation refuses to repent and return to the Lord,
the prophet foresees their fate as that of a terrible famine.
His picture of what awaits them is vivid indeed. God's verbal artist depicts a once-healthy, robust man who has become frail, thin, and weakened.

> And in that day it shall come to pass, that the glory of
> Jacob shall be made thin, and the fatness of his flesh
> shall wax lean (Isa. 17:4).

Isaiah adds still another picture to his description of
what awaits an unrepentant people. This picture seems to
be one of population decline, perhaps because many will be
carried away into the bondage of a hostile country.

The handful of people left behind after such captivity
would be like a field of corn which has been harvested.
Only a few ears are left on the stalks. There are just enough
ears to be pulled by one harvester and collected under but
one of his arms.

> And it shall be as when the harvestman gathereth
> the corn, and reapeth the ears with his arm; and it
> shall be as he that gathereth ears in the valley of
> Rephaim (17:5).

The third picture Isaiah sees, however, is the most graphic. He says if the nation does not return to the Lord it will be like unto an olive tree, once abundantly fruitful, but that has become almost barren.

> Yet gleaning grapes shall be left in it, as the shaking
> of an olive tree, two or three berries in the top of the
> uppermost bough, four or five in the outmost fruitful
> branches thereof, saith the Lord God of Israel (17:6).

The fate of God's own people, if they insist upon neglecting and disobeying Him, is described by the prophet's picture of a tree after the olive-gatherers have shaken the limbs and beaten the branches. Nothing is left but a few olives in the uppermost bough with a few more on an outermost limb.

The olive tree pictured, then, is not one of total barrenness but of near barrenness. The tree can still claim to be an olive tree, but there is no productivity left. The ultimate proof of its identity is all but gone. Save for a lone olive here and there, what distinguishes this tree from a fig tree or a sycamore?

Like Isaiah's descriptive near-barren tree, when Christians have lost their obedient closeness to the Lord, they too become unfruitful, indistinct, and unusable. They are still the Lord's own but, spiritually, they become almost barren. It is as Jesus said, when He used a similar word-picture:

> Abide in me, and I in you. As the branch cannot bear
> fruit of itself, except it abide in the vine; no more can
> ye, except ye abide in me. I am the vine, ye are the
> branches. He that abideth in me, and I in him, the
> same bringeth forth much fruit; for without me ye
> can do nothing (John 15:4-5).

Our concern in this message, however, does not stop
with the barren times upon which an unrepentant people
in the Old Testament would come. Our interest is upon
avoiding the condition of spiritual unfruitfulness in daily
Christian living. We have been given a specific admonition
on this subject in Peter's second New Testament letter.

> Grace and peace be multiplied unto you through
> the knowledge of God, and of Jesus our Lord, Accord-
> ing as his divine power hath given unto us all things
> that pertain unto life and godliness, through the
> knowledge of him that hath called us to glory and
> virtue: Whereby are given unto us exceeding great
> and precious promises; that by these ye might be par-
> takers of the divine nature, having escaped the cor-
> ruption that is in the world through lust. And besides
> this, giving all diligence, add to your faith virtue;
> and to virtue, knowledge; And to knowledge, temper-
> ance; and to temperance, patience; and to patience,
> godliness; and to godliness, brotherly kindness; and
> to brotherly kindness, charity. For if these things be
> in you, and abound, they make you that ye shall nei-
> ther be barren nor unfruitful in the knowledge of our
> Lord Jesus Christ (2 Pet. 1:2-8).

Notice, Peter reminds us it is possible to be barren and
unfruitful while having a knowledge of the Lord Jesus
Christ. However, it is no more desirable and purposeful for
a Christian to be saved and unfruitful than it is for an olive
tree to be rooted but barren.

If we are to be fruitful, then we must know how to
avoid being barren. That's where a deeper study of Isaiah's
verbal olive tree can be so helpful.

Just how did the people of Isaiah's day come to the
state of spiritual fruitlessness? Interestingly enough, some
of the same things which led to their spiritual condition on
a national scale, can lead to our barrenness as individual
Christians. Isaiah mentions three causes which lay behind
the declining, weakening condition of God's people in his
day:

A Love of Idols
A Lapse of Memory
A Loss of Concentration

I. A Love of Idols

Knowing the aversion the ancient Hebrews had toward idols, it seems ridiculous to suggest they would ever have a problem with them. By the same token, we evangelical Christians would be quick to deny having any attraction to images of wood or stone, fetishes or trinkets, statues or shrines.

The ancient Jews did have problems with idols, however, and Ezekiel's treatment of the subject provides real insight into the problems with idols we may have.

> Son of man, these men have set up their idols in their heart, and put the stumblingblock of their iniquity before their face: should I be enquired of at all by them? Therefore speak unto them, and say unto them, Thus saith the Lord God; Every man of the house of Israel that setteth up his idols in his heart, and putteth the stumblingblock of his iniquity before his face, and cometh to the prophet; I the Lord will answer him that cometh according to the multitude of his idols; That I may take the house of Israel in their own heart, because they are all estranged from me through their idols (Ezek. 14:3-5).

It seems when Isaiah spoke about the idol problem in his prophecy, he described it as something which could be more clearly recognized after repentance had revealed past sins for what they had really been:

> At that day shall a man look to his Maker, and his eyes shall have respect to the Holy One of Israel. And he shall not look to the altars, the work of his hands, neither shall respect that which his fingers have made, either the groves, or the images (17:7-8).

As modern-day Christians, our idol problems are not to be found on window sills or dangling from walls or within

temple shrines. The idols which infatuate us are more subtle competitors for the love which legitimately belongs only
to our Lord.

One such subtle idol which can capture our attention,
our energies, and affections, so that we lose our interest in
being useful and fruitful to the Lord, is the *idol of affluence.*
Especially do Christians living in the 1980s need to be
warned of the idolatry of affluence. Evangelical Christians
in the United States now are blessed with more social acceptance, more national profile, and more opportunities for
benefiting from the trappings of success than perhaps we
have ever been.

This is not to say that all Christians who live in wall-
to-wall carpeted worlds, who drive late-model, air-
conditioned automobiles, and who can afford exotic,
lengthy vacations are unspiritual as a result. There is nothing inherently evil about material comforts. There is, however, a danger to be found in such a high status of
well-being and in such material abundance. The danger is
that one discovers he has little need, or desire, to be rich in
spirit. For a Christian to be detoured by an attraction to
material things, and to be fulfilled in their acquiring, is to
be susceptible to a very alluring form of idolatry. Adding to
the subtlety of the idolatry of affluence is the emphasis
some versions of modern Christianity place upon physical
and material well-being as sure and ultimate signs of godli-
ness.

In the face of such misleading ideas, we would do well
to be reminded that God's greatest desire for us is not that
we become wealthy, popular, and successful, but that we become Christ-like! To cultivate a love for wealth and the
things it buys, regardless of how sanctimoniously we may
explain it, is to be captured by an idolatry which is servant-
less in its mind-set and spiritually fruitless in its end
result.

Another idol, which can so enamor us that we become
its servant, is the idol to which we often refer as *"success."*
Success, no more than material comforts, is not evil in itself.

In fact, it is a good witness for any Christian to exert every effort to succeed in whatever the Lord has assigned him or afforded him. Success becomes an idol problem when thoughts of self-glory and peer-recognition surpass the desire to glorify God. If our obsession is toward self-glory, we certainly cannot be content simply to bear the fruit God produces.

In no area of life are we modern-day Christians more susceptible to the idolatry of success than in the standards we use to evaluate someone's ministry. We often use the same standards to determine with which ministries we wish to be identified. When we excitedly give creditability to highly-profiled, numerically-overwhelming ministries, while at the same time according little appreciation or interest in less spectacular places of service, we are flirting with a pride-level the Lord resists. We will not be, for we cannot be, fruitful by God's standards, if our chief desire is to be successful by worldly standards or by those of our peers.

While we are fashioning labels for idols which enthrall and entice us, so that we lose all interest in being spiritually fruitful, we would do well to recognize one other. We might call this one the *idolatry of "elitism."* There is an attitude we can entertain which is so exclusively impressed with whatever our own beliefs are, concerning the style or the approach or the measurements of quality-Christianity, that we can refuse to recognize the indwelling Holy Spirit in other twice-born believers. Entertaining this attitude finds us trapped in one of the most subtle of idolatries.

Do not misunderstand! This is not to suggest there are no specifics by which to "try the spirits," nor is it to suggest there be no guidelines on which to base our fellowships. It is to say, though, that we dabble in the idolatry of elitism when we judge other Christians on the basis of:

> code words. . . . preferred politics. . . . the "theological company" one keeps. . . . bellwether interpretations of biblical passages (designed to test intelligence or "soundness" of position—not tests of The Faith).

That this type of elitism is an adulteration of a Christian's love for the Lord, which can strip the branches of his life of their intended spiritual productivity, should be quite obvious. It is little wonder, when the Apostle John came to the close of his first Epistle, he appropriately warned his Christian readers: "Little children, keep yourselves from idols" (1 John 5:21).

II. A Lapse of Memory

Isaiah prophesied:

> In that day shall his strong cities be as a forsaken bough, and an uppermost branch, which they left because of the children of Israel: and there shall be desolation. Because thou hast forgotten the God of thy salvation . . . (17:9-10*a*).

When God's people forget from whence they came, when Christians forget the simple faith and conversion which brought them from enmity with God to become children of God, then the vital "juices" flowing from the Vine to the branches begin to go dry; we become spiritually barren. To be certain, if Christians "pitch their tents" at the crossroads of their conversion experience and travel no further, they are just as likely to become barren as those who lose touch with their new-birth experience. Obviously, the need is to stay in touch with our redemptive beginnings as we continue to "grow in grace and in the knowledge of our Lord and Saviour Jesus Christ" (2 Pet. 3:18*a*).

In the late fall of 1968 I joined some thirty-five other Southern Baptist pastors and musicians and traveled to the Philippines to participate in a month-long evangelistic crusade. After three days of orientation, led by some of our missionaries there, we scattered over the islands to our various assignments. My first assignment was as the evangelist in the Baptist church located in the village of Babak on the island of Samal. Our first service was held on Saturday night, following our arrival that afternoon. As I was staying in the home of the host pastor, we went home together after that service and continued to get more acquainted with each other, even as we prepared for bed. I remember as we lay on our cots, beneath mosquito nets, talking in the dark, I asked my Philippine Christian brother to tell me about himself.

Since I had been particularly inquisitive at the point of how he had come to accept Jesus Christ as his personal Savior, my new friend related the story of his conversion. It had happened as a result of the witness of Southern Baptist missionaries in Davao City. My friend briefed me on his call to the pastoral ministry, told me of his plans to attend the seminary in Baguio, and shared with me his plans for marriage.

Then my turn came. My host pastor said, "Brother Charles, tell me about yourself."

In a way similar to my Philippine brother, I related my conversion experience. In the midst of unfolding the details of my conversion, I suddenly realized I was beginning to choke up and that tears were flowing freely. Within myself I thought, *Charles Fuller, how long has it been since you wept like this, rejoicing in the recollection of your saving encounter with Christ?*

In that moment, half-way around the world, lying on a cot, under a starlit Philippine sky, I realized how vital it is that we never lose touch with the vivid joy of the forgiveness of our own sin and our new birth in Christ. To do so, regardless of how well-traveled or seasoned we may become, is to lose that tenderness and verve so necessary to be the kind of branch on which Christ can produce His fruit!

Isaiah provides still another insight regarding the cause of barrenness among God's people. The insight is . . .

III. A Loss of Concentration

. . . thou . . . hast not been mindful of the rock of my strength (17:10*b*).

Notice! Isaiah says just what the problem was. They had lost their mindfulness (their concentration or reliance) regarding the rock (the source or foundation) of their strength. With respect to their lapse of memory, those ancients had lost touch with the grace of God which had given them their spiritual beginnings. Thus, we can readily see how they would not rely on the Lord to lead them in their continued spiritual pilgrimage. Knowing those Israelites had forgotten the power of the God who saved them, it is not difficult to understand how they mistakenly looked to their own resources for sustenance. They were attempting to meet their own needs, rather than relying on God for the strength and resources they needed to meet the demands and struggles of life.

Many years later, our Lord Jesus also spoke to the futility of a self-effort approach to Christian living:

> I am the vine, ye are the branches. He that abideth in me, and I in him, the same bringeth forth much fruit; for without me ye can do nothing (John 15:5).

Needless to say, there are some things God expects us to do. He will not do those things for us. But for a Christian to undertake, in the flesh, what can be accomplished only by the leadership, intervention, and gifts of the Holy Spirit, is folly of the worst sort.

Several years ago, at a time when I was unusually busy with preaching opportunities and denominational leadership responsibilities, our family was thrust into a sequence of painful difficulties. Within a matter of days, my wife underwent extensive back surgery, our youngest son (then eleven) entered the hospital on an emergency basis and required tedious surgery, and I snapped my achilles tendon while playing racquetball. Suddenly, my busy life came to an understandably abrupt halt. I was confronted with an enforced period of self-evaluation.

I had been stripped of my sense of well-being, mobility, and overrated usefulness. Impeded by a heavy cast on my leg and a prayerful burden for a wife and son recovering from surgery, I began to realize how much I needed to renew my dependence upon the God of my strength. As is the case with so many people, I had become far too impressed with my ability to handle life. It seemed ironic, too, that I should find myself in that self-reliant condition, even when my life was filled with vast and sundry sacred assignments.

Our family fully recovered from that intense period of testing, but I never want to forget what happened to my spirit in the midst of it all. Then I learned how essential it is that a Christian never lose his concentration upon the God of his strength. Life, even a life of busy, Christian service, lived in one's own strength, will eventually be discovered to be as barren as it really is.

Isaiah's lesson is plain. When there is a spiritual barrenness among God's people, there needs to be a removal of the subtle idols which have usurped the Lord's rightful place. There needs to be a refreshment of gratitude regarding one's spiritual beginnings. And, there needs to be a constant renewal of reliance upon God's strength.

It's as Jesus said, "Ye will know them by their fruits" (Matt. 7:16a). Or the implication is plain. We can know them by the lack of fruit.

The Power of Prevailing Prayer
Luke 11:5-13

Our Lord understood both the power and the priority of prayer. Though He was God, He lived in that daily dependence that comes only from fellowship with the Father. Often Jesus would rise a great while before dawn and spend those first waking hours in prayer. In the evenings, He would find a quiet place and there commune within the mystery of the Triune God. His days were interjected with great needs and therefore Jesus prepared in prayer, and His daily life was punctuated by powerful, prevailing prayer.

Have you noticed that Jesus walked through life with measured and unhurried steps? Though there were great demands placed upon His life, He never seemed harassed or harried. Though He was constantly pressured by people, He gracefully met their needs. Why such serenity? Jesus was on the Father's timetable. He lived according to a precise plan which unfolded daily in Heavenly fellowship. Our Lord moved about with the complete awareness that there was a divine timetable for every event in His life. He accomplished so much in such a short time because He practiced the priority and lived in the power of prayer.

So dynamic was our Lord's life of prayer that His disciples requested one day, "Lord, teach us to pray." It is significant that they did not say, "Lord, teach us to preach" or, "Lord, teach us to perform miracles," but "Lord, teach us to pray."

The sincere desire of the disciples is the heartcry of every growing Christian. Though most of us have been praying since early childhood, we never seem to be satisfied with our prayer lives. Most Christians will readily admit that prayerlessness is their most common and besetting sin. I know in my own life that every failure is ultimately a prayer failure. Prayer is the oldest and most universal of all religious experiences, yet we feel like beginners. Even though we believe that God hears and answers prayer, there seems to be a principle within that resists the incredible prospect of supplication. We, like the disciples, exclaim, "Lord, teach us to pray!"

Jesus is the Master Teacher. Like all good teachers, He begins at an elementary level and then advances to deeper levels of truth. In the beginning verses of Luke 11, we are introduced to the first level of prayer which is commonly called the "Lord's Prayer." This prayer is best described, however, as the "Model Prayer," giving believers a beautiful and simple pattern of personal prayer. Each sentence of this prayer for disciples illustrates the various elements to be included in daily prayer. It is not a prayer simply to be memorized and routinely repeated. Rather, it is an outline of principles which guide us in speaking to God our Father. This prayer could be called supplication and is the initial lesson in the Lord's school of prayer.

Immediately following the first lesson on prayer, Jesus moves to an even more profound level of prayer, which is intercession or praying for others. The first lesson concerns our personal requests while the second moves beyond ourselves to others. For example, in the first prayer we are taught to pray for our daily bread, but then we are taught in the ensuing lesson how to pray in order to get bread for others. As we move beyond ourselves, intercession becomes the ultimate in the life of prayer as we become mediators with Christ for the souls of men. This kind of praying is costly and demanding. By sacrificial and selfless prayer we become channels of blessing to a hungry world.

I know this, nothing will ever be accomplished for the cause of Christ until someone pays the price in intercessory prayer. Churches will not grow, the lost will not be won, nor will the saints be productive until we boldly knock at heaven's door in behalf of a world in great need.

Do you have a desire in your heart to see your friends come to Christ? Do you long to make a difference in your place of influence? Are you willing to engage in spiritual warfare, that the kingdom of God will advance? Do you want to experience the power of prevailing prayer, prayer that prevails with God and man? If so, this message is for you! Join with me in the school of prayer, and learn from the instruction of our Lord.

The Lord introduces the subject of praying for others with a parable known as "The Friend at Midnight." This poignant parable first illustrates what I want to call:

I. The Desperate Need of Prayer

And he said unto them, Which of you shall have a friend, and shall go unto him at midnight, and say unto him, Friend, lend me three loaves; For a friend of mine in his journey is come to me, and I have nothing to set before him? And he from within shall answer and say, Trouble me not: the door is now shut, and my children are with me in bed; I cannot rise and give thee. I say unto you,Though he will not rise and give him, because he is his friend, yet because of his importunity he will rise and give him as many as he needeth (Luke 11:5-8).

We are immediately introduced to a man who is surprised by the arrival of an out-of-town guest. It would be unthinkable for this man not to provide for his visitor, yet to the chagrin of the host, he realizes that his cupboard is bare, and there is no burger place in sight! Desperate, he rushes next door in the middle of the night, bangs on his neighbor's door, and explains to his startled friend (perhaps a former friend by now) that "a friend of mine in his journey is come to me, and I have nothing to set before him" (Luke 11:6). This man was both desperate and determined to meet the needs of his friend.

We, like that man at midnight, are facing a crisis. We look at our world and are overwhelmed by the desperate needs of people without Christ. Sin, sorrow, and death are the common destroyers of our families and friends. Divorce, drug abuse, poverty, immorality are well-known agents of terror. The emptiness of hurting humanity has come for a stay, and to make matters worse, our cupboards are bare, and we have nothing to set before them. We are driven to our knees by our own failures to provide for the urgent needs of our friends.

May I remind you that we have nothing in and of ourselves to place before a hungry world? All of our human efforts to alleviate suffering are overwhelmed by the pressing conditions of a Godless society. Dare we think that we can address the hurts and hungers of humanity without the power of God upon our lives? It is foolish and sinful to try to do God's work without God's power, and there is no way for Christians to have God's power except by prayer. Our plans, our programs, our preaching, our proclamation are worthless unless they are divinely energized by the power of Almighty God through prayer. Prayer is that slender nerve which moves the muscles of His omnipotence and links our nothingness to His almightiness. It has been said many times that we can do more than pray after we have prayed, but we cannot do more than pray until we have prayed.

Our failures, our inadequacies, our insufficiencies are constant reminders of our desperate need of prayer. Not only our failures but our friends also impress upon us the demand for prayer. All around us are people in need of the Bread of Life. They will never be saved until we learn to pray. This kind of prayer is costly. Notice in Jesus' story the man came at midnight in behalf of his friend. He went boldly and audaciously with his plea. It cost him both his sleep and his pride, but he was willing to pay the price for his friend.

The Bible describes Christians as a kingdom of priests. It was the responsibility of the Old Testament priest to intercede for the people at the Mercy Seat of God. Similarly, it is our role as New Testament priests to stand in the gap for the needs of people. Men and women without Christ are blinded by Satan (2 Cor. 4:4) and bound by Satan. Friends who know Christ are facing a hostile world and the daily difficulties of life. It is by prayer that we engage in spiritual warfare for their needs. Only by prayer will we be victorious in advancing the kingdom of God into the empty hearts of the lost. By the power of prayer we are enabled to march into the very headquarters of hell, delivering men from the burning and to "snatch them in pity from sin and the grave."

The largest church in the world is in Seoul, Korea. The church claims a half-million members and adds tens of thousands of new Christians each year. Reading the story of this congregation is like reading new chapters in the Book of Acts. What is the secret of the unparalleled growth of the church? The Pastor, Paul Yonggi Cho, reveals it by writing: "In our church we have committed ourselves to enter a ministry of intercession. We have learned petition in prayer, so we are seeing needs met. We are committed to devotional prayer, so we are enjoying fellowship with our precious Lord. Yet, we are more committed to the prayer of intercession; therefore we are seeing revival in our country and will see it in the whole world.

"No other plan on earth has three to ten thousand people fasting and praying continuously. We are serious about the battle God has commanded us to fight. We are serious about the spiritual weapons that will insure our victory. We are conscious of the battlefield, the hearts of men throughout the world."[1]

The possibilities of prayer are unlimited! Do not think anything or anyone is beyond the power of prayer. The man at midnight asked for three loaves of bread which is comparable to a day's provision of food. His request was large, but he received an abundant supply because he boldly asked. Our friends and family members may seem too difficult to reach for Christ, but the God Who is "not willing that any should perish" (2 Pet. 3:9) is the same Lord who said: "Call unto me, and I will answer thee, and shew thee great and mighty things, which thou knowest not" (Jer. 33:3). "Now unto him that is able to do exceeding abundantly above all that we ask or think . . ." (Eph. 3:20). Our Lord has declared: "Behold, I am the Lord, the God of all flesh: is there any thing too hard for me?" (Jer. 32:27). No, nothing is too hard for God, including saving the soul nearest hell.

> Thou art coming to a King,
> Large petitions with thee bring;
> For His grace and power are such
> None can ever ask too much.
>
> *Anonymous*

After portraying the desperate need of prayer, our failures, and our friends, Jesus then gave us:

II. The Descriptive Nature of Prayer

And I say unto you, Ask, and it shall be given you; seek, and ye shall find; knock, and it shall be opened unto you. For every one that asketh receiveth; and he that seeketh findeth; and to him that knocketh it shall be opened (Luke 11:9-10).

Three simple words describe the nature of intercessory prayer: Asking, seeking, and knocking. Asking infers petitioning prayer. Seeking involves perceiving prayer. Knocking illustrates persisting prayer.

To ask means to ask specifically and to make a particular request. In our parable, the man at midnight made a direct and definitive appeal to his neighbor. Therefore, to intercede is to ask specifically and express purposefully what we desire God to do.

So much of our praying is too general and indirect. We pray, "Oh God, bless the church, save the lost, forgive my sins." We live retail but pray wholesale and miss the joy of answered prayer! After all, if we do not ask God to do something specifically, we will never know if He answers prayer. How long has it been since you have asked the Heavenly

Father to do something so explicitly unique that when He gave you the request, it was beyond question that He answers prayer?

The next time you pray, instead of mumbling, "Save the lost, bless the missionaries," why don't you pray, "Oh God, my heart is burdened for John, for Joe, for Mary, and Sue. Touch their hearts, show them their need. Send some witness to tell them the Good News or, if possible, use me to bring them to the Savior"? Then when your friends trust Jesus and profess faith in Christ by walking down the aisle in your church, you will come apart with joy! Oh, if we could just realize the incredible resources made available to us in prayer. The Bible says, " . . . ye have not, because ye ask not" (James 4:2). I often wonder how many rich blessings intended for believers are never claimed and therefore never received.

In addition to asking, Jesus said that prayer was seeking. This involves perceiving prayer. Jesus used the word "seek," which means careful investigation and diligent pursuit. When we pray, we must seek to know God and His purpose in each situation of need. We are to carefully, not casually, spend time with God in order to recognize what He wants to do in and through our lives. The disciple John, known for his closeness to the Savior, wrote: "And this is the confidence that we have in him, that, if we ask any thing according to his will, he heareth us: And if we know that he hear us, whatsoever we ask, we know that we have the petitions that we desired of him" (1 John 5:14-15). This means that prayer is *not changing* God's mind *but finding* God's mind. Seeking God's will in prayer builds confidence and certainty into our lives and puts us on the pathway of fulfilling His purpose in us and through us.

Perhaps the greatest lesson that can be learned concerning prayer is knowing that the prayer which starts in heaven is the prayer that gets to heaven. That is, God has a desire, a purpose, that He wants to achieve in our lives. When we seek Him and His will, He places that desire in our hearts. "Delight thyself also in the Lord; and he shall give thee the desires of thine heart" (Ps. 37:4).

When we perceive the will of God, we simply pray the desire back to Him in the Name of Jesus. The prayer that was conceived in the heart of God is now delivered in prayer and placed in His loving hands unto the praise of His glory! Imagine the joy of participating with Almighty God in accomplishing His will on earth as it is in heaven. To know and do God's will is the greatest achievement in life, and it is all accomplished in perceiving prayer. Jesus promised ". . . seek, and ye shall find . . ." (Luke 11:9).

We are to ask; that is petitioning prayer. We are to seek; that is perceiving prayer. We are then to knock; that is persisting prayer.

Again in our parable, the man persisted in asking for bread. He knocked and continued to knock until the answer came. He bruised his knuckles for his friend. He was willing to lose prestige and dignity in order to get bread for a hungry house guest. Jesus said it was "because of his importunity he will rise and give him as many as he needeth" (Luke 11:8). That resolute inquirer took home a basketful of bread because he kept knocking. The door of blessing was opened because he meant business.

Certainly God knows when we mean business in prayer. We know that we are not heard for our much speaking, but away with half-hearted, half-serious, lukewarm, and lazy praying! "The effectual fervent prayer of a righteous man availeth much" (James 5:16). We are to pray with passion and intensity until the answer comes. The old-timers called this "praying it through." The answer may come years later, but the God who is always on time will come through. When Jacob wrestled all night with the angel of the Lord, he finally cried out ". . . I will not let thee go, except thou bless me" (Gen. 32:26). This does not mean we must twist God's arm to receive a blessing or get our prayers answered, but it does mean we are to make persistent, continual prayer a priority of our lives. If we are to learn how to pray, we must practice discipline and determination.

Paul commanded Christians to "Pray without ceasing" (1 Thess. 5:17). Therefore, to be effective in prayer, we shall not only schedule daily times of prayer, but we will be always ready to make our requests known throughout the day. May our familiar knock be well-known at heaven's door!

This brings us to our final consideration of the power of prevailing prayer, which is what I want to call:

III. The Dynamic Nearness of Prayer

> If a son shall ask bread of any of you that is a father, will he give him a stone? or if he ask a fish, will he for a fish give him a serpent? Or if he shall ask an egg, will he offer him a scorpion? If ye then, being evil, know how to give good gifts unto your children: how much more shall your heavenly Father give the Holy Spirit to them that ask him?" (Luke 11:11-13).

Jesus concluded His lesson on prayer with the most penetrating truth of all. Because we have a vital, living relationship with God in Christ, we have a constant connection and union with our Father in Heaven. Our Lord is not a distant Deity beyond our reach. Neither is He a God who withholds good gifts from His children. Prayer is not overcoming God's reluctance but laying hold of His highest willingness to bless His children.

What is the dynamic that makes such blessing possible? Please note that prayer is linked to the ministry of the Holy Spirit. "How much more shall your heavenly Father give the Holy Spirit to them that ask him?" (Luke 11:13). Our Lord is reminding us of the glorious truth that if an earthly friend and an earthly father willingly give to those in need, our loving Lord will most certainly give abundantly to His own. Paul captured this same reality when he wrote: "But ye have received the Spirit of adoption, whereby we cry, Abba, Father" (Rom. 8:15). The Spirit of supplication intercedes in our behalf, helping us to ask and receive from the Father all that He desires to give.

> Likewise the Spirit also helpeth our infirmities: for we know not what we should pray for as we ought: but the Spirit itself maketh intercession for us with groanings which cannot be uttered. And he that searcheth the hearts knoweth what is the mind of the Spirit, because he maketh intercession for the saints according to the will of God (Rom. 8:26-27).

Prayer is dynamic because we pray to the Father, through the Son, and in the Spirit! We are weak and often do not know what to say or how to pray. Our minds often wander, we become distracted and discouraged, but it is the work of the Holy Spirit to bring about that dynamic nearness with our God. He helps us to pray just as He helps us to work and witness. Specifically, the Holy Spirit solves the problem of distance between us and the Heavenly Father. We have a way prepared into His presence by the blood of Jesus while the Spirit carries us through the door. "For through him we both have access by one Spirit unto the Father" (Eph. 2:18).

The Spirit helps us with the problem of discernment for He interprets the will of God when we pray. "And the spirit of the Lord shall rest upon him, the spirit of wisdom and understanding, the spirit of counsel and might, the spirit of knowledge and of the fear of the Lord" (Isa. 11:2).

The Spirit puts life into our praying and even prays through us when we intercede. Imagine that! You are a prayer partner with the Holy Spirit who wants to pray through your mouth, agonize through your spirit, feel through your heart, and think through your mind. The most glorious ministry of all is to pray in cooperation and compatibility with the Holy Spirit.

So many are defeated in the matter of prayer. Having failed so many times, you have almost given up. You wonder if it is worth it to keep trying. Oh friend, listen to Jesus. Your Heavenly Father loves you, longs to supply your every need, and use your life as an extension of His grace and power to others.

Come to the Father with your weakness and emptiness and allow Him to fill you to the brim with Him. Place yourself before Him, think of His love, tell Him your needs and the needs of others. This kind of praying will prevail with God and men, transforming your prayer life from drudgery and discouragement to delight. Learning to pray is the most fulfilling prospect of life. Enroll in the Master's School of Prayer today!

Joel C. Gregory

When God's Servant Is Depressed

Perhaps we should take depression for granted as a part of life itself. The old spiritual says, "Sometimes I'm up and sometimes I'm down." Dr. Tim LaHaye claims to have asked 100,000 people if there were any among his audiences who had never been depressed. Among 100,000 people no one has ever said, "I have never been depressed." In fact, sometimes people who live in optimistic surroundings seem to be the most depressed at all. Someone said that a pessimist is someone who has to live with a constant optimist.

Depression is both ancient and universal. The Psalmist implored, "Why are thou cast down within me, O my soul?" Hippocrates, the ancient physician, wrote a treatise on melancholy. Winston Churchill, during the Battle of Britain, was a bastion of strength, but at the same time underwent severe bouts of depression. Edgar Allan Poe is said to have been depressed for four days after he wrote *The Pit and the Pendulum*. Svetlana Alliluyeva, the daughter of Joseph Stalin, recalled that the bloodthirsty dictator was the victim of deep and dark depression. Charles Spurgeon, arguably the greatest preacher in Christendom since apostolic days, knew weeks on end of darkness and melancholy.

Today we have with us the Moral Majority. When you look through the Bible you seem to have the "Miserable Majority." So many of God's greatest men were, at critical moments of their lives, depressed. Moses asked God to take his life. Job asked the Lord, "Kill me." Elijah wanted God to slay him. Jonah wanted God to do away with him. And

125

Saul, the king of Israel, destroyed himself and those around him because of his fits of depression. But when you look at the prophecy of Jeremiah 20, you find the most miserable one of all when it comes to the matter of depression. Jeremiah was a man who hit rock bottom. His experience should be helpful to every one of us who must deal intermittently and periodically with depression. I am encouraged by the very degree of Jeremiah's discouragement. The very fact that Jeremiah is in the Bible and that God could accept him and use him, in spite of his depression, is a redemptive encouragement to my life and may be to yours. Look at the *reasons* God's people may be depressed, their *responses* in the midst of depression, and their *resource.*

Why are God's people depressed? They sometimes are depressed because they imagine themselves to be victims of *divine deceit.* Jeremiah cried out to God a terrible prayer:

> O Lord, you deceived me, and I was deceived; you overpowered me and prevailed. I am ridiculed all day long; everyone mocks me (Jer. 20:7, NIV).

Psychologists inform us that one element in nearly all kinds of depression is a sense of disappointment. If that were the case, then Jeremiah had the greatest disappointment of all. He looked up to high heaven and said, "God, You Yourself have deceived me." He was so disappointed in God that he used some of the most violent, blasphemous language to be found in the Old Testament. Literally, the words he used in speaking to God are, "God, you seduced me. You enticed me. You ravished me." He used the most unusual language to speak of God's relationship to himself. He stated this still another way elsewhere. While speaking to God in a bout of melancholy, he pointed his finger at heaven to say:

> Why is my pain unending and my wound grievous and incurable? Will you be to me like a deceptive brook, like a spring that fails? (15:18, NIV).

When God called Jeremiah, He told him:

> My people have committed two sins: They have for-
> saken me, the spring of living water, and have dug
> their own cisterns, broken cisterns that cannot hold
> water (2:13, NIV).

Jeremiah replied, "I have ministered now for these two decades, but instead of being a perennial spring, I have found
God to be like a deceptive brook." All around Judea there
were dry river beds, the ever-present wadis which at a distance showed the promise of water, but when one came to
them, were as dry as dust. Jeremiah, in this moment of in-
dicting God for divine deception, accused God of promising,
but not delivering. He had preached for twenty years, and
Jerusalem was the same as when he had started. Nebu-
chadnezzar was still on the march. The politicians and the
established religionists were still against him. In a moment of darkness Jeremiah accused, "You deceived me."

Ere some of you finish this year of service, the dark
shadow is going to fall across your hearts. "Did God deal
falsely with me in bringing me to this place? I was up-
rooted from over there; I came here because I sensed that
God had spoken to me, but ever since I have come here I
have faced nothing but one difficulty after another. Has
God dealt with me deceptively?" When that shadow falls
across your heart in a moment of depression, you will sit
where Jeremiah sat.

Added to that, Jeremiah experienced *repeated rejection:*

> O Lord, you deceived me, and I was deceived; you
> overpowered me and prevailed. I am ridiculed all day
> long; everyone mocks me. Whenever I speak, I cry out
> proclaiming violence and destruction. So the word of
> the Lord has brought me insult and reproach all day
> long (20:7-8, NIV).

> I hear many whispering, "Terror on every side! Re-
> port him! Let's report him!" All my friends are wait-
> ing for me to slip, saying, "Perhaps he will be
> deceived; then we will prevail over him and take our
> revenge on him" (20:10, NIV).

Jeremiah literally says in the Hebrew of the text, "I have become a day-long joke. Ridicule, mockery, insult, reproach belong to me." His enemies had fallen to calling him names. He heard men whispering around him, and it gave him a sense that bordered on paranoia that everyone was against him. Earlier his own family at Anathoth had plotted against his life. He cried, "Even my friends [literally those who ought to say *Shalom* to me on the street] are those who are saying, 'We just can't wait until Jeremiah slips.'" He had experienced repeated rejection. Every resource system in his life had been blocked; personal rejection could cause even a giant like Jeremiah to fall. He tried to find a solution in not speaking the Word of God:

> But if I say, "I will not mention him or speak any more in his name," his word is in my heart like a burning fire, shut up in my bones. I am weary of holding it in; indeed, I cannot (20:9, NIV).

The same word of God that brought him reproach when he spoke it on the outside, became fire in the incombustible on the inside. He was depressed because he had experienced repeated rejection.

Likewise, some of you will face the reality of rejection. You may go out to some little church in the country, preach for them, and sing to them, and find out that they have not been waiting for your gift to the kingdom. Or what is more than that, they may ask you to serve with them; and once you get there, you may find rejection. That is even worse. You may experience rejection from peers; you may experience rejection from those above you. You may experience it even from those who love you and have pledged to share a life of ministry with you. Whenever you experience rejection and are depressed about it, you are sitting where Jeremiah sat.

Those are only two of the reasons that God's people may experience depression. What about their *responses?*

Jeremiah responded with a *black bitterness*. He spoke some of the most violent words of the Old Testament:

> Cursed be the day I was born! May the day my
> mother bore me not be blessed! (20:14, NIV).

In the Hebrew economy it was a capital offense to curse
one's parents. Jeremiah walked the line coming just as
close as he could to it. He cursed the day he was born, and in
so doing he cursed the very call of God on his life, for the
Lord had told him in the first chapter of the book, "I ordained you to be my spokesman from your mother's womb."
He was so low in black bitterness that he came to curse the
very God who had called him and the very call that had
come to him. In fact, he was one who said, like you may
have sometimes said, "I wish I had never been born." Added
to that black bitterness was an *irrational unfairness* and
anger:

> Cursed be the man who brought my father the
> news, who made him very glad, saying, "A child is
> born to you—a son!" May that man be like the towns
> the Lord overthrew with pity (20:15,16*a*, NIV).

That poor, hapless man! All he said to Jeremiah's father
was, "You have a new boy." Jeremiah was so irrationally
unfair that he said, "May that man be like Sodom and Go-
morrah. May brimstone rain on him from heaven." I am
sure if that man had been there he would have said, "All I
said was, 'You have got a boy.'" Dr. Mortimer Ostow, who
wrote *The Psychology of Melancholy,* says,

> Depression at every phase of its development in-
> cludes a component of anger. This anger is directed
> against the individual who is expected to provide
> love, but who disappoints at different phases. The an-
> ger may arouse a man's wish to irritate, to hurt, to
> destroy, depending upon the degree of pain that he
> faces.[1]

Jeremiah became irrationally angry, blackly bitter,
when he was depressed, and finally he entered into his *suicidal despair.* You will not find in all of the Old Testament
more vehement words than these:

> For he did not kill me in the womb, with my
> mother as my grave, her womb enlarged forever. Why
> did I ever come out of the womb to see trouble and
> sorrow and to end my days in shame? (20:17-18, NIV).

This was a complete blackout in the life of one of God's
greatest men. "I wish I had been slain from the womb, my
mother forever my grave." What would you have told Jeremiah, had you been his counselor? Do you suppose his case
would have responded to a glib, "Oh, why not cheer up?
Things will be better"? Martin Luther, who himself knew
depression deep and dark, speaking of this passage, wrote,

> Those who condemn this impatience and call at-
> tention to the need of patience are mere theoretical
> theologians. If you have met with such experiences in
> practical life, you will understand that stories such as
> this one are too great than that we should should dis-
> pute about them in theoretical fashion.

What do you say to a man like Jeremiah? What do you
say to yourself when black bitterness, dark despair, and de-
spondence become your lot—even in the Lord's service?

*First, one resource is the understanding that even in the
silence God is working.* Sometimes it belongs to the evangelical environment to think that if God is working in your
life, there must be some constant chit-chat coming from
heaven to you. When the psalmist was at the very lowest,
he cried out to God, this God who had spoken volumes to
him—even the longest book in the Bible. When Jeremiah
asked God for help, there was silence. You need never think
that because God does not thunder through the heavens He
is not doing something redemptive in your life. It was when
Jesus cried out, "Eli, Eli, lama sabacthani, why have
you forsaken me?" that God was strangely silent. But in
that silence, in those six hours, God was redeeming the human race. There will be days when you may walk around
and ask, "Why doesn't God say something to me?" God
may be saying more to you than He has ever said before, if
you will listen.

Jeremiah found another resource in that, even while he was at the bottom, he kept on talking to God. Now his prayers would not make very pretty devotionals for the WMU! And yet, the one redemptive factor in the depression of this giant for God is that it made no difference how far down he had gone, at the very bottom he was still saying something to God. God is a gracious enough Heavenly Father, knowing the dust of our frame, that He would even put up with listening to what Jeremiah said.

Jeremiah found the greatest relief from depression when he discovered something in the mist of his darkness to express as an act of praise to God. The only relief in this passage is the praise found in between two bouts of dark depression. Jeremiah found something verbally with which to express his praise to God. He praised God for His vindicating power,

> But the Lord is with me like a mighty warrior; so my persecutors will stumble and not prevail. They will fail and be thoroughly disgraced; their dishonor will never be forgotten (20:11, NIV).

. . . for His discerning power,

> O Lord Almighty, you who examine the righteous and probe the heart and mind, let me see your vengeance upon them, for to you I have committed my cause (20:12, NIV).

. . . and for his rescuing power,

> Sing to the Lord! Give praise to the Lord! He rescues the life of the needy from the hands of the wicked (20:13, NIV).

When Jeremiah began the overt, open praise of God, he started up out of the pit. Now that may not be the answer for pathological depression, or for depression that is organically caused, but I know this in my own heart. When I am in the bottom of the pit, I find something to look up to and to thank God for. I start up out of the pit when some days all

I can thank Him for is everything that has *not* happened to me. The great evangelist, John Haggai, in his book *How to Win Over Worry,* tells that as a young minister he was pastoring a church where there were troubles. At that time a baby was born to their family. Because a drunken doctor placed it in an overheated incubator, it suffered permanent brain damage. With troubles at church, and a baby with irreparable brain damage, he wrote, "I almost went out of my mind. I drove my car out to a country road where no one could hear me. I threw open my door and got out of the car, and I walked up and down that lonely lane with my hands in the air, thanking God for everything; praising Him for anything that He had ever done for me. I kept my sanity that way."

Now I share a leaf from my own journey, if you will permit me, this one moment.

In my middling years at Southwestern Seminary I had spent a year and a half at a wonderful little pastorate in a village a half hour from school. Despair and depression sneaked up on me, and I became disobedient and despondent, disillusioned and depressed. Like Bunyan's giant, Despair, it slew me so I stood up before that little congregation and shocked them one Wednesday night by saying, "I resign." I moved back to Seminary Hill into a little house, as low as I had ever been in my life. A friend, wanting to cheer me up, sent me down to his weekend pastorate to preach. I preached the worst sermon I had ever preached in my life. It was so bad that everyone in that country church drove off and left me standing there without asking me to dinner— that bad! I would have had to dig a hole to get any lower than I was then.

I came back to seminary and walked the halls for weeks, disillusioned, cynical, hoping to finish that semester, and then decide what I would do next. If you had told me that five years later, "You are going to be the pastor across the street from seminary at Gambrell Street Baptist Church," I would have called you a fool. If you had told me that a handful of years later, "You are going to have more doors open than you can go through to minister, more opportunities than you can take to minister," I would have laughed at you with a hollow, hellish cacophonous kind of laughter, and said, "Get out of here, I am finished!" If you had told me I would become the pastor of this great church, Travis Avenue Baptist Church, I would have roared. But somewhere in the midst of that, I kept talking to God. And somewhere in the midst of that I found out that, even in the silence, God can work. I found some ground to stand on to praise God for something. I want to testify now, I would not trade you everything I have learned about the will of God on the mountain top for anything I have learned about it in the bottom of the pit. I got up out of that, went back down to that little country church, and confessed, "I made a mistake." They called me back, unanimously. That was better than they had done the first time. And God gave me some more time of ministry in that place.

When you fall into despondency in your ministerial career, remember the example of Jeremiah, think of the testimony of this preacher, and realize you know a Lord whom Jeremiah never knew, but about whom I can testify with the song writer:

> From sinking sand, He lifted me.
> With tender hand, He lifted me.
> From shades of night
> To plains of light,
> O praise His name,
> He lifted me.

Lord, when we're down and we will be, keep us talking to you. And when the pit is deep and the way looks dark, help us to look up from the pit to the power and find something to praise you about, and remember that even when we've given up on You, You never give up on us. For Jesus' sake. Amen.

NOTE

1. Mortimer Ostow, *The Psychology of Melancholy* (New York: Harper & Row, 1970), p. 104.

Brian L. Harbour

Faith Is the Victory
1 John 5:4-5

Followers of Jesus have been given different names over the centuries. At first, they were described as "followers of the way." Then, at Antioch, they were called "Christians" which means Christ-ones (Acts 11:26). The most common word for those committed to Jesus is "disciple," which means a learner (Matt. 5:1). In his epistle, Paul addressed the Christians as "saints," those set apart for God (Rom. 1:7). They are also called "believers" (Acts 5:14), "beloved" (1 John 3:2), or "children of God" (Rom. 8:16-17).

Each of these names describes a distinctive characteristic of those who follow Christ. In our text, John suggests another name for Christians: "overcomers." A Christian is one who overcomes.

This description of a Christian as an overcomer is confirmed in other places throughout the New Testament. Revelation says this about the saints of God: "They overcame him because of the blood of the Lamb and because of the word of their testimony" (Rev. 12:11). Paul wrote to the Romans: "But in all these things, we overwhelmingly conquer through Him who loved us" (Rom. 8:37). To the Corinthians, Paul urged that they give thanksgiving to God "who gives us the victory through our Lord Jesus Christ" (1 Cor. 15:57). God's children are to be overcomers. We are to experience victory in our Christian lives.

What does it take to be an overcomer? What does it take to experience that victory? Notice how John answers that question in our text.

Acknowledges the Problem

First of all, an overcomer is one who acknowledges the problem. The word "overcomer" implies that something stands in our way. We are confronted by an obstacle. We have problems which we have to overcome. An overcomer is not someone who breezes through life without any opposition or obstacles. An overcomer is one who realizes each day will present another problem, another barrier, another obstacle that stands in his way, another opponent who criticizes him. He acknowledges the problems and then sets out to deal with them.

Whether or not we are overcomers has nothing to do with the circumstances around us. It has everything to do with the commitment inside us. Everyone has circumstances. The key is what we do with those circumstances. Things happen to everyone. The key is *what happens to what happens to us*. Problems will constantly confront us, even as Christians. These problems must be overcome to win victory in our Christian lives.

What is the problem that Christians have to overcome? Three times in the text John says that the Christian overcomes the world. Our problem is the world.

What is the world? The world is Satan and his plans. The world is sin and its pressure. The world is suffering and its pain. The world is sensuality and its pleasure. The world is anything and everything which stands in opposition to God.

What does the world do? It tries to destroy our Christian witness. It tries to distort our desires. It tries to confuse our value system. It tries to dilute our interest in God's Word. It tries to squeeze us into its mold. It tries to draw us away from God.

The problem of the Christian is the world which tempts us to forget who we are and whose we are and to live beneath our privileges.

A man approached a Little League baseball game one afternoon. He asked a boy in the dugout about the score.

The boy responded, "Eighteen to nothing—we're behind."
"Boy," said the spectator, "I bet you're discouraged." "Why
should we be discouraged?" replied the little boy. "We
haven't even gotten up to bat yet!"

That's the spirit of our text. The Christian is surrounded by problems, but he is not discouraged, for he sees
those problems as challenges he has to overcome. An overcomer acknowledges the problem.

Accepts the Promise

An overcomer also accepts the promise. John says in
1 John 5:4, and he repeats it in verse 5 for emphasis, that
the Christian can overcome the world. That is the promise
of God's Word. That means we do not have to be defeated by
the devil. We do not have to be disgraced by sin. We do not
have to be destroyed by suffering. We do not have to be distracted by sensuality. We can win the victory. We can overcome. That is the promise of God's Word.

Many Christians need to refocus on that promise, for
they are walking through a dark and deep valley right now.
They are the "walking wounded" in God's army. They need
to remember this great truth: God has never been totally
defeated by the events of the past, nor will He be by the
events of the future.

Joseph was in the dungeon, but God released him
(Gen. 41). The Hebrews were in slavery, but God delivered
them (Ex. 1—15). David was overwhelmed by the guilt of his
sin, but God forgave him (Ps. 51). Daniel was in the lions'
den, but God preserved him (Dan. 6). Jonah was in the belly
of the fish, but God retrieved him (Jonah 2). Peter was in
the depths of despair, but God renewed him (Mark 14:72;
John 21). Jesus was in the tomb, but God raised Him (John
20). No problem has been so great that God in His power
has not overcome it. That is God's promise to each of us.
What God has done in the past, He will do again today.
Through God's power, we can overcome.

A young man in a wheelchair, crippled by an accident,
asked his friend, "Do I have a future?" The friend re-

sponded, "As a pole vaulter, no. As a man, yes." An overcomer accepts the promise of God's Word that, no matter how great the problem, he can overcome. He has a future. He can win the victory.

Applies the Principle

This promise of victory belongs to those who apply the principle. What is the principle that will enable us to realize the promise and be overcomers? John answers that question in our text. He says, "This is the victory that has overcome the world, our faith." We overcome by applying the principle of faith.

What is faith? All of life is lived on faith, and every person has faith in something. We open a can of food and eat it because we have faith that it is not harmful to us. We get on a plane and sit back with assurance because we have faith that the pilot who is flying the plane knows what he is doing. We go to a doctor whose name we cannot pronounce. He gives us a prescription we cannot read. We take it to a pharmacist we do not know. He gives us medicine that we do not understand. Yet, we take it, all on faith! Faith means to trust someone else. That is the general meaning of faith.

John is not talking about this general kind of faith, however. He is talking about a particular kind of faith, and he describes it in verse 5. He who overcomes the world, John explains, is "he who believes that Jesus is the Son of God." Christian faith means to put our faith in Jesus Christ. A faith in Jesus which causes us to believe in Him, talk to Him, walk with Him, and abide in Him—that faith is the key to overcoming the world.

What does faith do?

First, faith makes available to us *the presence of God.* When David Livingstone, the inimitable missionary to Africa, was called back to London to receive an honor, he was presented the award before a vast gathering of well-wishers. Someone asked him how he had been able to make it when the natives rose up against him, and when the powers of darkness seemed ready to overwhelm him. He opened his well-worn New Testament and said, "Let me share with you the verse that helped me make it through: 'Lo, I am with you alway, even to the end of the age'" (Matt. 28:20).

Because of our faith, we know that God is with us every step of the way, and the promise of His presence provides victory.

Second, our faith opens to us *the power of God.* Many years ago, A. J. Gordon went to the World's Fair. From a distance, he saw a man in a brilliant suit, pumping water with a hand pump. The water was pouring out, and he said, as he looked from a distance, "That man is really pumping water." When he got closer, he discovered that it was a wooden man connected to a pump powered by electricity. The man was not pumping the water—the water was pumping the man!

So it is with us. From a distance, some might look at us and say, "That guy really has power. Look at the way he lives. He is really living for God." But when they get closer, they discover that it is actually God who is living in us.

The power of God is ample and available. Through faith, we plug into that power, and it begins to move through us. This power provides victory, because "greater is He who is in you than He who is in the world" (1 John 4:4).

Third, faith reminds us of *the plan of God.* In Revelation, John described a time in the future when "The kingdom of the world has become the kingdom of our Lord, and of His Christ, and He will reign forever and ever" (Rev. 11:15). God has initiated a plan in this world that is permanent and eternal. The things of the world will someday fade away, and every knee shall bow before Christ. Faith reminds us that the final victory belongs to God, and therefore faith encourages us to keep going.

Do you believe that God is with you everywhere you go? Do you believe God is able to provide for all of your needs? Do you believe the things of God are permanent and eternal and that God will ultimately win the victory? Do you really have faith? Then you too can be an overcomer!

O. S. Hawkins

All Things New
Ruth 1:16-17

In "the days when the judges ruled" there lived in the little town of Bethlehem a lovely family—Elimelech, his wife Naomi, and their sons Mahlon and Chilion. There came a famine to the land. There was no bread in Bethlehem. Instead of staying in Bethlehem and trusting the Lord as the others obviously did, Elimelech moved his family to the land of Moab.

As we recall, the Moabites were a race who began in incest. They were a godless people who worshiped pagan gods. Elimelech had no intention of staying there. The Bible records that he simply went to "sojourn." But like many of us who wander off into the fields of sin, what we sometime intend to be a sojourn ends up being a lengthy stay.

There is an interesting point that should be noted.

Elimelech did not transport his family to the land of Moab because "the grass was greener there." He left because it was dry in Bethlehem. There was a severe famine in the land. Many people today leave the will of God for their lives and journey into the "far country." I am convinced they do not do that so much because the grass is really greener there but because their own personal Bethlehem becomes dry. There is a spiritual famine in their hearts. So it was with Elimelech, Naomi, and their sons. They went down into the land of Moab, indicating they left the will of God for their lives.

After they had been in Moab for awhile, the two sons fell in love with two Moabite women, Orpah and Ruth. These women had been brought up in godless homes. Consequently Elimelech allowed his sons to marry women with whom they would be "unequally yoked." As time passed Elimelech died. Then the two sons Mahlon and Chilion died, leaving Naomi with her two daughters-in-law.

Following a succession of bad news, there finally came some good news. The Lord had visited his people in Bethlehem, and bread was there. The famine was over. Upon hearing this wonderful news, Naomi repented and headed back toward Bethlehem and the will of God for her life. She suggested that Orpah and Ruth go back to their people. Orpah kissed Naomi and left while Ruth clung to her.

I suppose we find ourselves here. That is, some of us are kissers and some of us are clingers. Opportunities come our way and some of us kiss them good-bye, just as Judas did with the kiss of betrayal in the garden. Others of us cling to those opportunities with the same intensity of Ruth. As Ruth clung to Naomi she said:

> Entreat me not to leave thee, or to return from following after thee: for whither thou goest, I will go: and where thou lodgest, I will lodge: thy people shall be my people, and thy God my God: Where thou diest, will I die, and there will I be buried: the Lord do so to me, and more also, if aught but death part thee and me (Ruth 1:16-17).

After revival comes you will say the same thing to the Lord Jesus. You'll say to him, "Lord Jesus, entreat me not to leave Thee, or to turn from following Thee: for wherever You go I'll go, wherever You lodge I'll lodge. Your people shall be my people, and Your God shall be my God."

Jesus declared, "Behold, I make all things new." He is the Giver of many new things. Revival, when it comes to our hearts, brings a newness. God is the God of newness. The Bible continually refers to this. In Isaiah 43:19 God promised, "Behold, I will do a new thing; now it shall spring forth; shall ye not know it? I will even make a way in the wilderness and rivers in the desert." In Ezekiel 11:19 He affirmed, "And I will give them one heart, and I will put

a new spirit within you; and I will take the stony heart out
of their flesh, and will give them a heart of flesh." Today
some of us are seeking to contain the new wine of revival in
the old wine skins of antiquated plans and programs, stale
institutionalism, and out-of-date traditions. But the river
of revival cuts its own course.

After revival comes God makes all things new. I contend that *Naomi* repented of her sin, and revival came to
Ruth's heart, leading her to say, "Entreat me not to leave
thee, or to return from following after thee: for whither
thou goest, I will go; and where thou lodgest, I will lodge:
thy people shall be my people and thy God my God: Where
thou diest, will I die, and there will I be buried: the Lord do
so to me, and more also, if aught but death part thee and
me." Revival brought a *new determination,* a *new direction,*
a *new dependence,* a *new desire,* a *new devotion,* a *new dedication,* and a *new destiny.* Yes, Jesus does indeed make "all
things new." After revival comes it brings:

A New Determination

Entreat me not to leave thee nor turn from following
thee.

Ruth was indicating, "Even though Orpah has gone
back, I will not leave you." "Entreat me not to leave thee
nor to turn from following thee." Naomi was making sure
Ruth realized the way was hard. She continually insisted
on her returning to her people. Note Ruth 1:8, "And
Naomi said unto her two daughters-in-law, Go, return each
to her mother's house: the Lord deal kindly with you, as ye
have dealt with the dead, and with me." Also Ruth 1:11
which records, "And Naomi said, Turn again, my daughters: why will ye go with me? are there yet any more sons in
my womb, that they may be your husbands?" And Ruth
1:15, "And she said, Behold, thy sister-in-law is gone back
unto her people, and unto her gods: return thou after thy
sister-in-law." Ruth's past and future both were against her.
But she clung to Naomi and pled, "Entreat me not to leave

thee nor to turn from following thee." Here was a *new deter-mination,* and the Bible says, "When Naomi saw that she was determined to go with her she said no more to her" (Ruth 1:18).

Jesus Himself always wanted a man to know the cost of following Him. Jesus never called anyone to follow Him under false pretenses. He challenges us, "If any man will come after me, let him deny himself, and take up his cross daily, and follow me" (Luke 9:23). On another occasion He said, "Whosoever taketh not his cross and followeth after me is not worthy of me." Once He said, "I send you forth as sheep in the midst of wolves." He never called anyone to follow Him under false pretenses. Like Naomi, he always wanted a person to know the cost of following.

After revival comes to our heart there is a *new determination.* Hear Ruth as she pleads, "Entreat me not to leave thee nor to turn from following thee." What determination! All influences were against her. Naomi's insistence. Or-pah's example. The religion of her childhood.

We will know when personal revival comes to our hearts. It will bring with it a new determination. It's one of the telltale signs of revival. We will say to the Lord Jesus, "Entreat me not to leave thee nor to turn from following thee." A new determination . . . that's what happens when Jesus makes all things new. There also comes:

A New Direction

Wherever you go I'll go.

Ruth was saying, "This is going to be my life's direction." "Wherever you go I'll go." Ruth had never been that way before, but revival had brought with it a *new direction* in life. This is always a reliable sign of genuine revival. One really begins to follow the Lord Jesus and commits to him, "Wherever You go I'll go."

After revival comes we become interested in what interests Jesus, and He said, "I came to seek and to save the lost." If we are true followers of Jesus we will be making

His way our life's direction, and we ourselves will be seeking the salvation of the lost. After all, it was Jesus Who said, "Follow me, and I will make you to become fishers of men."

To go where Jesus goes will carry many of us who find our retreat within stained-glass windows to places where we seldom go. When Jesus went to Jerusalem He didn't go to be seen with the religious leaders. He went to the Pool of Bethesda where lame and impotent people had spent a lifetime. When he went through Jericho he didn't go to meet the mayor; he went to a blind beggar, Bartimaeus, who was rattling a tin cup on the side of the road. When he went through Samaria he wasn't interested in meeting the governor; his interest was for a prostitute at a well outside the city of Sychar. Jesus loves the outcasts. They accused Him of being "a friend of sinners." Too few of us have ever been accused of such.

After revival comes it will bring to our lives a new direction. We will say to the Lord Jesus, "Wherever You go I'll go," and going in that direction will take us to those who are in need of a physician. Ruth followed Naomi and made it her life's direction. Has revival come to your heart? If so, a noticeable sign is: you will have a new direction in life, regardless of peer pressure, regardless of out-of-date traditions, regardless of antiquated plans and programs, regardless of stale institutionalism. Yes, Jesus makes "all things new." Revival also brings:

A New Dependence

Wherever you lodge I'll lodge.

Ruth was saying, I'm going to trust you, Naomi, to supply my basic needs. "Wherever you lodge, I'll lodge." What trust! Ruth had no place to lay her head. She was trusting totally in Naomi. She would later instill this dependence in her children, for she would marry Boaz, and they would have a son, Obed, who would have a son, Jesse, who would have a son, David, and David would one day write in Psalm

37:25, "I have been young, and now am old; yet have I not seen the righteous forsaken, nor his seed begging bread." He learned that dependence from his great-grandmother Ruth.

After revival comes there is a fresh, new dependence upon the Lordship of Jesus Christ. We are so prone to trust in so many things, but revival brings us to a new dependence and a new trust in the living Lord. We say to him, "Wherever You lodge, I'll lodge." That is to say, we begin to trust Him to meet our basic needs. And isn't it wonderful to know we can trust the Lord?

Has personal revival come to your heart? If so, some of the telltale signs are a new determination, a new direction, and a new dependence. Yes, Jesus said, "I make all things new." Revival also brings:

A New Desire

Your people shall be my people.

Ruth was saying, "There will be nothing between us. We will live in sweet fellowship. Your people will be my people." Ruth realized if she took the God of the Bible for her God she would have to separate from the godless crowd among whom she lived in Moab. It is impossible to fellowship with God and refuse to fellowship with the people of God. It's unfortunate, however, how so many of the people who are called by His name seek to fellowship only with the world.

I remember, as a seventeen-year-old young man in Fort Worth, Texas, when I was born again on a cold January morning in 1965. I had never read the Bible and did not even know that Matthew, Mark, Luke, and John were Books of the Bible. But that morning God changed my desires. It didn't take me long to learn that if I were going to go on with God, I had to go with His people. All of a sudden, things I loved before passed away, and things I loved far more were there to stay.

After revival comes it brings with it a *new desire*. We

say to the Lord Jesus, "Your people shall be my people." We have a new desire to fellowship with the people of God. After all, to love God is to love His people, fellowship with Him, and unite with Him. Some people who call themselves Christians may just be singing hymns, saying words, meeting with committees. Some people live like the world, talk like the world, look like the world, and then go to church and count the time on their watches until 12 noon. The same people can go to athletic events, ball games, movies, or the theater, and say, "My, how time flies by." And these people tell me they are going to heaven and spend eternity praising the Lord with the people of God . . . when they never do it here! Who are they kidding? It may be they are fooling themselves.

Has personal revival come to your heart? If so, a recognizable sign is a new desire. You will desire to find your fellowship with the people of God. There will be no barrier between you and another believer in Christ. Yes, Jesus said, "I make all things new." Fifth, revival brings:

A New Devotion

Your God shall be my God.

Ruth was saying, "I'm not only taking your people as my people, but I'm taking your God as my God. Your God shall be my God." If you are looking for an Old Testament conversion you need look no farther.

When we really think about it this was quite a decision for Ruth to make. Her past was against her. She was raised in a heathen home and worshiped immoral gods. Her present was against her. Naomi pled with her to stay and return to her people and her gods. Her future would be against her. She would be an exile from all that she knew— living in the strange city of Bethlehem among Hebrew believers who looked down on the Moabite race.

When we really stop to think about it Ruth was giving up all she knew to follow Naomi's God, and all she knew of Naomi's God was a God of suffering and sorrow! Think about that. What was it that led her to say, "I want your God to be my God"? After all, the only thing she knew of Naomi's God was a God who had brought suffering and sorrow to this broken-hearted woman. How could she say she wanted this God to be her God? She knew Naomi. She watched Naomi repent and turn her face as a flint toward Bethlehem.

Friend, the way to lead people to our God is to let them see Him in us. The truth is, when the lost world sees us heading for home, repenting, getting right with the Lord, they will follow. It begins to dawn on them that this God is not the good person's God, but he's the sinner's God, and so he could be their God also! We help others far more by being broken and open than we do by preaching from a pedestal.

Ruth said, "Your God shall be my God," not because she saw a God of pleasure or a God of prosperity or a God of health and wealth or because Naomi preached to her. She came to this new devotion because she saw Naomi repent. She watched how Naomi dealt with the discipline and saw her repent and head toward Bethlehem.

After revival comes there arises a new devotion. Has personal revival come to your heart? If so, there are some definite signs which always follow. A new determination, a new direction, a new dependence, a new desire, and a new devotion. We will say to the Lord Jesus, "Your God shall be my God." Yes, Jesus said, "I make all things new." There also comes:

A New Dedication

Wherever you die, I'll die.

Ruth was saying, "This is for life. Wherever you die I'll die." This was a life decision. Ruth was affirming that she was not coming back if things didn't work out in Bethlehem just like she thought they ought to work out. This was a life dedication!

It is the same in following our Lord. We will say to him, "This is for life." Recently I heard a television preacher say

something to the effect of, "Give your heart to Jesus tonight, and if you don't want to follow Him tomorrow, then
go back, but at least try!" No! It costs you your life to follow
Jesus. B. B. McKinney expressed it well:

> Take up thy cross and follow me
> I heard my Master say
> I gave my life to ransom thee
> Surrender your all today
>
> My heart, my life, my all I bring
> To Christ who loves me so
> He is my Master, Lord and King
> Wherever he leads I'll go.[1]

Ruth would die, but before she did, she would marry
Boaz and live on in history and in heaven because she
found a *new dedication*. After revival comes it brings a new
dedication. It is for life! God wants our whole life in a fresh
and new dedication. Has personal revival come to your
heart? There are some definite signs, not the least of which
is a new dedication. We will say to Jesus, "Wherever you die
I'll die. This is for life." Yes, Jesus said, "I make all things
new." Finally we see that revival brings:

A New Destiny

And there I will be buried.

Now, do you have the whole picture? Ruth was saying,
"Not even death can separate us. Wherever you die I'll die
and there be buried."

After revival comes there is a new sense of destiny
with us. "Nothing can separate us from Christ." Paul put it
this way:

> Who can separate us from the love of Christ? shall
> tribulation, or distress, or persecution, or famine, or
> nakedness, or peril, or sword? As it is written, For thy
> sake we are killed all the day long; we are accounted
> as sheep for the slaughter. Nay, in all these things we
> are more than conquerors through him that loved us.
> For I am persuaded, that neither death, nor life, nor

angels, nor principalities, nor powers, nor things
present, nor things to come, Nor height, nor depth,
nor any other creature, shall be able to separate us
from the love of God, which is in Christ Jesus our
Lord (Rom. 8:35-39).

Yes, Jesus is alive, and not even death can separate us.
Has personal revival come to your heart? If so there are
some telltale signs. Not only is there a new determination,
a new direction, a new dependence, a new desire, a new devotion, a new dedication, but there also comes a *new destiny.* Jesus said, "I make all things new."

We all know the story. Ruth went home with Naomi
and became the bride of Boaz, the kinsman redeemer, the
lord of the harvest. She was completely separated from her
old life, and the whole course of her life had been determined by another. All things were made new for her.

There is an interesting afterthought found in the genealogy of Jesus which we often overlook in reading the Gospels. In Matthew's account of the genealogy, four women
are mentioned. This was unheard of in that first-century
world. Tamar is there. She one day dressed as a prostitute,
seduced her father-in-law, and had an illegitimate child.
And there she is listed in the lineage of our Lord for all
posterity to see. Rahab is there. We all remember her. A
label sticks to her as though it were glued to her—Rahab
the harlot. She was the town prostitute of Jericho. And Rahab is listed with Tamar in the lineage of our Lord. Another woman listed there is Bathsheba. Of course, she lived
in adultery with King David. The other woman listed in the
genealogy of Jesus is Ruth, the godless Moabite woman
brought up in a heathen home whose very race began in
incest. What is Jesus trying to show us by listing such
women here in His own genealogy? I believe He is trying to
show us that he "makes all things new." After all, He said,
"If any man be in Christ he is a *new* creature. Old things
are passed away, Behold, all things are become new!" What
a wonderful Savior is Jesus our Lord!

Will you be a kisser or a clinger? As opportunities to make a certain sound come your way, will you kiss those opportunities good-bye or cling to them with a new intensity? Yes, Jesus said, "I make all things new." After revival comes it brings a new determination, a new direction, a new dependence, a new desire, a new devotion, a new dedication, and a new destiny—as we share the good news with the lost and dying world . . . as He makes all things new!

NOTE

1. Words and tune Falls Creek, B. B. McKinney, 1936. Copyright 1936. © Renewed 1964 Broadman Press. All rights reserved.

Jim Henry

God's Guidelines for Giving
1 Corinthians 16:1-4

I understand there is a preacher who has a special sermon from the Book of Acts dealing with Ananias and Sapphira. They were the two people who apparently were Christians that sold a piece of property and gave part of it to the Lord, but they lied about what they had given. If you remember, the Holy Spirit struck them dead. The pastor preached this sermon and called it his annual stewardship sermon on Ananias and Sapphira. It had three points:

1. It is more blessed to give than to buy.
2. It is more blessed to give than to lie.
3. It is more blessed to give than to die.

Chapter 15 of 1 Corinthians is a tremendous chapter on the resurrection, the rapture, the new bodies we are going to have someday, and immortality. Paul soars with these thrilling promises for Christians.

But chapter 16 is different. It is as if he took a coffee break before he sat down to write. Suddenly, there is a shocking reentry from outer space and things to come, to a mundane and practical matter, and that is "how we handle our money." The Holy Spirit told Paul to write something to His people about their giving. It is important for us to understand that, as the Holy Spirit speaks so much of giving, our Lord Jesus made that the theme of nearly 50 percent of His teachings and parables. In fact, sixteen of His thirty-eight parables deal directly with possessions. He knew there was something crucial to our spiritual pilgrimage in the way we practice stewardship.

In 1 Corinthians 16:1-4 the Apostle Paul, speaking to

150

the church at Corinth, began to deal with the important matter of money.

First, notice the reason for the giving in verse 1. The reason in this particular church that Paul was speaking about money is because the church *in Jerusalem was having a difficult time financially.* Jerusalem was economically poor.

Jews would move to the city, many of whom had become converts to Jesus Christ. As they came to the Lord from outlying areas, they came without much money. As a result, the church at Jerusalem had strained its resources trying to meet the needs of the new converts coming into the church. To make things worse there had been a famine. Many who were receiving Christ were losing their jobs because of antipathy to the new Christian movement. The church was facing a tremendous need of financially ministering to those in their midst who were economically distressed.

Paul was speaking to the church at Corinth about how to meet that need for their brothers and sisters in Christ. Now who was it for? For God's people! Always in the Bible you'll find that the Scriptures stress that our first giving is to God's people. There are many worthwhile needs around the community. But the Bible teaches that we, as Christians, should look after the family of God first. When we give our money every week, we're giving for God's people. We're giving it locally, and we're giving it to touch people around the world.

Through our missions giving program, our missionaries are reaching millions of people. Every time we give on Sunday we are helping our mission force, feeding them, helping them educate their children, providing for them, enabling them to share the good news of Jesus Christ with more than 100 nations and the fifty states in our union. We are giving to meet the needs of God's people.

Notice that Paul did not apologize for asking for the offering. He said, "Do what I told the Galatian church to do."

He didn't come in and say, "Now, brothers and sisters, if you don't mind I would like to ask you to make a little offering, and I hope nobody's offended." Paul said, "Do what I tell you to do."

The reason he did not apologize was because he was speaking a blessing to the church. Any pastor or Christian who does not understand that it is more blessed to give than to receive, has missed what the Bible has to say, because Jesus said that (Acts 20:35). If I held back from preaching on stewardship and finances, I would not be telling you all the Scripture truth. In that sense, you would not be receiving the whole counsel of God.

Some may be thinking, *I haven't been to church in a year, and the Sunday I come the preacher is talking on money. Every time I go to church all I hear is money!* My response is you shouldn't have missed for a year. You should have been here before now.

If you're a Christian, and you worship regularly, and the message is bothering you, it's probably because you are not doing what God wants you to do. I'm not going to come apologetically to teach you what God tells you to do. It's a blessing, and I don't want you to miss the blessing. I'll tell you what God says to do so you'll get in on what God wants you to be and what God wants you to do. I realize through counseling that many of you have financial problems and have had them through the years. One of the major causes for divorce is the poor handling of money. If you'll get in on God's program and make your priorities Jesus Christ first, your family second, and then your work, and get your money lined up with God's Word, He will bless you and help you straighten out that part of your life.

Second, notice the regularity of giving. When do we do it? Verse 2 (NIV): "On the first day of the week." Now two things are established quickly. First, the church met and worshiped on the first day of the week, which is Sunday.

This book was written about 50 to 60 AD. By that time the church had its regular worship service when they all gathered on the first day of the week. They didn't do it on

Monday, though many have met on Monday. They didn't give on Saturday, though many have worshiped on Saturday. But their prime worship time was Sunday, the first day of the week.

Second, a regular part of the worship was to give.

He says, "When you're worshiping, bring your offering." When we come to worship, we come to give. We really don't worship unless we give. I was preaching a revival in another state. When time came to pass the plate, they did not pass the plate for me. When I stood up to preach I said, "I'm used to giving, and I didn't get to worship this morning by giving. I'd like to give my offering if somebody will come get it." Well, fourteen people jumped up, so I got to give my offering! To me worship is giving. All of worship is giving. When we pray we give our prayers unto the Lord; when we sing we sing unto the Lord; when we fellowship we fellowship and give ourselves to one another. When I'm preaching, I'm giving the Word of God back to the Lord and the people, and when we give we're giving to the Lord. Worship is giving.

You can give one of several ways. You can give in a calculating way. You can sit there like the Pharisees did and say, "I'm going to give this much. This is the requirement, 10 percent. That's what I'm going to give." You can calculate how much you're going to give, and you can be a calculating giver.

There's a second way you can give. You can give as a comparison giver. You can look around and say, "Well, I believe I'm giving better than they are. I heard about what they're doing, I know what they've got, and I know what I've got. I just believe I'm probably doing better percentagewise than some of those folks." So you become a comparison giver.

There's a third kind of giver. That's a conviction giver. A conviction giver is a person in whom the Holy Spirit freely moves and brings them to conviction to give. Sometimes that happens in a worship service, an emotional moment, a divine impulse, and the Holy Spirit may say give

$10,000, $5,000, or one dollar—whatever it may be. You are moved to obey Him and you give. Nothing is wrong with that. But the fourth kind of giver is the most steadfast and best.

The fourth kind is a consecrated giver. A consecrated giver looks at what the Bible says, makes a commitment to the Lordship of Christ, and on the basis of God's blessing in his life, love for Jesus Christ, and the teaching of Scripture, gives in a consecrated way. Sometimes there may be a surge because of an appeal or special need, and that's above and beyond. But there is a consecrated, consistent, willful giving.

How are you giving? Do you bring an offering on the Lord's day? There is a time to do it—on the first day of each week.

Third, notice the responders who were to give. In the second verse Paul says, "Let each one of you." That's everybody! Nobody was left out. The poorest person in the church was not left out. Some people tell me occasionally, "I can't afford to give." Let me tell you something: *You can't afford not to give.*

Do you remember the story when Jesus went to the Temple and watched the people giving? A woman came to give. She had only "two mites" or next to nothing. The Bible said that was all she had. She was very poor, but she gave it to the Lord. You might think Jesus should have said, "No, lady, don't do that. You keep that. That's all you've got." Did Jesus reprimand her for giving all she had? No! You know what Jesus said? "This woman has given out of what she didn't have, and that's the kind of giving I'm looking for." Jesus didn't reprimand her. He congratulated her. What I'm saying is this. As long as you have anything, there ought to be an offering to the Lord. Jesus by His teaching, by His giving, by the Scripture tells us that we are to give. Everybody should give something.

I learned that early from my grandmother, Hazel Fisher, "Momee" to me. She and my grandfather lived in a little country house on forty acres of land. They didn't have a car or many of life's luxuries. Some weeks I would see her gathering eggs, and I'd say, "Momee, what are you doing with those eggs?" And she'd say, "I'm getting my church money." She sold eggs and ran a small home barber shop. From that small income, she would give to the Lord at the Hopewell Baptist Church in Springfield, Tennessee.

I learned from my Momee early on in life: It's not how much you give, it's that you give. You see, if God can't trust you with a little bit, how can He trust you with a lot? So our deepest generosity really starts when we're poor or don't have much. It is not when we are financially secure that we begin to give to God! God says, "No, let me see what kind of generosity you have when you don't have it. Then I can trust you with the true riches."

I will never forget Mrs. Hamblen in that rural church I pastored in Mississippi, who came to me one Christmastime and stuck five dollars in my hand. She was a widow who lived in a little ramshackle house down the road from the church, and who walked to church if someone didn't give her a ride. She stuck that five-dollar bill in my hand and said, "this is an offering." I said, "Don't do that. You haven't got it." Tears came up in her eyes, and she said to me, and I will never forget it, "Don't you rob me of the privilege of giving."

Everybody is to give. Each one is to bring something. How is your church doing? I was interested in how our church was giving so I checked it out. At the time, we had about 3,600 church family units. A family unit can be one person or ten. In the first six months of that year, 32 percent of our church families gave nothing. One-third gave zilch! Another 22 percent gave less than ten dollars per week. That meant that more than half of our church family gave next to nothing. I do not understand that. I do not understand it biblically. I do not understand it spiritually. I do not understand folks that just don't love Jesus enough to give Him something.

Have you ever heard of a UFO? Do you know what one is? That is supposed to be an Unidentified Flying Object.

I'm going to tell you what a UFO is. In this church and probably in most of them because, believe it or not, we give above average: a UFO is an "uncommitted freeloading on-looker." If you don't like that, don't get mad with me! You are not mad with me. You are crossways with God because you are disobedient to the clear teaching of the Word of God.

I'm going to have to be like a preacher friend of mine who wrote about a man who was always wanting to do something. The pastor told him that he had some inactive members in the church, and urged the willing layman to write them a letter and encourage them since they were not giving anything and were not attending. The man told the pastor he would love to do that and asked the pastor to give him some of his personal stationery on the church's letterhead. The pastor gave him ten pieces of paper and ten family names. The man wrote the families. About one week later, the pastor got a letter from one of his wealthy members who had not been to church and had not given. This is what it said:

> Dear Pastor: I want you to know that from this time on I will be back in church. I will give. Enclosed is a check for one thousand dollars. I'll catch up. You can count on me from this day forth. Sincerely, (and the man signed his name). P.S. Please tell your secretary that you don't spell "dirty" with two "t's," and you don't spell "skunk" with a "c."

Now I don't know who our "dirty skunks" are, but we have some! I don't know who you are, but you are "UFO." A freeloader, a hitchhiker to Glory. You need to get in here and carry your weight. Do your part because the Word of God is clear. The responders in giving are to be each one of us.

Where do you take it? That is the next thing that he talks about. Where is the repository? He says in verse 2,

"Each one of you should set aside a sum of money, in keeping with his income, saving it up."

Saving it up to do what? Take it somewhere. The words "saving it up" is where we get the word "thesaurus." A thesaurus means a treasury or chest or collection. Paul says to save it, collect it, get the treasury together, and where do you take it? Let's backtrack a little in church history. In Acts 2, the early church saw someone with a need and gave to them. But by Acts 4 the church was growing, and they had to have a system. They brought the money and gave it to the apostles. In Acts 5:2 they did the same thing and asked the apostles to help meet the needs the church was beginning to have.

In a short period of time they went from helping each other person-to-person to bringing it and letting someone distribute it to meet the needs of the body. In those days every pagan temple had a repository, a place where one made an offering to worship god. This thesaurus, this collecting place, became the spiritual treasury in the church. The church leaders and deacons would distribute it according to need.

Where do we bring our offerings? Our primary place is through the church and at the church. There are many good needs in the world, many of them Christian. We get dozens of letters, phone calls, and personal requests from people asking, "Would you help our organization?" or, "Would your church sponsor this cause?" We help as much as we can. We cannot meet every need. No organization or church can. We do what we can as we feel led of the Holy Spirit, but our basic giving is through the church for God's people, God's pastors, and God's ministries through our local church and to the world. There are many fine parachurch groups, but our basic giving is here. My wife and I give to other good Christian causes, but our primary thrust is through our home church. Where do we give it? The repository. The local church first and then through that body to the world.

Notice the requirement in giving. "How much should I give?" Paul says . . . "in keeping with your income." In verse 2 he says, ". . . set aside a sum of money in keeping with his income."

What does that mean? In the Old Testament, a Jew was required to give between 20 and 30 percent. That was his tithe, not 10 percent. Devout Jews gave between 20 percent and 30 percent, but it was a required gift. They didn't have any choice. They had to give that every year.

When you come to the Book of Proverbs (3:9-10), the writer said that there was to be a different kind of giving. That giving was to be a generous giving, and it was to be a first giving. In other words, God gets the first, and He gets it generously. In the New Testament there is no specific amount stated. So you are saying, "How much should I give?"

Let it be in your heart to give generously and to give the firstfruits of your income to God. A tithe, 10 percent, is a good place to start, but a poor place to stop!

I was a tither for years, but I didn't know anything about giving. I was a preacher for years, and I didn't know anything about giving. Nobody taught me. God sent some people into my life who said, "Preacher, this is how you learn to give." I thank God I was taught to tithe; I am even more grateful the Lord has led us to go beyond that. You will not hear me say that you have to give at least a tithe. I will teach giving, and that will probably be more than a tithe! I will urge you to give God the firstfruits of what He blesses you with.

If you need a percentage goal, shoot for 10 percent to start with, but don't say, "Whew, I got there," then relax and quit. Say, "Lord, I've got to a good starting place. Now what can I do beyond that?" Some people have gone to 15, 20, 25 percent as God blessed them, and they have matured in the faith. They have learned, instead of spending it on extras, to keep some of that to give more to the Lord.

R. G. LeTourneau, who built big road building equipment, came to a place where he could give 90 percent and live on 10 percent. Colgate of Colgate toothpaste fame did the same thing as God blessed him. So did Kraft of Kraft Cheese, and countless millions of ordinary people who have learned the joy of generous giving. Don't stop at 10 percent. Just say, "Lord, I want to give generously, and whatever I get, You get the firstfruits of it." You will enter a new era in your life.

What is the responsibility in it being handled properly? Verse 3 tells us. "Then, when I arrive, I will give letters of introduction to the men you approve and send them with your gift to Jerusalem."

What does that mean? That means proper responsibility is required for handling the money God's people give. In our church let me tell you how it is handled.

When you give every week, every day our business administrator and our finance office monitor our giving to see it is spent wisely and used right. Every month a budget committee meets with our business administrator to see that it is handled securely and properly. Once a year we have an audit done on our finances so we know where we are and how it is being spent. In my more than a quarter-century as a pastor, there has never been a financial problem in the handling of money in any church I have pastored, and I don't want it to happen. What you give is a sacred trust. You are giving it to God, and you are trusting us to handle it properly. It will be handled properly.

On a Sunday night at the invitation, down the middle aisle came a young woman in tears. I had never seen her. She met one our pastors at the front. She told him this story:

"This afternoon in a restaurant I heard a man and a woman arguing about the existence of God. He said that there wasn't a God, and she said that there was a God. I got so drawn into the argument that I turned around and said to her, 'Hang in there, there is a God.'" Then she said, "I realized I probably shouldn't have said it and turned back around and minded my own business. I said that, but I didn't know God. I got on the Interstate and said, 'Lord, I want to know if you are real. I believe you are. Help me.' I started down I-4. Going down I-4, I was holding the wheel of my car saying, 'God, if there is a God, help me.' I saw the cross at your church from the Interstate. I pulled into the lot and came in halfway through the service. I felt and sensed the love of God for me. So I came forward."

That night she accepted Christ. She was a barmaid working in a lounge. She said, "I quit that. I want to work in a legitimate business."

What happened? Because we have been faithful in proclaiming, living, and giving, the church is a lighted cross in our city for the men and women driving the highways of life and wanting to know if God is real. Our giving is an avenue to express the reality of God and lead them to repentance and faith in our blessed Lord Jesus Christ.

These are God's guidelines to giving. We can be disobedient; that is our choice, or we can be obedient and let God bless us. We choose to be a blessing, and let the light of God's grace and love shine bright in our Jerusalem and around the world through our faithful giving.

William E. Hull

"Multiplying ... and Murmuring"
Acts 6:1

How strangely our text begins: "Now in those days, as the disciples were steadily *multiplying,* there arose a *murmuring...*" (Acts 6:1).* What an unusual combination to find growth and grumbling linked together! We tend to equate expansion with optimism, enthusiasm, and success, but here it is associated with dissension, criticism, and tension. Let us look more closely to understand the background of the problem that had surfaced.

I. The Context of the Conflict (6:1)

The first five chapters of Acts describe the "honeymoon days" of the early church. After personal encounters with the risen and ascended Christ (1:3-11), the followers of Jesus prepared themselves through prayer and fellowship (1:12-14) for an outpouring of the Holy Spirit which resulted in three thousand conversions on the day of Pentecost (2:1-42). So filled were they with divine power that, publicly, they worked mighty miracles (2:43, 3:1-10) and proclaimed the word with boldness (4:13,33). Privately, this same power fused them into one loving fellowship where they shared all things in common (2:44-47, 4:32-35) and where their ranks were purged of unworthy members who betrayed this selfless ideal (5:1-11).

By the time chapter 6 opens, growth had continued to the point that Hellenistic Jews comprised a significant segment of the church (6:1). We read in this passage, for example, of Nicolaus, "a proselyte of Antioch" (6:5), who was already a leader "of good repute" (6:3). Probably a high

161

percentage of these members from the Diaspora were widows, "for many pious Jews in the evening of their days settled in Jerusalem so as to be buried near the Holy City."[1] Widows with no relatives nearby in Palestine to look after them were almost completely dependent on charity for their very survival. Judaism provided an elaborate system of public welfare for the poor,[2] but Jewish persecution of Christians, which had already begun to emerge (4:3, 5:17-18,33,40), may have cut off this source of support.[3]

To be sure, the church had already set up its own benevolent plan based on a voluntary community of goods (2:44-45, 4:32-37), but the administration of this spontaneous approach was not equal to the growing complexity of needs within the fellowship. The problem was not so much that there were insufficient resources available as it was that one group of widows felt "*neglected* in the daily distribution" (6:1). Everyone involved had the best of intentions, nobody was accused of being at fault, yet the rancor of simmering criticism emerged to threaten the most idyllic expression of the Christian faith that had ever existed.

How could this ugly growl intrude itself into the sweet harmony of the Jerusalem church? What kind of "spontaneous combustion" allowed the spark of controversy to singe its seamless robe of love? A clue may be found in the description of the combatants as "Hellenists" versus "Hebrews." The Hellenists were Jews of Greek language, culture, and life-style, whereas the Hebrews were Jews of Semitic language, culture, and life-style. The former tended to be more cosmopolitan, sophisticated, and progressive; the latter tended to be more provincial, simplistic, and traditional. Even though both groups were Jewish by birth and Christian by rebirth, these shared experiences had not been sufficient to overcome the profound tensions that festered between Jewish and Greek culture in the first century.[4]

It was not so much a case of overt hostility as of benign neglect. Hellenists were the outsiders, Hebrews the insiders. Hellenists were the newcomers, Hebrews the old settlers. Each group talked differently, dressed differently, acted differently, and so became increasingly clannish. The Hebrews seemed to have all the power, since the Twelve came from that camp; thus it was easy to suppose that their widows were given preferential treatment in the daily dole. Nobody wanted to attack the original disciples of Jesus, hence the quarrel was driven underground and took the form of suppressed indignation rather than erupting openly as defiant criticism. There was no hard evidence of favoritism, only a lurking suspicion of slight that was all the more dangerous because it was inarticulate, and so could not be dealt with decisively.

There is much we can learn from these circumstances surrounding our text. Here was the most loving, sharing community in the history of Christianity, yet suddenly a group within it felt *"neglected"!* The church was growing, it was bursting with power, it had the greatest ministerial leadership ever known, yet suddenly a group already living off the generosity of others began to complain! What all of this conclusively proves is that even the best of churches can experience dissension, not just when they are failing but precisely when they are succeeding!

Why should this be so? Because church growth, by its nature, reaches out to include an ever-wider variety of individuals and groups. Ironically, the more people are reached, the more polarization must be overcome. If the Hebrews had not included the Hellenists, but had been content to limit evangelism only to their own kind, there would have been no occasion for murmuring. But from the very beginning, the miracle of tongues at Pentecost (2:4) had symbolized that the Gospel was for those "from every nation under heaven" (2:5). The apostles were well aware of the animosities between Jewish and Greek cultures, but they also knew that it was the "last days" when God would "pour out His Spirit" on *all* of "those who were being saved" (2:47).

The church is an amazing paradox. On the one hand, it reaches out to all persons in total and unqualified acceptance. Every human difference on the face of the earth is

welcomed within its fellowship. Hebrews and Hellenists
alike retain all of their cultural diversity, even after each
has repented, believed, been baptized, and been filled with
the Holy Spirit. And yet, on the other hand, this pluralistic
church is to be united as no other group on the face of the
earth. Each member is to experience a oneness of loving
fellowship, an intimacy of sharing, that transcends every
human difference. Thus, no church that reaches out to all
people can escape the dilemma of our text: namely, the
more a congregation *multiplies,* and so deepens its diversity, the greater the likelihood that newcomers will *murmur* because they feel neglected by those with backgrounds
different from their own.

II. The Cause of the Conflict (6:2)

If cultural differences contributed to the background of
this conflict, what was its immediate provocation? Our text
indicates that it was rooted in a decision of the Twelve, the
collective spiritual leaders of the Jerusalem Church, to give
priority to the preaching of the word rather than to the
serving of tables (6:2). In other words, the apostles had been
preoccupied with outreach rather than with inreach, with
winning the lost rather than with serving the saved. They
had been so busy meeting the need for evangelism that
they had ignored the need for fellowship. Unintentionally,
they had allowed the church to get so large and diverse
that the original plan for ministering to the material needs
of its members was no longer adequate.[5] In short, while the
apostles had been concerned with the *divine word,* some of
their members had been concerned with *human welfare!*

The reference to "serving tables" (6:2) was not intended to be derogatory, as if the Twelve were squelching
the Hellenists with the retort, "Do you want us to quit
preaching and wait tables for you ourselves to be sure you
get enough?" The word here for "serve" *(diakoneō)* is one of
the great words for ministry in the New Testament, which
was also used for "the ministry [*diakonia*] of the word" in
verse 4. The Twelve were saying there is an important ser-

vice to outsiders which must be rendered by preaching the word and an equally important service to insiders which must be rendered by distributing assistance to those in need. Their crucial point was that these two tasks must never be in competition or conflict with each other. Neither the church nor its leaders should ever have to choose between evangelism and ethics, between growing and giving, between divine word and human welfare. The relationship between these two emphases must be both/and rather than either/or.

The root problem in the "murmuring" of the Hellenists was the assumption that the church's leaders should "give up" one ministry in order to take care of another. Such a reordering of priorities was "not right" (v. 2). The Hellenists had a perfect right to expect their daily needs to be met in equitable fashion, but they did not have the right to expect such at the cost of neglecting another equally essential ministry of the church.

It is remarkable how the same issue confronts us today. On the one hand, there have never been more lost persons crying out for the saving word of the Gospel. On the other hand, there have never been more Christians crying out to have their personal needs met on a daily basis. These counterpressures have created a tension between saving-ministries and serving-ministries which divide Christians into competing camps. The Church Growth Movement, for example, tends to emphasize breadth of concern for outsiders while the Church Renewal Movement tends to emphasize depth of concern for insiders. We are all aware of the classic cleavage between personal Gospel and social Gospel which confronts us with a false dichotomy because, as we saw earlier, the more people we evangelize the more social problems we will be forced to solve.

Each local church is vulnerable to the danger posed by the Hellenists of minimizing saving-ministries in order to maximize serving-ministries. As a congregation grows, the pressure steadily mounts to meet the needs of its members on a daily basis. Many of the newer members that come from different backgrounds "murmur" ever more insistently for an expansion of services at points where they "hunger" for help. If church leaders do not respond promptly to their concerns, these modern Hellenists feel "neglected" in the distribution of available resources. They complain, often in clandestine fashion, that there is not enough money in the budget, or enough positions on the staff, or enough workers in the church organization, to satisfy their needs. As a pastor, I can remember numerous times when modern Hellenists wanted the church staff to spend more time "serving at tables" where member needs are met, but I can remember few instances when these Hellenists asked less for themselves so that the church staff could spend more time winning the lost!

In such situations, the words of the Twelve are God's words to us today: *"It is not right..."* (6:2). A church must not respond to needs of its "murmuring" members at the expense of "giving up" on those who have no Savior. It is a false understanding of priorities to suppose that we are to take care of our serving-ministries at the expense of our saving-ministries. Although we should not neglect the legitimate needs of any church group in the allocation of available resources, neither should we neglect those outside the fold who never request anything because they don't even know what they are missing. To be sure, a church is so close to its own members that it can hear even the most muted criticism, but such proximity does not make their concerns any more important than the concerns of those outside the church whose cries for help are beyond earshot.

Let us recover the apostolic priority: *"It is not right to give up saving for serving!"* It speaks to every Sunday School class so interested in its own members that it pays no attention to prospects. It speaks to every deacon who gladly visits an old friend on behalf of the church but never gets around to the stranger on an outreach card. It speaks to every committee so busy with finances or property or other "table"-tasks that it feels exempt from witnessing to the lost. Once more: *it is never right to meet one urgent need at the expense of failing to meet an equally urgent need!*

III. The Cure of the Conflict (6:3)

How did the Twelve propose to meet the internal need of the church to its members without giving up its external need to reach the lost? By enlarging the available leadership pool so that both tasks could be entrusted to a sufficient number of servants. In democratic fashion, the whole "body of disciples" (6:2) was asked to select seven persons with spiritual qualifications which suited them to administer the congregation's resources in such a way as to resolve any friction in the fellowship. Interestingly enough, all seven who were chosen had Hellenistic names, which may mean that, for the first time, the original Hebrew leadership was expanded to include those with a sympathetic understanding of the needs of the dissident members.

Notice that this solution was administrative in nature. The Twelve did not meet the problem of dissension simply by urging everyone to pray, or to love each other more, or to be guided by the Holy Spirit. While divine dependence was essential, a practical human plan was also needed to open fresh channels of cooperation. Organization, as such, is not the enemy of spirituality. God can use our orderly management just as He can use our spiritual resolves. To say to the Hellenists, "We will be much in prayer about your problems," would not have meant half as much to them as did this decision to restructure the "Benevolent Committee" from top to bottom with people whom they knew and trusted, and then to secure the support of the entire congregation for its ministry as symbolized by the laying on of hands (6:6).

To make this dramatic change required a great deal of openness and flexibility on the part of the Twelve. After all, the "murmuring" of the Hellenists was an implied judgment on their leadership which could have made them defensive. Doubtless it was a delicate, even painful, process to replace those who had been supervising the Benevolent Fund. Likely they were all Hebrews who could have caused just as much dissension on the other side if they became hurt over losing their responsibilities. But the Twelve had no desire to dominate everything that was done. They were happy for the Seven to work beside them so each ministry might be fulfilled without hindrance to the other. Every new need was really another opportunity for God to put more people to work in the service of His cause.

It has often been assumed that this division of labor in Acts 6 separated the spiritual and temporal tasks of the church and assigned them to two distinct groups. Nothing could be farther from the truth.[6] As already noted, both the saving and the serving responsibilities were called a "ministry" *(diakonia)*, and both were clearly essential to the spiritual vitality of the church. The qualifications of the Seven were just as spiritual as those of the Twelve: "men of good repute, full of the Spirit and of wisdom" (6:3). Most important, the only members of the Seven we know anything about, Stephen and Philip, functioned primarily as preacher (6:8—7:60) and evangelist (8:1-40). What this means is that specific assignments within a church, however important, do not exempt a leader from those tasks which belong to every Christian. The Seven saw to it that the serving-ministries of the church were properly handled, but it never occurred to them, in so doing, to slight the saving-ministries of the church.

The most encouraging thing about this incident is that God used "murmuring" as the catalyst to launch a bold new mission.[7] Out of ordinary jealousy and grumbling of the kind that can be found in any congregation, God raised up a Stephen and a Philip to blast the church out of its Jerusalem stronghold and launch it on an expansion that finally reached the gates of Rome. By effectively responding to this problem, the church became stronger than if it had never had a problem. By being forced to deal with the Hellenists, it learned to deal with the world!

That same victory can be ours as well. If we will learn

to deal with all of our cultural complexity and the murmuring it creates, if we will refuse to sacrifice saving-ministries for serving-ministries, and if we will raise up spiritual leaders who are willing to do both outreach and inreach with equal ardor, God will multiply the ministry of our church to the ends of the earth.

NOTES

*Author's translation throughout.

1. Ernst Haenchen, *The Acts of the Apostles* (Philadelphia: Westminster, 1971), p. 261. Based on a personal communication from K. H. Rengstorf.

2. On the Jewish system of the weekly "poor basket" for settled indigents and the daily "poor bowl" for itinerant paupers, see Joachim Jeremias, *Jerusalem in the Time of Jesus* (London: SCM, 1969), pp. 130–131. For a popular summary see William Barclay, *The Acts of the Apostles* (Philadelphia: Westminster Press, 1955), p. 50.

3. Johannes Munck, *The Acts of the Apostles* (Garden City, N.Y.: Doubleday and Co., 1967), p. 55.

4. On this theme and its implications for the early church see Gregory Dix, *Jew and Greek* (Westminster: Dacre Press, 1953).

5. Kirsopp Lake and Henry J. Cadbury thought that the experiment with a community of goods in Acts 2:44-45, 4:32-37 broke down because "the officers appointed to administer the dole were either killed or driven out of Jerusalem." See *The Beginnings of Christianity, Part I: The Acts of the Apostles,* edited by F. J. Foakes Jackson and Kirsopp Lake (Grand Rapids: Baker Book House, 1965 reprint), vol. IV, 63.

6. See William E. Hull, "Appointed Over This Business," *Church Administration,* vol. 2, no. 10, pp. 5-6, October, 1960.

7. R. B. Rackham, *The Acts of the Apostles* (London: Methuen, 1901), pp. 81,83; Frank Stagg, *The Book of Acts* (Nashville: Broadman Press, 1955), p. 92.

Warren C. Hultgren

Help for Our Whole Person
2 Timothy 4:9-13

God is concerned with our total life and experience. There is no problem too great or need too small for His strong and loving concern. We can compartmentalize Him. We can confine Him to a few high hours of crises and confrontation but leave the rest of life untouched by the Heavenly Father.

We must learn to see Him in majestic mountain peaks, magnificent sunsets, and the pounding surf of the sea. We can see His hand in the shading of a butterfly's wing, the blush of the rose, the microscopic eye of the fly, and the web of the spider. He is the same to us at work, at worship, and at play.

This was Paul's second imprisonment in Rome. It contrasts sharply with his first. The last two verses of the book we call Acts reports that he lived in his own rented quarters for two full years. There he preached, taught, entertained friends and foes without interference or intimidation. This was different from the conditions that seemed to exist when he wrote his last note to a young friend in the faith. In his rush to leave Troas, obviously he left behind with others a few possessions he needed now.

He asks for three specific things: "When you [Timothy] come bring the cloak which I left at Troas with Carpus, and the books, especially the parchments."

We can learn something about Paul's concern for his own well-being and God's concerns for the whole person.

1. We Are Human Beings with Physical
Needs ("Coat")

One of the prerogatives of soldiers in that day was to take a prisoner's possessions for their own use. They gambled for Jesus' garments at the Cross. Paul did not need much, but a coat was appropriate. Fall and winter were approaching (v. 21). A heavy goat-hair cloak would help warm his body in the humid chill of a dungeon. It was not a clerical vestment but a heavy, warm covering for his body.

It is obvious that even the choicest and most useful servants of God are not immune to or exempt from the ordinary needs of life. He knew now the loneliness of isolation. Demas had forsaken him, and others were on assignment. He needed the medical ministry of Luke and the encouragement of John Mark. The letter lifts us in verses 17 and 18 by reminding us that the tensions of our times and our warfare with evil can be overcome only by a sense of the divine presence, a sense of servanthood in preaching the Gospel, and confidence in the ultimate triumph of His heavenly kingdom. In the meantime we adjust and accommodate for things we cannot change and learn to be content in spite of the surrounding circumstances (Phil. 4:11).

We must never divorce the Lord from the common needs of life, what we eat, wear, how we feel or what we do. A physician friend, early in my ministry, helped me understand that money is important. It is not, however, all-important. Jesus paid the Roman tax and the Temple tithes. In spite of the Greek ascetics, the physical body is important. For the believer, it is the dwelling place of the Holy Spirit. It must not be ignored, neglected, or abused. "Glorify God in your body" (1 Cor. 6:20).

Archbishop William Temple suggested that the Christian faith is the most materialistic of all religions, materialistic in the sense that Jesus spoke often of money and drew His illustrations from life. The Incarnation itself gives divine dimension to our material substance. Jesus' work as a carpenter the greater part of His life sanctifies labor, sweat, and tears. The ultimate resurrection of our body, that is made new and in His likeness, suggests our accountability for its use in the common ventures of every day.

II. We Are Human Beings with Intellectual Needs ("Books")

There are many ways we enlarge and educate the mind. Schooling, travel, conversation, and reading. A king once said to his son, "Give yourself to reading." Even an Apostle read what he could. It should be part of every life discipline. Jesus encourages us to read the things that enlarge our capacity for more useful service. He said the mind is like a treasure chest. "A good person out of the good treasure of his heart [mind] brings out good things . . . an evil person, evil things" (Matt. 12:35; Luke 6:45).

We must read to stay abreast of the world in which we live. My brother is an aeronautical engineer. He said that unless he stays read-up on the current literature, he is behind. This would be true of the biochemist, physicist, and anyone in a fast-changing, specialized field. The responsibility of the Christian witness and disciple is to begin where people are and lead them to the Savior. Recently, the book review section of the *New York Times* estimated that 17 percent of Americans read books regularly and that 55 percent of people in England read books regularly. If these figures are not true or correct, we will still admit to reading too little and looking for predigested material.

The Apostle Paul was well-read in many fields. Some of it was part of his scholastic training in the school of Gamaliel (Acts 22:3). The request to "bring the books" could be to reference material and other important reading matter aside from the Scriptures. Many years ago, A. C. Dixon preached a sermon on "The Ethics of Novel Reading." His text was the same as ours, and one of his first points was that Paul read books. In his sermon at Athens in Acts 17:28, Paul quoted from Aratus, a classic poet of 270 BC. Aratus was poet, court physician, and astronomer. The poem from which he quoted was "Phenomena." The Romans were so impressed with it that Cicero translated it into Latin. Paul quoted from a philosopher in Titus 1:12, "The Cretans are always liars, evil beasts, slow bellies" [lazy gluttons]. Epimenides, 600 BC, was a pagan prophet and political commentator of his day. Paul quoted the Greek dramatist, Menander, in 1 Corinthians 15:33, "Evil communications corrupt good manners," which was written in 342 BC. Menander was a pagan Epicurean of wealth and wisdom. Some of his writings can still be seen. He did not believe the gods had anything to do with human affairs. Paul was used of God in certain situations by his understanding of what others believed.

In college days, one of the pastors in the city brought a noon Bible study. He made an effort to convince us that one need only to let God "fill your mouth and mind." Reading and listening to others was a detriment to the working of the Holy Spirit. He was consistent; he gave away all his books except a concordance and his Bibles. This would imply that God never said anything worthwhile or fresh to others, that the pastor lived close enough to the Word to get all there was in it, that even schooling itself with the study of language, history, and structure are not helpful or useful. "Who never quotes is seldom quoted."

There is a transforming power in good books. William Wilberforce read *Rise and Progress of Religion in the Soul.* He became a committed Christian and took the first significant strides for the abolition of slavery in England. Walter Scott claims he was kept from suicide by reading the hymns of Isaac Watts. Among Watts's six hundred hymns were "When I Survey the Wondrous Cross" and "O God, Our Help in Ages Past." The spark of foreign missions was kindled in William Carey when reading *Voyages* by Captain Cook. Carey was used of God to translate the Bible into the language of 200 million people.

Dwight Eisenhower was a high school student in Abilene, Kansas. He wondered what he would do when he graduated. He visited J. W. Howe, who edited the local paper.

Howe asked him to read a book and write a brief review. The book highlighted the life of Hannibal the Great and his amazing military career. It was the turning point that led Eisenhower to West Point, to supreme commander of the Allied Forces in World War II, and the presidency of the United States.

Joseph Henry was a watchmaker in Albany, New York. He wanted to become an actor. One who roomed in his mother's home left a book with the complicated title, *Lectures on Experimental Philosophy, Astronomy, and Chemistry*. To Joseph a new world opened. He taught at Princeton University, explored electro-magnetism, sun spots, weather reporting, and scores of other scientific innovations. He was a devout Christian and the first curator of the Smithsonian Institute.

Rudyard Kipling went to Bombay, India, at seventeen. He toiled at newspaper reporting. One hot evening he read a book with the unusual title, *All in a Garden Fair*. It was about a person who overcame obstacles to become a writer. At twenty-four, he returned to England, lived over a sausage shop, and began writing things the world still loves to read.

III. We Are Human Beings with Spiritual Needs ("Parchments")

Scholars are not agreed on what this represents. Some feel, as I do, it was scrolls of Old Testament Scripture. Paul would have had no difficulty with the Hebrew language. The teachings of the Old Testament saturate his epistles, especially Romans and Hebrews.

We are spiritual as well as physical beings. It is the inspired Word of God that is the seed and spark God uses to kindle the flame and regenerate the spirit. We cannot live by bread alone but by the Living Word of the Living God. J. B. Phillips, in the Preface to his translation of the New Testament, said that the translating process was like rewiring an old house. There was current and energy in the wires. It was the life of the Spirit still active and penetrating.

We find in the Word, God's great plan of salvation. A physicist I met in China told me about his reading of the Bible. He said, "It is the only book that answers the age-old questions of who I am, from whence I came, why I am here, and where I am going." It is the infallible, unerring guide out of sin through Grace to Glory!

In the Bible we find the answer to how life works best. No one breaks the physical laws of health; the laws of health break us. No one breaks the spiritual laws of God; we break ourselves upon them. All the world's knowledge cannot take the place of "God's Rules for the Road." We cannot live by bread alone. It is the Bread of Life alone that can feed the soul, direct our steps, and make life whole. The other evening I was watching an old black-and-white movie, one of the classics. Somehow, the picture ceased to synchronize with the action and the words on the screen. We ourselves get "out of sync" with God, His will, and His Word. The Word of God is the best basic text for human relations in office, factory, home, playground, or church. Paul wanted to keep his soul sensitized and saturated with the Word of God.

There are two great promises that are simply stated but contain the "how to" of God's will. Proverbs 3:5-6, "Trust in the Lord with all thine heart; and lean not unto thine own understanding. In all thy ways acknowledge him, and he shall direct thy paths." The other is the very familiar Romans 12:1-2, "I beseech you therefore, brethren, by the mercies of God, that ye present your bodies a living sacrifice, holy, acceptable unto God, which is your reasonable service. And be not conformed to this world: but be ye transformed by the renewing of your mind, that ye may prove what is that good, and acceptable, and perfect, will of God." Here are presentation, separation, transformation, application.

There are five overarching lessons that sum up this final record of the apostle's life. First: Friendships are important but can be brittle. Demas, who had been a companion, deserted Paul when his love for Christ was replaced by an infatuation with this evil age (4:9). We can easily feel betrayed by friends we trust, but we can be encouraged to go on by friends who enrich, enable, and inspire. Paul, in his writings, referred to at least a hundred by name who had shared and cared along with him. Some are mentioned only once. The last few verses of this chapter name people of whom we have not heard before. Learn to cultivate friends, develop a network of kindred spirits who will weep and rejoice with you. Paul had known desertion by those who ten years before had given him a triumphal entry into Rome (Acts 28:15-16).

Second: We need to accept the obvious. It is not always easy to be a Christian and disciple (vv. 14a,17). Alexander, the coppersmith, did much to hinder the work of God. There are some people whose agenda is evil, and of these we must be aware. In spite of this, he asked God's mercy upon them. It is in the best tradition of our faith to commit the enemies of the Cross and our personal enemies to Christ. He has the final verdict and disposition. There is the evil one himself, Satan, from whom God can deliver us "from the mouth of the roaring lion" (4:17; 1 Pet. 5:8).

Third: Death holds no horror for the child of God. Death is the worst and the best thing that can happen to us (vv. 6-8). D. L. Moody said, "Someday you will read that D. L. Moody has died. Do not believe it. At that moment I will never be so much alive and well as when you read that I have died."

Fourth: We are never alone. In verse 17, we are told, "the Lord stood with me and strengthened me." This truth has sustained God's children down through the centuries. The Chinese, during the Cultural Revolution, found a source of strength and confidence by repeating "Yea, though I walk through the valley of the shadow of death, I will fear no evil: for thou art with me." He was with them as He was with Daniel in the lion's den, as He was with his three fellow countrymen in the fiery furnace. In the trials and traumas of life, He is there. "Never a burden that He does not bear, never a sorrow that He does not share. Moment by moment I'm under His care."

Fifth: There will come a time when we cannot do what we want to do. Paul said, "Come before winter" (v. 21). Acts 27 gives us some insight into the fierceness of fall and winter weather on the sea. The violence of the wind and wave can break a sturdy ship apart. Do not delay in doing what you feel impressed to do, in giving what you have determined to give. We cannot know what a day may bring forth. Life at its best is brief and brittle. Life is subject to change without notice or warning.

There was a framed motto on a physician's wall in an American hospital overseas. As I recall, it said, "I shall pass through this world but once. Any good, therefore, that I can do or any kindness I can show to any human being, let me do it now. Let me not defer nor neglect it, for I shall not pass this way again."

Thomas Carlyle, the crusty Scotsman and writer, married a young woman, Jane Welsh. She was artistic, sensitive, talented, and beautiful. Upon her death, Carlyle was looking through her diary. Frequently, he would see a reference to the fact, "Thomas hurt my feelings tonight." . . . "Thomas embarrassed me this afternoon." . . . "I went to my room and shed a tear." Carlyle was suprised by the several comments on her reaction to his conduct. He could not remember the episodes. His reply, however, was classic: "I did not know how much she loved me until it was too late to correct it." "Come before winter." Make your commitment to Christ and His Will while it is still fresh on your mind. He is interested in your total life situation; commit it to Him before the winter of the soul.

Richard A. Jackson

A Glimpse of Glory
Matthew 17:1-13

Years have slipped by since Simon Peter stood at Caesarea of Philippi. The echo of his preaching at Pentecost has long since quit sounding. It is late in his life as he pens his epistle. We approach the apostle to interview him concerning this Christ.

Our question might be, "Peter, how can you be sure . . . how are you certain that this Jesus whom you know and love is really the Christ of God? You say He has changed you. We see some evidence, but how do you really know? How do you know what is to be your position in eternity?"

The answer comes thundering from the pages of Peter's Epistle:

> For we did not follow cleverly devised tales when we made known to you the power and coming of our Lord Jesus Christ, but we were eyewitnesses of His majesty. For when He received honor and glory from God the Father, such an utterance as this was made to Him by the Majestic Glory, "THIS IS MY BELOVED SON WITH WHOM I AM WELL-PLEASED"—and we ourselves heard this utterance made from heaven when we were with Him on the holy mountain (2 Pet. 1:16-18, NASB).

"Yes," Simon says, "this is a personal testimony. I am not speaking from hearsay or sharing a fantasy. I was with Jesus on the Holy Mount. I saw Him in all His holiness. I shall never be the same. I have had a glimpse of glory . . . I have seen Jesus 'as He is.'"

That is the same testimony John must have had in mind as he penned the second verse of the third chapter of 1 John.

> Beloved, now we are children of God, and it has not appeared as yet what we shall be. We know that, when He appears, we shall be like Him, because we shall see Him just as He is (1 John 3:2, NASB).

Surely John could say we shall see Him "as He is," for John, along with Peter and James, had seen Him.

As we come to Matthew 17, we are in the presence of things eternal. Here we see Jesus in His completed humanity. Here we have a glimpse of the glory which is to be revealed. Here we view the Master as He will make all men in Himself. The transfiguration does not so much prove His Deity as it decorates His humanity. It is a glimpse of what God has intended for man and what we can be in Christ.

To put this passage in its proper position, we must go back to the last verse of chapter 16. In that 28th verse Jesus said, "There are some of those who are standing here who shall not taste death until they see the Son of Man coming in His kingdom." Then chapter 17 begins, "And six days later Jesus took with Him Peter, James and John, and brought them up to a high mountain by themselves." There have been many things said and written about what that statement in verse 28 means. Most have concluded that it was fulfilled with the destruction of Jerusalem in AD 70. Indeed Jesus was there in judgment as He is in all judgment, but His kingdom obviously did not come at that time. It would seem most logical to say that these three chosen disciples did see Jesus coming in the glory of His kingdom. They did see Him as the kingdom would have Him in this transfiguration experience.

The Greek word for transfiguration is *metamorphō*. The English word "metamorphosis" comes from it. There is a great fascination in the study of phenomena to note the changes (metamorphoses) which can come to substances without destroying their essential nature. Charcoal, pure

carbon, under terrific heat and pressure turns into a brilliant, flashing diamond. Both are the same thing, the charcoal and the diamond. Whether it is black, lusterless coal,
or glorious, precious jewel, it is still carbon. Hold in your
hand a piece of hard, cold ice, warm it, and it is water to
drink. Heat it further, and it becomes an instrument of almost illimitable power—steam. Here is a pile of sandstone.
Pulverize it, heat it, add a little lime and soda, and it can
become beautiful transparent glass. Here is a little plot of
dirt and there a small seed. Behold the beautiful flower and
fruit rising out of the dirt of the soil. In a treetop is a little
nest, and in the nest are small speckled eggs. Behold the
transformation when the eggs are quickened in life, and
the mockingbird learns to sing. Without a doubt and without contradiction, that same vast, illimitable transformation can come to man. The cursing, swearing, fisherman
named Simon becomes the rock of God who delivers God's
message at Pentecost. The persecuting self-righteous Pharisee, Saul of Tarsus, becomes Paul, servant of Christ. Such
is the transforming power of God that we see all around us
in everyday life.

The remarkable transfiguration was an adumbration
of the glory that was yet to be and a harbinger of what was
soon to come. The immediate purpose of the miraculous
transformation of our Lord was to strengthen Christ for His
coming death and to encourage His disciples in the trial
they were yet to face. It was a dark hour for the disciples
and for the Messiah. Suffering and death and crucifixion
and cross-bearing are not easy. The easy way of possessing
all the kingdoms of the earth and the glory of them without
sacrifice and suffering had been offered to Christ by Satan
in the hour of temptation. Knowing that there is no crown
without a cross, Jesus had spurned that temptation. Christ
shows the way that leads to heaven and to glory, and with
Him He brought His many sons and daughters to that salvation impossible apart from blood and tears of sacrifice.

In the dark hour of trial a marvelous gift was bestowed
upon the Lord. On a high mountain was revealed to three of

His disciples His glorious Sonship. With Him appeared Moses and Elijah, representatives of the Law and the Prophets, who conversed with Christ about His approaching death. The disciples' hopes were revived. They had never dreamed of such splendor in their Lord. Jesus Himself found a sympathy and understanding in this high conversation with Moses and Elijah that was lacking on the earth. Surely they would be able to walk down from this mountain to the "valley of the shadow" in the strength of the Father.

Indeed these three disciples got a glimpse of glory on the Mount of Transfiguration. It is ours to examine what their experience was that we may see how that glimpse of glory may come to our lives.

I. The Election They Enjoyed

The witnesses of the transfiguration were Peter, James, and John. We might ask why these three? There are many reasons that could be given why these men were chosen to gain this glimpse of glory. Perhaps it was because these could be counted on to keep the instructions of Jesus in verse 9 when they were told not to tell this vision until the resurrection. Maybe it was because they were in somewhat deeper sympathy with their Savior and had a better understanding. These three were elect out of the elect and favored to see what none else in all the world might behold. Doubtless our Lord had reasons for His choice as He does for every choice He makes. These are the same three that beheld the agony in the Garden of Gethsemane. Perhaps the first sight at Transfiguration Mount was necessary to sustain that faith for that second sight. Whatever may be the case, the Lord makes the choice, and it is not necessary for Him to reveal to us His every reason.

All throughout the Bible the people of God are referred to as "the elect." Indeed it is clear that men are chosen for salvation. God always has His reasons for these choices, even though He does not make those reasons always clear. Writing in his first Epistle (1:2), Peter says of himself that he is "elect according to the foreknowledge of the Father through sanctification of the Spirit unto obedience and sprinkling of the blood of Jesus Christ." Surely that is the testimony of every saved individual. We are the "elect of God" (Matt. 24:22,31).

> And unless those days had been cut short, no life would have been saved; but for the sake of the elect those days shall be cut short (Matt. 24:22).

> And He will send forth His angels with a great trumpet and they will gather together His elect from the four winds, from one end of the sky to the other (Matt. 24:31).

> Who will bring a charge against God's elect? God is the one who justifies (Rom. 8:33).

> . . . knowing, brethren, beloved by God, His choice of you (1 Thess. 1:4, all NASB).

There is no way that anyone can receive the glimpse of glory that is in Christ Jesus until he is elect of God. Our salvation begins when the Holy Spirit initiates conviction of sin. Our salvation is sparked when the Holy Spirit imparts faith to believe in Jesus Christ. None of us is saved by accident or merely by our own choosing. We are the chosen of God, elect unto salvation. As He reveals Himself to us, so we gain a glimpse of glory.

II. The Revelation They Received

While in prayer, the splendor of the Lord shone out. His face lit up with its own inner glory and became like a sun. All of His dress was like clouds radiated by that sun. They became as white as the light itself. "He was transfigured before them." He alone was the Center of all they saw. It was a marvelous unveiling of the hidden nature of the Lord Jesus. In one way it was a fulfillment of the word of John: "The Word was made flesh and dwelt among us, and we beheld His glory."

Verse 3 of our text tells us "there appeared unto them Moses and Elias talking with Him." These departed saints

appeared probably as representatives of the ancient economy. Moses was the founder of Judaism and Elijah its re-
former. Now the system which one inaugurated and the
other ratified was about to undergo a change, not a destruction, but a transfiguration.

It is interesting that Moses and Elijah talked to Jesus,
according to Luke's account, about his impending death.
Moses, representing the Law, must have said something
like this, "I have come to talk with you about your death.
The Law requires a sacrifice. The Law says that it is the
blood that makes atonement for the soul. The Law says
that the substitute for the sinner must die. Lord Jesus,
every rite—every ritual—every ceremony—every sacrifice
of the Law points to you. You must bear the Cross, die upon
it, else all mankind will perish. The Lamb of Atonement,
the Blood of the Passover, are but pictures of You."

Elijah represented the prophets and may have said
something like this, "I have come to talk with you about
your death. Every voice of the prophets calls for the expia-
tion of sin by the death of the Son of God. All we like sheep
have gone astray; we have turned everyone to his own way;
and the Lord hath laid on You the iniquity of us all. The
chastisement of our sin is upon You, and with Your stripes
we are healed."

The finger that wrote the Law on Mount Sinai and the
hand that smote the prophets of Baal on Mount Carmel
both were lifted up to point to Christ as He approached the
hour of His death. The stern voice that spoke the commandments and the grim prophet that uttered the judgments of
God upon Israel both proclaimed "the lamb of God that taketh away the sin of the world." This is He whom they had
seen from afar.

The transfiguration, even though it spoke of His death,
was an adumbration of the glory that was yet to be. Jesus
was transfigured, and He now is and forever shall be in
heaven. On that day of His transfiguration both types of
kingdom citizens, Moses raised from the dead and Elijah
translated, immortalized in the moment—in the twinkling

of an eye were presented. So shall it be with us. Our beloved dead shall be raised incorruptible, and the living shall be changed in a moment, in the twinkling of an eye.

Thus the revelation was to them one of the complete economy of God's redeeming grace.

Verse 4 is also part of the revelation. It reveals the inadequacy of man in the sight of glory. The sight spoke to the three beholders. They felt bound to answer it. Peter must speak: "Lord, it is good for us to be here." Everybody was of this opinion. Who would not have been? Because it was so good he would stay in this beautiful state and still get more good from it. He has not lost his reverence, and therefore, he would have the Great One sheltered suitably. He submits the proposal to Jesus, "If thou wilt." He offers that he and his brethren will plan and build shrines. "Let us make here three tabernacles." He would not propose to build one for himself, James, and John. Who would not wish to abide in such society as this? Yet, how impractical is Peter—how selfish the one thought, "It is good for us." What was to be done for the rest of the Twelve and for the other disciples and for the wide world? Indeed, the excitement of the experience was not sufficient to bring wisdom of its application.

Verse 5 reveals that as we catch a glimpse of glory, we must listen to God. "While he yet spake"—such wild talk might well be interrupted. What a blessed interruption. We may often thank the Lord for stopping our babble. "A bright cloud overshadowed them." Surely they felt they were entering into that cloud and feared as they did so.

Then a voice out of the cloud, the Father Himself, spoke: "THIS IS MY BELOVED SON IN WHOM I AM WELL-PLEASED, HEAR YE HIM." Indeed it was clear that the Father was happy with Christ and therefore is happy with all who are in Him. It is not ours to want to build a tabernacle and escape the world, but as we tabernacle in Christ, so the Father looks upon us, and He is well-pleased. It is better to hear the Son of God than to see saints or build tabernacles. This will please the Father more than all else that love can suggest.

Verse 6: "And when the disciples heard it, they fell on their faces and were much afraid" (NASB).

Yes, the voice overcame them. They were in the immediate presence of God, listening to the Father's voice. They said no more about building tabernacles, but, "they fell on their faces." Awe is the end of talk. Indeed no one has really had a glimpse of glory who does not stand in awe in the presence of God.

In verses 7 and 8, we have the beautiful culmination of the revelation. Jesus had seemed to go away from them, lost in a cloud of brightness, but now He "came and touched them." His communion with pure spirits did not make Him disdain to touch feeble flesh. Oh, the sweet comfort of that gentle touch. It aroused, consoled, and strengthened His amazed and trembling disciples. A touch of manhood is more reassuring to poor flesh and blood than the blaze of the Godhead. The voice from Heaven had cast down, but the word from Jesus was "Arise." The Father's voice made them so afraid, but Jesus said, "Be not afraid." Such is our cry, "Glorious God, how much we bless Thee for the Mediator Thou hast given."

Verse 8 is extremely significant. "And when they had lifted up their eyes, they saw no man save Jesus only." When they opened their eyes at the touch of Jesus, they saw only Jesus. Moses and Elijah and the exceeding brightness had all gone. They had come back to the common places of their life with Christ. They saw no man, but they had lost nothing since Jesus remained. They had gained by the vanishing of the shining ones, since they could see Jesus all the better, and their attention was not divided. The vision of His transfiguration blinded them, but now to see "Jesus only" was to come back to practical life and have the best of all sights still left to them.

Indeed no man has ever had a glimpse of glory until he sees Jesus Christ and Him "only." Oh, that we might also have the eye of our mind so fixed on the Lord as our one Object that He may fill the whole field of our vision, and we may see "Jesus only." We have had a glimpse of glory when we see Jesus—come in the earth to be our Example, dying on Calvary to be our Sacrifice, arising from the grave to be our Sufficiency, ascending to the Father to be our Advocate, and coming again to be our Deliverer and King. It is my prayer today that you would experience the revelation of seeing "Jesus only" in your life.

III. The Assignment They Accepted

How are the believers to handle special experiences with God? When we have had a glimpse of glory, how are we to share it?

In verse 9, Jesus charged them: "Tell the vision to no man, until the Son of man be risen again from the dead." What they had seen would confirm their own confidence and remain a secret spring of delight to them, but since it would require great faith in others to believe it, they were to "tell the vision to no man." The transfiguration would be as hard to believe as the Incarnation itself. There could be no practical use of making demands upon a faith which scarcely existed. Until the greatest confirmation of all was given in our Lord's resurrection, the vision of the Holy Mount would be rather attacks upon the faith of those who had not personally seen it themselves.

It is wise not to overload testimony. There is a time for making known the higher truths. Out of season these may be burdens rather than assisting. We often should be charged to present "Jesus only" that men may see Him and have their own experience, rather than to seek to duplicate ours.

Now that the "Son of man" has risen from the dead, there is no need for us to hold back the full story of His life. His coming out of the grave has set free all buried truths.

Verses 10-13 show us something beautiful. The disciples now had seen Jesus as the full Messiah. Somehow

Peter, James, and John could realize, like Peter had not even when He had said, "Thou art the Christ, the Son of the Living God," that Jesus was all that God intended man to be. Yet they had a problem. They had been told that before the Messiah came, Elijah would return. Their deduction would be, "Messiah cannot come until Elijah has appeared; Elijah has not appeared; therefore, Jesus is not the Messiah."

Jesus answered. He has an answer to all questions. When we bring difficulties to Him honestly, He replies. Jesus said that Elijah had come in the person of John the Baptist, and as they had done unto him "whatsoever they wanted," so also would "the Son of man suffer." The plain truth was that when they had seen Jesus and understood Him as the Messiah, all other questions were answered. They accepted their assignment that they should not tell the story until after the resurrection, but when the resurrection was complete, the story became the theme of their lives.

Have you caught a glimpse of glory? Have you seen Jesus for yourself? The desire of my heart for fellow believers is that more and more the great Object of our thoughts, motives, and acts may be "Jesus only." Our faith is most vital when it is most full of Christ. When we are in the depths of sorrow, nothing will do but "Jesus only." In the higher, rich, spiritual moments of joy and ecstasy, it is always because of "Jesus only." If we would work effectively, we must rely on "Jesus only." If we would suffer patiently, we must feed on "Jesus only." If we would wrestle with God in prayer, we must find our intercession in the name of "Jesus only." If we aspire to conquer sin, it must be in the blood and by the name of "Jesus only."

Some who read this are not yet believers in Christ. As best I know my heart, I simply come to ask you to see "Jesus only." If you can see only Moses, you will see a Law which condemns you. If you can hear only Elijah, you will hear a prophet who frightens you, but if you can look and

see Jesus, you will see a Savior dying for you on a Cross and
hear the voice of a Redeemer who says, "Father, forgive
them, for they know not what they do."

May God grant us grace, everyone of us, that we might
have such a glimpse of glory that we will see Jesus and
trust "Jesus only" for our eternal assurance.

> Back to the cold world I will not go,
> > Back to the old paths of pain and woe,
> Back to the old life of sin, O no!
> > I've had a glimpse of Jesus.
>
> Back on the night-shrouded sea to die?
> > Back where the breakers of sin toss on
> > > high?
> Back, 'mid the billows of doubt? Not I!
> > I've had a glimpse of Jesus.
>
> Back to the boon friends of former days,
> > Still walking on in their sin and dismay,
> Back with a message of love and grace;
> > I've had a glimpse of Jesus.
>
> I've found a life that is sweeter to me,
> > Sweeter with peace, from unhappiness free,
> Fuller of joy than the old life could be;
> > I've had a glimpse of Jesus.
>
> Back to the cold world I will not go,
> > Back to the old paths of pain and woe,
> Back to the old life of sin, O no!
> > I've had a glimpse of Jesus!

Peter Rhea Jones

All I Need and More
Psalm 23

One of my warm childhood memories is of my three brothers and my parents and I repeating the Twenty-third Psalm as our blessing at the table. It was read at my grandmother's funeral. It may have made spiritual history in your life too. This beautiful psalm has been called by Scroggie "the simplest, sweetest song that was ever sung." It is a true masterpiece, a sacred poem of a mere six verses. Alexander Maclaren wisely said, "The world could spare many a book better than this sunny little psalm. It has dried many tears." Some of those tears may have been yours.

The famous preacher, Henry Ward Beecher, declared, "The Twenty-third Psalm is the nightingale of the psalms." Charles Haddon Spurgeon picked up on the beautiful metaphor of Beecher and agreed that the Twenty-third Psalm was the nightingale of the psalms because "it was sung sweetly in the ears of many a mourner in his night of weeping, and has bidden him hope for a morning of joy."

It is the favorite of favorites. Some Christians can say the words of the psalm by heart. Some can close their eyes and can hear the cadences of the psalm in the elevated language of the King James Version. As you read it over and over, savoring its sentiments devotionally, it begins to dawn on you that this psalmist had a great conviction. His conviction was that life is good because of God. Out of his own experience of living he reached a peace of mind flowing from a trusting faith. And it was not always in the sunny meadows that this poet lived. Likely he had himself been in the valley of the shadow of death. Here was a believer

189

whose hard-won affirmation was that life is good because of God. It also dawns on you from repeated readings that the famous passage is simply a prayerful testimony.

As you let this psalm touch your hearts and your lives, you see that the song pictures God as a shepherd who provides—not merely an abstract God or the Force out there in space—but a God who loves and cares and provides for His own in a gracious and generous fashion. We will divide this spiritual masterpiece into two parts, both under the theme of God's provision. In the first division, the first four verses, God provides for our needs. In the last two verses God provides more than our basic needs. He is a recklessly generous kind of God. Let us allow this psalm to alter our outlook. Let us hide its message in our hearts and let us allow its ministry to happen in our personal existences.

We are not sure who wrote the pearl of the psalms. Perhaps the shepherd king penned it, for David after all cared for the flocks of Jesse on the hills of Bethlehem (1 Sam. 17:34-35), and it is possible, as Kyle Yates suggested, that near the end of the king's life, after he had experienced many stressful stages in his life, he reflected back on his boyhood days as a shepherd. David may have recalled how he knew the name of every sheep and called them by name, and how the sheep responded to their shepherd when they heard his voice. He remembered how he cared for his flock and took them from meadow to meadow. Perhaps the spiritual masterpiece of the Psalms was the personal testimony of the shepherd king. It's not complicated, but simple. It's the testimony of a person who has lived the life of faith. Twice he breaks in with a kind of natural prayer to God (vv. 4-5). It was apparently written for worship, because that's where we do testimony and that's where we pray. It is a powerful psalm with a spiritual track record spanning centuries.

I. All I Need . . .

In the opening verses God provides all our needs if we follow. The very essence of faith is caught up in the very first statement: "The Lord is my shepherd." This is personal religion. It expresses the strong covenant between God and Israel. It expresses faith in the God who led the Israelites out of bondage in Egypt and led them safely through the wandering in the wilderness. The shepherd Lord was the God of Jacob who could say at the end of his life that the Shepherd God had led him all his life until his last hour (Gen. 48:15). But it is also the personal testimony of the psalmist: "The Lord is my shepherd." The Lord is the One the psalmist had chosen as leader of his life. For this psalm to begin to take root in your life and mine it is necessary for the God Who is Shepherd to be your shepherd and mine, and for us to be willing to follow His leadership in our lives. We often sing, "He Leadeth Me, O Blessed Thought," and we are encouraged to let Him be our shepherd and to follow in His way today. And let us sing, "Guide Me, O Thou Great Jehovah."

The psalmist declares, "I shall not want." I need ask for nothing. The Lord provides all I need. When the children of Israel had wandered forty years in the wilderness they were reminded that God had taken care of them so "you have lacked nothing" (Deut. 2:7). When they looked forward to the Promised Land they were promised, "You shall not lack anything in it" (Deut. 8:9). God provided for His people. Paul's testimony after a life of following faith resembled the confidence of the psalmist, "My God will supply every need of yours according to his riches in glory in Christ Jesus" (Phil. 4:19). And God still provides for our needs.

One of the things that we need from time to time—and there are some who need this a great deal— is to have a restoration of our souls. The poet says in the psalm, "He restores my soul" (v. 2e). Dr. J. J. Owens likes to translate the Hebrew "He gets me breathing again." The psalmist's personal experience with faith and with life was that the God he knows restores his vitality and his life. How does God restore souls? The poet is very clear how He does it. God gives rest for the body and peace for the troubled mind. You are greeted by the testimony, "He makes me lie down in green pastures" (v. 2a). What a pastoral picture. A shepherd who knows the grazing lands can find the meadows where the grass is thick. He leads his sheep to good pasturage where they can lie down. Now it is important to notice that it is not just grass for grazing. For the text speaks of lying down in some verdant valley (see Jer. 33:12). God restores your soul with rest for your body. This psalm offers rest to any of us who would follow God as our shepherd rather than merely the secular pace of life. Some have stressful jobs. There are some who face tense pressures daily. There are some who experience stress in marriage or in relationships in the office. You may need to draw these words into your heart and life. The Lord wants you to lie down in green pastures.

Dr. Charles Allen, who was beloved in Atlanta and went on to pastor the First Methodist Church of Houston, Texas, wrote many books, including a valuable one on the Twenty-third Psalm. But at one stage in his life, due to his heavy pastoral responsibilities, he suffered a kind of breakdown and was forced to go to the hospital for an extended stay. One of his friends came to see him. Immediately Dr. Allen sat up in his bed and began to speak vigorously about all that had to be done at the church and how eager he was to get back to work. His friend caught on quickly to the pastor's problem, and he said, "Dr. Allen, do you remember writing a book on the Twenty-third Psalm?" He answered, "Yes," puzzled. His friend confronted him, "Remember the words of the psalm, 'he maketh me rest'?" Here was a message preachers need to hear. In Dr. Allen's life it was time to lie down and to rest and to allow his body to be renewed and restored. One of the ways the Lord restores your soul is by leading you into places of rest. A Japanese man paraphrased the psalmist's sentiment, "The Lord is my pacesetter, I shall not rush." The Shepherd can save you from an early heart attack.

Another way the Shepherd King restores our souls is by giving us peace for our troubled minds: "He leads me beside still waters" (v. 2b). The eastern shepherd never drives but always leads his sheep. The "still waters" are those chosen by the shepherd to protect small ewe lambs from treacherous torrents of noisy rivers. It refers to water that is quiet and still. The Hebrew literally means "the waters of peace" or "waters of rest." The wise shepherd leads to the quiet places, to the still waters. And our God would lead you and me to the still waters. He will lead us to those times when we relax and can be still and be renewed.

There are times when what we need is quiet reflection, times when we need to meditate, and times when we need to pray. There are times when we need to worship in the sanctuary, in the presence of God and with all his people, in order to be renewed and to find fresh peace for our lives. The Shepherd offers quiet repose as a soothing remedy. Hannah Jelkes in an American play speaks profoundly to a disturbed Episcopal priest who had angrily driven his congregation away. She said that if he went back he would lead them beside the still waters because he knew how much they needed them.

So many decide when the pressures become too great in this highly competitive society that they will deal with the pressure by drinking excessively, or they will seek a release from their anxieties by popping pills, prescribed or otherwise. I read not long ago a heart-breaking paraphrase of the Twenty-third Psalm penned by a drug addict in East Harlem in New York:

> Heroin is my shepherd;
> I shall not want.
> It maketh me to lie down in gutters.
> It leadeth me beside still madness.
> It destroyeth my soul.
> It leadeth me in the paths of hell for its
>   namesake.

We share a Shepherd rather Who can restore the soul and lead into the paths of righteousness.

Our Shepherd God provides all we need. He wants to

restore your soul and mine with peace for our troubled minds and with rest for our bodies. Those of us who may be working too hard, who may be too involved, whose health and heart and muscles and whose quality of life are being wasted, need to respond to these pastoral, inspired words of God, for they are God's special delivery letter for us today.

We also find that this Shepherd God who provides sufficiently gives guidance in our temptations. You remember the familiar words, "He leads me into the paths of righteousness." The ancient shepherd would lead his flock from one meadow to another. He knew the right paths to take and the ones to avoid. He knew how to reach the destination most safely. The psalmist avers that our God, if we will follow Him, will lead us into the right paths, the paths of righteousness.

Sometimes we are tempted. We are tempted to take paths of unrighteousness. Sometimes we are tempted to do things we know to be wrong. We may feel in mid-life the power of temptation to withdraw from the world or compromise with it. Pearl Buck depicted in *The Good Earth* (p. 126) the temptations of the successful man who has money to spare and no need to work who turns for the first time to wine and dice and women. We may be inclined to go in the wrong direction, and we may wonder sometimes if there is any way out. Faith says there is. For God beckons us onward to the paths of righteousness and encourages us to follow. God provides the way of escape from temptation (1 Cor. 10:13). This God provides guidance for us in our temptations and also comfort for us in our deepest darkness.

The traditional translation in the King James Version of the next verse is hauntingly memorable: "Yea, though I walk through the valley of the shadow of death, I will fear no evil, for thou art with me; thy rod and thy staff they comfort me" (v. 4). The picture intended is not primarily the valley of death. The picture, from the Hebrew word *salmaweth*, is "deepest of darkness," a place of deep shadow, a glen of gloom. *The New English Bible* renders "a valley dark as death." And sometimes the shepherd cannot lead his flocks in the sunny places. Sometimes of necessity the shepherd must lead them down narrow, dark gorges and up steep, dangerous ravines. Jeremiah describes the Lord who led the house of Israel in the wildnerness "in a land of deserts and pits, in a land of drought and deep darkness (2:6). We sometimes enter the valley that is dark but with the Shepherd. And it is not just "though" we go through the valley; it's "when" we go. No one of our lives is so charmed, so untouched, that we are shielded from the dark valleys of sorrow, distress, and pain. Rather, everyone of us must walk the lonesome valley of the shadow.

Clarence Cranford, Baptist minister for many years in Washington, confided that he had read this passage over and over without paying enough attention to the words *"through* the valley." It dawned on him that the psalm does not say we walk into the valley of deep darkness but *through* it! God is there to meet us, take us by the hand, and see us safely home.

Dr. John McNeil told, out of his own childhood, of a memorable moment in Glasgow, Scotland. He had gone to the store, late at night, and then had to make his way back across a rough section in which was a dangerous ravine. There were actually robbers who hid themselves in some of the dark places to pounce on defenseless people and take away their money. John was scared almost out of his wits as he made the dangerous journey alone. He was walking as fast as a little boy could possibly walk. Suddenly he heard someone walking along the narrow path behind him. He backed up against an overhanging rock and stretched himself as thin as he possibly could, hoping the man would just walk by and not even see him. His heart was pounding in his throat. But then suddenly he heard a voice call out, "John! John!" Without a moment's hesitation he came running out of the shadows and wrapped his little arms around the knees of the man who had called. It was his father. Joy filled his heart as fear fled. No one could harm him now. His dad took the boy by the hand and together they walked through the valley of the shadow. Instead of fear and panic the boy's heart was bubbling over with joy and confidence. He understood what the psalmist meant when he said, "I will fear no evil for thou art with me." The Lord gives comfort in our deepest darkness. God spoke to Jacob at Bethel, "I am with you and will keep you" (Gen. 28:15). God said to Moses, "Certainly I will be with you" (Ex. 3:12). Joshua received the assurance, "I will not fail you nor forsake you" (Josh. 1:5). Jesus promised His disciples, "I am with you always" (Matt. 28:20).

The shepherd comforts with his rod and staff as well as his presence. The shepherd used the rod to defend against the wild enemies, the jackals and the wolves that attacked the sheep (Mic. 7:14). And the shepherd used the crook to lift up a little ewe lamb to put it back with its mother and would lean on the staff for support. Even so the good Lord, who is like a shepherd, offers a defense from dangers and a staff for support.

This summer our family did a stay-at-home vacation and made day trips. Our most exciting day was a raft trip on the Ocoee River in the mountains of Tennessee. There are dangerous rapids on the Ocoee. We were not entirely aware of the full challenge in advance. We had asked one of the friends in our church who had gone on the trip what it was like. Rather philosophically, she had said how the Ocoee was like life with its quiet, smooth-running places between the rough waters. We soon forgot the philosophy when we boarded the rubber raft and hit a rapid as soon as we pushed off. If it had not been for the guide, who sat in the back steering, and who told us how to paddle and when to paddle, we would not have made it. He knew the river intimately and how to approach each rapid and how to run it without crashing into the boulders. We certainly would not have challenged some of the rapids as we did. We did a three-sixty in swirling water. We had to paddle hard, hold on with our feet, and hang in there, but the guide brought us through the rough water. My friend's philosophy was right in her view that life has smooth places and rough, and we had better expect both. But after the raft adventure I would add the psalmist's philosophy. We have a Guide. We have a Shepherd. If we will follow, He will take us through the rough places. And Jesus is the Good Shepherd Who lays down his life for his sheep (John 10:11).

The Lord provides all I need. He restores my soul. He gives guidance in my temptations. He offers comfort in my deepest darkness.

II. More Than I Need

The Lord is so generous in His provision to us that He graciously gives not only what we need but even more than we need. "My cup runs over." In the last two verses of Psalm 23 the portrait of God shifts from leading shepherd toward loving host. Perhaps the role of the shepherd remains in the background. Samuel Terrien points out that the task of the shepherd included preparing the pasture ahead of his flock. He carefully surveys the grazing area:

> He uproots poisonous weeds that sheep never
> learn to avoid;
> He cuts off thorny thistles or cacti that scratch
> ears and eyes and noses and legs;
> He uncovers nests of snakes and scorpions; and
> He prepares safe pasture ground in the presence
> of the many enemies of sheep.

Bruised and bloodied heads were anointed with oil and an earthen cup contained medicine made of hemp or barley mixed with honey and herbs. And a shepherd serving as host would spread a cloak or leather skin on the ground in order to serve a guest.

Whether the predominant picture is a shepherd preparing a pasture or hospitality in a desert tent, the loving host offers even more than we need. These closing words bestow a climactic significance. They represent the testimony of faith.

We are welcomed warmly to extravagant hospitality (v. 5). "He prepares a table before us. He anoints our head

with oil" (v. 5). Here is an overflowing abundance. We are
privileged to be guests at the Lord's table. We live on the
Lord's bounties. Here we are safe from our enemies. Our
host has made a covenant of protection. Our Lord went
even further to challenge, "Love your enemies" (Matt.
5:43).

The Shepherd graciously invites the weary pilgrim to
come in after the toil and the stress of the day are finished.
It reminds you of the little girl retelling the Old Testament
story of Enoch's walk with God: "The man walked and
walked and walked, and when it became dark God said,
'Enoch, you are nearer my home than yours so you should
come on in with me,' and he did."

Our experience in accepting the warm hospitality of
the Lord is a staggering extravagance of His grace.

God provides more than we need with His active pursuit of lovingkindness (v. 6a). This is humbling and overwhelming. It is a conviction that grew out of a lifelong
experience with God. Criminals are pursued by justice.
Christians are pursued by God's lovingkindness. The Hebrew word *chesed* means loyalty born out of love. The Hebrew verb does not merely mean "follow" but "pursue." The
one who trusts in God is openly exposed to the pursuit of
divine love and affection. A Scottish preacher put it, "The
Lord is my shepherd, aye, and He has two fine collie dogs,
goodness and mercy. They will see us safely home."

One last gracious provision is a home at the end of the
journey. "I shall dwell in the house of the Lord forever"
(v. 6b). The guest was so warmly received and enjoyed fellowship with the loving host so much he wanted to remain
in the house forever.

Some interpreters take the reference to the house of
God as meaning the Temple and so understand the sentiment that he so enjoys God in worship he intends to continue faithfully in the sanctuary as long as he lives. We do
not become more strongly conscious of the nearness of God
in the hallowed atmosphere of worship than is possible in

the noise of the streets. And so we make our commitments to enjoy the worship of God as long as we live.

But Dr. Kyle Yates went on to say that he took the verse further to point by inspiration to the mystic beyond. We are invited home to spend all the ages of eternity with the Shepherd. At the family funeral you attended your heart was lifted by the promise of a home at the end of the journey.

Jesus Christ is the Good Shepherd who invites you to spend all eternity with Him in the Father's house.

The Lord provides even more than I need. My cup does overflow from His extravagant hospitality, His active pursuit with lovingkindness, and His promise of a home at the end of the journey.

Clearly these immortal six verses are the Word of God. To know them is to love them. To live them is to claim them. Let your testimony and mine be, "The Lord is my Shepherd."

Don M. Kim

The Gospel of Jesus Christ in Genesis 1—3

The purpose of this sermon is to bear my humble witness to the fact that Genesis 1—3 does bear witness to my Lord Jesus Christ whom this sin-sick world so urgently needs to know.

Genesis 1—3 has been the battleground between the Christians and non-Christians, and even between the Bible-believing brothers themselves. I wonder whether I am mistaken to believe that some of the controversies could have been avoided if we all had heeded what our Lord said to the Pharisees and scribes: "You search the Scriptures, because you think that in them you have eternal life; and *it is these that bear witness of me*" (John 5:39).

Why did the Pharisees clash with Jesus when they loved and believed the Scriptures so much? Could it be because they looked in the Scriptures for something else other than Jesus Himself? Aren't some Christians today making, though unwittingly, the same mistake? It is my prayer that the Spirit will help me to seek only Jesus in Genesis 1—3, not something else.

Christians have taken Genesis 1—3 very seriously for different reasons. So do I, because it tells about the beginning or the origin. The Book of Genesis is called in the Hebrew Bible, "B'r'eshith" which means, "In the beginning." Knowing about the beginning is important and profitable.

First of all, we can learn what our God was like in the beginning. We know about God who was revealed by His Son, our Lord. Is the God of Jesus the same as the God of the Old Testament? As a child in Korea, I used to believe

that the God of the Old Testament was spooky and tyrannical while the God of Jesus was gentle and loving. And I was
more confused because preachers tried to justify the seeming contradictions with the scoldings and harassment.
Don't many today receive the same impression from the Bible and from preachers and then get confused?

One's faith is the manifestation of his concept of God,
as W. T. Conner said. Confusion of theology seems to be the
root of today's problems. The concept of God has been polluted by many, such as Pharisees, scribes, and theologians.

Genesis 1—3 tells us what God was like from the beginning. Our Lord said, "I and my Father are one" (John
10:30). If we find that God in the beginning and Jesus are
truly one through this study, our faith will be clarified and
strengthened.

*Secondly, Genesis 1—3 teaches the meaning or purpose
of man and of the world because it tells us about the beginning.*

Suppose I have a watch here which has been trodden
over by people. It is so disfigured we cannot tell what it is.
But suppose we can somehow see the original state of this
watch; then we can know what this timepiece is for—its
meaning and purpose. It will be thrillingly better if we can
meet the watchmaker who made this watch because we can
ask him everything about this puzzling watch.

Today, the world and everything in it, including man,
have been so deformed that we cannot tell their purpose or
meaning, no matter how hard we try. Philosophers tried
without much success. What is man? What am I? What is
life? What is death? Why is the world like this? Many despair, and others give up, but questions keep haunting
them. Many therefore try to cover up with agnosticism or
atheism. But thank God that Genesis 1—3 beautifully answers all these questions because it is the story about the
origins.

*Thirdly, Genesis 1—3 tells us about the paradise, sin,
and salvation in the beginning.* By knowing their origins
we can know the real nature of these important matters.

By knowing the origin of sin, we learn the real nature of sin. By finding what God did for the sinners in the beginning, we can learn the real nature of God's plan of salvation.

Genesis 1—3 is indeed filled with the treasures of God's truth. We cannot cover much in this sermon. We shall note only a few. Amazingly, the teachings of Genesis 1—3 are identical with those of our Lord Jesus Christ. That is the reason why I titled this sermon, "The Gospel of Jesus Christ in Genesis 1—3."

I. God in the Beginning

First of all, what does Genesis 1—3 say about God? "In the beginning God created the heavens and the earth" (1:1). The first proclamation of the Bible about God is that God is the Creator. This is the most important truth. This is the central message which the entire Bible tries to convey to every man and woman. God is the Creator!

But in a way it does not look very important because even non-Christians already know this. Mere knowledge of it does not seem to make any difference upon the lives of the professors. Doesn't the devil even know this?

Once I asked this question to a group of students: "Would it make any difference to your life if the Bible said, 'a dog created the universe'?" Many thought it was only a silly question. But it was not. It was a matter-of-life-or-death question, because if a dog is the creator we must worship a dog.

Therefore, when the Word of God tells us that God is the Creator, it means that He is the Lord. God is, in fact, saying, "I am your Lord; worship Me, obey Me, and serve Me."

This is indeed the central message of the entire Bible. What was the purpose of God's Son coming and dying on the cross? To crown God as the Lord. Didn't our Lord ask us to pray, "Thy kingdom come!" so that God would be enthroned as the Lord? We do long for that blessed day when every heart and every nation fall prostrate before Him. God longs for that day, too. That is why the last word of the Bible is, "Yes, I am coming quickly." And all who know His heart say, "Amen. Come, Lord Jesus" (Rev. 22:20).

Genesis 1:1 thus proclaims that God is the Lord, which is the theme of the entire Bible, of our Lord's entire ministry, and of the prayers of all His children.

Secondly, the text tells us that God creates by His Words. Genesis 1:2 says, "The earth was chaotic and empty and darkness was over the surface of the deep." It does not explain why the earth was in this condition. Apparently, that was not its concern. But the Bible says that God spoke to the earth in this condition; and everything has changed. God spoke to the darkness, "Let there be light," and there was light! and the darkness was dispelled. God spoke to the empty universe, and the empty universe became full of life. And God spoke to the chaotic earth, and there came order. God created this beautiful, orderly universe with His Words.

This was His way of creation in the beginning; and we should learn that this is also His way of re-creation today. Genesis is very emphatic that God works through His Words.

The Samaritan sister's life was chaotic, empty, and hopelessly dark. When Jesus came and spoke to her, light began to shine in her soul; her chaotic life became orderly; and her empty, thirsty heart became full of life as to coax the barren Samaritan desert into full bloom. We can say the same thing about Zaccheus. My life also was chaotic because no one could rein it. My heart was empty and dark. And Jesus came; He became my Lord; and everything has changed.

How is America today, the richest nation in the world? Do lawlessness, emptiness, and darkness characterize her? How is the world today? Is it in the same condition? According to Genesis 1, America and the world still have hope, if the Word is brought to them. America and the world need God as the Lord. Why? Think of a division of an army without a commander. Think of a herd of sheep without a shepherd. Their condition would be chaotic, empty, and dark, wouldn't it?

The fundamental problem today is not material, not political, and not even moral. It is the lack of Jesus-God as the Lord; and He is more than sufficient. And only the Word of God can melt the stubborn hearts to enthrone Him as the Lord.

In Genesis 1, the word "God" appears thirty-two times as the subject. When we read Genesis 1, it sounds like a composition of a first grader who doesn't even know the use of pronouns. Why should he repeat "God" thirty-two times in this short essay? Was the author a first grader? Could it be the expression of his anxious desire to have God enthroned, in view of the fact that everyone in his day, including the government, business, education, art, home, and even churches, left God dethroned despite all the pious talk and outward prosperity? The message of Genesis 1 is very contemporary. It insists that God is the Lord. God can become our Lord through His Word. Is He our Lord in reality?

II. Man and the World

What does the text say about the world and, most of all, about man? In Genesis 1, we find the statement, "And God saw that it was good," repeated five times. This statement seems to suggest God's feeling toward His creation. He seemed smiling as He looked over His wondrously beautiful creation. When He completed the work of creation by creating man and woman in His image, Genesis 1:31 says, "And God saw all that He had made, and behold, it was very good." God looked jubilant. This was how he felt about man and the world. Now, what do we learn from this?

First of all, we learn that the God of Genesis is not like the gods of human imagination. All man-made gods are spooky and fearful without exception. But the God in the beginning is the almighty Creator and yet so attractive. His creation manifests His character. Look at the flowers, fruits, trees, hills, the sunset, and the like. He is a superb artist. He is a wonderful musician. He put songs in the beaks of birds and in the flowing streams. He is most humorous; He made monkeys and piglets. He created everything so good and smiled and smiled. He is good. He is *not* "mysterium-tremendum." He is like our loving Jesus around Whom little children loved to swarm. Who wouldn't love Him? Who wouldn't adore Him? Genesis 1 says He is our loving Lord.

Secondly, we learn that everything God created was good in the beginning. We know this is true. How wonderful and marvelous are His handiworks? If we see anything bad today, it may be because the good things have become polluted due to man's sin, as Genesis 3 suggests.

At a home Bible study in Paraguay on this passage, a young Korean, Mr. Park, asked, "Pastor, did you say that everything God made was good?" Mr. Park was known for his notoriety. "Yes," I said. "Did God make these mosquitos, too?" I knew what he was getting at. Unlike the timid Korean mosquitos, the Paraguayan mosquitos are like "Kamikazes." I said, "Yes, I am positive that God made the mosquitos. But you know that good mosquitos can change to bad ones like some people do. They may be biting you to tell you to wake up and get saved. If you get saved as a result, you would be grateful to these mosquitos, wouldn't you?" Everybody laughed except Mr. Park. I was not sure whether I gave him a right answer or not. The problem of evil is so difficult. But Mr. Park is a wonderfully born-again Christian today and still remembered my mosquito story when I saw him a few months ago. I don't know whether the mosquitos became bad or vicious from the beginning. At any rate, they helped Mr. Park.

One thing is very clear: Genesis 1 is emphatic that everything God created was good because such a good God could not have done otherwise. And this fact assures us that He will not stand by for long allowing His beautiful world to be polluted. He will soon bring the day when "the nursing child will play by the hole of the cobra and the weaned child will put his hand in the viper's den" (Isa. 11:8). In the meantime, "We know all things work together for good to them that love God" (Rom. 8:28).

Thirdly, what does Genesis 1 say about man? It says that God created man and woman in His own image, blessed them so blissfully, and set them above all creation to rule.

What is the image of God in man? The capacity to fellowship with God, according to Dr. Conner. Only to man was this special privilege granted. What God actually did was that He handed Himself over to man to worship and to enjoy forever. Genesis 1 says that we are very special to Him.

His deep love for man is also shown by the fact that He created man at the very last. He wanted to prepare everything just right for us. When He created the sun, the moon, air, trees, fishes, and every good thing, He had you and me in mind. How thoughtfully He prepared everything just right for us! He did not forget to tilt the earth's axis 23½ degrees toward the sun so we could enjoy four seasons! I am awed by the thought that God had me in mind when He made apples so delicious, nutritious, and beautiful in the beginning. When He smiled and said, "It was good," He was apparently thinking about me enjoying the apple just as my mother used to smile when her cooking came out just right. Genesis 1 is saying that everything around us is soaked with His love for us.

God loves us with His unfathomable love. Modern man needs this knowledge so desperately. He does not know who he is. He needs self-discovery. Until we meet the God of Genesis, we do not know what we are. The Samaritan woman, Zaccheus, and many others did not know who they were, but they met God in Jesus and had self-discoveries. They found the meaning of their lives. Their eyes opened and began to have right perspectives on everything. Modern man needs to meet the God of Genesis. Then, he will know what he is.

III. The Paradise and the Forbidden Fruit (Genesis 2)

God placed His beloved in the Garden of Eden (2:8). Eden means "joy." Man was made to live only in the Garden of Eden. When God made fish He put them in the water; fish were made to live only in the water. Since man was expelled from the Garden, he could never be happy. Money and fame could not make man happy any more than juicy worms could make fishes out of the water happy. Ever since, man has been seeking the Garden every moment, whether he was conscious of that or not. Man goes to college, finds jobs, and gets married in order to find the Garden. The problem is that man seeks the Garden in a wrong way.

Where is the Garden? Genesis 2 does not tell us where it is, but it tells us about some of the things which were in the Garden. They seem to be the same items we find in heaven as described by John in the Book of Revelation. If we can somehow secure these items, we shall have the Garden, I am sure.

The most puzzling thing in the Garden was the tree of the knowledge of good and evil. God placed it right in the center of the Garden and said, "From this tree you shall not eat, for in the day that you eat from it you shall surely die" (2:17).

Since God who loved man so dearly put this tree there, it must have been essential for the Garden. What is this tree? Surely, it is not an apple tree as some Americans believe. I do not believe that it matters much to know what kind of tree it was. The important matter is God's command attached to it: "Thou shall not eat from it." The tree symbolizes God's Word, such as "Thou shalt not kill," "Thou shalt not commit adultery," and so on. It is the Word. It is Jesus! If man had kept God's Word, he could have enjoyed the Garden forever. Where is the Garden? It is where Jesus is. When we abide in Him, we live in the Garden.

Did man die when he ate the forbidden fruit? God had said, "In the day that you eat from it, you shall surely die." How did man die? He died spiritually and morally, and that is the real death because man is man, due to his spiritual nature, the image of God. When man sins, he is dehumanized; he becomes animal-like. Animals help themselves to the forbidden fruit. Many a man today helps himself to the forbidden fruit. Man, the most glorious and the most beloved of God, has given the loving God the bitterest pill, the greatest disappointment and grief.

IV. Sin and Salvation (Genesis 3)

1. Man, a Rebellious Doubtor

When Adam ate the forbidden fruit he actually rebelled against the loving God. Why did he rebel? Because the fruit looked so good and delicious. All sins are attractive. Man both loves and hates sin, as Augustine said.

However, the root cause was that man forgot or began to doubt God's unfathomable love. If he had remembered His love he could have tried to resist the temptation. Man's attitude toward God looked like that of today's rebellious juveniles toward their "tyrannical" parents. Eating the forbidden fruit was therefore not some isolated mischief but a symptom and result of their hearts' alienation from God.

Man's bitterness to God is apparent in Eve's conversation with the tempter. She deliberately misquoted God. What God said was, "From *any* tree of the garden you may eat *freely*." But she changed it to, "From the fruit of the trees of the garden we may eat." She also changed from "You shall not eat" to "You shall not eat it or *touch it*." She misrepresented our generous and blissful God as a narrow-minded, oppressive God. Unbelief of God's love was the root of sin. Unbelief thus alienated man from the loving God.

What was the result of sin? The wages of sin was death, as it is today. Man lost peace, joy, self-respect, and everything wonderful—the eternal life. Instead, he "gained" shame, guilt, fear, and the eternal death.

2. *God Who Seeks with a Bleeding Heart*

What was God's reaction to the ungrateful, rebellious couple? God did not send His fury or punishment. Rather, He set out to seek the prodigals. He cried, "Where are you, Adam?" (3:9). Do we feel His pathos? His pathos is well expressed in Isaiah 1:2-9. There was more than the pathos; there was the bleeding in His heart. His heart was broken because He dearly loved the prodigals, however sinful they were because sin consigns His beloved prodigals in hell. His love was redemptive from the beginning. His love was a costly love from the beginning. The cross of His Son on Calvary was the supreme revelation of such a loving heart of God in Genesis 1—3.

Genesis 3:8 says the prodigals heard the sound of God "in the cool of the day," when they felt the day was about over: when they are aged or sick or feel helpless. Even the prodigals feel the need of God in the cool of the day. Thank God for the cool of the day.

God caught up with the prodigal couple and asked, "Have you eaten the forbidden fruit?" (3:11). They put the blame on others. Why? Because they were afraid of God's punishment. They misunderstood God. A good shepherd does not seek the lost sheep to punish. God came to restore the fellowship. He loved them; but they could not believe. As long as they feared Him, a warm fellowship with Him was an impossibility.

If the couple had knelt down and confessed their sin before God, what must have happened? Needless to say, their sin would have been forgiven; a warm fellowship would have been restored; and they would have been overwhelmed by His amazing grace and would have sung, "Where sin abounded, grace did more abound." All the prodigals had to do was to trust His love. But, alas, man persisted in unbelief and lost the Paradise.

Moreover, he became a curse to the beautiful universe. Man was originally made to rule over the creation. God gave him His blissful image to be a blessing. Degraded

man had become a degraded ruler and a curse to the creation. Man is still polluting His creation.

Genesis 3:23-24 says that God drove the couple out of
the Garden. Did He really do it? Yes and no. I used to be a
math teacher in a girls' high school in Korea. I had to give
some students "Fs." When the girls complained about their
"Fs," I used to tell them, "Girls, you know I did not give you
Fs. I did give you Fs but I didn't. You got them yourselves." Girls can say I gave them "Fs"; but in reality I did
not. God, in reality, did not expel the prodigals from the
Garden. He rather tried to bring them back to the Garden.
Thank God!

V. Conclusion

We have glanced together through Genesis 1—3, the
story about the beginning. We learned that the God of Genesis 1—3 is the loving, redemptive God of our Lord Jesus
Christ. The God of the rest of the Bible is also the same God
Who is seeking His beloved prodigals with pathos and with
a bleeding heart. The Scriptures do bear witness of Jesus
and Jesus alone, not science.

Since the root of sin is unbelief of God's unfathomable
love, God's effort to save the prodigal has been to make his
heart known. As a last resort, He sent His only begotten
Son to reveal His bleeding heart to today's "Adams and
Eves." The cross of our Lord is the supreme revelation of
God's bleeding heart for us. His heart broke; and He bled to
death for a prodigal like myself.

What should be our response to such a loving God? We
do magnify Him; we enthrone Him as the Lord. Is that all?
No! We rise up to join with another forgiven prodigal who
said, "Now I rejoice in my suffering for your sake, and in
my flesh I do my share on behalf of His body in filling up
that which is lacking in Christ's affliction" (Col. 1:24).

The forgiven prodigals do not merely glory in the
Christ crucified. They take up their crosses to participate
in His suffering. Many Korean Christians bled and died in
His name.

To take up the cross is to join in the suffering of our Lord in seeking the prodigals. The cross-bearing is an essential sign of His disciple. I believe God of Genesis 1—3 demands this just as our Lord lovingly demanded His disciples.

I praise Him to learn that God of Genesis 1—3 and Jesus Christ our Lord are amazingly one.

Phil Lineberger

Love One Another
1 Thessalonians 4:9-10

"There is no real religious experience which does not express itself in love."[1] Would you agree with this statement? It was made by the great New Testament scholar, C. H. Dodd. Long before Dodd, however, it was Jesus who said in reply to an "expert in the law," "Love the Lord your God with all your heart and with all your soul and with all your mind. This is the first and greatest commandment. And the second is like it: Love your neighbor as yourself. All the Law and the Prophets hang on these two commandments."[2] Jesus taught that there is no real religious experience that does not express itself in love.

The apostle Paul was anxious for the church members at Thessalonica to increase in their love for one another. He wanted them to grow in real spirituality. He wanted their lives to be pleasing to God and pleasant to their brothers in Christ. The most impressive way for them to accomplish this goal was to love one another.

Listen to the reading of Scripture from 1 Thessalonians 4:9-10. Paul urges his readers to increase their love for one another. What a worthy encouragement for his or any age! We as twentieth-century Christians, and as Southern Baptists, would do well to pay close attention to these words. More than anything else in our day we need to increase in our love for one another.

The word translated "brotherly love" in verse 9 is *philadelphias*. It narrows the scope of love from everyone in the world to one's brother or sister in the Christian faith. Paul emphasizes this again in verse 10, referring to "all the brothers throughout Macedonia." Christian brothers and sisters must first learn to love each other before trying to love those outside the faith. Otherwise, their love for others carries a hypocritical ring. The definition of this kind of love is that of seeking the best for the other person—being concerned with the other person's welfare.

Tertullian, born in Rome a pagan, converted to Christianity and closely tied to the church in North Africa, a second-century church father (ca. AD 192), said, "The heathen are wont to exclaim with wonder, see how these Christians love one another! for they [the heathen] hate one another; and how they are ready to die for one another! for they [the heathen] are more ready to kill for one another."[3]

This love Paul is encouraging involves fellow believers and is characterized by service (What can I do for you?) and sacrifice (What can I give for you?).

Why would people who identify with Jesus Christ Who "first loved us" need to be encouraged to love one another? That's a good question. It is addressed specifically in these verses. We are taught here that loving one another, even as Christians, is not our natural disposition. We are naturally, Christian or not, competitive. We are selfish, egotistical, arrogant and self-serving. It is not our first inclination to seek the welfare of fellow believers. Our first inclination is to help ourselves—self-preservation, the highest law of nature.

Paul teaches through these verses that the kind of love he is encouraging is "taught by God" (v. 9)—*theodidaktoi*. The key to loving one another in the Christian faith is to understand the full implication of this idea of being "taught by God to love each other" (v. 9). We'll seek to understand by addressing and answering two questions from these verses. First, how are we taught by God to love one another? Second, why are we taught by God to love one another?

How Are We Taught by God?

There are at least three ways that God uses to teach

Christians to love one another. The first is by example. Our premier historical example of sacrificial brotherly love is found in the life, works, death, and resurrection of Jesus of Nazareth. In Romans 5:8, we read, "But God demonstrates his own love for us in this: while we were still sinners, Christ died for us" (NIV). God did not wait for mankind to change before He set His example of love through Jesus Christ. He loved first that men might see an example of how to love one another. Jesus is our example or hero to follow. In John 13:34 Jesus told his disciples to love as He had loved them. William Barclay says Jesus loved His disciples in these four ways: selflessly, sacrificially, understandingly, forgivingly.[4] Who is your example today? Who is your hero? Are you loving as Jesus did, or are you following some man's example? The church desperately needs to follow the example of Jesus in loving one another. In fact, John says, "We love because he first loved us. If anyone says, 'I love God,' yet hates his brother, he is a liar. For anyone who does not love his brother, whom he has seen, cannot love God, whom he has not seen" (1 John 4:19-20, NIV).

Second, we are taught to love one another by command. Brotherly love is not an option to exercise when one feels like it. It is an imperative from Almighty God. Anyone who leads a brother to treat another brother in an unloving manner lives in open disobedience to God. The Proverbist would say that God "hates . . . a man who stirs up dissension among brothers" (Prov. 6:19, NIV). The church of the twentieth century needs to be obedient to the command of her Lord to love one another.

Third and finally, we are taught by God to love one another by relationship. The relationship I am speaking of is the relationship each believer shares with and through the Holy Spirit. John says, "But the Counselor, the Holy Spirit, whom the Father will send in my name, will teach you all things, and will remind you of everything I have said to you" (John 14:26, NIV). If we will listen to the Holy Spirit, He will remind us to love one another.

Several years ago I was watching a television special

concerning a blind skier. When asked how she negotiated turns and stayed out of trouble, she related that her instructor skied behind her, yelling instructions. He was with her to be her guide. Our unloving behavior toward one another is evidence of a poor relationship to God through His Holy Spirit. We are listening to other voices rather than listening to His. We are being reminded of fleshly hurts and worldly concerns rather than being reminded of what God has said, "Love one another."

If we will pay attention, we are told that the anointing of the Holy Spirit, the personal touch and power of God, will be a moment-by-moment experience (1 John 2:20 and 27). Moment by moment we are being taught to love one another.

Why Are We Taught by God?

The second question addressed to this Scripture is, why are we taught by God to love one another? There must be a good reason for Christians to love as Jesus loved. In fact, there are at least three good reasons.

First and foremost, it is a testimony or assurance of one's own personal salvation. Some of the most insecure and frustrated people in the world are those who are uncertain of their own salvation. The Bible declares, "We know that we have passed from death to life because we love our brothers. Anyone who does not love remains in death" (1 John 3:14, NIV). There you have it. People who feel unloved have a difficult time loving others. Instead they are critical, hateful, and unloving. Unable to manage their own lives, they strike out to try and manage the lives of others through anger, fear, and criticism.

Cecil Osborne wrote: "I am neither good nor bad, I am both; and because God loves me, I will love myself properly. I am neither guilty nor innocent, I am both; and because God forgives me, I will forgive myself. I am neither loving nor hateful, I am both; and because God loves me, I will love myself properly. I am neither pure nor impure, I am both; and because God accepts me, I will accept myself."[5]

On the other hand, if we do not love one another we testify to our lostness. It is often amazing that we have enough religion to make us hate, but not enough to make us love one another. John says, "Anyone who claims to be in the light but hates his brother is still in the darkness" (1 John 2:9, NIV). One can be orthodox in his belief and lost in his behavior.

Several years ago I heard an interesting story which illustrates this point. A child was killed by a mad dog. The neighbors turned on the dog's owner, not realizing the guilt and sorrow the man already felt. He became a marked man, avoided and ostracized. This went on for a long while. Finally, a drought came. The land was bare and seed scarce. The man who owned the dog sowed the last of his seed, and the wind blew it out. The neighbors said, "It is a curse on him!"

But the father of the dead child went and sowed the other man's field in the night. When the neighbors found out what he had done, they asked, "Why did you do that?" The grieved father answered, "Because I couldn't let God die in my heart!" Isn't it a shame for one, born of God, to let Him die in the heart through an unloving spirit?

Love for one another stands as a witness in our heart to say, this is a child of God. The warmer our love for one another, the deeper our assurance of God's love for us.

Second, we are taught by God to love one another because it is evidence to the world of our discipleship. We have both the internal witness of passing from death to life and the external witness, verified by others, that we know Jesus. Jesus said in John 13:35, "All men will know that you are my disciples if you love one another" (NIV). All men may not agree with you or like you, but they will know! Again in John 17:23, Jesus prayed, "I in them and you in me. May they be brought to complete unity to let the world know that you sent me and have loved them even as you have loved me" (NIV). How can Christians think that the world will see them as ministers of reconciliation when they cannot even be reconciled to one another? Most likely the world will say, "No thanks! I'll not be a part of that fussing and feuding family. I think I'll live longer and happier on the outside."

General Robert E. Lee, in those terrible days of what we call the Civil War, was bitterly, caustically, nearly inhumanly criticized by General Whiting. Then at a staff meeting, Jefferson Davis, the Confederate president, asked General Lee what he thought of General Whiting's qualifications for a certain responsibility.

"I believe him to be an officer of unusual capacity," replied General Lee, and he went on to say several good things about his enemy's ability. Another man called General Lee aside and warned, "You evidently have not heard what General Whiting has been saying about you."

The grand Southern general, a great Christian and peacemaker, pulled himself erect and said crisply, "Oh yes, I know. But Mr. Davis did not ask what General Whiting thought of me. He asked what I thought of General Whiting."6

What a great example of discipleship—a man disciplined to bring every thought into captivity to Christ.

Third, and finally, we are taught to love one another because it completes God's love in us. First John 4:12 declares, "No one has ever seen God; but if we love one another, God lives in us and his love is made complete in us." That word complete, *teteleiomene,* is a perfect passive verb. The subject is acted upon, and the action is completed. Time and again, as we love one another, God's love is reaching its goal in us—this goal whose purpose is that we may love others as God has loved us. What a shame constantly to thwart the love of God as it is about to reach its goal. Unfortunately there are Christians whose lives are like the Dead Sea—all intake and no outflow. That isn't God's plan. We are to be channels of love for others.

Anthony Campolo, chairman of the Department of Sociology at Eastern University in Pennsylvania, has illustrated this principle beautifully. He relates his work with an orphanage in a Third World country. The orphanage was designed to house fifty children, some so debilitated that unless they received intensive treatment they would die within a few months. The day the orphanage was completed, Campolo and his group took a bus and drove to a slum region where these desperate children lived. When the bus arrived there were over two hundred children waiting. Over the next few hours a process of selecting only fifty was completed. The rest would simply stay in the slums until death overtook them.

After the bus had been loaded, the priest who served the Catholic church in the slum expressed his gratitude and asked if the children who had been left behind could sing a song for Campolo's group to show their appreciation for the help given to the others. These emaciated and malnourished children began to sing a familiar gospel chorus:

> God is so good, God is so good,
> God is so good, He's so good to me.
> He loves me so, He loves me so,
> He loves me so, He's so good to me.

Campolo said his heart began to cry out in protest. "It's not true! God isn't good to them. He doesn't love them or else He would not leave them in this condition!" Suddenly it dawned on Campolo as it must dawn on us. God *did* love them. He had a plan to deliver them. That plan was to bring His love to them through other believers.[7]

What a revelation! God's love is complete in us as we love one another!

Conclusion

I would agree with C. H. Dodd, "There is no real religious experience which does not express itself in love."

John Killinger, in a sermon entitled "The Great Importance of Little Deeds," concluded by saying, "It's an exciting thought . . . that when we die and come into the presence of God in all its fullness, it will not be our major achievements that speak for us . . . 'He was president of a bank,' 'She was the first woman senator from her state,' 'He was the author of twenty-two books' . . . but the small, apparently inconsequential things we long ago forgot: 'He mowed my lawn when I was sick,' 'She cared for my child while I went to the market,' 'He sent me flowers when I needed them most,' 'She washed and mended my socks.' These are the little things that hold the world together. They are the small stones that comprise the great cathedrals where God is worshipped. And they shall be remembered like stars in the crowns of all the saints."[8]

These "small stones that comprise the great cathedrals where God is worshipped" are simply the deeds of brotherly love. No one has encouraged this in more powerful terms than the Lord Jesus who said, "Love the Lord your God with all your heart and with all your soul and with all your mind. This is the first and greatest commandment. And the second is like it: love your neighbor as yourself. All the Law and the Prophets hang on these two commandments" (Matt. 22:37-40, NIV).

Let's be about the work of building a great cathedral of brotherly love testifying to ourselves and to a lost world that God is real and has shown His love to us in Jesus. Let's make Jesus our hero and love as He loved, selflessly, sacrificially, understandingly, and forgivingly. Let's have this world saying again, "See how these Christians love one another!"

NOTES

1. C. H. Dodd, quoted under "Love" in illustrations from *The Pastor's Professional Research Service* (Knoxville, TN: Christian Communications Laboratory, 1986).

2. Matthew 22:35-40 (NIV)

3. *The Ante-Nicene Fathers,* Vol. III, edited by Alexander Roberts and James Donaldson (Grand Rapids, MI: Eerdmans, 1978), p. 46.

4. William Barclay, *The Gospel of John,* Vol. II (Philadelphia: The Westminster Press, 1955), pp. 174-175.

5. Cecil Osborne, *You're in Charge* (Waco, TX: Word, Inc., 1973), p. 128.

6. C. M. Bess in *Proclaim,* O-N-D, 1982, p. 27.

7. Anthony Campolo, *It's Friday, But Sunday's Comin'* (Waco, TX: Word, Inc., 1984), pp. 95-97.

8. John Killinger, *Fundamentals of Preaching* (Philadelphia: Fortress Press, 1985), p. 99.

Kenneth L. Mahanes

In His Steps

One of the books that influenced my Christian life most profoundly during my teen years was Charles Sheldon's *In His Steps*. The book tells the story of a pastor who challenged a handful of congregants to make no decision or take no action for one year without first asking themselves: "What would Jesus do?" The simplicity and sincerity of the story challenged me to follow in the steps of Jesus, a challenge I still feel deeply today.

Some time ago, I perused the Gospel of Matthew to discover anew the message of Jesus. Reading the verses printed in red, which record the Lord's spoken words, I found five recurring principles from the teachings and example of Jesus that have helped me walk in His steps.

The first principle emerges from an incident recorded in Matthew 11:16-19. Simply stated, Jesus was willing to risk His reputation to reach sinners. I have learned in achieving spiritual goals, it is often necessary to risk in order to reach. The passage reads:

> But whereunto shall I liken this generation? It is like unto children sitting in the markets, and calling unto their fellows. And saying, We have piped unto you, and ye have not danced; we have mourned unto you, and ye have not lamented. For John came neither eating nor drinking, and they say, He hath a devil. The Son of man came eating and drinking and they say, Behold a man gluttonous, and a winebibber, a friend of publicans and sinners. But wisdom is justified of her children.

Jesus begins this pericope by finding fault with fault-finders. John came neither eating nor drinking, and the faultfinders accused him of having a demon. Jesus came eating and drinking, and the faultfinders accused him of being a glutton and a winebibber. Jesus reveals how childish faultfinders are in verses 16-17. They are like temperamental children who can never be pleased: ". . . we have piped unto you, and ye have not danced, we have mourned unto you, and you have not lamented."

Not only are faultfinders childish, they are reputation ruiners. With their inclination towards exaggeration, faultfinders often distort the motives or intents of others. Jesus' sincere desire was to reach sinners. But to reach sinners, He found it necessary to identify with sinners. That required risking His reputation. Inevitably the childish faultfinders exaggerated Jesus' actions. Identification with sinners was construed by them to be the same as participation in sin.

A pastor friend of mine in South Florida shared with me a revealing incident in his own life. A member of his church had been saved out of a homosexual life-style. Unfortunately, the new convert had contracted the horrible disease of AIDS due to his promiscuous behavior prior to his conversion. The new Christian asked the pastor to go with him and his family to a meeting where AIDS victims and their families would receive information and counsel for dealing with the disease. The pastor readily agreed. Some days later as he was leaving the meeting, it suddenly occurred to him that the meeting had taken place in a hotel in the city that was notorious as a gathering place for homosexuals. The thought that flashed across the pastor's mind was how could he explain his true purpose for being there to others who might have seen him coming out of such a disreputable place. Would judgmental church members accuse the pastor of mixing with the wrong crowd, or worse, of being a homosexual himself? But, the more important question was: "What would Jesus do?" Jesus frequently mixed and mingled with "the wrong crowd." He ate and drank with publicans and sinners. He spoke to Samaritans and prostitutes—taboos for respectable Jews. His association with sinners was necessitated by His mission to reach them.

One of our most obvious problems in evangelism today is our lack of significant contact with the very ones to whom we have been sent to reach. Our church began an aggressive evangelism training program a few years ago. At that time we discovered the pyramid principle. The principle states that the longer one is a Christian the fewer lost people the Christian knows. When we first become believers, we are at the base of the pyramid. We know dozens of lost people. But the longer we are Christians, the greater is our tendency to associate with other Christians only. The number of sinners with whom we have meaningful contact, like the rising sides of a pyramid, sharply narrows.

The real tension for a Christian who desires to walk in Jesus' steps is created by the pull of two extremes. We are pulled between separatism on the one hand and secularism on the other hand.

I have many sincere Christian friends who practice extreme Christian separatism. Admonished by Scripture to shun the very appearance of evil and to come out from among the world and be separate, these believers avoid any contact with sinners. But a separated life does not mean an isolated life. Jesus did not save us *out of* the world; in fact, He sends us *into* the world as salt and light. Our responsibility is to maintain contact with the world without becoming contaminated by the world. The only way we can maintain meaningful contact with the world is to walk among the people among whom Jesus walked. If we follow His steps, we must be willing to risk our reputation in order to reach sinners.

A second principle is revealed in Matthew 12:1-8. The confrontation described in the passage demonstrates that Jesus broke man-made rules to meet mankind's needs.

> At that time Jesus went on the sabbath day through the corn; and his disciples were an hungred, and began to pluck the ears of corn, and to eat. But when the Pharisees saw it, they said unto him, Behold, thy disciples do that which is not lawful to do upon the sabbath day. But he said unto them, Have ye not read what David did, when he was an hungred; and they that were with him. How He entered into the house of God, and did eat the shewbread, which was not lawful for him to eat, either for them which were with him, but only for the priests? Or have ye not read in the law, how that on the sabbath days the priests in the temple profane the sabbath, and are blameless? But I say unto you. That in this place is one greater than the temple. But if ye had known what this meaneth, I will have mercy, and not sacrifice, ye would not have condemned the guiltless. For the Son of man is Lord even of the sabbath day.

The background of this recorded incident is found in the strict Old Testament observance of the sabbath. Clearly, the Decalogue prohibited work on the sabbath (Deut. 5:12-15). But the Pharisees of Jesus' day had felt compelled to define work by specifying certain activities that were either permissible or not permissible. Their elaborate system of rules permitted the plucking of corn on the sabbath but forbade gathering more than one lamb's mouthful. Nor were the Jews allowed to cut grain with a sickle on the sabbath. The rules also disallowed threshing and cooking grain.

The passage in Matthew reveals that Jews openly broke the Pharisees' arbitrary rules. When accused of being a lawbreaker, Jesus reminded the Pharisees of an incident out of their own history. David, the venerable and revered hero of the Jewish people, had broken the rules governing the showbread. Each week twelve loaves of bread were placed in the house of God. The bread replaced by the fresh loaves was given to the priest to be eaten. David had broken the rules by eating bread consecrated to the priests.

When is it right to violate arbitrary, man-made restrictions? The example of Jesus reveals that relieving human need takes precedence over the ritualistic observance of rules. Rules can be indispensable in helping individuals and groups establish order and consistency for their lives. But when rules become cruel and heartless, they have lost their original intent, which is to serve the needs of the people who devised them. One should not be held guilty for temporarily setting aside an arbitrary rule to extend mercy and help to a needy person. The teaching of Jesus is most direct in verse 7. "But if ye had known what this meaneth, I will have mercy, and not sacrifice, ye would not have condemned the guiltless."

Several months ago, I was invited to attend a banquet honoring a local congressman for his years of humanitarian service. Since I am a friend of the congressman, I was asked to share a brief word and conclude the evening's activities with prayer. The invitation presented me with a difficult decision. The banquet was planned for a Sunday evening. The unwritten but strictly observed rule of some of our church members is that the pastor should be at church on Sunday evenings discharging his preaching responsibilities. A few exceptions are allowed, but I knew that to some of our people, this would not be one.

The few folks in our church who are religious legalists would view my absence from the evening service to attend a banquet to be a desecration of the Lord's Day. To add to their consternation was the fact that the banquet was to be held at a Jewish synagogue and was sponsored by a prominent Jewish organization in our city. A decision to absent myself from the Lord's house on the Lord's Day to feast with Jews in their synagogue would certainly violate the rules of these members. But, the question I asked myself was: "What would Jesus do?" I sincerely believed Jesus would make an exception to the rule in order to bear witness to His lost kinsmen. I could do no less. The opportunity to represent Jesus Christ before the very people He came to seek and to save seemed compelling enough to me to set aside a time-honored, normal rule governing Sunday evening church attendance. To walk in Jesus' steps means placing mankind's needs ahead of man-made rules.

A third principle is found in Matthew 15:1-9. Jesus warned against making the traditions of men more important than the commandments of God.

> Then came to Jesus scribes and Pharisees which were of Jerusalem, saying, Why do thy disciples transgress the tradition of the elders? for they wash not their hands when they eat bread. But he answered and said unto them. Why do ye also transgress the commandment of God by your traditions? For God commanded, saying, Honour thy father and mother; and, He that curseth father or mother, let him die the death. But ye say, Whosoever shall say to his father or his mother, It is a gift, by whatsoever thou mightest be profited by me; And honour not his father or his mother, he shall be free. Thus have ye made the commandment of God of none effect by your tradition. Ye hypocrites; well did Esaias prophesy of you, saying, This people draweth nigh unto me with their mouth, and honoureth me with their lips; but their heart is far from me. But in vain they do worship me, teaching for doctrines the commandments of men.

In the preceding verses, Jesus' disciples offended the elders by not washing their hands before eating. The failure to wash their hands had nothing to do with personal hygiene. It had everything to do with ceremonial uncleanness. Jewish traditions stated that certain activities, such as touching a dead body or walking in the path of a Gentile, rendered a Jew ceremonially unclean. The Jews required that worshipers undergo a series of ritual washings to symbolize their purity before God. Not only the act but the manner of the washing was meticulously prescribed. Such traditions, which were originally passed on orally from one generation to the next, were eventually written down. Whether oral or written, the traditions were as binding upon the life of a Jew as were the commandments of God.

Unfortunately, the traditions were used by some Jews

to circumvent God's commandments. For example, Jesus accused the Jews of violating the commandment of God to honor one's parents by practicing an ancient tradition regarding the designation of gifts offered to God. This obscure and strange tradition allowed someone to pronounce land or possession to be a gift to God, which thereby prevented the gift from ever being given to anyone else. It appears that some unscrupulous Jews were actually withholding for themselves possessions needed by their fathers or mothers by pronouncing the items to be a gift to God.

In addition to the misuse of tradition as demonstrated by the example Jesus gives, the Jews elevated their own teachings to the status of divine pronouncements. Jesus accused the Jews of "teaching for doctrines the commandments of men" (v. 9).

During my years of pastoring, I have encountered many oral traditions. In one of my first pastorates, I innocently promoted a church dinner to be held in the church's basement before realizing that some of the people had for years opposed the practice of eating inside "the Lord's house." The prohibition against eating inside the church building was a tradition that had been passed down from one generation to the next, like a family heirloom, until it was revered as if it were a direct command from God. The chains of oral tradition are not easily broken.

I recall the strong opposition voice by a devout church member against the hanging of a picture of Jesus in his Sunday School classroom. Oral tradition had taught him that an artist's rendering of Jesus is a graven image and was idolatrous. I was never able to help him see the difference between actual idolatry and artistic imagery. The chains of oral tradition are hard to break indeed.

I know I am on dangerous ground, but I often wonder if our church's practice of baptism is based more upon the writings of J. R. Graves and J. M. Pendleton than upon the written Word of God. When the authenticity of baptism is determined primarily by its identification with the name

Baptist, we risk "teaching for doctrines the command-ments of men." To follow in the steps of Jesus requires the subordination of the traditions of men to the command-ments of God.

Fourthly, a similar principle is taught by Jesus in Mat-thew 15:10-11. Without question, Jesus preferred inward righteousness over outward righteousness. "And he called the multitude, and said unto them, Hear, and understand: Not that which goeth into the mouth defileth a man; but that which cometh out of the mouth, this defileth a man." When Jesus encountered the hypocrisy of the Pharisees, He called them "whited sepulchres" (Matt. 23:27). Outwardly, they appeared clean, but inwardly they were like decaying corpses. Jesus' Sermon on the Mount deals extensively with matters of the heart. The Beatitudes, a significant part of the Sermon on the Mount, reflects an emphasis upon the inward qualities of purity of heart, meekness, a hunger and thirst for righteousness, and an inward spiritual depen-dency upon God.

The evidences of the Spirit-filled life are not seen in one's outward veneer but in one's inward virtue: i.e. love, joy, peace, patience, gentleness, goodness, faith, meekness, and self-control (Gal. 5:22-23). Jesus is more concerned about who we are than He is about what we do. Those who follow in His steps must prize inward righteousness above outward righteousness.

A fifth principle is discovered in Matthew 22:36-40. It is the principle of love which Jesus Himself embodied. "Master, which is the great commandment in the law? Jesus said unto him, Thou shalt love the Lord thy God with all thy heart, and with all thy soul, and with all thy mind. This is the first and great commandment. And the second is like unto it. Thou shalt love thy neighbour as thyself. On these two commandments hang all the law and the prophets."

Although every commandment of God is great, this is the greatest. It is the pinnacle of Jesus' accumulated teach-ings. William Hendriksen observes: "This two-fold commandment, love for God and love for neighbor, is the peg on which the whole Law and Prophets hang. Remove the peg and all is lost; for the entire Old Testament with its commandments and covenants, prophecies and promises, types and testimonies, invitations and exhortations, points to the love of God which demands the answer of love in return."[1]

The Apostle Paul, who was undoubtedly expressing the mind of Christ, wrote: "And now abideth faith, hope, love, these three; but the greatest of these is love" (1 Cor. 13:13).

My first pastorate was in a small town in the foothills of the Appalachian Mountains. A couple of years into my ministry at the church brought me to a point of spiritual introspection. What was I supposed to be doing as a pastor? How effectively had I achieved my purposes? These and similar questions were bouncing around my mind during a reflective moment of personal and professional inventory.

My initial conclusion was that I should preach the Bible—a slightly ambiguous but safe answer. How was I doing? *Great!* I thought. After all, the people seemed doctrinally sound, some to a fault. Most every member could give a reason for the hope that was in him (1 Pet. 3:15). But like the jolting streak of lightning that flashes in the midst of a thunderstorm or the jarring sounds of the ringing of the telephone in the middle of the night, an uninvited thought suddenly flashed across my mind. Many of the most doctrinally correct people in the church were the same ones who were often the most unloving and unkind. How could the same people who would make the top scores on Bible knowledge tests and could so quickly and correctly answer any Bible question be uncharacteristically hateful and cruel in their attitudes and relationships toward others, as they often were? The incongruity and tragedy of the thought both confused and troubled me.

I concluded that my ministry had been incomplete. Not only must I preach the teachings of Christ, I must impart the *spirit* of Christ. A follower of Jesus who knows what to believe but does not know how to love is not walking in Jesus' steps. I determined from that moment to broaden the scope of my ministry. My purpose would be twofold. My ministry would be directed, first of all, toward helping people to know Jesus and, secondly, toward helping people who know Jesus to become like Jesus. Jesus' words in John 13:35 have been embedded in my consciousness since that day: "By this shall all men know that ye are my disciples, if ye have love one to another."

To walk in Jesus' steps means (1) risking our reputation to reach sinners, (2) placing mankind's needs ahead of man-made rules, (3) making the traditions of men subordinate to the commandments of God, (4) emphasizing inward more than outward righteousness, and (5) acknowledging love to be the greatest commandment.

The hymn writer beautifully expresses the appropriate response to Jesus' call to follow Him:

> Sweetly, Lord, have we heard Thee calling, Come
>   follow Me
> And we see where Thy footprints falling, lead us
>   to Thee
> Footprints of Jesus that make the pathway glow,
> We will follow the steps of Jesus, where'er
>   they go.

NOTES

1. William Hendriksen, "Matthew," *New Testament Commentary* (Grand Rapids, MI: Baker Book House, 1973), p. 810.

Wayne McDill

How to Work with God

The other day I was stopped downtown in a line of traffic while a trucker backed an eighteen-wheeler into an alley. Talk about nerve. There he was stopping traffic while everybody watched him slip that thirty-foot trailer into an opening with only a foot or two clearance on each side. But he did it. I wanted to applaud.

You see, I don't believe trailer backing is natural to man. I'm not sure God ever intended us to back trailers. Did you ever notice how things don't work the way they're supposed to? Left is really right, and right is left. You almost have to turn your brain over to get used to it.

I'll never forget my first attempts to back our tent camper into the driveway. No matter what I did, the thing would go the wrong way. I had mirrors on both sides but still couldn't see what was happening back there well enough to do much about it. And, of course, everybody was there in the front yard to see this great feat.

There are a number of difficult and rather unnatural things we learn to do. Ask any five-year-old learning to ride his first two-wheel bike. It just takes patience, some help from a friend, and a bit of instruction as to the secrets of success.

One of the hardest things I have ever tried to learn is how to work with God.

Since I was a teenager I have known that God wanted me to be his servant. He had great and marvelous things He wanted to accomplish through me. "The things that I do will you do, and greater things than these" (John 14:12), Jesus had promised. What a challenge!

231

But working with God doesn't come easy.

I have some ideas about what should be done. Are these good ideas? Are they God's ideas? Are my big plans for life something God can support?

I have some abilities. Can God use my abilities? Or does everything have to be done in the special power of the Holy Spirit? How do I get God's power in my life?

Have these questions come to your mind? Do you have answers that satisfy?

Only recently I saw a passage in the Bible in which Jesus answers these questions. In these verses in John 5 he sets out His own strategy for working with the Father. Turn with me to John 5, and let's explore how to work with God.

This passage tells about the healing of the crippled man at the pool of Bethesda. With this miracle Jesus stirred up trouble for Himself with the Jewish leaders, because the man who was healed was carrying his mat on the sabbath day.

When they challenged Jesus about this, He explained what had taken place at the pool. He gave a simple and clear description of how He had worked in partnership with the Heavenly Father to heal the man. Against the background of what took place in the healing of the crippled man, let's focus our attention on Jesus' explanation for answers we need to our questions.

Look with me at John 5:16-20 (NIV).

> So, because Jesus was doing these things on the Sabbath, the Jews persecuted him. Jesus said to them, "My Father is always at his work to this very day, and I, too, am working." For this reason the Jews tried all the harder to kill him; not only was he breaking the Sabbath, but he was even calling God his own Father, making himself equal with God. Jesus gave them this answer: "I tell you the truth, the Son can do nothing by himself; he can do only what he sees his Father doing, because whatever the Father does the Son also does. For the Father loves the Son and shows him all he does."

Remember that this passage records Jesus' explanation for what happened in the healing of the man at the pool. In essence, then, He gives His methodology for ministry, principles for working with the Father.

The first principle here for working with God is this:

God Involves His Servant in His Work

Look at Jesus' words in verse 17, "My Father is always at his work to this very day, and I, too, am working."

At the Pool of Bethesda He had not acted on His own. He was rather responding to what the Father was doing.

I can imagine Jesus, with some of His disciples accompanying Him, moving through the crowded streets of Jerusalem. He is calm and secure, but alert to every face, reading every situation.

They come to the Pool of Bethesda, by the Sheep Gate. A large number of disabled people are gathered there. Some have relatives or friends with them; some are alone. Jesus stops at the edge of this scene to look at the people. One catches His attention, a crippled man in shabby clothing who had obviously been long disabled and poor.

Jesus moves toward the man for a closer look. As Jesus stands over him, the man looks up hopefully. The disciples draw near to see what will happen.

Jesus asks, "Do you want to be healed?" The man responds that he has no one to put him into the pool when the water is stirred. He wants healing. He is there in hope of it. Every day he could, he has been at the pool, as close as he could get to the water.

He believes what most people do, that occasionally an angel visits the pool and stirs the water. Whoever is first into the water when that happens will be healed, but only the first.

Jesus sees his faith. He sees the desperation, the hoping against hope. Perhaps He even knows of the tears which have accompanied the man's lonely prayers to Jehovah. For many years he had cried out to the God of Israel to heal him from his long nightmare of helplessness.

His brief conversation with the man convinces Jesus that the Father has indeed prepared the man for this day and is ready to heal him. He commands the man to get up and walk.

Had you and I been among those disciples, we would never have suspected that Jesus was only responding to what He saw the Father doing. We would probably have wondered why everybody wasn't healed and why we shouldn't franchise this marvelous program all over the city.

Answer this question: Is your strategy for ministry based on the confidence that the Father is already at work in your place of service? Or do you feel it is up to you to start some work you hope God will bless?

Don't most Christian workers go into a field with an agenda of work already in mind? We do not need to wait and watch and listen to see what God is doing. We already know what to do. In fact, it never occurs to us to look for what God is doing. Our minds are preoccupied with the plans and strategies we bring with us.

As we set about the work of the Lord on our own initiative, we assume that we can do His work. We believe that the Father will involve Himself with us when we are doing something for Him. We assume that our intentions are worthy. We assume that the Father is obligated to support our work because we are doing it for Him and in His Name.

We are busy, too busy to look for God. We do not notice what He is doing, except as we occasionally stumble upon it. Even then we may try to reshape what God is doing to fit into our plans!

The affirmation of Jesus in this verse is clear: "My Father is always at his work." Wherever God takes us, whatever our circumstances, the Father is at work.

Also clear in Jesus' statement is the relationship of His own work to the work of the Father. The Father takes the initiative, and the Son responds. The Father *always* works; the Son *also* works. Jesus never acted independently of the Father. He was convinced that the Father was already and always at work, and that His own part was to respond to what the Father was doing. He did not take initiative, even though He was the Son of God. He participated, but he didn't push ahead.

God has made it His method to use men. But He never allows himself to be used by men. Even for the noblest and most biblical efforts, He will not take the support role with man in the position of control. God must always be in the control position and man in the support position.

This is a great source of encouragement and hope for us. If God is in control and He alone takes the initiative in kingdom work, then He is finally responsible for making the plans, providing needed resources, and guaranteeing the results.

We can trust Him completely and joyously as He involves us in His great redemptive work. We can know that because He is *always* at work, we can *also* work.

So the first principle of how to work with God is clear. The Father involves His servants in His work as He Himself takes the initiative and maintains control.

Look now at the next statement Jesus made to explain what was going on in His ministry. Here is a second principle for us in working with God:

God Limits His Servant to His Work

Look again at Jesus' words, this time in verse 19: "I tell you the truth, the Son can do nothing by himself; He can do only what he sees his Father doing, because whatever the Father does the Son also does."

This is indeed a startling admission for the very Son of God. "The Son can do nothing by himself." What a limitation for the Savior of the world to accept.

The Father never intended Jesus to strike out on His own. It was disobedience and mistrust on Adam's part which brought sin into the world. It would be complete submission on Jesus' part which made a remedy for sin available to lost humanity. Jesus came to reestablish as man that complete harmony with the Father which had been lost. He subordinated himself to the Father so the principle of authority could be reestablished in the world.

That was Satan's appeal in the temptations, that Jesus act by Himself and for Himself. The enemy came to a hungry, weary Jesus in the wilderness, after forty days of fasting and praying about his calling.

"You are hungry," the devil said, "Turn these stones into bread and feed yourself." Of course much more may have been said as Satan tried to persuade Jesus to act on His own.

Jesus replied that He would never live by bread but by every word from the mouth of God. If the Father did not give Him instructions, He would not act. If the Father did not feed Him, He would willingly starve.

The purpose of those temptations was to break that harmony with the Father which made Jesus' mission a serious threat to Satan. Satan never fears a man doing some great work for God, as long as he does it on his own. Satan was even willing for Jesus to rule over all the kingdoms of the world, as long as He was not under the authority of the Father in doing so.

"The Son can do nothing by himself; . . . only what he sees His Father doing." If this severe limitation were necessary for the divine Son of God, how much more is it necessary for us? In fact, Jesus said it directly in John 15:5 in His analogy of the vine and the branches. "I am the vine; you are the branches . . . apart from me you can do *nothing*."

We are generally under the impression that we can go ahead and take the initiative to do any work which is in keeping with Scripture. We see the will of God as all the Bible says God intends to do. If some proposed activity is forbidden by Scripture, of course it is not in God's will. But what are we to do with the clear commands of the Bible about missions, evangelism, ministry, and personal responsibility?

In this ministry strategy of Jesus we have guidance. Not only are we to pray and act according to the *intention* of God (the content of His will), but also according to the timing of God for a specific situation. God intends to direct not only *what* work is done, but *when* it is scheduled and *how* it must be done. He reserves to Himself the authority to determine all these factors.

When I was a college student, I played for a time in the symphony orchestra of our town. My instrument was bass violin. I was, at best, a marginal player. But then, our orchestra was not the Philadelphia Symphony.

The conductor had already chosen a repertory of music for the orchestra, so we practiced to play everything in that collection. But we were not free to play anything in the repertory anytime we wished. The conductor insisted that we not only play the right music, but that we play it at the right time and in the right way. He would stand and hold his baton aloft to be sure he had our attention. Then came the first downbeat. And we made music, after a fashion.

In the same way, the servant of God must not assume that he is free to launch out on any work within the bounds of biblical authority. If we do that we do not make music. We make noise.

Paul warns that the ministry we build on the foundation of Christ must stand the test of judgment. While the wood, hay, and straw of self-effort will not survive, the work of God is like gold, silver and costly stones (1 Cor. 3:10-13). In the analogy of the Vine and the branches this is equivalent to the "fruit that remains."

The Father insists that we involve ourselves only in the work He is doing where we are. This partnership with the Father requires that we forego all independent initiative. We do not call on Him to respond to us. We respond to Him—*His* initiative to do *His* work in *His* time. Only then can we work in harmony with the rest of the body as well.

I believe much of the discouragement and frustration common to pastors is due to their efforts to "get something going" in their fields of service. But this may represent a misconception about how to work with God, or a doubt that He is at work at all. Whether we like it or not, we are limited in our ministries to what God does. And God can involve us in His work only as we abandon any hope of getting Him to support our efforts.

But, oh the joy of being carried along in a movement of God! What a matchless privilege to work with God in the miracle of His direction and power!

We have seen that the Father involves us in His work and that He limits us to His work. Now notice the third principle for how to work with God.

The Father Shows His Servant His Work

Look at what Jesus says in verse 20. "For the Father loves the Son and shows him all he does."

It is obvious that we cannot be consciously involved in the work of God if we cannot see it. But God is a God of revelation. He wants to show His servant where He is at work in the world.

I like to call this the "burning-bush" principle. Just as Moses' attention was arrested by the burning bush, so can we see "burning-bush" signs of the work of the Father where we are.

Imagine the difference in the story of Moses if he had not turned aside to check out the burning bush. There he was, keeping the sheep of his father-in-law on the backside of the desert. And there, on the mountainside, was a strange bush that burned without being consumed.

Suppose Moses would have responded like this. "Would you look at that," said Moses. "In all my years here I've never seen the like. But then, strange things happen. Too bad I don't have time to check it out. I have these sheep to take care of. There are always repairs around the tent. And the children require so much attention. I can't imagine what that bush means, burning like that without being consumed. But it's getting late. I'd better get home for supper!"

Many a servant of God is too busy with the work of God to stop and see the burning bushes. Schedules are packed with important tasks. Planning, setting goals, pursuing the work all make for an agenda not receptive to interruptions. And the missing ingredient in such a ministry is, unhappily, the holy ground where we see God at work and become involved in what he is doing.

With just a little thought, you and I can see the difference it makes when we approach a day with a deliberate intention to be on the lookout for what God is doing. We pay attention to the people in our paths. We look deeply into their faces for some signal of God's work in their lives.

We watch for need, hunger, receptivity. We look at our own lives for what God is doing. We notice circumstances that open the way for grace. We stop. We look. We listen for the voice of the Spirit. Because we know the Father is at work, we expect to see what He is doing.

He wants us to see what He is doing. He wants to involve us in His work. As he sets a "burning bush" afire where we can see it, He is inviting us to draw near. The closer we get, the more we understand what God is doing. Finally He draws us onto holy ground and involves us in the miracle of partnership in His redemptive work.

How often those who would serve the Lord are weary and want to give up. How often they long for a renewal of their strength and do not know where to get it. How often they wonder why serving God should be so hard and so fruitless.

David writes in Psalm 27:14 just what we need to hear in our weariness. "Wait for the Lord; be strong and take heart and wait for the Lord."

We can determine to follow the biblical admonition to "wait on the Lord." This is indeed an exciting commitment. What promises are given to those who wait on the Lord! That favorite passage in Isaiah 40:31 takes on new meaning in light of Jesus' strategy for working with God. "Those who wait on the Lord will renew their strength. They will soar on wings like eagles; they will run and not grow weary, they will walk and not be faint."

But it takes courage to wait for the Lord. It calls for a deeply held conviction that only in waiting for Him will we see His hand at work. Only in seeing Him at work will we be able to become involved in that work. Only as we are involved in what He is doing will fruit be borne. Only as God Himself produces that fruit will it remain to His glory.

We have seen that working with God can be guided by principles Jesus gave in explaining His own ministry. We can know that He involves us in His work, that he limits us to His work, and that He shows us His work. These insights are simple. But applying them will revolutionize our approach to serving God.

The Jews came to Jesus one day to ask the question, "How can we do the work of God?" Jesus answered that question in John 6:29, "The work of God is this: to believe in the one he has sent." Our faith is to be in the presence and reality of Christ in the church, in our lives, in the world. He is alive! He is here! He is at work. He is faithful. He is doing what He promised to do.

We are His people. His agents for doing His work. We are His voice for expressing His thoughts and words. We are His hands to affect this world according to His will. We are His body to be His physical presence in the world. Through us He will make material and tangible what is spiritual and supernatural.

In his book, *Eternity in Their Hearts,* anthropologist Don Richardson gives striking accounts of missionaries finding God already at work, even among the most primitive tribes.[1] Upon their arrival the missionaries were often welcomed as the ones long promised to bring them news of God. Though the tribal name for God was strange in their ears, the missionaries could recognize that He had indeed been at work already to prepare them for His messengers.

The missionaries' role was not to get something started in that remote place. It was rather to be God's instruments for the fulfillment of what the Father had already been doing. However dim the light of revelation, the loving God had "made his light shine in their hearts" (2 Cor. 4:6). Those missionaries who learned to respond to that work found a receptivity others did not see.

Rather than thinking we must do the work of God if any is to be done, we too can see that God is already at work. Our role is to be available to Him for bringing that work to the fulfillment prepared for this moment. Ours is to listen and learn, to probe for signs of His presence. Ours is to search for that holy ground He calls us to.

You and I can work with God. We can become involved in the redemptive work of a loving Heavenly Father as he touches us with His grace and draws us to Himself in Christ. What a privilege! Praise the Lord!

NOTE

1. Don Richardson, *Eternity in Their Hearts* (Ventura, CA: Regal Books, 1981).

Alton H. McEachern

Communication—God's Problem Too

At various times and in different ways God spoke to our fathers through the prophets. Now in these last days he has spoken through his Son (Hebrews 1:1).

In the beginning was the Word, and the Word was with God, and the Word was God (John 1:1).

I. Communication Is a Miracle

It is such a common occurrence that we take it for granted. We live with communication every waking hour, even when we're holding onto the phone or riding in an elevator. It is so commonplace that it seems startling to think of communication as something miraculous, but it is.

Packaging is a powerful form of communication. On your next visit to the supermarket or discount store, stand for a moment and look at all the silent screaming. Ten thousand items are silent salesmen pleading for your attention and dollars, crying, "Buy me! Buy me!" Packaging is a powerful means of communication and sometimes costs more than the contents.

While communication can be nonverbal, most of our communication is verbal. Think about this for a moment: we make marks, more or less legibly, on a piece of paper, or we wag a red muscle between our jaws, and ideas are conveyed from one mind to another across the room, across the nation, across the years. This is a miracle beyond denial.

Words are the principal tools with which we communicate. They can hurt or help, bless or blight. When we were children and someone would call us an ugly name, we would recite a ditty: "Sticks and stones may break my bones, but words can never hurt me." Not so. Words are powerful, and they can hurt or help, very much indeed. The Second World War was a battle of words, propaganda, and oratory as surely as it was a battle with bombs and bullets.

Words represent the condensed experience of the race or, if I may borrow a Kentucky phrase, the distilled experience of the race. Words are seldom created in a vacuum. They most often have their own distinctive history. Consider some examples: South of the city of Rome, an entrepreneur built a tavern, an inn, at a place where three roads came together. Not surprisingly, he called it Tri Via Inn, or Three Ways Inn. The Roman soldiers would hang out at Tri Via tavern. When there were no campaigns on, they passed the hours with a lot of small talk. After a while their small talk became known as "tri via" talk—or trivia.

Ancient Greek charioteers would whip their horses in an effort to win the race. The whip cut the flesh on the backs of the horses. The Greek word for flesh is *sarx,* and we came to have the term "sarcasm" for cutting words.

A vehement man is one who is adamant and says, "By God, I won't!" He became known as a "by-God" man, or bigot. Some of those have even come to occupy responsible positions.

In Medieval England, a hospital was built and named St. Mary of Bethlehem Hospital. With the passing of time, it became an asylum for the incurably ill. The name of St. Mary of Bethlehem Hospital was telescoped into the term "bedlam," our word for confusion. Words are powerful. Jack London observed that printer's ink is more intoxicating than whiskey. He had plenty of experiences with both and should have known. Never underestimate the power of words, for good or evil.

II. Communication Is a Miracle, but Communication Is Also a Problem

It is an international problem. In the United States and the U.S.S.R., we both speak about democracy and free elections, but we mean something entirely different, though we use the same terms.

One summer I attended the Baptist World Alliance meeting in Buenos Aires, Argentina. I attended a Rotary meeting where I was seated beside the secretary of commerce for Argentina. We had an interesting conversation. He told me that he had just returned from spending the month of June at an international conference of commerce ministers in Yugoslavia. I asked him what they accomplished. He replied, "Nothing! Absolutely nothing, because the super powers will not communicate with each other. And that leaves other nations in the breach."

Communication is a problem between various groups: labor and management; students, faculty and administration; parents and children; pastors and deacons. Communication can be a problem between couples. There is a story about an old man in the mountains of Western North Carolina. One evening he was feeling romantic, and he complimented his wife, "I'm proud of you, Ma." She was only half listening and replied, "I'm tired of you too, Pa!"

Alice of *Alice in Wonderland* was honest, if not especially helpful, when she emphasized, "A word means what I want it to mean."

One of the sources of our problems with communication is that words change meaning. When I was in high school, we would talk about having a gay old time. We don't use that term anymore. Or we would speak about going on a trip. I hope my high school senior doesn't "go on a trip"! Those perfectly good words have taken on bad connotations with their use or misuse.

Once I had a double wedding when I was pastor in Louisville, Kentucky. It was a monstrous event, and almost a logistical nightmare, deciding which bride's bridesmaids should enter first. There were eight bridesmaids, eight groomsmen, two bridegrooms, two brides, two ministers, two best men, two maids of honor, and *one poor father* paying for the whole thing! The other minister who shared the ceremony with me was an Episcopal rector. I enjoyed getting to know him, and frankly he seemed impressed to meet a Baptist minister who could read. He was especially impressed that I used the wedding service out of the Episcopal Prayer Book. I explained to him that I had to make some revisions in that ceremony in order for it to be appropriate for Baptists.

For example, the Episcopalians say "amen" at the end of every paragraph. If you did that in a Baptist church, they would think the meeting was over, get up, and go home. I also had taken out the phrase where the couple says, "And thereto I plight thee my troth." We don't really understand what that old English phrase means anymore. I further revised the ceremony to leave out the phrase in which the bride promises to "obey" and "serve" him. The Episcopal rector told me that originally, in the English prayer book, brides promised to be "boughsome"—that is, they would give in to their husbands as a bough on a tree gives in to the wind. Isn't that interesting? In the history of the English wedding ceremony, brides have promised to be boughsome—to obey—and now they don't make any such promise. Words and their use change over the years.

In the Bible itself, we are in need of constant translations because our language changes, though the Scriptures do not change. For example, in 1 Thessalonians 4 (King James Version) we read that, "We who are alive and remain until the Lord's coming shall not *prevent* those who are asleep." This does not mean we will keep those who died before Christ's return from going to heaven. It means we will not go to heaven before them: prevent has changed meaning. Words and the usage of words change, and this can create problems with communication.

III. Communication Is God's Problem Too

How does God, who is Spirit, communicate His nature, will, and love to mortal men and women? How could we understand His communication? Think about how we communicate human love. Recall when you fell in love for the first time. I was in the third grade and remember it vividly.

She was the cutest little girl I had ever seen. Strange, after all these years I don't remember her name. I communicated my affection for her by writing notes and passing them in class. I also communicated my love for her by saving my allowance for months one summer to buy her the largest box of chocolates I could find in Atlanta. It was really extravagant. I couldn't afford it, but I wanted her to know how much I loved her.

I once heard a man ask, "Wouldn't it be nice if we treated our wives all our married life the way we treated them when we were courting them?" Another man replied, "Yes, but we certainly would be broke!"

The ultimate communication of human love is when we stand before the altar in the presence of God, family members, and friends, and make a life commitment to our beloved. The basis of marriage is not romantic love; it is commitment.

It seems there are parallels between the way we communicate human love and how God communicates His love and divine purpose to mankind. The Scriptures are examples of God's love letters, His self-revelation of how He feels toward us and what He requires of us. They are both windows to show us the Father and mirrors to show us ourselves, in both our worth and our sinfulness. The Bible discloses God's redemptive purpose for mankind and the world itself. God has communicated with us in writing. His Holy Word is ours to read and understand.

God has also given us wonderful, extravagant gifts. He has given us what the astronaut from space called "the good earth." This earth is vast in its expansiveness. I read that if we could travel from where we are to the center of the universe and return at the speed of light, we would be ten years older when we returned. That is not bad. It takes us that long to learn to parallel park! But when we returned, the earth would be thirty thousand years older! God is the Creator of all the universe in its loveliness and its complexity.

God has given us the beauty and grandeur of the earth itself. He has given us food and water, shelter and safety. He has given us color and flowers. He has given us a child's smile and the warm embrace of love. All of His good gifts are meant to point us to the Father, to elicit our praise and gratitude. "Great is the Lord and greatly to be praised" (Ps. 48:1, RSV).

God's supreme communication of His love is found in the person of His Son. "The Word became flesh and dwelt among us" (John 1:14). God became a man in the Person of Jesus Christ in order to show us how much He loves us and His purpose as our Redeemer. Paul Scherer called the birth of Jesus "that night of nights when God walked down the back steps of Bethlehem, with a babe on his arm." The late J. Wallace Hamilton of Florida declared, "Clarity, poetry, vitality! Make it clear, make it sing, but above all, make it live!"

As Christians, you and I are in the communications business, and we are communicating the most important message of all, the glorious Gospel of Jesus Christ. This is the message of divine love for which mankind longs. We have the Good News, and it has transformed our lives. Let us dedicate ourselves to share the Gospel effectively, near and far. Anything less would be irresponsible—in fact, desperately tragic.

God has spoken, in the Person of His Son. Are you listening?

Calvin Miller

The Evangelist As . . .
the Rebel Lover
2 Samuel 15:1-5, 18:5-9,14,33

Introduction

In 1 Samuel 15 is the heart of the rebel disclosed. What lies in his heart? If only he *were king, he would do it better!* It is always easy to see how we would do it until it is our time to do it! I watched from the bottom of a waterfall in Oklahoma as various men dove from the top of the falls to the frothy, blue pool before me. A group of young people bet that I could not do it. In that group was the young girl I later wanted to marry.

With their daring taunts in the porches of my ears, I decided I would do it, and I began to climb to the top. I pictured in my mind the marvelous cliff-dwellers of Acapulco—I saw my arms, swan-like, swept back, sleekward. I saw my chest and abdomen bent like the glorious hood ornament on a '47 Buick. My legs tapered off in a graceful arc of intention with only the tiniest jet stream facing backward from my pointed toes. Today, Turner Falls! Tomorrow the Black Cliffs of Acapulco!

Then suddenly I was there, and I turned to look where I must dive. I must hit the tiny little patch of blue between the huge rocks, like shark's teeth reaching upward to devour the divers. Finally I did not dive at all; I only fearfully jumped and perished beneath the pounding waters seemingly for hours, before I finally came to the surface again.

In 1 Samuel 15 is hidden the lament—"If only I were King, I would do it better," cried Absalom. He, of course, never lived to be king, so we have no idea how he would have managed.

But rebels are dreamers, and all they envision is utopian. As the rebel Lenin would improve on Czar Nicholas II, or Castro would improve on Bautista or Ortega on Samosa, so Absalom would improve upon David.

Rebel dreams usually are more savage than kind! They pick the moments when the establishment is at bay.

So Lenin rode through Sweden on a sealed train when the Czar had resigned, and the imperial army was in rags.

Mao moved against Chiang when Japan had China at bay.

Absalom, well, he moved against a father whose age and house had lost their taste for war.

But never mind the son—what was the father doing? Did he rage and rail against his self-serving son? Did he want to crush him in the coils of war, of hate and destruction?

Hardly.

As the soldiers left, he whispered to his high general, Joab, "Deal gently with the young man Absalom, for my sake! No matter his hostility—answer him only in love!"

"Care, Joab!" cried the weeping king.

Joab curled his lip and moved out to lead the army.

The helmets caught the sun. The king cried over the battlements in a voice made faint by iron rims on cobblestone, and winding, dusty distance.

"Care, Joab!"

Every rebel is loved: swallowed up in his self-concern, he is loved. And every rebel might be saved. That is what it means for Christ to enter the pain of this world. If we would help Christ with the rescue, we must enter the world beyond the church. We would rather do our saving work where almost no one is lost—the church. So we sing thirty-two verses of "Just As I Am" for three struggling children who are standing in the pew, trying to think what Big Bird would do. But at last they come, saving not just their souls but our reputations. Now at last we can go to the Evangelism Conference with confidence.

Children are precious to God, but are they our best

shot at evangelistic reputation? Are there rebels with more stature? Is there not someone not already wooed by the Gospel Network—a genuine non-cable-watching sinner not traumatized by overexposure—a macho sinner with a one-*Playboy,* three-wife, four-martini-per-day aroma about him? What of these class-A renegade, lost-forever rabble? Where were they? How did we miss them? They were there all around our churches, yet never in them. Between margaritas, they often sobered enough to answer the doorbell and answer the Kennedy questions, if anyone had been there to ring and ask.

The first question in caring is *not,* "If you were to die, do you know for sure . . ." The first question is, "How are you?"

"How are you?" I ask you! I am struck dumb that no plan of salvation I know teaches us to ask three questions, only two. But those who care begin by asking, "How are you?" and after that, "How are Madge and the kids?"

"Madge and the kids?" I ask of you. Simple and lovely niceties that show how much we care and, as the cliché goes, people don't care how much we *know* till they know how much we *care.* Rebel-catching . . . is rarely done by our clever schematics. We waste a lot of time trying to question and answer people into the kingdom of God. Maybe we ought to try *caring* people into Christ.

Rebels rarely ask for rescue, yet there is something in them that cries out for it. Do you not see that some of Absalom longs for his father? In his mind, and only in his mind, will he help seize the royal palace and kill his father. In his heart there is a yearning to embrace the very father his heart would kill. Rebels always have two forces tearing their insides out—they want to fight and they want to be loved.

Can you not remember that awful struggle of your rebel heart against God? You fought Him as he tried to lift you from your sin, yet you reached for His embrace. You did not want God, yet you wanted all of God that you could hold. "Crucify" we cry against Christ while we choke the words to silence, dumbfounded at our words. We are the rebels and hateful lovers, the loving haters of the great Almighty who loved us, and we too have philosophically been like Pooh walking the river bank and making conversation while Eeyore is in great trouble, floating downstream on his back:

> *Pooh*—"Did you fall into the river, Eeyore?"
> *Eeyore*—"Silly of me, wasn't it?"
> *Pooh*—"Is the river uncomfortable this morning?"
> *Eeyore*—"Well, yes, the dampness you know."
> *Pooh*—"You really ought to be more careful!"
> *Eeyore*—"Thanks for the advice."
> *Pooh*—"I think you're sinking."
> *Eeyore*—"Pooh, if it's not to much trouble, would you
>   mind rescuing me?"[1]

How can we know or understand the rebel's burden of heart?

We are Christians, little Christs—little rescuers of a sinking world. How do they tell us they are sinking? How do they cry out to us? By ignoring us. By closing the door in our faces, even when we have the Four Spiritual Laws written all over them. How do they say, "Would you mind rescuing me?"

They speak their needs in hidden phrases. Listen to their crying hearts and know their self-protective rhetoric. "If you died today would you . . . ?"

"Please . . . please . . . I think my spiritual life is a very personal thing . . ."

"I never discuss religion!"

"I'm quite happy in the church I never go to."

"'I'm Episcopalian, you know—thoroughbred—registered, papers and all."

"I gave my heart to 'Brother Moseby' when I was ten. It is enough."

"I send ten dollars to Sister Victoria of the Miracle Crusade every time her make-up gets thin."

"I don't believe in organized religion."

"My father was a Baptist, my mother was a Methodist, and I'm a somnambulist."

"Yes, I understand, but would you mind if I ask you a couple of questions? Nothing hard, it will be like on 'Jeopardy.' Your category is 'chest pains, I.C.U. and paramedic evangelism.'"

Still, there is something to this question-and-answer business. They are there longing for the encounter if we can get the questions and leave all the answers right. Fight it out with life. And they are loved and we are their lovers—we bear the word of faith—saving faith. But hear the last thing our King whispers over the battlements as we choke down the last donut and leave the evangelism training room, "Please care. Deal gently with the young rebel, for my sake."

Apathy is the great sin of the church.

If there was anything Absalom prided himself on it was his wild hair. Naturally, his father's cabinet had protested. Most of the time when they passed Absalom in the corridors of the palace, and Absalom said "Shalom," they said, in flawless Piel imperative, *galech*—which, being interpreted, is, "Get a haircut, you crazy kid!" Absalom got a little tired of it all.

Rebels sometimes have a way of wearing their hair a little funny. If the straights have long hair, the rebels get crew cuts. If the straights have crew cuts, they wear it long. The key thing is, just don't look like the establishment. Well, most of the king's men looked like Daddy Warbucks, so Absalom decided to look like Ted Nugent. It took him a long time, but sometimes as he'd gaze into a mirror he could hear them saying, *galech,* and he'd fluff his hair and think, *Oh, that I were King!* His hair got so thick that he couldn't even get his helmet on. Rebels are not always too practical. He was a fighter; that's all that mattered—he could assault his assailants, helmet or no! And he would win! And he would slaughter the sleazy little sabers of Sion—the imperialists of Jerusalem. The king would pay in blood when he faced Ted the Terrific—Rambo of Judah—and the Bolshevists of Beersheba.

It amazed King David how no one saw Absalom's finer points. He was a child of God! Unaccepted, ridiculed, social outcast. Yet, his very name, Absalom, meant "Father of Peace." And it is funny that the king never noticed how long his hair was! My, how God loves those we feel are so very odd, so different. God loved him from the womb, and so all rebels. The king had watched the child grow, and each new step had held promises of life.

Rabindrinath Tagore wrote, "Every child comes with the message that God is not yet discouraged of man." And even as the king, like every father with a new son looks at his baby, his heart too hopes. "My son will succeed where I stumbled. He will love where I have lusted. He will serve God where I have served only myself!" And David held that little lump of life called Absalom, lifted him into the sun, and cried: "You are my sunshine and my rain. My son, already you are all I wanted to be but have not been. All of my aspirations and dreams are fulfilled in you." Now the child, all bright with hope, is a lost rebel.

Still, rebels have dreams. They are beautiful dreams; plans, life-sized blueprints that always spell success. The boy turned man cannot see the truth of Freud's dictum. He is driven by that odd "castration complex" that he will yet best his father, own more, and be greater. *Yes,* he thought one night as he fluffed his mane and inserted three rings in his right ear, *I will be greater than my father!* He looked again at his magnificent hair and thought of his father's thinning, graying pate.

Tomorrow we will meet, and after the battle all of my dreams will be a reality, thought Absalom.

Life sometimes knows only the management of demons. It is Joab, not Absalom, who picks the battlefield. Joab—establishment—who greased his hair down and looked like an old hair-oil advertisement. Still, Joab could get his helmet on! And he did pick the battlefield—not the plains of Ephraim but the thickets of Ephraim, not at all the kind of place you should wear your hair long.

So the day ended in tangled shame, and they met; the slick-back wethead and the "Borneo Wild Man." And Absalom was hanging by his hair in the tree. His rebellion was now dreamless. And somewhere in some old Aramaic inclusion it must say that the old warrior looks at his hated foe and says again *(galech)!* And then he listened, and the very breezes whispered the old king's words, "Care Joab . . . care Joab . . . care Joab!"

But Joab took three spears and drove them through the heart, and the rebel died! He was dead! Caught in the tangled thickets of an existentialism he did not understand.

But the rebel was not the only thing that died—it was the major part of the old man's heart. And as each messenger came he asked again, "Is the young man Absalom safe?" Ahimahaz was sure they had won the battle! But that was not what the old man wanted to know. The Cushite came and told the rebel's final tale:

> MAY THE ENEMIES OF MY LORD THE KING,
> AND ALL WHO RISE AGAINST YOU TO DO YOU
> HARM BE AS THAT YOUNG MAN IS!

And the father wept, like King Lear holding the dead Cordelia: "Oh, Absalom, be not dead!"

> Please stay a little—I am old now and these same crosses spoil me . . .

No, no, no—no life!

> Why should a dog, a horse, a rat have life
> And thou no breath at all.
> Oh, Absalom, thou'lt come no more[2]

And the King was deeply moved, and went up to the chamber over the gate and wept! And as he went, thus he cried,

> Oh, my son Absalom,
> my son, my son, Absalom,

if only I had died in your place
Oh Absalom, my son, my son! (2 Sam. 18:33).

And thus is the unclaimed love of a father, like a great diamond Star of India, exposed in the window of a pawnshop. A treasure of vast value made cheap, even lost.

It is the parable of the prodigal son dying in the pigpen far from the father who would have embraced and loved him. And what is the sin of the elder brother in this Old Testament parable? Not bitterness but apathy.

God alone grieves the loss of rebels! Apathy—who comforts a king when a rebel dies? No one much. They saw only the rebel's long hair and remembered his Bolshevism. But not the king! He wept. Apathy—it bakes casseroles for church fellowships while battles rage in the woods of Ephraim. And turnpike-wide, they drive forward like lemmings into hell. Churches don't cry. Seminaries don't cry. Book stores don't cry. Only God cries!

For they are lost—perished and gone!

Not just lost. Not just perished in hell, but hanging in the tangled thickets of life, trying in their last moments or first to make meaning of it all. Waiting for a kinder Joab who can weep with God. We shoot our wounded, too—Joab-like in the thickets of Ephraim.

Drugs, booze, the cancer ward, the divorce courts—*the cities themselves are the thickets!* And God weeps and waits, and Jesus, levitating from Olivet, cries out: "Into all the world . . ."

Please care, please care, please care.
Don't take a plan of salvation—or any other plan.
Take me, the dying Christ, and get to the hurting
world before Joab does! For they hang in tangled
woods with tangled minds

There was but one word which would have delighted David that day. And only one word which will delight God in our day,

There is a Cushite at the door. He brings with him a
rebel he spared in a tangled wood. The soul he brings
weeps and begs for forgiveness.

And the young Absalom would cry:

Oh, Father, I have sinned against heaven and in thy
sight! I am no more worthy . . ."

And the father would draw his kneeling form into an
embrace and cry,

Nonsense! Your brokenness has made you worthy!
Bring forth the best robe and put it on him, and shoes
for his feet and a ring for his hand—For this my son
was dead but is alive again! He was lost and is found.

But unlike Jesus' parable, the joyous father would continue,

It is not just the found that are special. The finders,
too, are special. Wait, young Cushite—where do you
go? Why do you leave this party? The lost is found.

And the Cushite would say,

Oh, Father, the world is a tangled, dying place. The
woods are full of hanging forms. Be ready with your
love—I'll bring another! I must go now! Joab—the
heartless, loveless secularian . . . walks the woods
killing your children.

And the Father would say,

Yes, go . . . tell them all to wonder at my love.

And Carlyle cries,

(For) the man who cannot wonder is but a pair of spec-
tacles behind which there are no eyes.

God challenges, "Tell each hurting and lost person of
My extravagance."
God offers every lost one:

More sky than he can see
More seas than he can sail,

> More sun than he can bear to watch
> More stars than he can scale.
> More breath than he can breathe,
> More yield than he can sow.
> More grace than he can comprehend.
> More love than he can know![3]

NOTES

1. Quoted in William M. Fletcher, *The Second Greatest Commandment* (Colorado Springs, CO: NavPress, 1983), p. 57.
2. William Shakespeare, *King Lear,* V, iii, lines 278*ff.*
3. Ralph W. Seager quoted in *The Treasure Chest,* Charles L. Wallis, compiler (New York: Harper and Row, 1965), p. 26.

Jess Moody

The Most Encouraging Verse
in the Bible

His face was drawn, more troubled than I had seen it before. It framed two haunted, deeper set eyes than normal. His need was obvious.

"I feel so left out of it. My family would prefer me dead. My business has practically folded due to intrigue on my partner's side of the firm.

"The firm is not firm—and neither am I. I cannot honestly say that I have one true friend on this planet. I even fondled my thirty-thirty rifle last Monday with the first stages of premeditated self-murder in my mind."

"How deep is your loneliness?" I asked, probing clumsily.

"As the sea . . ."

He knew, and I knew that his depression was so deep he was bathing in despair.

At this point I felt Satan's subtle whisper, "Now, don't quote Scripture to him—that's the last thing he needs." But I proceeded to tell him I was preaching the next Sunday on the most encouraging verse in the Bible.

"God knows, I could stand a lot of that," he said wistfully.

"Would you like to see how a pastor prepares a sermon like this?"

"Yeah, sure—you're going to show some of the tricks of the preaching trade?"

"No tricks, not even clean ones—just straight digging until the Bible gold vein is found; then you yell 'Eureka.'"

I read the verse I considered the most encouraging

verse in the Bible, Hebrews 13:5b, "I will never leave you nor forsake you."

Now, this is either a bland sentence, or it is God's solid gold.

We must dig deeply into this rock to see what it yields. We must ascertain the answers at least.

1. What does *never* mean?
2. What does *leave* mean?
3. What does *forsake* mean?

What does *never* mean? I discovered a true nugget when I investigated the semantics of this negative word. It doesn't mean simply a bland never. It is a compounding of five negatives, not each negative added to another, but multiplied by the other. It should read, "I will never, no not ever, no never leave you, nor forsake you . . ." It is a synergistic compounding negative. It is a forever never which has no exceptions ever!

If God will never leave you, He has not now left you because never includes now. Can you accept that in your mind? In your will? In your emotions?

I want to put the branding iron of this great never into the white-hot heat of God's love and brand it upon your eternity-destined psyche so you will never, no not ever, no never forget it.

"I will never, no not ever, no never leave you."

You can get well if you will yield your whole mind to this powerful positive negative never.

"Leave" . . . she was a shambles. He, the earthly source of her life's garden, had left a note on the refrigerator: "You have posted the Orders of the Day on this refrigerator for years. Now, I want you to know that this Buck Private has gone AWOL."

She never saw him again until that terribly barren day in the divorce court.

The judge's gavel hammered horror into her heart with the casual, "Divorce granted."

It was like the four-thousand yards from Pilate's Hall

to Golgotha as she walked from the courtroom to this Pastor's study.

God will never leave you like that.

In this verse, in this context, let us discover gold mine number two. What does *leave* mean?

This is a little Greek word, *aniemi:* it is the second aorist active subjunctive which translates "to leave behind, to abandon, to give up on, to send back."

Now, let's see what we have: "I will never, no not ever, no never leave you behind, abandon you, give up on you, or send you back." Get these burning words into your soul, your emotions. How can you feel left out if you haven't been left behind?

If He doesn't leave you behind, He is taking you along with Him.

If he hasn't abandoned you, why do you feel so alone?

Your emotions are lying to you. Your emotions are whispering to you, "I have abandoned you." God says, "I will never leave you behind, give up on you, abandon you, send you back." So, right now, I want you to call your emotions a liar and God's Word the truth. Get your mind, will, and emotions converted to God's Word. If He hasn't "given up on" you, then why have you given up on yourself? If He will never leave you behind, then He is taking you with Him. Instead of your going along with God, God is going along with you.

Wherever you go, whatever you do, this verse says right clearly—you're together.

If God has "not abandoned" you, why do you feel so abandoned?

Because your unconverted emotions have lied to you. Get your emotions in tune with God's Word. If He will never "send you back," why do you keep thinking you can lose your salvation? Because your emotions have your ear and you listen to your temperamental emotions instead of the non-temperamental Bible.

Your emotions lie if they don't comply with the Word of God.

There is another important word in this text. It is the word *forsake*. What does it mean?

The father's face was buried in his hands. The tears were coursing through his fingers; his son had confessed to being homosexual. The father had reacted in such a way as to alienate the son.

Now, three years later, he and his wife were in Los Angeles to bury their engineer son who had died of AIDS. Their arrival in the City of Angels was greeted by a contingent of homosexuals who informed them that his lover had made all the funeral arrangements, and he would be buried with a homosexual church service under the leadership of a gay minister.

The bereft mother thought for a moment, then stepped up to them, and said, "I brought him into this world. I will plan his departure. He was led to Jesus by an old-fashioned Bible preacher. He will be buried by one."

It fell my lot to do the deed. We met on a cold day at the graveside at Valhalla Cemetery. The mother and father sat at one side . . . isolated . . . alone.

Seventy hostile homosexuals stood at the other side . . . His lover sat weeping, holding a picture of the boy and clutching an armful of flowers. My heart went out to all of them, but especially to the father and mother.

Before I stood to preach, the mother signaled for my attention. "Please tell these young men how much Jesus loves them and that He can save them."

I tried to preach Jesus as the only Savior, the Holy Spirit as the key to power of self-control, and the Father as the Guide and Stay of us all.

While I preached, the father wept through his hands, and the tears fell on the cemetery grass.

But the mother's face drew my attention. The chill had drawn her flesh tauntly about her face. The sorrow had taken the gleam out of her eyes. She was wintered in by a blizzard of grief; she looked totally withered.

Old.

Then the sheer force of our verse of concentration hammered into my soul. "I shall never, never, never, never, never leave you, forsake you, turn My back upon you."

To my mind, *forsake* is one of the most interesting words in all the Word of God. It is the word *encatalipō* which translates "to leave one in a helpless state, to disregard." Now, how is it used in other biblical references?

Jesus Whose hands had never done harm to anyone, Whose hands had always reached out in love to little children, had touched the fevered brows of sick people, had touched a dead little girl into life—now had nails driven through those loving hands.

Jesus Whose feet never walked a wayward step, had taken Him on many a wearying journey to missions of love—now had nails driven through His loving feet. Fever rising, pain wracking His body, limestone dust drying out His thirsty mouth, pectoral and leg muscles wracked with cramping, the crowd hooting their taunts, the disciples, save John, had run the coward's trail to the hills.

Then He used a word related to this text, "My God, my God, why hast thou forsaken me?" (Matt. 27:46, Mark 15:34). The same Father God who seemed to forsake His Son on the cross (though He did not), has promised never to forsake you. The same God who allowed His Son to be put in a helpless state will never allow you to be put in such a helpless state—the translation of the word.

Now, look at another use of that very same word as it is used in Hebrews 10:25, "Not forsaking the assembling of yourselves together." It is exactly the same kind of forsaking of God's Son that God had to do to His Son, that we do to God's church when we forsake the assembling of ourselves together.

When you stay away from God's church, you are doing to the church what God had to do to His Son, disregarding it, rendering it into a helpless state. We are to be as faithful in attending God's church as God is faithful in not forsaking us.

The word forsake also translates to mean relax (A. T. Robertson).

So, now, let me give you a full, more amplified translation of our text: "I WILL NEVER, NO NOT EVER, NO NEVER GIVE UP ON YOU, ABANDON YOU, LEAVE YOU BEHIND, CAUSE YOU NOT TO SURVIVE, LEAVE YOU HELPLESS, NOR SHALL I EVER RELAX CONCERNING KEEPING MY PRESENCE WITH YOU."

We can cash a promissory note only one time. Here is one you can cash a thousand times, and it will still be good. It is universally applicable. It applies to the businessman, the housewife, the student, the young person, the retired. It covers all time, all space, and all circumstances.

This verse will give you comfort, courage, confidence, and compassion. Who backs up this verse? "I will never . . ."

God Himself is the presence behind the promise. Behind the presence is omnipotence, omnipresence, and omniscience.

Omnipotence answers when you say, "I don't have the strength."

Omnipresence answers when you say, "I'm so lonely."

Omniscience answers when you say, "I don't know what to do!"

The God Who didn't leave the children of Israel in the wilderness will not leave you. The God who didn't forsake Elijah on Mt. Carmel will not leave you.

So, practice the presence behind this promise. Note that the sentence begins with "I" and it ends with "thee." This is the first of the "I-thou" relationship.

The good news is that God really cares about having you in His heart.

Arthur Ray Ebersole had drowned.

The paramedics were working over his body. The frantic father was begging the paramedics and the boy to start his breathing.

In the background, I heard a voice, clear-as-crystal, ringing with hope.

All our eyes turned to the source of the song.

It was Arthur's mother, sitting in the cab of the paramedics' truck. She was looking through the sun-roof and affirming her faith skyward.

> I've seen the light'ning flashing
> I've heard the thunder roll,
> I've felt sin's breakers dashing.
> Trying to conquer my soul.

> I've heard the voice of Jesus
> Telling me still to fight on
> He promised never to leave me,
> Never to leave me alone.

> No! Never alone.
> No! Never alone.
> He promised never to leave me,
> Never to leave me alone.

W. Winfred Moore

Who Shall Reign Over Us?
Judges 9

Judges 9:14 reads: "Then said all the trees unto the bramble, Come thou, and reign over us." This is a portion of an unusual parable which was related to Jotham, the youngest son of Jerubbaal (more familiarly known as Gideon). In chapter 8, verses 30 and 31, we are informed of Gideon's "ten sons of his body begotten: for he had many wives."

"And his concubine that was in Shechem, she also bare him a son, whose name was called Abimelech" (8:31). Verses 33 and 34 record that this was a son who should never have been born. Why? As soon as Gideon was dead the children of Israel again turned—"went a whoring"—after Baalim. That facilitated Abimelech's political maneuver to capture for himself the place of esteem and leadership.

At the outset of chapter 9 Abimelech contacted the men of Shechem and offered himself as their king, explaining in effect, "You ought to elect me because I am one of you. Of course, being one of you I will care for your own interests better than anyone else." What a politician! They gave him their vote of confidence and elected him to rule.

Abimelech turned out to be a dirty, ruthless ruler. Chapter 9, verse 5, is a shocking revelation:

> And he went unto his father's house at Ophrah, and slew his brethren the sons of Jerubbaal, being threescore and ten persons, upon one stone: notwithstanding yet Jotham the youngest son of Jerubbaal was left; for he hid himself.

Later when young Jotham heard what had happened, he stood on the top of Mount Gerizim, lifted up his voice, crying out to the people and speaking to them the parable of our text.

The parable of Jotham had a near and distant fulfillment. First of all, a kingdom under the leadership of a rascal like Abimelech will ultimately be overthrown. There is a penetrating message in that parable for America today. We must not become too busy for civic affairs. We become so caught up in our own business that we seem to have neither time nor interest in saving the political and social structures. Ours is a "government of the people, by the people, and for the people." But democracy is also the most difficult to manage and to keep alive. To manage it judiciously and to keep it healthfully alive requires continuous thought and sacrifice by all.

Notice in 9:15 that the bramble, a symbol of the curse, degradation, and rejection, boasts, "If in truth ye anoint me king over you, then come and put your trust in my shadow..." What a paradox! The bramble is not timber and has neither fruit nor shade. It is neither substantial nor fruitful but is only capable of being combustible, as the latter part of the verse indicates.

The bramble never would have become ruler, except for the fact that those sturdier and better qualified simply had neither the time nor the interest to assume the responsibility. The indifference of good persons to civic duties is appalling. I remind you of Edmund Burke's oft-quoted observation: "All that is necessary for the triumph of evil is that good men do nothing." A man or woman may be effective and true to their home or church and yet ineffective and false toward their community and nation.

Some of us came to this country as immigrants—if not we ourselves, then our fathers or grandfathers. We have enjoyed all the advantages of this great "land of the free and home of the brave." Yet, we are unwilling to make any sacrifice to ensure that the political structure remains sound and vibrant. But let us remember: Whenever and wherever good men flee their governmental obligations, there is always a bramble asking, "Put your trust in my shadow." The neglect of civic duty is one of the saddest chapters in our nation's history. In most elections here only 50 percent of the registered voters cast their ballots on election day.

Who is responsible for this neglect? The pulpit must share in this responsibility. Many of us have failed to impress upon our people their duty in the civic arena. We have feared that some would accuse us of neglecting our primary calling, the proclamation of the Gospel of the Lord Jesus Christ, and instead dealing with secondary matters. But I remind you that the church of the Lord Jesus Christ never functions as she ought where her members neglect their civic obligations, where brambles rule over the people. Beloved, all that is totalitarian is opposed to all that is Christian—and all that is totalitarianism is opposed to all that is Americanism, as we have known it.

But laypersons must also share the blame for the reign of the bramble king, for many of the laity have neglected their duty, some through inadequate information, others because civic duty is often disagreeable and tedious, and others because of sheer selfishness. The truth is: we have treated the community like it were a cow. We have filled our own pails with milk, gone into the house to drink it, neither caring nor giving thought to feeding and providing for the cow.

Let those of us who pride ourselves on being church men and women be reminded that we have a Scriptural admonition to care for the matters of the government. We have the stark testimony of history that where brambles reigned, because men and women have neglected their governmental duties, the church has never for long remained missionary and strong.

The parable of the bramble also looks to an hour when nations shall make another foolish choice and invite the Antichrist to be their king. In Judges 9:8*ff.* the parable goes that, "The trees went forth on a time to anoint a king over them; and they said unto the olive tree, Reign thou over us. . . ." He declined. So did the fig tree and the vine.

Does that sound familiar, not only in civic but also in church business? "Not me." "George'll do it." "Get somebody else." "I have too much on me already." The olive tree, the fig tree, and the grape vine sound like Baptists at nominating committee time! They were actually capable and worthy, but they were not willing to pay the price of leadership.

So the bramble became king, a plant that seemingly has no reason for its existence in nature's economy. "Fatness, sweetness, fruit, wine" were too important to the olive tree, the fig tree, and the grape vine, but surely not so important as to leave rulership to one who would beckon, "Put your trust in my shadow." The biblical record relates the disaster which befell the men of Shechem, the ones who were duped by the political chicanery of a dastardly "bramble," Abimelech.

The truth taught is that Israel, ordained by God to bear witness to the entire world and to provide spiritual nourishment for them (symbolized by the olive tree, the fig tree, and the grape vine), failed miserably so the nations turned to a bramble. Remember that a bramble is a shrub that scratches, hurts, bruises, wounds, but is quick to seize opportunity when others default.

I believe the bramble is a type of Antichrist who, when he becomes king, will demand absolute submission from all his subjects—or death. The devil will send the Antichrist into the world. The Antichrist will epitomize all that is corrupt, evil, gross, and wicked, but he will craftily cover his nefarious intent. God Almighty will send back His only begotten Son, the Lord Jesus Christ, to defeat and banish the Antichrist into the pit. Now, prophecy is not really all that mysterious, for it is nothing more than prewritten history. All that prophecy predicts, history will produce.

At this juncture let us look at the coming heyday of the Antichrist. The time of the Antichrist will be during the tribulation period, the period after all born-again believers have been raptured, "caught up . . . to meet the Lord in the air."

Now the world has seen many tribulations. There are severe afflictions in the world right now, but these conditions only foreshadow the monstrous darkness that is to break over the world in that great tribulation. Jesus Himself described it in Matthew 24. After Jesus had declared that many would be offended and betray one another, hating one another, and many false prophets would arise, he continued:

> But pray ye that your flight be not in the winter, neither on the sabbath day: For then shall be great tribulation, such as was not since the beginning of the world to this time, no, not ever shall be. And except those days should be shortened, there should no flesh be saved: but for the elect's sake those days shall be shortened (24:20-22).

This will be the period which will reveal the worst persecution the Jews have ever known. Jeremiah prophesied of it: "Alas, for that day is great, so that none is like it; it is even the time of Jacob's trouble; but he shall be saved out of it" (30:7).

For a moment view the personality of the Antichrist. The bramble represents the worst evil personality the world will ever know, with the single exception of the devil himself. Listen to John the beloved, "Little children, it is the last time: and as ye have heard that antichrist shall come, even now there are many antichrists; whereby we know that it is the last time" (1 John 2:18).

Paul wrote in 2 Thessalonians 2:3-4:

> Let no man deceive you by any means, for that day shall not come except there come a falling away first and that man of sin be revealed, the son of perdition, who opposeth and exalteth himself above all that is called God, or that is worshipped; so that he as God sitteth in the temple of God, showing himself that he is God.

The Antichrist will appear as a peerless personality, intellectual, a flatterer, a humanitarian, offering material and political salvation to the whole world, and he will be admired as no other personage by a Christ-rejecting civilization. I believe he will be a Gentile who will make a covenant with the Jews, granting them religious privileges and rights to their own land. His political power and statesmanship will attract worldwide attention, and a whole unregenerate world will be anxious to follow him, the Bramble of brambles.

Consider the power of the Antichrist. What a thorny shrub he is compared to mighty trees! It is unbelievable that majestic trees would submit to such low-grade, bramble, thorny leadership. Yet look at the brambles around the world today—Castro, Khadafi, Khomeini, and countless other ruthless, bloodthirsty dictators over the earth. Yet, man in folly will turn to any madman who offers him comfort and material prosperity. By this and other strategems the power of the Antichrist will be all but universal.

> And it was given unto him to make war with the saints, and to overcome them: and power was given him over all kindreds, and tongues, and nations. And all that dwell upon the earth shall worship him, whose names are not written in the book of life of the Lamb slain from the foundation of the world (Rev. 13:7-8).

Preparation is being made now for the appearance of the Antichrist, for a jittery world longs for the entrance of someone who can offer security and stability. Uncertainty is the word of the hour, and people can stand uncertainty within and without only so long. Then they are willing to sell themselves away to a mere bramble who promises peace and prosperity, whatever the price.

Thank God, you and I who have crowned Jesus Christ as the King of our hearts will not have to face that great tribulation when Satan's beastly bramble, the Antichrist, will reveal himself. We shall have been "caught up together with them in the clouds, to meet the Lord in the air" (1 Thess. 4:17a). With our King we shall be awaiting His and our triumphant return *(apokalupsis)* to earth to establish His millennial kingdom. We are spoken of in Revelation 20:6: "Blessed and holy is he that hath part in the first resurrection: on such the second death hath no power, but they shall be priests of God and of Christ, and shall reign with him a thousand years."

One of our deacons, James Franklin, used to observe, "There are no human solutions to human problems. There are only divine solutions to human problems." Our answer is not in the bramble but in the true Vine, the Lord Jesus Christ, Who is also our Lord, our Master, our Savior, our King of kings and Lord of lords!

Charles D. Page

Victory Over Depression
Philippians 4:1-13

Introduction

One of the saddest things I know is the sight of a person who has stopped growing in life. It should be our profound desire to be always more than we are and all we can be. Depression is hindering the growth of many of God's people and keeping them from being all they can be.

In speaking about depression, we recognize that there are varying degrees ranging from simple mood swings to utter despair. Somewhere it touches all our lives, whether in the life of a friend, business associate whose work is affected, family member whom we worry about constantly or an acquaintance. Everyone has mood swings. We go through a twenty-eight-day emotional cycle. For some there is little difference between the high periods and low periods. These people stay on an even keel most of the time.

For others, the swing is more noticeable, even to the point of grave concern. It is like the black spiritual which says, "I'm sometimes up, and I'm sometimes down, Lord." The psalmist asked in one of these swings, "Who shall deliver me from this miry pit?" The psychologist tells us that the person with these moods is probably more normal than one who never varies in their moods. A man suddenly left a religious cult he had been very enthusiastic about. When asked why he left, he said, "I got tired of always being so happy."

Some dark nights of the soul can be of great value. We cannot really appreciate the good times of joy and excitement if we have never experienced the "blahs," and we can't fully appreciate the mountain top unless we have done some time in the valley. We can't really minister to others if we ourselves have not experienced some of their pain. Many of God's choicest servants have suffered greatly from depression.

Elijah is a classic case. His depression had already settled into self-pity, the terminal stage of depression. As he sat under the juniper tree, he cried to God, "Take my life away, for I am all alone in the battles of life." Abraham Lincoln was called by an enemy "the most perfect leader of men of all the ages," yet he often suffered deep valleys of despair. When Ann Rutledge died, he was totally incapacitated for weeks and when he was to be married to Mary Todd, he did not show up for the wedding, moaning his unworthiness. His sensitivity made him the perfect leader for a nation in the throes of civil war, for he could understand even the views of the other side. What a rare quality.

There are times when depression ceases to be positive. It dips over into the area of the negative and the harmful, and it robs the person of power, and even usefulness. It renders them ineffective. At this point solutions need to be found.

Our text has as its backdrop the church at Philippi. They seemed to be in the "blahs." Their newfound faith was being sorely challenged and tested. Here is one of those paradoxes in the Scripture. Paul, writing from a jail cell, had to encourage those who were free. The causes and answers to depression are not to be found predominantly in circumstances. In our text we will look at the situation in Philippi that contributed to their spiritual "blahs" and then the solution Paul gives them in his letter to them.

The Situation at Philippi (vv. 1-4)

We have to read between the lines here because we do not have the correspondence from the church at Philippi to Paul that precipitated the writing of his letter to them. We do have recorded history, and in history we discover that

the Christians there were enduring great difficulty. In the
first four verses of this chapter, we can read between the
lines a very pessimistic mood that produced the most positive letters we have in the Scriptures. As we use reverse
interpretation, we can perhaps discover some of the causes
of their pessimistic mood, and these correspond with some
of the causes of depression. We do have to be careful here so
we do not oversimplify.

Feeling Defeated by Life's Circumstances: Verse 1

"Stand fast in the Lord," Paul says. They were almost
ready to buckle under the pressure of the persecution they
were facing. Paul used the term, "My dearly beloved,"
which is a term of warmth, for he hoped to relieve some of
the pressure. One of the causes of depression is the feeling
of inadequacy or the inability to cope with life's problems.
Imagine a balance scale. On one side of the scale we find
the positive attributes we have, either real or imagined.
The only thing that carries weight is what we perceive we
have available to do battle in life. Most of us have more
than we think or use. On the other side of the scale are the
weights or problems we have. These also can be real or
imagined. Imagined problems are as heavy as real ones.
Now, if the problem side in our mind outweighs the attributes side, depression sets in, for we begin to doubt our ability to cope.

Circumstances often seem to warrant depression. In
his book, *Psychology and Religion,* Charles T. Holman tells
the story of a young man who seemingly had everything
going for him. He had a successful business and a wonderful family. Then the war came, and he was drafted. While
serving in the service, he lost his business, a child died, and
he was terribly injured. He became very depressed and
even suicidal. His circumstances seemed to warrant his depression. Yet we read the story of H. G. Spafford who lost
his home in a fire and both of his daughters in a shipwreck,
and he was able to write, "When peace like a river attend-
eth my way, when sorrows like sea billow roll. Whatever

my lot, Thou hast taught me to say, 'it is well, it is well with my soul.'" Similar stories and yet different responses. We must remember there are two sides to that balance scale.

Relationship Problems: Verse 2

This passage has our only biblical mention of the two women, Euodias and Synthyche. We can assume that they both were very faithful women in the church, but they were not getting along, and this is very clear in the text. This relationship problem was affecting their spirit and the spirit of the church. We can see the seriousness of this conflict by the word Paul uses to address both of them. He repeats the same word. It is the word *parakalleō*. I beseech you. He besought them to be of the same mind, not to agree on everything, but in everything to be agreeable. To be in the right spirit, different but not divided.

Broken relationships are a great cause of depression. These are found in the home between mates, in the office between coworkers, and among longtime friends. Even the church is not immune from fractured relationships. Underline this in red, "Broken relationships destroy inner harmony."

I usually have a very slow thermostat when it comes to anger, but the other day I got angry at some news I heard, and I began to boil on the inside. It was amazing what happened to me. I lost my appetite, my ability to concentrate was decimated, and my stomach began to churn. I stopped and thought how foolish that was and dismissed it before it made me sick! It is no wonder people go around depressed with unresolved anger inside.

Years ago a woman came to see me, and she was indeed miserable and very depressed. The longer we talked, the more it became evident her major problem was a fractured relationship with a neighbor. She did not want to correct the situation. Finally she got so low, she would do anything. She made things right with her neighbor and over the succeeding months, became a radiant Christian. A fractured relationship is like holding onto a rattlesnake while it repeatedly bites you, putting its venom into your body. That is why Paul "beseeched" these two women to get their relationship straightened out.

Self-centeredness: Verse 3

Paul uses a very significant word here. It is the word "yokefellow," which means helper. He is saying, "Helpers, help them." Get your mind off your own insignificant problems and involve your energies in the problems of others. The yoke was a very useful tool for carrying or pulling a heavy load. It fit over the ox's neck and was designed often so you could put two oxen together to pull a load one could not pull by himself. It kept them from pulling in two different directions.

So often we are so busy doing our own thing that our energies are dissipated. Depression by its very nature causes a person to turn all energies in on self. This causes our burdens to grow out of their normal proportions. They become unreal to the extent that the mind begins to feed on itself until self-pity sets in. Paul says for us to get involved in the lives of others. One of my greatest disappointments in the ministry is seeing the self-centeredness of Christians more concerned about being ministered to than ministering. Sure, we all need ministering to at times and we should be willing to accept the help of others, but not feed on ourselves.

Negative Thinking: Verse 4

They had become downcast in their thinking. It had become predominantly negative, and Paul had to use shock therapy. He said, almost as if shouting, "Rejoice, and again I say, rejoice." It is so easy to get in a rut of negative thinking, and subtly the rut gets deeper and deeper until there is no way out. It is like a mole. He lives so much underground that he eventually is blind to the light.

Years ago we had a dog name Heidi. She was more nervous than "Jello." At the slightest sound in our house, she would begin running around and around the house. Gradually a rut began to form around our house, and it got deeper and deeper until, before long, you could hardly see the dog's legs as she ran in that rut. Some people get in such a rut of negative thinking that they see only the negative by habit. You cannot reason with them for when you mention something positive, they have an arsenal of negatives to counter with. That is the stuff of which depression is made.

The Solution at Philippi: (4:5-13)

Moderation: Verse 5

Paul says, "Let your moderation be known unto all men." Barclay calls this one of the most untranslatable words in the New Testament. It was never meant in Paul's writings to justify a little bit of wrong. We can think of it as between strictness on the one extreme and total abandonment on the other extreme. The Pharisees represent the one extreme as they meticulously kept the law to a fault, to the exclusion of joy. The Herodians represent the other extreme as they knew no self-discipline at all. Too much of a good thing in many instances will kill, as well as too little. A friend in Africa loved the little African bananas. They are so tasty and so small, you can eat a number of them. He overdid it because they are not filling. He became dangerously ill as they overloaded his stomach. We can get so meticulous about detail that it adds too much weight to the burden side of the scale.

A preacher had a little black book in which he wrote everything and kept minute detail of every place he was to be and everything he was to do. He was fanatical about it. He had a nervous breakdown because of the stress of his perfection. As they carried him from his home on a stretcher, he threw his black book in the trash can, and that was the beginning of his recovery. A person too bound to rules never will run a risk and experience the miracle of God in that risk. They will hardly ever laugh for they will constantly be taking themselves too seriously. They are like the woman whose girdle is too tight or the man who continues to buy the same caller size, even though he knows his neck size has grown. This is not an admonition to forsake any of the moral laws of God or any of His precepts, but rather an admonition to enjoy His marvelous grace a little more.

Prayer: Verse 6

This is probably one of those exceptions to the rule just stated. I don't think there is any danger in the world of anyone getting too much prayer. I don't think we need to carry the moderation idea into this area. Prayer is a very broad subject, and there is no way we could ever cover it all in one message or a portion of one message. Let's analyze what Paul says in this next verse about prayer.

There are three distinct ideas of prayer here. When he used the word "prayer," he was denoting an attitude of worship; whatever it takes for us to come into the presence of God. In includes confession, rededication, and yielding. When he uses the word "supplication," he is referring to the asking of God specific petitions or requests based on need in our lives. He stresses everything in this, for there is nothing too large or too small for God to be concerned about in our lives, or to be able to fulfill within His will.

This includes solutions to specific problems and for direction in certain decisions we need to make. Here he uses the word "thanksgiving." He is referring to that attitude of praise or bragging on God. The more we brag on Him in prayer, the bigger He becomes in our lives, and the smaller our problems become to us. Paul says the result of this kind of praying is a wonderful kind of poultice to the soul and the emotion called peace. Isn't this what the depressed person really needs. During my dark nights of the soul, prayer became more essential to me than food. My physical appetite was gone, but my spiritual appetite was magnified beyond measure. Each time I came off my knees, I was a little nearer to victory. I had experienced a little more of the "Balm in Gilead."

Thinking Good: Verse 8

We do become what we think day in and day out. Paul reminds us of this as he tells us to think on those things that are good and pure. We live in a world that is wallowing around in the gutter and in filth. Everywhere you turn, you see it and hear it. I grieve over what our children are having to battle in order to keep their minds dirt-free. Our world is involved in an organized effort to wipe from the earth that which is pure and good. It is seeking total depravity. We ask "Why?" The answer is clear. If the whole world is depraved, the depraved minds will not be reminded of their depravity and will not feel any guilt for their depravity. Rest assured, the evil and negatives of this world will take over your mind, for your mind is programmed that way.

The question then is how do we counteract all this? We must reprogram our minds with the things of God and the things that are good. We must replace the carnal and the negative with the Holy and the positive. You will have to set your own sentry on your mind and have a built-in censor, for we have seen that the world is not going to do it.

Oh, we might get a few half-hearted warning labels on filth records just to get the criticism to die down, but that will keep no one from buying them. If anything, it will increase their sales, and the record people know this. You will have to be your own censor and teach your children to censor themselves. Set up in your mind an in-and-out basket, and you will be amazed at how refreshing this will be to your soul. It's little wonder there is so much depression today, and it will continue until we clean up the alleys of our minds.

Doing Good: Verse 9

Doing good follows thinking good. Our actions hinge on our thinking. In many cases depression is a result of unresolved guilt. It forms a vicious cycle. We feel guilty and try to hide that guilt by engaging in sinful pleasures of this world, adding then to the guilt, driving it deeper into our hearts. Paul says we need some good examples to follow. He is bold enough to say, "Follow me." Today we need some idol changes. Because persons play or sing music well does not mean they are good examples to follow. Because a person is a good athlete does not mean he is a role model.

A number of years ago, I was counseling with a lady laden with depression, and we were not making progress at all until we began to deal with guilt out of her past. The guilt was killing her until she got it resolved with God, and then gradually peace began to return to her. Some say that is old-fashioned, but so is God and so is peace.

Contentment: Verse 11

Paul, in this verse, is urging us to simplify our needs and our material expectations. This also is hard to do in today's world for every time we turn on the TV, someone is trying to sell us something or tell us of something that we simply cannot do without. But, when we do simplify our needs, more things thrill us and fewer things disappoint us. This takes a lot of the pressure off us because our material expectations are lower.

In my home as a boy, we did without a lot of things, but as I think back on it, I was a lot more thrilled with the simple things we did get to enjoy. We never had a TV when I was growing up, for my father felt it would draw him away from his studies, but the beauty of that, as I look back on it, is that we did a lot of talking to one another as a family. When our expectations outweigh our realities, it lessens the load on the burden side of the scale. A key word then is to simplify.

Confidence: Verse 13

The depressed person suffers from an ebb in self-confidence. Paul tells us we can have perfect confidence in Jesus Christ for any situation. Paul could not be intimidated by any person or circumstance. His confidence was not in his looks, for the descriptions we have are atrocious.

He admits himself that his speech was contemptible. He seemed to have the personality of a manikin. His confidence was in the Lord Jesus Whom he trusted with his past, his present, and his future.

Conclusion

The depressed person must get outside of himself if he is to find confidence that will stand the stress of today's world.

We can find victory over the valleys we now walk through, and those valleys, whether they be just low mood swings or dark nights of the soul, can be our best teachers, for they teach us about God and all His power.

Franklin D. Pollard

When the Light Goes Out Inside You
1 Samuel 16:14

It is a sad day when you realize the light has gone out inside you.

Tom Shipp was one of the greatest men *I've never known*. He was a minister in Dallas, Texas, a former professional baseball player, and a recovered alcoholic. I never met him, but I heard him tell this story.

One day, late in the afternoon, a man met Tom in the hallway of his church. "Say, Buddy," the man asked, "can you spare me a couple of bucks for a meal?"

"No, I can't," said Tom, "but I'll be glad to take you to dinner."

During the meal the unshaven, shabbily dressed beggar became uncomfortable when he noticed the preacher was looking at him.

"Why are you looking at me like that?"

"Because," said Tom Shipp, "I believe there's a lot more to you than can be seen right now. I have an idea the next time we meet you may be so changed I'll not recognize you."

An hour or so later, during a wedding rehearsal, Tom saw someone in the balcony of the church. The lights were not on in the balcony, but he could see a person in the shadows. When the rehearsal was over, he went up in the balcony and found his former dinner companion sitting there. Tom Shipp sat down beside the man. Neither of them said a word. For two hours they sat in silence. About midnight Tom said: "I've really got to go. I need to lock up the church. There's a funny thing about this church. When the doors are locked they can't be opened without a key from either side. You're welcome to stay but if you do, you won't be able to get out until the morning."

Now the beggar told his story. He had been a frustrated and defeated pastor of a fairly large church. One day the burden became too heavy. He simply walked away from his family and his ministry and for the past many weeks had just drifted from one city to another, living off the benevolence of churches. To complete the story, Tom Shipp says the man did return to his family and his church.

Yet here was one whose light went out for a while. Surely there once was a thrill in his calling, a joy in serving our Lord. But the light went out inside him. It happens.

The Light Goes Out

It happened to one of the most promising and powerful people in Israel's history. His name was Saul, the first king of God's people.

The ninth chapter of 1 Samuel tells us Saul was a favored son of a prosperous landowner. Verse 2 declares he was more handsome than any other man in the kingdom—and a full head taller.

One day Saul's father, Kish, sent him and a servant to find a strayed herd of donkeys. They searched long and hard but without success. Finally Saul said to the servant: "We'd better go back. My father will soon stop worrying about the donkeys and start worrying about us" (see 1 Sam. 9:5).

The servant had heard of a highly respected prophet who was nearby. The servant persuaded Saul to stay longer in order to find Samuel and ask for his help.

In the meantime God had revealed to Samuel that He had heard the people's prayers for a king and soon Samuel would meet God's choice for king of the land. The next paragraphs tell of God's convincing both Samuel and Saul that Saul was to be the king. The word declares the "Spirit of God came upon Saul" (1 Sam. 11:6). Immediately he became a valiant and wise warrior and leader. He was crowned king, the first king over Israel.

What a man! More handsome and at least six inches taller than any other man in the kingdom. He was *brave and wise.* He was *not proud and arrogant, but humble* and *reluctant to receive honor* from his people. He was *not vengeful* to those who opposed his appointment as king. You understand in those days, there was no two-party system because the defeated party was eliminated immediately after the election! He was blessed with the Spirit of God. The light of God's Spirit shone within him.

A few years later we see the same man. Still tall, of course, still handsome, *yet his face is changed.* There is a hardness, and a look in the eyes betrays the difference. Now he is vengeful, violent, suspicious, and unloving. Rest comes hard for him, and he must have music to soothe his frayed nerves. Once he commanded an admiring and committed army of thousands, but now his troops number in the hundreds, and they serve for reasons other than admiration of their commander. His own courage is gone. This once fearless warrior sits quaking in his tent while Goliath hurls insults at Saul, his army, and worst of all, at God every day for more than a month. *The dark around him mirrors the dark within him.* His light has gone out.

In 1 Samuel 16:14, we read the chilling words: "Now the Spirit of the Lord departed from Saul, and an evil spirit from the Lord terrorized him."

Reading through this section of Scripture brings both encouragement and warning. It floods our emotions with the thrill of the story of David's rise and the agony of Saul's tragic decline. *It pictures the joy of a sunrise in one life and the anguish of premature loss of purpose and light in another. Saul's decline was not a sunset. It was too early for the sun to set on his life.* It was an eclipse at midday—a sinful eclipse marked by decline and disobedience which led to frustration, darkness, and death. James 1:14-15 could be a commentary on the decline of Saul or any of us: "But each one is tempted when he is carried away and enticed by his own lust. Then when lust is conceived, it gives birth to sin and when sin is accomplished it brings forth death."

The Spirit of God departed from Saul. In the Old Testament the Spirit of God would come as God blessed and empowered people for their calling. His Spirit would leave when sin started the process of disqualification and death. With Pentecost, the Spirit came to stay in believers' hearts; but the power, the filling of the Spirit, is a thing we must seek continually in our daily walk.

The Presence of an Absence

It's a terrible thing Saul experienced. He experienced the agonizing presence of an absence. When that light in his life, that empowering presence of God, was no longer there, what great sadness and agony must have filled the dark hole it left! In fact, the next line in God's Word tells us the place the Spirit of God once had in his life was replaced by an evil spirit which terrorized him.

It is a tribute to the successful salesmanship of Satan that so many are missing the sweet spirit of God. Such an absence brings ultimate terror and death.

When the Bible tells us this evil spirit came from the Lord, it may be reflecting the Old Testament view that everything good or bad came from God—in the sense that God allows us a free will, which means we must face the consequences of our behavior, it is true. When our Lord Christ came, He taught there is a battle raging, and we are the objective of both sides. To choose to follow the leading of the Spirit of God is ultimate victory and heaven. To follow the way of sinful self and Satan is to experience ultimate defeat and hell.

Saul was experiencing this tragic absence of the presence of God.

This is a hard thing for anyone to be out of touch with the best in them. But it is a most difficult time for a Christian. When once you've known the blessing of His filling, and you've lost that, it is a tragic loss. Although people without Christ are facing the judgment of God and eternity without Him, it doesn't bother most of them. They simply refuse to think about it. The first chapter of Romans declares that they choose to darken their minds. In the name of wisdom they became fools (Rom. 1:22-23).

But when someone has known the exhilarating presence of our Lord, has gloried in the glow of new life in Christ, and then lost that awareness of His presence, how hard it is.

How Does It Happen?

How does it happen? Why did Saul lose the blessing of God in his life? Why do we? Saul disobeyed God. He thought his way was better than God's way. He lost purpose in life.

It doesn't happen all at once. Even the road to hell is a gradual slope. Most on it don't even sense they're going downhill. So it is with sliding out of fellowship with God. It begins with a spiritual pride which assumes we know as much as, or sometimes more than, God about some things.

Of course a "spiritual giant" doesn't need to pray all that much. There's no need to spend time in God's Word. Gradually other things fill that space He once occupied. You may begin to become a religious critic. Instead of worshiping God, you become a sermon taster or a music critic. You pass judgment on everything and everyone around you. Your pet sins come back and are invited in for a visit. Then they move in.

Now your spirit is hard, critical. You don't enjoy being with God's people. Finally you realize your spirit is no longer in tune with His Spirit. Your light has gone dim. It is winter in your soul, and you begin to pray: "Lord, to my heart bring back the springtime. Take away the cold and dark of sin. Come into my heart, sweet Holy Spirit. Make me warm and tender once again."

It happens to most of us. Even David, "a man after God's own heart," yielded to the sin of "leaning to his own understanding," and thus started the death-producing sin cycle in his life. In Psalm 51 we read the lines most of us have felt: "Have mercy upon me O God . . . My sin is ever before me . . . Purge me . . . Cleanse me . . . Wash me . . .

Make me to hear joy and gladness. Hide Thy face from my
sins . . . Create in me a clean heart, O God . . . Don't take
your Holy Spirit from me . . . Restore unto me the joy of Thy
salvation . . ." Oh, the agony of the absence of God!

We Can Come Back

You know, of course, we can come back. We don't have
to stay in a cold spiritual winter. It can be spring again in
our hearts. David came back. Elijah did. Peter did, too. So
did the prodigal son. The Bible is a book about the Gospel of
beginning again. Ours is the God of the second chance, and
the third, and the fourth . . . and as many chances as we
need.

Paul W. Powell

How God Helps Us
2 Timothy 4:16-17

What the unbelieving world wants to know about Christianity is: Does it work? When the chips are down, when the heat is on, when the pressure mounts, can it stand the test? When the storms of life come, does faith in God make a difference?

The answer of both Scripture and experience is a resounding, "Yes! Christianity works!" The Lord does help us in life.

But how? The apostle Paul relates an experience out of his own spiritual autobiography that tells us how the Lord helped him and how He in turn can help us. Paul's experience occurred during his first imprisonment in Rome (2 Tim. 4:16-17). At that time Paul was required to stand trial for his life before a Roman court. The charge? Sedition. He was accused of being the ringleader of a group of insurrectionists. The outcome of that trial was acquittal of the charges made against him. Paul was set free to continue his missionary work. Years later, back in prison and facing almost certain death, Paul reflects on that first trial and tells us how God helped him.

Paul's testimony is filled with legal, technical language. It is language used in a courtroom and trial proceedings. Paul writes, "At my first answer no man stood with me, but all men forsook me."

The word "answer" means to make a verbal defense in one's own behalf. The word "stood" refers to the appearance of one person in a court of justice in behalf of another. It means to serve as a character witness in behalf of the accused.

At his trial, when Paul was called on to defend himself against the trumped-up charges alleged against him, no one came to his defense. No one stood with him or spoke up for him. All of his friends deserted him, and he was left to face his accusers all alone. Then he adds, "I pray that this will not be laid to their charge."

Paul then turns to the bright side of this difficult ordeal. He declares that while everyone else forsook him, the Lord stood with him and strengthened him, so he was able to turn his trial into a preaching opportunity. He used his defense arguments as a means of making the Gospel fully known to his accusers. If Nero presided over the trial of the apostle Paul he heard the Gospel that day.

Paul then says that the Lord delivered him out of the mouth of the lion. Who or what is "the lion" Paul refers to? It is not Nero, the emperor, for he ultimately won over Paul. It is not the lions of the arena because Paul was a Roman citizen, and Roman citizens were never thrown to the lions. The lion referred to here was Satan himself. Remember, Peter described Satan as "a roaring lion going about, seeking whom he may devour" (1 Pet. 5:8).

At the trial Satan would like to have silenced the apostle Paul so the Gospel could not have been preached. That would have been a decisive victory for Satan. But the Lord stood with Paul. God strengthened Paul, empowering him to preach the Gospel under the most trying of circumstances. Thus, God through Paul snatched victory from the jaws of defeat.

Paul concludes his testimony by saying, "And the Lord shall deliver me from every evil work, and will preserve me unto his heavenly kingdom."

In these words the apostle Paul describes how the Lord helped him, and how in turn the Lord helps us. If you examine Paul's testimony carefully you will note there are three ways the Lord helped him. First, He gave him grace for the disappointments of life; second, He gave him strength for the trials of life; third, He gave him hope for the end of life.

That's how the Lord helped the apostle Paul. That's

how He will help you and me today. If you are wondering, "Does Christianity work? Will it stand under the stress and strain of life?" the answer is an emphatic, "Yes. It worked for Paul and it will work for us."

How does God help us? In three ways:

Getting Even or Getting Ahead

First, He gives us grace for the disappointments of life. At his trial, when he was called on to make a defense of himself against the false charges of sedition, Paul declared, "No man stood with me, all men forsook me." The word "forsook" is the same word he used earlier in this chapter to describe the actions of Demas. Demas was one of Paul's fellow workers who had deserted him and the work of Christ because of the lure of the world (2 Tim. 4:10).

In the same way that Demas had deserted him, Paul's other friends also deserted him at his trial. No one stood with him; no one spoke up for him.

Obviously, there were some people whom Paul had reason to believe could have come to his defense. They knew full well that he was not an insurrectionist. They should have attested to his innocence. But, for some reason, perhaps out of fear for their own lives, they didn't. At a time when Paul needed support and encouragement the most, everyone let him down.

This had to be a great disappointment to Paul. It could easily have made him bitter and resentful. But there is none of that in Paul. He would not allow the fact that his friends had let him down, get him down. Instead of trying to get even with them, Paul rises above them and prays for their forgiveness. He writes, "I pray God that it may not be laid to their charge." Paul seeks no vengeance nor does he want God to.

This prayer of Paul's was not an original with him. It was a copy. He had heard it prayed in his own behalf years earlier. Before he became a Christian, Paul had been an accomplice to the stoning of Stephen. He hadn't actually thrown any rocks, but he had held the coats of those who did. As Stephen died, he prayed for his executioners, using the same words Luke later wrote, "Lord, lay not this sin to their charge" (Acts 7:60).

But this prayer didn't even originate with Stephen. Jesus was the first to pray it Himself when He cried from the cross, "Father, forgive them for they know not what they do" (Luke 23:34).

This prayer of forgiveness is nothing less than the work of grace in Paul's life. The same love of God that flowed from Calvary through Stephen now flowed through Paul and enabled him to pray for those who disappointed him and let him down.

What happened to Paul can happen to us. People disappoint us and hurt us. At a time when we need them the most, they let us down. Sometimes it is a mate. Sometimes it is a child. Sometimes it is a best friend. Sometimes it is a Christian brother. It may even be your pastor.

When that happens we can become so disappointed in them that we become angry and resentful toward them and toward God. We can nurse and rehearse our hurts until they smolder into bitterness. One of the sure signs a hurt has turned into bitterness is that we relive it, rehash it, and retell it again and again. We have not dealt with our hurts sufficiently until we dismiss them first from our conversation and then from our minds.

Bitterness is an emotional cancer. If you do not rid yourself of it, it will ultimately consume you. It will shrivel your soul like a raisin. Carrying resentments in your heart is like carrying a bag of stones. The longer you carry them, the heavier they become. And, if you aren't careful, you will eventually stumble beneath the weight of them and be crushed by them. So, collect postage stamps or coins if you will, collect autographs or bubble gum cards if you must, but don't collect resentments.

Dale Carnegie, in *How to Stop Worrying and Start Living*, wrote, "When we hate our enemies, we give them power over us—power over our sleep, our appetites and our happiness. They would dance with joy if they knew how much they were worrying us. Our hate is not hurting them at all, but it is turning our days and nights into hellish turmoil."[1]

Bitterness is the fruit of an unforgiving heart. We must therefore never allow our disappointments in others to canker into resentment by harboring them in our hearts. We must rise above resentment at all costs. We must remember the best and forget the rest. If we spend our time trying to get even we will never get ahead.

But how do we do that? Is it possible for us to really forgive those who let us down and disappoint us? Yes. Yes, it is. There is a way. It is by God's grace.

Just as it did with Paul, the grace of God that flows from Calvary to our hearts can enable us to rise above the disappointments and hurts of life and pray for those responsible for them. This grace to forgive is one of the ways God helps us.

Let the judges judge. Let the prosecutors prosecute. Let the juries condemn. You forgive and pray for those who hurt you. Never let the failures of others make you bitter or a quitter. God's grace will enable you to do that. That's one of the ways He helps us.

The Word of a Gentleman

There is a second way God helps us; He gives us strength for the trials of life. While all his friends forsook him, Paul declared, "Notwithstanding, the Lord stood with me and strengthened me; that by me the preaching might be fully known, and that all Gentiles might hear: and I was delivered out of the mouth of the lion."

The word "stood" as it is used here means to stand beside another in order to assist them. So, the Lord stood beside Paul and enabled him successfully to fulfill his mission of proclaiming the Gospel to the Gentile world.

I want you to note that the Lord did not save Paul from his trial, nor is he likely to save us from our trials either. He did not spare him from it, He rather strengthened the apostle in it and saw him through it. That is most often the way of God with His people.

The Lord didn't save Daniel *from* the lion's den; he saved Daniel *in* the lion's den. He shut the mouths of the lions to keep them from devouring Daniel.

God did not save the three Hebrew children *from* the fiery furnace; He saved them *in* the fiery furnace. He entered into the furnace with them and became their shield to keep the fire from consuming them.

God did not route David around "the valley of the shadow of death"; He became David's shepherd and walked with him through it. God did not save Jesus from the cross; God glorified Him and saved us through the cross.

There is no promise from the Lord in Scripture that we as His people will be exempt from any of life's trials. Christians get cancer. Christians suffer heart attacks. Christians are involved in automobile accidents. Christians lose their jobs. Christians go broke. Christians die young. Christians experience every heartache imaginable.

Health and wealth are not our automatic birthright. Strength and success are not fringe benefits that come with salvation. We are promised no exemptions from and no explanations for the trials of life. What we are promised is that the Lord will be with us in them and see us through them.

Listen to the promise of Isaiah, "When thou passest through the waters, I will be with thee; and through the rivers, they shall not overflow thee; when thou walkest through the fire, thou shalt not be burned; neither shall the flame kindle upon thee" (Isa. 43:2).

The favorite text of David Livingstone, the early English missionary to Africa, was the promise of Jesus. "Lo, I am with you alway, even unto the end of the world" (Matt. 28:20).

For thirty-two years he planted his life in that dark continent. Some men set themselves to evangelize; some make it their business to explore; others feel called to emancipate; but Livingstone undertook all three!

Evangelization!
Exploration!
Emancipation!
Those were his watch words. No man ever set himself a more tremendous task. No man ever confronted his life's work with more serene and joyous confidence! At times he was surrounded by hostile and infuriated savages. At times his life was in imminent peril. At times his body was so wracked with pain he could hardly keep going. At times he was the victim of merciless and scandalous gossip. Disease and death, disappointment and discouragement were his constant companions. But again and again Livingstone came back to this text on which he staked his life. A thousand times or more he would put his finger on that verse and say, "It is the word of a gentlemen of the most strict and sacred honor, so there's an end of it!"

But let me quote from his own journal; it will give us the rest of the story.

"January 14, 1856. Evening. Felt much turmoil of spirit in prospect of having all my plans for the welfare of this great region and this teeming population knocked on the head by savages tomorrow. But I read that Jesus said: 'All power is given unto me in heaven and in earth. Go ye therefore and teach all nations, and *lo, I am with you alway, even unto the end of the world.*' It is the word of a gentlemen of the most strict and sacred honor, so there's an end of it. I will not cross furtively tonight as I intended. Should such a man as I flee? Nay, barely I shall take observation for latitude and longitude tonight, though they may be the last. I feel quite calm now, thank God!"[2]

The words in italics are underlined in the journal, and they were underlined in his heart.

He anchored his life to the promise of Jesus, and so must we. We may have to sleep in the lion's den as Daniel did. We may have to stand in the fiery furnace as the three Hebrew children did. We may have to walk through the valley of the shadow of death as David did. We may even have to die on a cross as Jesus did. But if we do, He will be with us and strengthen us. And I believe that if he is with me, He and I can handle anything life brings. I can count on His promise, "I will never leave thee, nor forsake thee" (Heb. 13:5). That is the word of a gentlemen of the most strict and sacred honor, so that's the end of it.

The Lord strengthened Paul, and He will strengthen you. That's how He helps us.

Horizons Now—Heaven Then

There is a third way the Lord helps us: He gives us hope for the end of life. Hope, according to the Bible, is not mere expectation. It is a well-founded, well-grounded expectation for the future. What then is our hope? It is the hope of heaven.

Listen to the apostle Paul! Having affirmed that the Lord had delivered him out of the mouth of the lion, he then declares, "And the Lord shall deliver me from every evil work, and will preserve me unto his heavenly kingdom."

When Paul penned these words his own death was imminent. Earlier in this chapter he had said, "The time of my departure is at hand. I have fought a good fight, I have finished my course, I have kept the faith: henceforth, there is laid up for me a crown of righteousness, which the Lord, the righteous judge, shall give to me at that day: and not to me only, but unto all them also that love his appearing" (2 Tim. 4:6-8).

Paul had run out of time, but he had not run out of hope. He looks beyond this life and sees heaven awaiting him. Time eventually runs out for all of us. George Bernard Shaw was right, "Life's ultimate statistic is the same for all men, one out of one dies." But Christians never run out of hope.

Bishop William Quail boarded a train one day and sat down next to a group of salesmen. They did not know he was a minister, and one of the turned to him and asked, "Sir, what do you sell?" He replied, "I sell horizons now and heaven then."

Heaven then! That is our hope, and it is well-founded

and well-grounded. It is founded on and grounded in the death, burial, and resurrection of Jesus Christ. Because He lives, we shall live also (John 14:16).

An unknown poet expressed this hope when he wrote:

> The hands of Christ
> Seem very frail.
> For they were broken
> By a nail.
>
> But only they
> Reach heaven at last
> Whom these frail, broken
> Hands hold fast.

Eric Nelson was a pioneer missionary to the Amazon Valley of Brazil. For years he sailed the Amazon on riverboats establishing churches in the villages along its banks. In his biography, *The Apostle of the Amazon*, he speaks of our hope. At a Sunday service on one of the ships, the daughter of the captain seemed in perfect health; the next day she was dying. The girl had been studying medicine. When the father was informed that her condition was hopeless, he told her to listen to the advice of the missionary and prepare to die.

She fixed her eyes on him and said, "Dad, since Mother died two years ago, you have been telling me that there is no heaven or hell; and now you are telling me to prepare for death."

"Do not think of what I have told you, but remember what your mother taught you," he replied. "Believe in Christ."

"Then this is the end of it all," she said. "I have been preparing myself to be useful as a doctor; now this is the end of it."

She was told that this was not the end. If she would believe in Christ, she would have all eternity to serve her Savior. She was able to grasp the truth that had been taught to her by her mother and retaught by the missionary.

"Dad, what do you want me to tell Mother?" she asked.

"Tell Mother that I am coming, too," he replied.[3]

No matter what happens to us in this world, as the people of God we are never without a future hope. The promise of eternal life is always before us, "He shall preserve us unto His heavenly kingdom." And with that hope we can cope!

Do you see, then, how the Lord helped Paul? He gave him grace for the disappointments of life, strength for the trials of life, and hope for the end of life.

There is a famous story of Roland, an officer in the army of Charlemagne. He was in charge of the rear guard of the army, and he was suddenly caught by the Saracens at Roncesvalles. The battle raged fiercely against terrible odds. Now Roland had a horn called Olivant which he had taken from the giant Jatmund. And its blast could be heard thirty miles away. So mighty was it that, as they said, the birds fell dead when its blast tore through the air.

Oliver, Roland's friend, implored him to blow the horn so Charlemagne would hear and come back to help. But he was too proud to ask for help. One by one his men fell fighting until only he was left. Then at last, with his dying breath, he blew the horn, and when Charlemagne heard it he returned quickly. But he was too late. Roland, too, was dead.

Roland was too proud to ask for help. It is easy to be like that—to think we can handle life's problems all by ourselves. What a tragic mistake.

Do you need help with life? If so, don't be too proud to ask the Lord. He's in the helping business (see Heb. 4:16). In the same way the Lord helped Paul, He will help us if we will let Him.

NOTES

1. Dale Carnegie, *How to Stop Worrying and Start Living* (New York: Pocket Books, Inc., 1953), p. 114.
2. George Seaver, *David Livingstone: His Life and Letters* (New York: Harper & Brothers, 1957), p. 85.
3. Lewis Malen Bratcher, *The Apostle of the Amazon* (Nashville: Broadman Press, 1951), p. 83.

Nelson L. Price

Overcomers

1 John 5:1-5

Jesus Christ said, "In the world you will have tribulation; but be of good cheer, I have overcome the world" (John 16:33).[1]

He spoke of a complete and abiding victory, as is indicated by the perfect tense of the verb form rendered, "I have overcome."

The peace of Christ which a believer can experience on the inside should be completed and complemented by "cheer" on the outside.

As I have often heard, "If you have Christ in your heart, notify your face."

Christ met His and our worst enemy, Satan, and was victorious over him. Because of Christ's victory, we work *from* victory, not *for* victory. It is Christ's victory in us that enables us to be victorious.

By total confidence in and dependence upon the Father, He won the victory. All that the Father was to the Son, the Son wants to be to us. All that the Son was to the Father, we are to be to the Son.

Our King has met the "prince" of this world and defeated him. The world is still the same, and the battle must constantly be enjoined, but the victory is assured. Take courage. As with Him, so it must be with us: no compromise, no fellowship with the world, and no surrender to it.

Our Lord's shout of victory is: "To him who overcomes I will grant to sit with Me on My throne, as I also overcame and sat down with My Father on His throne" (Rev. 3:21).

Jesus in finishing His discourse with the disciples in

the upper room on the eve of His execution spoke these words. Referring to the fact that the prince of this world, Satan, had come, Jesus said, "Arise, let us go . . ." The battle in which He was to win the ultimate victory for us was at hand—Calvary.

Application in daily life is essential in order to enjoy His victory. Simply greeting some Christians can be depressing. Just a casual, "How are you?" can break your heart. You run the risk of being pulled aside and shown gall bladder X-rays. Depressing utterances such as, "Oh, pretty good under the circumstances," are intoned. In summary, most of our responses to greetings are negative.

Try this for style. "How are you?" "Thanks for asking. I'm overcoming."

Many people aren't overcoming because they live in a state of shock and surprise failing to realize Christ said there would be . . .

I. Opposition

You *will* have tribulation . . .

In 1 John 5:4 the word "world" translates *kosmos*. As used here, it refers to all forces opposing the new life principle found in Christ.

The prophetic pen of the poet William Wordsworth in part explains what often diminishes our victory.

> The World is too much with us; late and soon,
> Getting and spending, we lay waste our powers;
> Little we see in Nature that is ours;
> We have given our hearts away, a sordid boon!

John appeals: "Love not the world or the things of the world. If anyone loves the world, the love of the Father is not in him" (1 John 2:15).

Again, the word "world" is used in summary of Satan's system for opposing the Kingdom of God. With this in mind John writes, ". . . the whole world lies under the sway of the evil one" (1 John 5:19).

The world system is dedicated to opposing every be-

liever in every act of faith. Don't, therefore, be shocked
when opposition is encountered. Expect it and be prepared
for it. As combatants preparing for engagement with the
enemy, so must believers. Regimentation results in rejoicing. Daily exercises in prayer, Bible study and memoriza-
tion, meditation on the Word, and verbalizing your faith
help prepare for combat. A state of perpetual alert avoids
surprise attacks. Don't just expect adversity; anticipate
victory through Christ. Live with the dynamic of an . . .

II. Overcomer

He who overcomes the world . . .

The very word "overcome" implies opposition. The
greater the obstacle to be overcome, the sweeter the victory.
Victory by Christ over the world's triumvirate of sin, death,
and the grave should stimulate us to rejoice. He has overcome the maximum opposition the world could marshal.
Sweet is His shared victory. If He has overcome the ultimate enemies—and He has—that should give us confidence
in His capacity to enable us to overcome a defeated foe.

A. *The Reason*

Cheerfully, not begrudgingly, we should approach our
challenges. "Overcomes" is a verb form which speaks of a
continuous victory in a continuous struggle. There will be
no time in this life we can take off the "whole armor of
God." Don't be preoccupied and wearied by the fact that
ours is a "continuous struggle." Fix your faith on the "continuous victory." To live expectantly is to live cheerfully. Be
of good cheer.

The word "victory" in the text is a verb form which
speaks of a single victory. The single victory was Christ's
victory over the world. Because of that single victory, we
have the potential of a continuous victory. Because of His
victory, we are called "overcomers."

Hate is overcome by love (1 John 2:9).

Lust is overcome by temperance (1 John 2:17).

Deception is overcome by consistency (1 John 2:19).

Death is overcome by life (1 John 2:25).
We must not merely talk tough but rather walk triumphantly. We must live out our quotes from God's Word such as . . .

> My God shall supply all your need according to His riches in glory (Phil. 4:19).

If you believe that, act with the cheerful expectation of one awaiting His imminent delivery.

> I can do all things through Christ who strengthens me (Phil. 4:13).

If you believe that, flex your faith and respond courageously, even boldly.

Nature abounds with physical illustrations of physical overcomers. Just outside Tucson, Arizona, is the captivating Desert Museum. The variety of wild life displayed in a natural habitat is extensive. Creatures of all sizes are exhibited: bear, panthers, hogs, eagles, beaver, and mountain sheep are a few. Many of these animals would not be expected in the desert. However, they have adjusted and overcome the desert. Walking through the museum one can find inspiration for living in a spiritual desert and overcoming. They have done so by physical adjustment. We can overcome our spiritual desert by internal, eternal resources.

B. The Resources

There are two resources noted in 1 John 5:4.

1. BIRTH—". . . whatever is born of God . . ."

A believer's birthright makes available indispensable resources. At the time of natural physical birth, all resources of the father that the father wants to share with the child are immediately the assets of the child.

At the moment of spiritual birth the inventory of assets belonging to the Heavenly Father, which the Father desires to give, become yours. In failing to know this fact and the facets of it, we lay waste our powers. When engaging in spiritual warfare, we need to use the weapons in our arsenal and not those of the world. To fight with the weapons of the world against the world is to lose. When the King's weapons are used, the world does not understand them and has no defense. Truth, love, grace, joy, patience, faith, hope, steadfastness, consistency, temperance, and a thankful heart are winning weapons.

The word translated "victory" was used to mean "to have knocked the weapons out of the hand of the enemy." Thus, Satan and his worldly warriors are seen as defenseless against our Lord. He being our Champion assures us of potential victory if we only properly align ourselves with Him.

There is a counterpoem to "Invictus" by W. E. Henley written by Dorothea Day entitled "My Captain" which expresses our victory through Christ.

> Out of the light that dazzles me,
> Bright as the sun from pole to pole,
> I thank the God I know to be
> For Christ—the Conqueror of my soul.

That kind of confidence comes from . . .

2. BELIEF ". . . our faith . . ."

Faith is mere confidence in God's character. If you believe God is as good as His Word, then you can believe that His Word is as good as He. It then becomes a matter of confidently relying on Him and His Word.

In the introduction to his commentary of Romans, Martin Luther defines faith for us: "Faith is confidence in God's grace so strong and so confident that a man will stake his life on it a thousand times." He then went out and provided us a living example of his definition. The lost world is awaiting your demonstration of this definition.

Everyone has faith. It is not a question of whether or not one has faith. It is a matter of in what one places their faith. Everybody has strong faith.

Robert Jastrow, noted astrophysicist, not a professing believer, in an address to the American Association for the Advancement of Science, noted: "For the scientist who has lived by his faith in the power of reason, the story ends like a bad dream." He was thus saying that even scientists operate by faith. If not in God, at least in his own power of reasoning.

Every time we drive in the rain, fly in a plane, buy or sell on credit, make a date, or get married, we are exercising faith.

To eat in a restaurant is a classic exercise in faith.

We go to doctors we don't know. They give us a prescription we can't read. We take it to a pharmacist we may never see, and he gives us medication about which we know nothing. We then take it—by faith.

Faith is not saying that we believe what God says is true; it is acting on it because it is true. It is not blindly believing in spite of evidence; it is boldly obeying in spite of consequences.

"Faith . . . is the victory that overcomes the world." It enables us to overcome twin threats of faithfulness.

Temptation is one. The world invites every believer to its perennial vanity fair. It appeals to our cravings and fantasies with craftily varied displays. Faith gives us victory by reminding us of the following:

The passing nature of temptation. The "pleasures of this world are but for a season," but "at His right hand are pleasures forever more."

The product of yielding. Grief and guilt are unheralded results of yielding of which faith reminds us.

The pleasure of faithfulness, its gratification and rewards, His "well done" is kept in focus by faith.

Terror is the other. The world seeks to intimidate us. Faith reminds us of:

The *support* given in trial. He is with us and will never leave us. He will be with us always, even to the end of the world.

The *strength* of our Lord's example and those who have faithfully followed in His train.

The *stimulus* resulting from our eternal hope in Christ.

Hebrews 11:1,3 notes faith as being: "substance . . . evidence . . . understanding."

The word rendered "substance" is a term used to describe a chemical compound which has been shaken up. When it settled that which collected at the bottom was called the "substance." When a life-shaking experience happens, faith might well be all that is left. Often believers are heard in times of crisis to say, "My faith is all I have." In such an uncomfortable and uneasy moment Christ often becomes most trusted. He is always trustworthy when trusted and dependable when depended upon.

The term "substance" was also used of a title deed. Thus, it suggests that faith is our title to victory. If you have the title to a piece of property, you have the property. When you have faith, you have the product of its object— Christ. The product is victory.

Remember, He warned there will be "tribulation." When it comes, don't act betrayed. God has at no time promised immunity to anyone from trouble or exemption to anyone from problems. The "trouble" is the combat. Overcoming it through faith is the victory. If you want the *victory*, you must have the *venture*.

J. B. Phillips' *New Testament in Modern English* translates James 1:1-4 in such a way as to help us interpret tribulation.

> When all kinds of trials and temptations crowd into your lives, my brothers, don't resent them as intruders, but welcome them as friends! Realize that they come to test your faith and to produce in you the quality of endurance. But let the process go on until that endurance is fully developed, and you will find you have become men of mature character with the right sort of independence.

Bronze that and put it on the mantel of your mind.

In George MacDonald's work entitled *Robert Falconer* he wrote: "This is a sane, wholesome, practical, working faith: first, that it is a man's business to do the will of God;

second, that God takes on Himself the special care of that man; and third, that, therefore, that man ought never to be afraid of anything."

That is an overcoming life of faith. We seem to pretend to trust God but not to believe He is trustworthy. That is, we talk tough but walk timid. Our faith is embellished with words, but our works aren't garnished with victory. If we profess to have faith in God, we should act as though what He has promised has already been received. Perhaps it hasn't; but based on His character, you can be assured it is in the process of being delivered. Faith is "substance."

Faith is "evidence." The term was used to speak of convicting testimony given in court. Faith is demonstrable proof that we trust God.

By faith we "understand." It gives life meaning. We are thereby enabled to comprehend God's Word and will. Where faith abides, a confidence remains that there is a purpose in what is happening in our life.

When we know, understand, and trust the object of our faith, this becomes more reasonable. The God who conquered Cana is waiting upon your faith to enable you to conquer currently. The God who spoke galaxies into existence is the God deserving to be the object of your faith.

John bears record of Whom we are to have faith in. He speaks of Him as "Jesus is the Christ . . . born of God . . . the Son of God."

His three-fold ministry meets the needs of man's three-fold nature. Our nature consists of intellect, emotions, and will.

There is threefold sin in our life.

a. Intellectually we have our "understanding darkened" (Eph. 4:18).

b. Emotionally we are "unhappy" (Rom. 7:24).

c. Our will is "evil" (John 3:19).

Christ has a threefold office.

a. Prophet

b. Priest

c. King

Christ offers threefold salvation.

a. As Prophet, He enlightens our darkened understanding.

b. As Priest, He cancelled our guilt and delivered our feelings.

c. As King He rules and guides us on the path of holiness.

This is the Christ deserving and desirous of our faith. In this fact we place our faith and rest our feeling.

An old story illustrates this. Allegedly, Feelings, Faith, and Fact went walking one day. Their path took them along a perilous mountain trail that seemed to grow ever more narrow.

Fact knew the way and walked out front. Faith walked close behind and kept his eyes on Fact. As long as Faith did, he was stable. Feelings kept wavering and complaining as a result of constantly looking at the circumstances. Faith was soon distracted by Feelings and, looking around to consider Feelings, lost his footing at the same time Feelings did. They both, having their eyes off Fact, fell from the path onto a narrow ledge. Fact reached down and helped Faith back onto the path. They together struggled to get Feelings back on the path also.

That parody is descriptive of the sequence of events involved in many of our life experiences. Faith must ever look forward to facts and never back at feelings. Fact and faith together must often superimpose their will on feelings.

III. The Obedient

Keep His commandments . . .

"His commandments are not burdensome." His instructions are not irksome because they are insights for victory.

Soldiers who know their orders are being given them directly from a successful, schooled, and skilled strategist listen attentively and respond faithfully. Their victory will depend upon their knowing and executing faithfully the orders of their advisor/commander.

Our obedience to Christ goes even further. We should take delight in doing His commandments because of the love factor involved. No lover finds it burdensome to do what pleases the one dearly loved. Christ loves us. He has never asked us to do one thing that was not birthed by love. He has never asked us not to do anything for any reason other than love. Love lives to please.

The sooner we realize that His commandments are expressions of His love for us, the more gratified we will be in doing them. They are actually statements of His best wishes for our welfare. His is the counsel of Heaven intended for earthly application.

Persons who have faith in that fact look for occasions to make application for His commandments. The greater our faith the stronger our desire to do His will.

In a crisis moment the day before General Eisenhower was to lead the Allied Forces in one of the most decisive battles along the Rhine River, he was approached by a panicked young soldier. The lad pled to be sent back because he was sick. His appeal was denied by the field general. He then begged to be sent home to help his mother in her time of need. Again the request was turned down.

As the general was about to leave he turned to the youth and said, "Would it make you feel better if we met here tomorrow morning and went down to the river together?" Biographers tell of the young man bravely walking down to the river by the general's side with great courage. The victory was theirs. Together they overcame. Guess who was the greater contributor to the victory?

The general's commands were not irksome. Not only were they not a burden, but they were a blessing.

A perfect God has no problem authorizing a perfect Bible. If it is His Word, and it is, it is authoritative because of its Author. If it is authoritative, and it is, it should be allowed to exercise authority over our lives. It, being His command, should be joyfully obeyed. When it is, the obedient one is a victor.

In an athletic contest, even when the victory is conclusive but the game still not over, every participant wants to do his best until the final whistle. There is a desire for victory to be paralleled by personal faithfulness. Christ's victory has assured the believer of victory. Nevertheless, there should burn within each of us a desire to be found faithful right through our final brain wave.

Faith is foundational to faithfulness. Faith is the only basis for co-victory with Christ. Faith is the divinely appointed means for conveyance of God's power to us. It is the unalterable condition of salvation, the first breath of new life, and the basis for the coronation of Christ in our hearts.

Only one who is "born of God" and who "believes that Jesus is the Son of God" is partaker of His victory and overcomer of the world. This occurs when the three aspects of our nature concur and unconditionally commit our love to Christ.

Our intellect confesses acceptance of the historical truths and spiritual nature of Christ. That is good, but that is not good enough.

Our emotions concede expressively deep feeling about the love of God—and sow it variously. That is good, but that is not good enough.

Then our will concurs with our intellect and emotions, confessing, "I will that my will be Thy will." That is good. That is good enough to be "born of God."

This repentant, receptive response to Christ as Savior by faith enables one to be "born of God" into the Kingdom of Overcomers.

NOTE

1. Unless otherwise noted, all Scripture in this chapter is from the *New King James Version*.

Joe Samuel Ratliff

From Whence Cometh the Power?
Isaiah 40:31

> But they that wait upon the Lord shall renew their
> strength; they shall mount up with wings as eagles;
> they shall run, and not be weary; and they shall
> walk, and not faint (Isa. 40:31).

The modern church boasts of her capacity to reach millions through her massive buildings, with all the machin-
ery in place and the manpower properly trained and
assigned. She stands dazzled, awed, and even confused in
the keen awareness of the growing gap that exists between
"what the church is" and "what the church ought to be!"

This agonizing experience has taught us some things.
We've learned that religion reforms; sin deforms; education
informs; and that only the Spirit transforms. Knowing this
truth, then why can't we fill the gap between our "isness"
and "oughtness"? From whence cometh the power for us,
the church, to become the salt, the light, the change agents,
the transformers?

The prophet Isaiah found himself attempting to speak
to a people in Exile and forewarn them of their impending
fate. Noting their inability to control their situation, he
points them to the God of their fathers as the source and
resource of their needs and wants.

This generation is so far removed from the Exodus
event. The dramatic assurances and confidences garnered
by those of prior ages lose their appeal and poignancy.

Is this not what is happening to us? The more time
removes us from the watershed experiences of our collective
existence, are we not leaning toward our own understand-

ing and knowledge of the problems that haunt us and the facts that stunt our growth? These are too much for us!

What a waste? To know you have a problem, be in the reach of a solution, and stand powerless to change! From whence cometh the Power?

I've noted the people I've labored with over the years, and recently there has been a growing number who seem to be experiencing *burnout*. They're tired, weary, worn, and simply out of fuel. Their source of energy does not match their responsibility. All the efforts to better themselves and the world seem futile. Many are exhausted, detached, cynical, irritable, and suspicious! How can we expect such to be salty, the light to the world, change agents, transformers?

The church must constantly redefine its mission statement. The Great Commission summons us to go, to wait, and to be. We are to be the expression of His person and presence in this world and, more importantly, exhibitors of His Power.

We must deliberately work to make sure our calendars are not full of activities only and void of ministries.

Jesus summons us to go into Jerusalem, Samaria, and to the most distant "uttermost parts" unknown. This is not to be done in any particular order—but all at once. What a task? Such a task is too much for us! From whence cometh the Power?

The church then becomes the church on the move! Given these marching orders we must go! And as we go we must attack evil systems, and evil moves by evil men which produce evil results that threaten our physical, social, and moral existence.

Our reason to go is our reason for being. We must be His witnesses. His desire to be our liberator from sin and oppression must be understood, accepted, and acted upon! We must never become so heavenly righteous that we are no earthly good.

To ignore the evils of a South African system of apartheid, or even worse to remain silent about such injustice, makes our purposes and witness suspect. Such an issue points to our perceived powerlessness. For what can we do? Such a task is too much for us! From whence cometh our Power?

Rehearsing the perils of their exilic state and noting their encroaching captivity, Isaiah challenges the hopelessness of their obvious inability to alter the prophecy with the words of our text.

I have long argued that these words spoken to heathens would not have meant much. But to believers, they are powerful! Many who have not exercised faith in their lives when crises come ask for Scriptures to inspire or comfort. But one must note quickly that for the believer to hear again the promises of God based upon experience is music to one's ears. Such rehearsals induce confidence in a God who is willing and able to liberate from sin and oppression.

In verse 28, he asks "Hast thou not known? Hast thou not heard, that the everlasting God, the Lord . . . fainteth not, neither is weary?" This summons us as a people, when faced with things too much for us, to be reminded from whence cometh our power.

For whatever is before us can be obtained, conquered, handled! For verse 29 says, "He giveth power to the faint and to them that have no might He increaseth strength." The church needs the power of God to infuse us so we can serve this present age. Isaiah divides the house and notes two characteristics: some are weary, and some are faint. A man once had two mules. One was named Able and the other Willing. Able was able but not willing! Willing was willing but not able. He had very little if any results.

The modern church is plagued with such a problem: some willing, some able; some weary, some faint. For those who are weary have lost their enthusiasm. They don't enjoy working in the kingdom anymore. They don't see anything changing. They think their labor is in vain. Others are faint, for they lack the strength to get anything done. How do we harness the latest energy of the church? How do we convince ourselves that God is able to pull off everything He promised? For when we are faced with our situations, with evil and corruption in high places, and then examine our resources and what we have as a people to work with, we get discouraged. "Even the youths shall faint [lose strength] and be weary [lose enthusiasm], and the young men shall utterly fail" (v. 30). But they that wait upon the Lord shall receive power!

Waiting is not idle, listless activity. It is an attitude of expectancy rooted in the hope of our salvation. It is the assurance that the God of our fathers insures the outcome. Waiting on the Lord is akin to watching a TV Western movie rerun and knowing the outcome.

They that wait shall renew their strength. God promises to exchange His strength with ours, to enable us to accomplish the impossible, the spectacular—to mount up with wings as eagles. Then He promises to give us the adrenalin to struggle, to run, and not be weary (lose enthusiasm). Moreover, He says He will prevent us from becoming bored with the mundane. We shall walk and not faint (lose strength). For it takes more power to walk than to run. Walk together, children, don't you get weary.

From whence do we get our Power? It is from the Lord. Since He calls us, He insures us. He gives us the power we need. He guards us with His presence. He bids us to go! Then He teaches and reminds us as we wait, and then He empowers us to be what He would have us to be.

How can we lose? Praise God from whom all blessings and power flow! "For I don't feel no ways tired. I've come too far from where I've started." Nobody told me that the road would be easy. But I don't believe He brought me this far to leave me. God is our Liberator from sin and oppression. He can match our energy with our responsibility. For when you are His, you can rest in the fact that He will protect you against failure. For when you are weak, He is strong.

For this is His battle, His Kingdom, His Power, and His Glory!

Darrell Robinson

And in Hell . . .

In the sixteenth chapter of the Gospel of Luke, our Lord Jesus Christ draws back the veil that separates the earthly from the eternal. He allows us to focus on the spiritual rather than the temporal.

In Luke 16:19, Jesus speaks about hell. "And He said there was a certain rich man." Jesus does not name the rich man, for there were still those where Jesus was speaking who were the man's relatives and friends. He names the poor beggar, Lazarus, who is in heaven with the Father. But not the rich man. But He says the rich man "was clothed in purple and fine linen and fared sumptuously every day." He had the finest of clothing. He had a splendid mansion in which he lived. He not only ate well, he had the delicacies of life. He had all he ever wanted to eat and wear. He was a very affluent person.

But the Scripture says, "There was a certain beggar named Lazarus which was laid at his gate, full of sores, desiring to be fed with the crumbs which fell from the rich man's table; moreover the dogs licked his sores."

The poor beggar, Lazarus, had not enough even to eat. He ate out of the garbage can of the rich man. And he was glad to get the crumbs. He was clothed in rags. His friends were the dogs of the street. The old street hounds rubbed against Lazarus's body and licked his sores.

"And it came to pass that the beggar died." There was no funeral mentioned for the beggar. His poor, diseased old body was simply raked up from the street by the street keeper and taken to the edge of the city of Jerusalem, cast down into the Valley of Gehenna where a perpetual fire burned, consuming the bodies of the dead like Lazarus.

But look! "The beggar died and was carried by the angels into Abraham's bosom." What a beautiful picture of the death of one of God's children. The angels carried him into the bosom of Abraham, into the presence of the Father, into the place of peace and rest. Lazarus received an angelic escort into the very presence of the Father.

Notice the teaching of our Lord Jesus about material things in this world. The pleasures, position, and power of this world really do not determine our status before God.

There is a brand of heresy common among us today that says if we really have faith in Christ, and if we really are abiding in righteousness with God, that we are going to be wealthy and affluent, and that God never withholds from one of His children any need or desire.

That is not true. The poor beggar, Lazarus, did not have enough to eat. His body was diseased. He was "full of sores." That same brand of religion says that if you really have faith, you will not get sick. Or if you do get sick, you quickly look to God and claim it from God, and God will immediately make you well.

But the beggar was full of sores. He died that way. Indeed, the condition of our physical body and our financial condition is *not* evidence of our soul's status before God. The poor man, Lazarus, was brought into the bosom of the Father.

But the Scripture says the rich man died and was buried. They had a great funeral for him. Without doubt, there was emblazoned across the headlines of the paper, "Philanthropist Dies." Listed are all of his wonderful achievements. His social, political, and civic contributions are enumerated. But the rich man died! There were eulogies at his funeral acclaiming the great exploits of this fine citizen.

The next verse declares, "And in hell he lift up his eyes being in torment, and he seeth Abraham afar off, and Lazarus in his bosom. And he cried and said, Father Abraham, have mercy on me, and send Lazarus that he may dip the tip of his finger in water and cool my tongue; for I am tormented in this flame."

This man prayed, but he prayed at the wrong time. He prayed the right prayer. But it was too late. "And Abraham said, son, remember that you in your lifetime received good things, and likewise Lazarus evil things; but now he is comforted and you are tormented. Beside all this, between us and you there is a great gulf fixed, so that those who would come from you to us cannot, and those who would come from us to you cannot."

Then he said, "I pray you therefore Father, that you would send to my father's house, for I have five brethren, that he may testify unto them, lest they also come to this place of torment.

"And Abraham said unto him, 'They have Moses and the prophets; let them hear them."

"And he said, Nay, Father Abraham, but if one went to them from the dead, they will repent."

"And he said, If they hear not Moses and the Prophets, neither will they be persuaded though one rose from the dead."

One DID rise from the dead. One DID come from the dead, declared the righteousness of God, and called men to repentance, *but* they *did not hear Him.*

Verse 23 of this passage contains the saddest words ever penned. "And in hell"—and in hell! The doctrine of eternal punishment is the most terrible of all the Scriptures. "In hell."

Although it is prominent upon the lips of the people of our world, the word "hell" today is noticeably absent from modern preaching. The average pulpit in our land has little to say about the subject of hell, if it is mentioned at all. But, if you leave the doctrine of "hell" out of your teaching, you literally cut the nerve of evangelistic fervency. For, if there is no hell, there is nothing from which people need to be saved. We preach hell as salvation by repulsion. We preach heaven as salvation by attraction.

There are two places of abode past this life, heaven and hell. We need to approach this subject with great solemnness and soberness. Our Lord Jesus warned, with tears in His voice, that men not come to this dreadful, terrible place called hell. A place of separation, eternally, from God.

The great evangelist of the past century, D. L. Moody, was seated around a conference table with the teachers of his institute. They were enjoying themselves, having fun as only Christians can have. They were telling their favorite stories and laughing. When one told a humorous story about hell, the others, except Moody, laughed.

Quickly, Moody was to his feet. He said, "Gentlemen, when you speak about hell, speak with tears in your voice."

Let us approach with our shoes off our feet, the holy word of warning of our Lord about this terrible place God calls eternal hell.

There are several words used in the New Testament translated, hell. One of them is the word, *Hades*. It is the equivalent of the Old Testament Hebrew word, *Sheol*. It means "the covered state." The state beyond which we do not go and cannot see. It is the realm of the dead. Jesus spoke about that realm of the dead as containing two areas or compartments.

First, paradise into which Lazarus was taken to be with the father, Abraham. In the bosom of Abraham there is joy and peace. There, all is well. Then Gehenna, the compartment of the dead without Christ, where the fire is not quenched and the worm never dies, where there is torment and separation from God forever and ever.

When the Lord Jesus died on the cross of Calvary, for three days and three nights He was in Hades, the Scripture says. He opened the compartment of Paradise, and He brought forth with Him the souls of the righteous dead into the presence of God the Father in heaven.

But the unrighteous and the ungodly remain in Hades in the place Jesus calls Gehenna. The word, Gehenna, is used twelve times in the New Testament. It comes from a Greek word which means "the son of Hinnom." It identifies a valley to the south of Jerusalem where Manasseh, the wicked king of Judah, set up idols and caused the people to worship them. He led them to offer their children as sacrifices to heathen idols. Human sacrifices were said to be made to pass through the fire. Manasseh even offered his own children as human sacrifices.

When Josiah, the good king, came to the throne, he destroyed the heathen idols and the altar. Josiah put a curse on the valley. He pronounced "anathema" over that whole valley. It was made the garbage dump for the city of Jerusalem. They brought the garbage and cast it down into the Valley of Gehenna. The bodies of the dead animals and the dead poor from the streets were cast into the Valley of Gehenna. A caretaker kept a perpetual fire burning. The maggots ate away at the dead bodies. And thus, Jesus speaks about the valley of fire, the Valley of Gehenna, the valley of filth, the garbage dump, where the fire is not quenched and where the worm dies not.

Another is the Greek word, *Tartarus.* In 2 Peter 2:4, he speaks about the wicked angels, imprisoned in Tartarus, in the bottomless pit of Revelation 9:11. Jesus speaks about hell in this story. Let us focus our thoughts on three ideas drawn from this passage.

    I. The Certainty of Hell

        Many deny hell and its existence. But it is declared by our own sensibility, by the Scriptures, and by the Savior Himself.

    II. The Characteristics of Hell

        What hell is like. It is a place of suffering. A place of sorrow. And, a place of separation.

    III. The Citizenship of Hell

        Who is going there? The Bible is explicit and definite about who is going to hell. You do not have to wonder, "Am I going to hell?" God pointedly declares who will be in hell.

Let us look first at:

I. The Certainty of Hell

The truth of hell is Scripturally irrefutable, yet many deny it. Many deny it like they deny the second coming of the Lord Jesus. In wishful thinking they block it from their minds, hoping it is not true. For they do not want to give up their ungodly and immoral way of living. They do not want to release the reins of their hearts to the Lord. In rebellion they live in opposition to God. They try to block out the reality of eternal retribution.

1. The Annihilationist Denies the Existence of Hell.

The annihilationist says that when you and I die, we simply cease to exist, like an animal—a dog, cat, or cow. He takes Ezekiel 18:4 and 20, where it says, "The soul that sinneth, it shall die."

He interprets that to mean the soul ceases to exist. But the Scriptures teach that spiritual death is not ceasing to exist. It is separation from God.

The annihilationist ignores Luke 16:19-31. Jesus *plainly* declared there are two places of abode after death— heaven with Him and an eternal hell in Gehenna fire, apart from Him.

2. The Universalist Denies the Existence of Hell.

This is the devil-inspired theory that ultimately all people will be saved. Such an ungodly doctrine literally cuts the nerve of evangelistic fervency. Sadly the heresy is creeping into many churches. It is rampantly spreading across our country.

The average congregation really does not believe in hell today. Oh, mental assent is given to the doctrine. But emotionally and spiritually, if we really believe in hell, we would go to those who are lost and declare the unsearchable riches of Christ, and warn them with tears in our hearts and eyes.

Do you believe that hell is real? If you do you cannot help but take the message of deliverance and salvation to the lost.

The report came to me that a certain preacher made the statement that he did not believe in hell. I couldn't believe it!

I picked up the phone and said, "My friend, I understand that it has been told that you do not believe the Bible, nor do you believe in an eternal hell."

He said, "Darrell, I can no longer build my life around an authoritative book, nor believe that when a man dies he will be eternally in hell, suffering forever. I can't believe in a God who will allow that to happen."

One of the greatest heresies pressuring the church today is the heresy of universalism. If the devil can convince us that there is no hell, we will have no concern about the destiny of our husband or wife. We will not care that our children do not receive Jesus Christ and confess Him. We will not care that the world around us does not acknowledge Jesus Christ. We will go on as if it doesn't matter.

The universalist denies the existence of hell.

3. The Sentimentalist Denies the Existence of Hell.

The sentimentalist says, "I believe in a God of love. I do not believe that God would send anybody to hell." And I tell you, He is right! God sends nobody to hell.

Second Peter 3:9 says that "God is not willing that any should perish, but that all should come to repentance."

If one moment after death you find yourself in hell, do not blame God! God has gone to the very limits of His being to rescue you and to save you. He has given His own Son to save you. If you go to hell, you will go because you have persisted to rebel against *every* appeal that God has given you to turn to Christ.

The sentimentalist denies the existence of hell.

4. The False Religionist Denies the Existence of Hell.

There is a heretical religion that has created a diabolical, mind-terrorizing doctrine of purgatory as a scheme to raise money and manipulate the minds of men. It tells us that there is a purgatory, an intermediate state into which man goes after he dies. There he burns out the dross of his sin and eventually is released to heaven, OR, if we who are left here will pay enough money, we can buy him out of purgatory.

It is a diabolical scheme to raise money and to control the minds of men. It has nothing to do with the Scriptures. The Bible never says any such thing.

The Declaration of the Certainty of Hell, of Its Reality

1. Sensibility Declares It.

Through the employment of human logic, we know there has to be a hell. With our finite system of justice, we confine the criminal, the rapist, and the murderer. We put them in prison, so they cannot walk in the midst of law-abiding citizens.

God with His infinite justice, with His perfect holiness, will not allow the unrighteous and the unregenerate sinner to stand in His presence in heaven. Besides, if He did, heaven would be hell to that one. If an unregenerate sinner were allowed into heaven, it would be hell to him. He could not stand it! Sensibility demands the reality of hell.

2. The Scriptures Demand It.

Someone says, "Oh, preacher, this stuff about hell I can't accept." With his sophistication and his pseudo-intellectualism he says something like, "I believe in a way of life based on the Sermon on the Mount. The Sermon on the Mount is my religion. 'Do unto others as you would have them do unto you.'"

That is a great religion to have. Have you read the Sermon on the Mount lately? Turn with me to the Sermon on the Mount. In Matthew 5:22 the Lord says, "But whosoever shall say, thou fool, shall be in danger of hell fire."

Look at verses 29 and 30. "If your right eye offend you, pluck it out and cast it from you. For it is better for you that one member of your body should perish, and not that your whole body should be cast into hell." The Gehenna fire! Look at it! In the very Sermon on the Mount, whatever in your life keeps you from Christ and commitment to Christ, cast it from you, for it is better to be rid of that thing than to be in hell forever.

Look at Matthew 7:13-14, the Sermon on the Mount again. The Lord Jesus said, "Enter the straight gate, for broad is the gate and wide is the way that leads to destruction, and many there be which go in thereat."

I could go on and on through the Scriptures, Matthew 8:12, 10:15, 13:40, 18:8, and 25:41. That is just in Matthew, not to mention countless other Scriptures where the Bible declares that hell is a reality and warns man to repent and turn to God to escape an eternal hell. The Scriptures declare the certainty of hell.

3. The Savior Declares It.

Jesus, as the greatest preacher on the subject of hell, marches through the Scriptures warning, warning, with tears for men to turn from that awful place of hell.

II. The Characteristics of Hell

Jesus told us what hell is like in Luke 16:19 and following.

A. It is a Place of Suffering.

The rich man in hell "lifted up his eyes." It is a place of physical suffering. With his physical eyes he looked up. He said, "Send Lazarus that he may dip the tip of his finger in water and cool my tongue for I am tormented in this flame." It is unthinkable and unspeakable, the physical agony of hell.

Our family was enjoying Fourth of July fireworks just outside the town where we pastored. Suddenly we heard the scream of an ambulance siren. We knew there had been a tragedy. Police sirens were also wailing. We rushed to the hospital just in time to see them take the body of a twelve-year-old boy whom we knew into the emergency room of the hospital. I had led his grandfather to the Lord and baptized him.

The little boy was visiting with his grandfather who lived next to an electrical plant. The boy had climbed the fence and up into a transformer to get a bird's nest. He was caught in the electrical current. Now he lay with his appendages burned from his body. His body was red with raw, burned flesh. He was in the greatest agony I have ever beheld. I simply cried, "Oh God, if you will, take him on from this suffering and agony."

But the boy lived on and on, day after day, in the agony of physical torture. As awful as that physical suffering was, it cannot compare to the physical agony and the inescapable misery of hell. But even that is not the worst part about hell.

B. It Is a Place of Sorrow.

The rich man cried. And Abraham said, "Son, remember, remember!" From the painful memory of past sin man forever attempts to escape. But in hell there is no escape! Man attempts to drown it with alcohol. To "drug it" with pills. If to no avail, he will pull down the shutters of his mind to block out the thought of the agony of his sin, of his misspent life, of his spurning appeal after appeal from God. Then, he will take an overdose or put a pistol to his head to "end it all." That does not end the anguish of the mind.

I preached the funeral of a forty-one-year-old woman who was unfaithful to her husband. She was with child by another man. She said, "There is no use, life is not worth living." The note she left said, "Hell could be no worse than this." But there is no escape from the agonizing memory of past sin. In hell the memory is intensified forever and ever. There is no escape.

C. It Is a Place of Separation.

It is separation from all that is good. Separation from God. It is the place of the hypocrite. It is the place of the filth of this world. It is the bottomless pit where man forever and ever descends deeper and deeper in moral and spiritual degradation. It is the refuse heap of eternity. The self-righteous are there. The proud are there. The hardened are there. It is a place of eternal separation from God.

Abraham said that no one can come from hell to heaven. There is "a great gulf fixed." There is NO HOPE! The most awful thing about hell is its hopelessness.

If one could go to hell for a thousand, a million, a billion years, with a hope that one day it would be ended, hell would not be hell. Its hopelessness is the awfulest aspect of hell.

III. The Citizenship of Hell

Who is going to hell? While none of us have the knowledge or the capability of answering this question, the Bible is very explicit about this. There are two groups. First, the unregenerate religious. Second, the unregenerate rebellious.

A. The Unregenerate Religious

There will be religious people in hell. Some who have been strongly involved in religion are not saved. They are religious but lost.

How sad are the words of Jesus in Matthew 7:21. "Not everyone that says to me, Lord, Lord, shall enter the kingdom of heaven. But those who do the will of my Father which is in heaven. There will be many in that day who will say to me, Lord, Lord, did we not do many wonderful deeds in your name? Did we not cast out devils in your name? But I will say to you, depart from me you that work iniquity, I never knew you." I never knew you! Does He know you? Is your name written in the Book of Life? Have you received Him as your Savior and Lord? Or have you just joined a church, been baptized, gone through the ritual, and done many good works? Jesus declared that unless one is born again, "he cannot see the kingdom of God."

The unregenerate religious will be in hell.

B. The Unregenerate Rebellious

In Revelation 21 is a list of people who will be in hell. "But the fearful and the unbelieving, the abominable and murderers and whoremongers and sorcerers, and idolators and all liars shall have their part in the lake which burns with fire and brimstone which is the second death" (Rev. 21:8).

Who will be there? Listed are the abominable. These are those defiled by the spirit and ways of the world. Their hearts have turned from God.

Murderers will be there. These are those who take the lives of others. God has given human life. It is sacred. Only God has the right to take life.

Whoremongers will be there. That is, those who are sexually impure.

Adulterers, fornicators, homosexuals. Those who reject the way of God morally and sexually for their lives.

Sorcerers will be there. Sorcerers include those into witchcraft, the binding of spells, soothsaying, astrology, worshiping the creation rather than the creator. There are those who live by their astrological charts. They guide their lives by what the stars say. They make decisions by their sign and its prediction for that particular day. God says they will have their part in hell. The Creator, God, is the only one who is to have authority over our lives. Not the creation, but the Creator. Order your life according to the Creator and God's will and Word for you.

The Greek word for sorcery is *pharmakia*. We get our word pharmacy from it. It means "drug users." There were those in that day, as this, who used drugs to superimpose a synthetic experience upon their lives. This gives a superficial kind of life. Life becomes unreal.

Somebody says, "What is wrong with drugs?" Drugs destroy the body, mind, and soul of man. Drugs cause one to approach life from an unreal perspective. The Lord cannot really govern a life controlled by drugs. They will send a person to hell.

Idolators will be in hell. These are those who give their lives to something other than God. All liars will have their place in the lake of fire.

Look at the head of the list. "The fearful and the unbelieving." The fearful is the Milquetoast character who is afraid of what others will say if he turns to Christ. Christ calls us to openly confess Him. Some are saying, "If I give my life to God, what are others going to say? If I really obey and follow Him, what are my friends going to say? What are the others in church going to say? I will go back to work; what will they say?" They are afraid to take their stand publicly for Christ and to walk with Him. They are fearful.

When Nicodemus and Joseph of Arimathea came to the cross to behold our Lord, they could no longer be secret disciples. They came forward in open confession of their commitment to request His body for burial. A true believer lays aside his cowardice and fear and takes his stand for Jesus Christ regardless.

The unbelieving is the person who refuses to receive Christ, commit his life to Him, and confess Him as Lord.

Who, then, can go to heaven? "Surely, everyone will be in hell," you might say. Yes, you've got the point. That is the point. We are sinners! We live in a world that is separated from God. There is no hope for any of us apart from Jesus Christ Who came into this world and gave His life for our sins on the cross. It is only by His forgiveness that you and I can escape hell and come to heaven. It is only as we are washed in the blood of Jesus Christ and cleansed by His Spirit and blood that we are saved.

Jesus said "I am the way, the truth, and the life; no man cometh unto the Father but by me" (John 14:6).

An old man was walking to church with his Bible under his arm one Sunday morning. He passed by three young skeptics. They decided to have some fun with the old man.

"Where you going, old man?" one shouted.

"I am going to church," he answered quietly.

"What is that under your arm?"

"It is my Bible, God's Word," answered the old man, holding up the Bible.

"Ah, old man," snarled one of the youth, "Where is hell?"

The old man paused, looked him in the eye, and said,

"Young man, hell is at the end of a Christless life."

You live your life without Christ, and one moment after death you will find yourself in hell.

But I ask you just now to come to Jesus. He is the Lord Who has given His life for you. He calls you to come to Him. It behooves us to come when He calls. He is calling your heart today. Come now. Do not hesitate. None of us have the guarantee of a second chance or of another appeal. Come to Jesus now!

Adrian P. Rogers

Mending Broken Brothers
Galatians 6:1-2

In this touching passage is more than a tremendous word of advice. It is an admonition and a commandment.

> Brethren, if a man be overtaken in a fault, ye which are spiritual, restore such an one in the spirit of meekness; considering thyself, lest thou also be tempted. Bear ye one another's burdens, and so fulfil the law of Christ (Gal. 6:1-2).

Do you know someone who used to walk with the Lord but who is not close to Him now? All through this message, think of the person who has been ambushed and sabotaged by the devil and who has fallen into sin and disrepute. They are broken, discouraged, and in the bondage of guilt.

Once that person loved God with all his heart, all his mind, all his soul, all his strength, but now he is a broken brother or a broken sister. Image that person in your mind, and even now begin to pray for that broken one.

Our Scripture is about God giving to us a ministry of restoration. Let us ponder this ministry which is imperative from God's standpoint.

In verse 1 we are instructed to "restore such an one." That word restore carries with it the idea of *setting a broken bone.* That is exactly how the word is used—to set a broken bone, but also to make it useful again. Now the word was also employed in reference to mending a broken net, to restore, to put it back, so it can be useful once again.

When I was a boy in West Palm Beach, money was scarce for snacks, so I'd climb coconut trees. One day I shin-

327

nied up a thirty-foot tree (it was at least that tall). While perched in the top I put one arm around the palm frond, and with the other I began to unhook the coconut. The coconut didn't want to let go, so I put my hand around the coconut and gave a yank. When I did the coconut came loose, but the palm frond also came loose The boy also came loose, and all three of us went hurtling to the ground!

A sidewalk was alongside that tree. The rest of me fell onto the grass, but my left arm crashed onto the sidewalk and the arm was broken. It was a compound fracture—that is, the break was right in the elbow, and the shattered bone was protruding through the skin. Oh, it hurt indescribably!

At that moment my brother saw what happened and ran and called a neighbor since our parents weren't at home. The neighbor put me in his car, and I held that arm the best I could clear to the Good Samaritan Hospital. The doctor there put me to sleep. When I awoke, my arm felt so good because it was in a cast, and they had given me a painkiller. The arm was lying still, and it felt so much better since the doctor had restored it. He had put the bones back in place so the arm could heal and mend.

In a spiritual sense that is what Paul has in mind here. What could they have done when I fell out of that tree? Well, they could have seen me on the ground, gone and found a gun, and they could have shot me as if I were a horse with a broken leg! "He said he has a broken arm. Kill him!"

Someone has commented that the Christian church is the only army in the world that kills its wounded! They could have shot me. They could have lectured me, "Young man, you need to be more careful when you climb trees, and after all, couldn't you see the limb was turning yellow? You should've known that the limb was going to come loose, and why weren't you holding on better? After all, what were you doing up there in the first place?"

I didn't need a lecture, even though I got one later on. But no lecture while I lay on the ground! Or they could have ignored me, shrugging, "That's none of my business. That's his problem. Let him squirm. He made his bed. Let him lie in it!" Or they could have run around yelling everywhere, "Hey, Adrian's got a broken arm. He's got a broken arm. Look at him!"

Does that remind you of what believers do when people stumble, trip, and fall? Hmmmm? Criticize them? Lecture them? Ignore them? Disown them? I'm thankful, not only that they didn't shoot me, but also that they didn't amputate my whole left arm. They could have advised, "His arm's shattered. Let's get rid of it." They didn't amputate it. They restored it. They put it back in place. I still use it after all of these years. It was a good arm, but at the time it was broken. It didn't need to be discarded or amputated. It needed to be *mended*. It needed to be *restored*.

That is what Paul means here. He is talking about a "brother" in these verses. If he is overtaken in a fault, if he is overtaken by sin, we are to restore him. Fix him. Mend him. Heal him. He is not referring to an unbeliever, a person whose sin is his way of life. He is dealing with a born-again, blood-bought child of the King who is somehow "overtaken" in sin and stumbles.

What is the difference between us now and before we were saved? We still sin sometimes. We don't want to. We hate to sin, and we are ashamed when we sin.

Before I was saved I was running in sin. Now I'm running from it. Yes, sometimes we are overtaken, but it is not an habitual life-style. God's people may be overtaken, may sin, may fall out of fellowship with God.

As you read and study God's inerrant Word, which is inspired by the Holy Spirit, you discover how candid it is. When it paints a picture, it shows "warts and all." It reveals people for what they are. Think of the godly heroes in the Bible who were overtaken.

Think of Moses the Lawgiver. Moses was a great man, so great that only he and Elijah appeared in Jesus' transfiguration experience to the awe of Peter, James, and John. Yet there was a period when he ran from God. He started out to be a missionary and ended up a murderer and spent forty years on the backside of the desert. Yet, God restored him.

Consider Simon Peter, the mighty apostle. He really loved God. But there came a barren time when Simon Peter cursed and swore and denied the Lord Jesus Christ. What a field day the gossips could have had! "Old Simon Peter, old Reverend Peter. The rock. Hah! I never had any confidence in him, anyhow. He was always running off at the mouth about how he would defend his Lord. Why, he even pulled out his sword in Gethsemane and cut off Malchus's ear—which Jesus restored. That old hypocrite—the rock was nothing but grains of sand. I am finished with him!" But God wasn't finished with him. And that same Simon Peter, when restored, became the Spirit-filled apostle of Pentecost.

Focus on David, "a man after God's own heart," the sweet singer of Israel. He truly loved God. Yet, he was trapped; he tripped and stumbled. He became entangled in lust, murder, cheating, and lying. He disgraced God, ushered in heartache, shame, and reproach. But David loved God, and God restored him. He even prayed, "Restore unto me the joy of thy salvation . . . that the bones which thou hast broken may rejoice," and God set those broken bones. God put King David back on a life of service, and David, at the end of his earthly life was still serving the Lord God, because he was reclaimed. There was a prophet, Nathan, who restored such an one in the spirit of meekness.

Let your mind fall on John Mark, who wrote the Gospel of Mark. At one time he became a coward, a turncoat, and quit the ministry, returning home to hold his momma's hand. But there was a Barnabas ("Encourager") who restored Mark, prayed for him, believed in him, and now we have the Gospel of Mark. And Paul, who at one time withdrew from young Mark, later wrote from prison, "Bring Mark with you because he is profitable for the ministry."

The ministry of restoration. At one time or another every one of us has gotten out of the will of God, haven't we? Thank God for His restoring us! Many times God has used a friend to restore us.

There is a ministry of restoration. How we must restore wayward believers back to fellowship with Christ! That is second only to our responsibility of soul-winning.

When a brother or sister falls, what are we to do? Are we to alibi, "This is none of my business"? Are we to criticize and condemn? Are we to report him? "Tell the preacher. Tell Brother Rogers." There is not enough of me to do it.

How often people have come to me with, "Brother Rogers, there is a member of our church who is living in sin. He is out of fellowship with God. I wish you would go see him." Friend, my calling is to preach and teach you so you will become a bonesetter, a minister of restoration. It is biblical and logical. I am to equip you for the work of the ministry.

There are too many who need you. One person cannot do it. It is not merely a task for the "professionals." It is for all of us, and the only qualification is what? "Ye which are spiritual . . ." Now if you do not care for this ministry, you have already classified yourself as unspiritual. Amen? "Ye which are spiritual, restore such an one in the spirit of meekness, considering yourself."

There is someone who needs your ministry of restoration right now, someone who used to be in your Sunday School class, someone who used to be in the ministry, someone who used to be a deacon in the church, who used to be a servant of God. And they have gone down ignominiously. Do you think God is finished with them? No! That person can and should be restored.

Second, I want you to see not only the *ministry of restoration,* but also the *manner of restoration.* Look at our text again. "Restore such an one in a spirit of meekness."

Paul speaks three truths about the manner of restoration. One, it is to be done gently. "The spirit of meekness." Other translations may have it "gentleness." The words meekness and gentleness are essentially the same. When a person is broken, you have to handle him firmly but gently. Tender, loving care in Christ. The last thing a broken brother needs is a harsh, censorious, critical person. But all too often in our Baptist churches that is what the backslidden brother finds. Rather than being taught gently, that person is often condemned and criticized.

Some teenage girls were talking about falling into moral difficulty. One of them commented, "If I got into trouble, those people down there at the church would be the last people on earth I would want to know about it!" What a tragic commentary. The people down at the church should be the first ones to know, if they were spiritual and in the business of restoration.

Not only are we to restore the broken with a gentle spirit but also with an humble spirit. "Considering thyself, lest thou also be tempted." Believe it or not, the time may come when you yourself will need this ministry. Paul is warning us, "Don't let the same happen to you." He gives us a warning and a possibility. You may answer, "Not me, Pastor, not me." When you say "not me," and you say it in the wrong attitude, you may be fulfilling the statement of the apostle Paul in 1 Corinthians 10:12—"Let him that thinketh he standeth, take heed lest he fall."

There are three persons sitting in your seat. You respond, "No wonder it's so crowded." There is the person you are right now, and there is the one you have the potential of becoming for God's good pleasure. But there is also the broken person who could be in depravity, sin, and wickedness. I do not think we ever realize the propensity for sin in our hearts. That which is flesh is still flesh. I preached a while back on "Victory in Jesus," and I mentioned Romans 8:2, "For the law of the Spirit of life in Christ hath made us free from the law of sin and death." There is the law of the Spirit of life that lifts us, but there is also the law of sin and death that drags us down. And little do we realize how filthy and how foul the flesh is.

Even if you have been saved for a hundred years, your

flesh is still flesh. And the flesh is not subject to the law of God; neither indeed can it be. Within you there is a proclivity for sin if you move out of "that good, and acceptable, and perfect will of God" (see Rom. 12:2).

What is sin? It is a built-in weakness plus an opportunity. Perhaps some of you have not yet had the circumstances for plunging into disobedience. You are walking in the Spirit, and the only reason you have not fallen into sin is: you have not had the opportunity.

Take heed! The proud person tempts the devil to tempt himself, even dares him. Knowing your own frailty, then restore your broken brothers and sisters with humility and gentleness. Jesus reminds us, "Blessed are the merciful, for they shall obtain mercy." The next time you may be begging for mercy, so always be merciful.

Third, you should restore him gently and humbly, but also sympathetically. Look at verse 2: "Bear ye one another's burdens, and so fulfil the law of Christ." Some have supposed a contradiction, because Galatians 6:5 teaches, "Every man shall bear his own burdens." In our text it states, "Bear ye one another's burdens." These two verses are complementary, not contradictory. Two different words are used for burden. In verse 2 *burdens* means "oppressive weights." But in verse 5 it means a load like a soldier's pack or a backpack. It is a load you must carry for your own benefit and safety. Indeed, it may save your life. That kind of burden is nontransferrable. You must carry it for yourself.

Let me illustrate. No one else can repent for you. Nor can they receive Christ for you. No one else can serve for you, tithe for you, pray your own prayers, do your own soulwinning. Love God for you. Proxy religion is not true.

But verse 2 refers to a burden which a person cannot carry by himself. Like the hymn, "I must tell Jesus, I must tell Jesus, I cannot bear these burdens alone." In our text these burdens are brought on by the weight of sin. One sure way to know you are saved is: when you sin, it becomes a heavy, weighty burden which pulls you down. If sin does not burden you, it is probably a sign that you have never been saved. A saved person is burdened and oppressed when he sins.

What is the burden of sin when a person falls out of fellowship with God? There is a guilty conscience. When David sinned he was crushed, pulverized, in agony. In Psalm 51 he cried out, "Against thee, and against thee only, have I sinned and done this evil in thy sight." God, I have sinned against You. It broke his heart, it grievously pained his conscience. No torture the poets name can match the fierce, unutterable pain he feels who, day and night, devoid of rest, carries his own accuser within his breast.

But not only is there the accusing conscience with which to contend—but the accuser himself, the devil, who comes along and adds to the burdensome weight. He will whisper, "You're no good. You're not a Christian. You don't love God. God is through with you. You'll never be able to hold up your head again in public. The church will not receive you. Your friends are gone, and you're better off dead." He is a liar, and his dirty work is to make you feel hopeless, even though you are looking toward that "blessed hope."

Then there is the burden of shame. The burden of unanswered prayer. The weight of a heavy heart. David prayed, "Make me to hear joy and gladness that the bones which thou hast broken may rejoice."

Friend, when God saves you, He doesn't fix you up where you can't sin anymore. The most miserable person on earth is not an unbeliever—he is a saved person out of fellowship with God!

Those people who laugh and call themselves "old backsliders," and they're happy about it, are not backsliders. They are going straight to hell. They have never been saved.

If you are saved, if you are born again, when you sin the Holy Spirit of God inside you is going to lay that burden on you. In this passage Paul is talking about the believer who has that burden on him. Verse 2 is an imperative for us to bear one another's burdens. When a brother is overtaken in a fault, we are to be sympathetic, empathetic, and to help him lift that load.

Not only the ministry of mending broken brothers, and the manner or method of it, but also the motive of it . . . What is the motive of this ministry? "Bear ye one another's burdens, and so fulfil the law of Christ." What is the law of Christ? Go back to Galatians 5:14: "For all the law is fulfilled in one word, even this, thou shalt love thy neighbor as thyself." The law of Christ is fulfilled in one word—love.

The law of Moses has ten commandments, but the love of Christ has one. *Love.* There it is. That is the motive. He loved us. We ought to love one another. "And be ye kind one to another, tenderhearted, forgiving one another, even as God for Christ's sake hath forgiven you" (Eph. 4:32). Christian, hasn't the Lord restored you repeatedly? Therefore, we ought to restore one another. We ought to fulfill the law of Christ, which is love, LOVE. "We love him, because he first loved us" (1 John 4:19).

We are members one of another. When I suffer, you suffer. When I rejoice, you rejoice. We are tied heart to heart and life to life by the blood of Christ.

When my arm was broken, all of me suffered. Whether or not you understand it, every broken brother is a wound in your life. We are that inseparably linked together through Christ. When one suffers, we all suffer. When one member is joyful, we are all joyful. If you want a healthy church, then help to mend our broken brothers and sisters. That is the motive, love, which fulfills the law of Christ.

Is God laying someone on your heart at this moment? Go to him or her. Offer that person the TLC of the Lord Jesus.

If you are a broken brother, your failure is not final. The Gospel is one of the second chance. That does not mean you can pick up exactly where you were when your fellowship with God was disrupted. It will require a time of healing for your brokenness. I couldn't use the arm exactly like

I used to—in fact, it is still not completely straight. Healing and mending take time.

Charles Haddon Spurgeon was asked, "When can a brother who has fallen into sin be used of God again?" He answered, "When his repentance is as notorious as his sin." David was a great sinner, but he was also a great repenter, wasn't he? You can be restored.

Don't mistake the moment for the man. Don't think an isolated moment in the life of Moses, David, John Mark, Peter, or anyone else, was a true measure of what the man was. That was the moment. Many people stumble. You might trip. It does not mean God is finished with you.

It is extremely important in the matter of soul-winning that we bring these broken brothers back into fellowship with the Lord Jesus once again. What is more pivotal? To mend a broken brother or to win a new soul to Christ Jesus? Please don't try to answer, because you can't. That is like saying which wing on a bird is the most vital.

This word *restore,* as I explained, is also used in reference to mending a net. There are many fish going out through a hole in the net, and the hole is the broken brother. Because of broken brothers, the body of Christ is crippled and limping, when it ought to be leaping.

Can you imagine what Bellevue Baptist Church would be if every broken brother were mended? May God give us a heart of compassion and love, and so fulfill the law of Christ. Is there someone you need to approach carefully, privately, and prayerfully, and with tender, loving care? Make yourself available to mend them. They may need counsel, prayer, encouragement. You may need to slip your arm around them and say, "I love you. We miss you. We need you. We care for you and want you."

God help us to mend broken brothers and sisters!

Perry R. Sanders

A Portrait of Christ
John 5:1-9

Behind the pulpit of the First Baptist Church in Lafayette, Louisiana, where I have preached for twenty-eight
years, is a plaque given to me by the late J. D. Grey. On it is
a quotation from Holy Scripture which simply says: "We
would see Jesus." Every preacher who stands behind that
podium to preach—the choir members and every singer
who stand to sing—are reminded that the waiting congregation is interested in one thing—seeing Christ.

The sculptor, with hammer, chisel, and stone, leaves
for us his image of Jesus. The artist, with canvas, oils, and
brushes, renders for the world his conception of Christ. The
skilled musician, with marvelous renditions such as Han-
del's "The Messiah" and Beethoven's "Mount of Olives,"
shares with us his impressions of Jesus.

In this homily, with words I trust the Holy Spirit will
direct, I wish to paint a portrait of Christ from which you
can never escape.

I. The Compassionate Christ

The first thing that leaps out at us from this story is
the fact that He is the *compassionate Christ*. He walked
into the porch where for thirty-eight years this man had
lain ill, and He cared for him.

Whenever you begin to describe Jesus, you may talk of
His power and, indeed, He was powerful. He took a few
loaves and fishes and fed thousands. He stood on the prow
of a small boat on the raging bosom of the Sea of Galilee
and commanded the winds to go howling back to their

337

caves and the waves to subside. You may speak of His exalted ethic. Surely, in all of literature there is nothing to compare with the socio-ethical implications of chapters 5—7 of Matthew, that incomparable "Sermon on the Mount." You may speak of His wisdom. The distilled truth of all the ages is in His relatively few sayings that are recorded in Holy Scripture.

However, the most brilliantly glowing facet in the many-sided personality of the Son of God is the fact that He loves us. This is what drew me to Christ. I did not become a Christian because of fear of hell or judgment, though I surely do believe in retribution for sin and in a place of eternal punishment. I was drawn to Jesus by the fascination of His magnificent love for me. The very first time it dawned on me that Christ died for my sins, it broke my boyish heart, and I found myself saying, "Jesus, if You love me that much, I am going to give my life to You." I had an experience as a young preacher that has fashioned and shaped my entire ministry. While walking down the streets of Knoxville, Tennessee, on my eighteenth birthday, a bitterly cold day in February, I encountered a small boy selling newspapers. The chill factor was probably in the low teens. His clothes, though ragged, were very clean. His lips were literally blue from the biting cold as he called out, "Get a paper, mister!"

I responded by taking a quarter from my pocket for the five-cent paper. Upon looking at his ragged clothes and his obvious need, in an impulsive and uncharacteristic moment of generosity, I said, "Keep the change, buddy." He said, "Gee, thanks, mister," and flashed a big smile. Something touched my heart, and I said, "Friend, do you know Jesus as your Savior?" He said, "No, sir, but I would like to." I said, "Do you have time for me to talk to you?" He said, "I'll take the time." He then put his newspapers in a deserted doorway, out of the cold, biting wind. We sat on that bundle of papers, and with New Testament in hand, I pointed out the Scriptures that tell about Jesus and salvation. I concluded with the story of the cross in that magnificent Scripture—John 3:16.

After he had read it through, I said, "Harold, what does it mean when it says, 'God so loved the *world* . . .'?" He responded by saying, "Well, I guess it means everybody in the world." I said, "That's right. Then it means YOU." He said, "Yes, if it means everybody, then it means ME." I then said, "What does it mean when it says 'whosoever . . .'?" He scratched his head for a moment. This was a rather big word for an eleven-year-old boy. He said, "Well, I guess it means just whoever, just anybody." I said, "Right. In other words that means YOU." He said, "yes."

I said, "Harold, read it again and put your name where the words 'world' and 'whosoever' appear. That would be all right since they refer to you, wouldn't it?" He began reading. "For God so loved . . ." He got to the word "world," where his name was to be inserted, and he paused, looking up at me. I said, "Go ahead." "For God so loved Harold that He gave His only begotten Son, that . . ." When he got to the word "whosoever," where his name was to appear again, he could go no further. He dropped his head down on his scrawny little knees, and he began to sob. I was embarrassed and scarcely knew what to do. I placed my arm around him, held him tightly, and just let him cry for a moment.

Then, I asked, "What's the matter, buddy?" I will never forget his answer. He lifted his face to mine, and with tears streaming down those cheeks, he said, "Perry, God loves ME! God loves ME!" There on the streets of Knoxville, Tennessee, that young lad gave his life to Christ. Shortly thereafter he united with a Baptist church, and the last I heard, he was a faithful Sunday School teacher and worker for the Lord. Captured by the love of Christ! An unknown poet wrote:

> Some love is like a valentine,
> All trimmed with lace and garlands fine,
> As fancy, fragile as the air,

Whose gilded words this legend bear:
I love you.

Some love stands recorded in the toil-worn hands
Of those whose labors have smoothed along
        life's way
And proved that sacrifice can say:
I love you.

But greater love than all was shown
By one, so young and so alone,
Whose matchless words by Galilee ring on
Through all eternity:
I love you.

II. The Challenging Christ

Jesus approached this man who had been ill for thirty-eight years with a challenge. He said in verse 6, "Wilt thou be made whole?" Christ is still the challenger.

Coaches, politicians, military people—all have long since discovered that one of the best ways to elicit a favorable response from their adherents is through a challenge. Who could forget the ringing words of that indomitable Englishman, Winston Churchill, who, when England was on the brink of her political disaster, rallied them together with this stirring challenge, "We will not capitulate, though blood, sweat, and tears lie in the path to victory"?

However, no challenge ever issued by anyone compares with the challenge our Lord issues to us. He said, "If any man will be my disciple, let him take up his cross and follow me." He said, ". . . Whosoever he be of you that forsaketh not all that he hath, he cannot be my disciple." He said, "Go ye therefore, and teach all nations . . ." The challenging Christ!

Upon reflection, all of us have to concede that it takes no character, no discipline, no commitment to live for the world and for the devil. Jesus said, in Matthew 7:13, "Wide is the gate and broad is the way that leadeth to destruction and many there be which go in thereat: . . . strait is the gate, and narrow is the way, which leadeth unto life, and few there be that find it."

That narrow way is "straight," but this old English word "strait" refers to the disciplined demands of the Christian life.

It is glorious to walk with the Lord, but it is never easy. A huge throng of people around us is living for the devil, serving the world and headed for hell—a broad road—"and many . . . go in thereat." No discipline, no character, no commitment, no will is required to go with that crowd. Just relax, and you will be swept along with the pagan group. Once one decides to follow Jesus, great discipline and commitment are required for this "pilgrim's progress."

Let me illustrate. One can go down to the broad Mississippi River, and all sorts of things may be seen floating downstream—flotsam, jetsam, trash, dead fish, sometimes dead people. But, any time anything is seen going against the tide of that mighty river, there is force, vitality, power, dynamism. So it is with this age. Any time anyone cuts across the grain of this age, you can be sure the driving force is the challenging Christ in his life.

III. The Commanding Christ

After Jesus had challenged the man, He said, "Rise, take up thy bed, and walk." This is in verse 8. Jesus was in charge—I like that picture of Christ. I have been in most of the great art museums in the Western world, including the Hermitage in Leningrad, Russia; the Louvre in Paris, France; the Vatican in Rome, Italy; and many others. With but few exceptions, the pictures of Jesus that come out of the Renaissance portray Him as weak, effeminate, vacillating—a "little Lord Fauntleroy." This is not the biblical picture of Christ. He was wind-bronzed and sunburned. He slept out-of-doors once for forty days and forty nights without the benefit of modern camping equipment. He was a man from the top of His head to the soles of His feet.

There were callouses in His hands from wielding the

foot adze and the saw in His father's carpenter shop. There were sinews in His arms from chopping wood and carrying water in small-town Nazareth where He lived.

I believe there was such a charisma and dynamism about the Son of God that, were He to walk into this room today, not clad in the Oriental garb of the first century, but in typical twentieth-century attire (whatever that is), we would immediately be drawn to our feet by the dynamic of His presence.

Perhaps some would ask, "But doesn't the Scripture say He is meek and mild and like a lamb led to the slaughter so He opened not His mouth"? Yes! Yes! But the same Bible that calls Him the Lamb of God also calls Him the "Lion of the tribe of Judah," the "captain of the Lord's host," and "King of kings and Lord of lords."

The church of our Lord Jesus and God's people need a picture of Jesus as our great Commander-in-Chief. When I hear His name, I want to click my heels together, stand at attention, and salute, because He is my Leader. He is my Commander. He is in total charge of every situation.

IV. The Conquering Christ

With great joy I am glad to be able to tell you that He is the conquering Christ. In the ninth verse, the Scripture says: "And immediately the man was made whole, and took up his bed, and walked." Back of every command Christ gives, He places His divine omnipotence. To say it in another way—He never orders anything He can't pay for. When Jesus gives a clear command, we have only one adequate response: Do it!

Notice the contrast with Jesus and the would-be "healers" of today. No suggestion that the man wait in a "prayer line." No suggestion that he send in a "free-will offering." No suggestion that he order a "prayer cloth" or "healing oil"—just the instant divine mandate to be healed. The full compliance of all forces and powers were at the Savior's command. What a wonderful thing to say to a sin-sick, sin-cursed, ailing, hurting, bleeding humanity—Jesus is the conquering Christ!

You may be faced with a challenge today, and you say, "I can't." Oh, yes you can! You may have received a challenge to start a new church, to build a new class, to witness to a friend, and your response may be, "I can't." Oh, yes you can! You can do anything your Savior has asked you to do.

Let's let this picture of the compassionate, challenging, commanding, conquering Christ totally dominate our lives for Him!

William L. Self

Any Old Bush Will Do
Exodus 3:1-7

For one year after my wife, Carolyn, had gone to Mt. Sinai, she talked about it continually. Morning, noon, and night I was reminded that next year I would be going to Sinai. I used every excuse that I could think of not to go, but finally my wife said, "You are going, and I'm going to give you the trip." So, for Christmas I received a trip to Sinai, and on January 2 we left.

After we had spent some time in Israel, we went down into the desert and on to Sinai. I do not want to give you a verbal slide show, but I do want to paint a picture for you. First of all, it was the coldest day Israel had had in fifty years. We started the trip at 5 in the morning to the city of Elat, which is on the Gulf of Aqaba, and spent the night there. Early the next morning we boarded our bus for Sinai. We drove down the road that the Israeli government had placed down by the Gulf of Aqaba; then we came to a pile of stone along the road that was about the size of this pulpit. I watched the bus drivers as they turned our bus by the stones into the desert. There was no road except for a slight indentation in the desert earth.

As we went into the Sinai we could feel the stillness of the desert. Some people have remarked that it's 24,000 square miles of nothing. That is not true. The Sinai is a holy place, and you can sense the holiness about it when you are there. After a long, arduous, bumpy, dusty ride, we came to Mt. Sinai itself. We got out of the bus and had about a mile to walk before we could come to the Monastery of St. Catherine. St. Catherine dates back to 600 AD, but it has roots that go back to 300 AD. It is the oldest monastery on the face of the earth now in existence, and it has a treasure in its library that is incomparable. It was from this monastery that the oldest manuscript of the Bible was stolen. Count Tischendorf found it, stole it, and took it to Europe to sell to the Russians. It was later acquired by the British Museum and is on display there. St. Catherine's has a letter from Count Tischendorf written to the Greek Orthodox monks, apologizing for taking it. The letter is 110 years old, and over it is an inscription which reads, "The letter from the thief." You can go into the chapel and see the doors that were erected by the Crusaders in the year 1090.

All of this gives a very strong sense of history. While we were there, we went over behind the main chapel to another small chapel called the Chapel of the Burning Bush. We couldn't go in because of some activity transpiring there, so the guide took us around to the back and showed us a very beautiful bush. He told us it was supposed to be a part of "the burning bush." We didn't believe that, but it's nice for somebody to point to a bush, and say, "This is the burning bush that Moses saw." We saw that the bush was red, and somebody has said that maybe the sun hitting the red bush made it look like it was burning.

Where Was He?

You know the story of Moses. He was with his father-in-law's sheep on the backside of the mountain of God, even Horeb, and he saw a bush burning that was not consumed. Then he heard the Lord speak to him out of that bush. God told him to take off his shoes, for he was standing on holy ground, and then God commissioned Moses for a mighty act.

The first thing I want us to see is *where he was*. He was on the backside of God's mountain. I have been on the backside of that mountain—in two ways. I have literally put my feet in that place; there is no real contest among biblical scholars as to where this was. I have been to the place and want you to know it is desolate. But I have been to that place personally as well. I want all of us to understand again that life is not an even terrain. Life is a journey from desert to oasis. All of the theology being preached now that claims we are just to breeze through life with nothing ever going wrong if we are Christian does not face up to the biblical revelation. It is not New Testament religion. The biblical revelation has a cross in the middle of it and a resurrection. It does not have life always sweet and kind; it has death and depression. It has deserts, it has desolation, it has poverty, it has famine, but in the midst of it, it has the hand of God holding it together.

A wise king asked one of his philosophers to write the history of the world. The philosopher came in with five hundred volumes of the history, and the king said to him, "That is not adequate. Go back and condense all that you have written into one page." The philosopher came back with this line, "This is the life experience of all men who have ever had sorrow and died." That is the history of the world. We did not come today without some pressure. I like the expression I discovered a couple of weeks ago, "Everybody has his own bag of rocks around his neck."

I do not know what your bag of rocks is, but everybody has one. John Bunyan had his. He was in Bedford jail twelve years, but while he was there God spoke to him, and in the midst of that experience he wrote *Pilgrim's Progress.* Abraham Lincoln, whose picture hangs in every sacred spot in American life, had the sorrow not only of being disappointed and deserted and of losing his own son; he also had the sorrow of not ever being appreciated in his own day. Yet, as he walked the halls of the White House, grieving over the death of his son, he found Bunyan's *Pilgrim's Progress,* picked it up, and read it. It changed his whole insight into the transformation that was going on in his own life. God speaks clearest on the backside of the desert. If we need the sunlight all the time, then we do not understand the ways of God in our lives.

What Did He See?

What did Moses see? He saw a bush not consumed. That is an interesting thing to see. When I had climbed Mt. Sinai, I came down early to wait for the rest of the group. I asked the bus drivers how we could keep warm. We decided to gather some sage brush to build a fire. We had a pile of tumbleweed as big as this pulpit, and I thought we would stay warm forever. We lit the brush, and I got ready for a long time of warmth, but the fire burned for about five minutes—then it was gone. It was absolutely gone in a very short time.

That's the way life is for most people. You think you are just about to get what you need out of life, and it disintegrates. You get on fire from something, and you are consumed inside. There is no need to try to decide what kind of bush it was that burned and was not consumed. We don't need to debate whether or not it was something that Moses imagined. What we need to see out of this particular part of Scripture is that when God gets ready to do something, when God wants to reveal Himself, when God comes to give us our commands, any old bush will do. We do not need a special bush. God can use the things of this world.

The Book of Exodus says that God does His act in history—any old bush will do. Not a perfect bush, not a beautiful bush, any bush. But look at that line, "It burned without being consumed." That's what we think we should do. I watch you, tired businessman, shuffling on and off airplanes in some kind of lockstep. I watch you, tired mother, running through town with a station wagon full of children and cocker spaniels, waiting at traffic lights forever. Living is a depleting experience! Just getting a check cashed, just getting your laundry, just getting your credit card straightened out—all of these things can absolutely destroy your life. It is a wonder we get anything done in this world, but man thinks he is not consumed. "I am the captain of my soul. I am the master of my fate. I am never consumed. I have inexhaustible energy. I can do anything I want to."

God can do anything He wants to, but we are consumable. Living makes you consumable.

The illustration here shows that God is the One who speaks through natural resources. God is the One who never has all of His being consumed. Man is the one who is finite and is consumed by living. How do we live that way? Some of us came to church today feeling consumed. We have been consumed with the tragedies of our own lives. We have been consumed by having to make a living, by traffic lights, and by credit cards. How are we going to get by? According to this Scripture, God is the One who has limitless resources; we are the ones who are limited. The limited man comes to the limitless God, and something begins to happen. In the next part of the chapter God tells Moses, "I have all you need, I made you, I give you what you need."

What Did He Do?

In the third verse Moses said, "I will turn aside." That's interesting. It is a good thing Moses was not a modern man. He would not have been able to do that. We do not turn aside much today. I came down from Mt. Sinai through a herd of goats that were being taken through the valley by a Bedouin family. That was an interesting experience. A Baptist clergyman from America out in the Sinai by himself, all of a sudden finds himself in a flock of goats. I didn't quite know what to do, but I noticed one thing. I saw there was an intensity in that family as they took care of those little animals. They were bent on going to another pasture. Moses turned aside.

Some of you have been rushing headlong in a direction. I do not know what kind of dead-end street you are going down. I do not know what kind of goal you are pursuing. I do not know what kind of place out there you are trying to get to, but you have been pursuing it so fast and so hard that God couldn't talk to you. If you saw a burning bush, you wouldn't stop because it's not on your calendar. "Busy man, you've had a little day." Have you really ever thought of taking time to smell the flowers? I know, we are American workaholics—we do not like to do that. What we like to do is work. Play is not what we are supposed to do. God knew that we can be consumed. He knows that He is the limitless One. So God has created a way for our burned-out situation to be brought to His limitless supply. You know what it is? God said there is a cycle in life about one day in seven; then everybody needs to stop. Did you hear that? One day in seven we need to shut everything down and let the body and soul catch up with each other. The Jews took it literally. We were in Jerusalem on a sabbath, and it was shut down. But I see America, technologically advanced, burning itself out because we will not stop. We have a holy day turned into a holiday. God wants us to recreate ourselves inside because we can be burned out. Man would rather recreate and destroy himself inside. What we need is not a weekend in the mountains. What we need is a weekend in His Word, on our knees, and in the place of God, worshiping to fill the inner man. No wonder we are so burned out. We come once a month and when we do, we are at a stadium event, seeing what is going to happen. No wonder we are so burned out; we do not stop to hear from the Highest. We do not give the holy a hearing ear. When the Bible says, "Be still and know that I am God," that, literally translated, means, "Be quiet so I can talk to you."

What Did He Hear?

Now, let us go to the last thing. Read the fifth verse. He said, "Draw not nigh hither, but put off thy shoes from off thy feet, for the place whereon thou standest is holy ground." I like that. The worship of God is high and holy. There is an awesome mystery about God. Do you know what the whole Book of Exodus is revealing? It is revealing the ways of God with men. You do not learn "about" God; God "reveals" Himself to you. You do not find God; God finds you. The whole Book of Exodus says this. What a scandal it is to think we can know anything about God on our own initiative. God does the coming and God came . . . in the burning bush to Moses. He said it was holy! We do not have a sense of the holy in our culture.

A couple of years ago I went to the Augusta Masters Golf Tournament. We had just finished this building, and I had watched the stadium mind-set of our people as we came into it, as though it were a fancy religious stadium. I was distressed. Going in at the Masters, the crowds were jubilant, just like any crowd going to an athletic contest. We were at a holy place, for this was the turf for which Bobby Jones had been responsible. This was the place where the great golfers of history had been. I noticed that people did not throw their cigarettes down and grind them into the ground, but they put them in their proper containers. I noticed that people walked with respect, awe, and honor there. People arrived on time and stayed until it was over. And if the player were having a little trouble moving along, they stayed with him until the tournament was over. There was a holy hush over the entire experience.

Then I came back to church, and I saw people coming late and leaving early. I saw people grinding their cigarettes into the turf of God, and I thought to myself, "Where are we in America that the holy is in athletic contests and the profane is in the house of God?" This is the holy house of God. We are here for the worship of the Lord God of all creation. We could claim with the saints that the Lord God Himself is among this body; the holy hush falls over the people. You don't judge the preaching; the Word of God judges us all. You don't judge the music; God speaks through the music to all of us. Take off your shoes, you are on holy ground. Maybe you are burned out because your priorities are mixed up. Maybe you are burned out because you have been worshiping at the wrong altar. Maybe you are depleted because your sense of the holy has been out of focus. You want your life right. You need to understand where it is. What this is, what that is, Who He is. That is what it's all about. Any old bush will do when God is burning.

This is a holy hour, and God is speaking now. Some of you are too busy to turn aside and see a bush aglow. Some of you are trampling through life because you have taken the values of our culture, and you believe them. This morning we are going to give you a chance to turn aside and to see a bush aglow and to hear the voice of God and to respond to the voice of the holy. When God chooses to appear, He does it with His people before the body of His people in any way He chooses.

Don Sharp

Will You Go?
Isaiah 6:1-8

In the year that King Uzziah died, I saw the Lord seated on a throne, high and exalted, and the train of his robe filled the temple.

Above him were seraphs, each with six wings: With two wings they covered their faces, with two they covered their feet, and with two they were flying.

And they were calling to one another:
"Holy, holy, holy is the LORD Almighty;
the whole earth is full of his glory."

At the sound of their voices the doorposts and thresholds shook and the temple was filled with smoke.

"Woe to me!" I cried. "I am ruined! For I am a man of unclean lips, and I live among a people of unclean lips, and my eyes have seen the King, the LORD Almighty."

Then one of the seraphs flew to me with a live coal in his hand, which he had taken with tongs from the altar. With it he touched my mouth and said, "See, this has touched your lips; your guilt is taken away and your sin atoned for."

Then I heard the voice of the Lord saying, "Whom shall I send? And who will go for us?" And I said, "Here am I. Send me!" (Isa. 6:1-8, NIV).

Introduction

Isaiah, whose name means "salvation of the Lord," was the greatest of the writing prophets, and he was unique in many respects. Although he was a prophet to the people of that day and age, his prophecy extended beyond that time period to the future event of the coming Messiah.

His conversation is perhaps representative of an experience we have had or need to have. The Scripture says, "In the year that King Uzziah died, I saw the Lord seated on a throne, high and exalted . . ." There is a great deal of truth to the statement that King Uzziah died before Isaiah could see the Lord. As it was for Isaiah, so it is for us today. In order that we might see God as He really is, and not only see God, but know God as He is, some things must be removed from our presence. Perhaps our worship is misdirected. Oftentimes we cannot fully commit to God because of the Uzziahs in our lives. Don't delude yourselves, my brothers and my sisters, all of us have someone or something which hinders us from having a complete relationship with God. One important aspect of our relationship with God is knowing him in His totality, which is the result of permitting those things which bind and shackle us to die. Certainly the Bible tells us about seeing God, but not with the physical eye; for God is a spirit, and He is bound neither by space nor time, nor a body with limbs and eyes. Therefore, those who worship Him and those who want to have a full relationship with Him must do so in spirit and truth.

Spiritual Elevation

The major hindrance in our relationship with God is due to the lack of spiritual elevation in our lives. Anyone who has ever flown in an airplane is aware of the view from a higher perspective. Or, if you have seen the view from the top of the Sears Tower you realize the difference. And so it is in our relationship with God. We must elevate our thinking, our minds, and our attitudes to a higher, spiritual plane. The advantage of elevation allows a broader range of vision, a better view, and a different insight. Once our minds are elevated, seeing and knowing God take on a new meaning.

Daily Communion

In the year King Uzziah died, Isaiah saw the Lord, and the train of his robe filled the Temple. Notice that Isaiah met God in the Temple, which was a special place of meeting and communing with God. Sometimes as I drive along in my car, I am in communion with God. The important factor is there must be an attitude of worship in order to be receptive of God. Daily communing with God is a privilege afforded all Christians, but we seldom take advantage of its benefits. Generally, our worship is limited to Sunday morning. However, worshiping God on a daily basis we then are able to see God as Isaiah saw him, which enables us to tell the story of how God has effected changes in our lives. Isaiah was able to commune with God because of an elevated mind, because he possessed the proper attitude of worship, and because he expected to meet and commune with God.

Expect God to Answer

Our prayers are evidence of what we expect God to do, but many really do not expect to commune with God. That is why it is very difficult for God to get our attention. You have heard the story over and over, but I will tell you once more just to remind you (certainly in light of the flood situation this past week) about the man who had been praying to God to rescue him because there was a flood and his house was covered with water.

He sat on the roof and as the water began to rise, a helicopter came by, and the pilot said, "Come on up, we are going to rescue you," but the man answered, "No, no, God is going to rescue me," and so the helicopter flew away. The man continued to pray and next, a motorboat came by and the captain said, "We came by to rescue you," but the man replied, "No, no, God is going to rescue me." You know the story, the water came up and the man drowned.

When he reached heaven and began to complain to Peter he said, "Look, Peter, I should not have died because I prayed and waited on God to rescue me, but He didn't rescue me and now I am dead—I died because God didn't come to rescue me." God answered and said, "I sent a boat by for you, and you refused it; then I sent a helicopter by for you, and you refused that." Oftentimes we are like that man. When God sends us a lifeline, and it does not meet our expectations, we refuse what He sends. But Isaiah expected God to commune with him and was greatly blessed thereby, for God revealed to him His holiness.

The Holiness and Magnificence of God

The seraphim proclaimed, ". . . Holy, Holy, Holy is the Lord Almighty, the whole earth is full of his glory." We have failed to understand the attribute of God's holiness and have become confused in what we think of God as one of the good ole' boys, an errand boy, or a good buddy; but God is neither an errand boy, a good buddy, nor "the man upstairs"—He's God Almighty—and when we talk or even think about Him, we should prostrate ourselves with the right frame of mind and attitude. It is imperative to recognize that we are communing with a Holy, Holy, Holy God. (I sat in a couple of the Sunday School classes this morning which gave me an opportunity to listen to some of the classes, and I heard some interesting observations about what people think about God.) I can think about the sky and realize God made it, no, God created it. He did not need cranes, bulldozers, or anything that man uses; he simply yet magnificently created it out of nothing.

Then I think in terms of air travel—I can go up and up and up, and yet there is no end. As finite things, we relate to a beginning and an end, but imagine boarding an airplane and continuing the flight indefinitely—you still would not have explored all that God has done. How then can he be classified as a good buddy, the man upstairs, or the great cowboy in the sky?

We must know that He is God, He is Jehovah, He is Almighty, He is El Shaddai. Communion with God necessitates that we understand the holiness of the Almighty. The seraphim understood and could say, "Holy, Holy, Holy is the Lord Almighty, the whole earth is full of his glory." The Psalmist understood and could say, "When I look at the moon and the stars, I know Who God is; when I look at the elements, I know Who God is; when I wake in the morning, I know Who God is; when I breathe, I know Who God is—Holy, Holy, Holy is the Lord Almighty, the whole earth is full of his glory—there is no place I can go to escape from the magnificence of God; if I took the wings of a dove and flew to the uttermost corners of the earth, He is there; if I made my bed in hell, He is there—He is Almighty God!"

Admit, Confess, Be Cleansed

When the seraphim announced the holiness of God, at the sound of their voices, the doorposts and thresholds shook, and the Temple was filled with smoke. Sincere communion and recognition of God's holiness lead one to concrete changes in life-style. Isaiah stood in the presence of the Almighty God, and something took place in his life; something started burning like the fire burning on the main altar of the heart.

As we relate to Isaiah's conversion, we understand that to stand before God means we are stripped bare. Gone are the phony facades, the false faces, the unclean hearts, the filthy minds, the adulterous thoughts, and the worldly life-styles. In their places God will create within us a clean heart and mind. One day I stood in the presence of a Holy God, and can say like Isaiah, "Woe is me, I am unclean." Standing in the presence of God makes you realize how holy and magnificent He is and how unclean you really are.

Not only are your thought patterns changed, but your actions and life-style are called into account. You desire to rid yourself of haughty attitudes, unloving ways, criticism of others, fault finding, back biting, and the list goes on. Instead, your awareness is heightened in relation to the things concerning God, and you will love those who do not love you; you will be more inclined to follow the words of Jesus as he says, "How can you get the mote out of your brother's eye and cannot see for the beam in your own eye? The positive results will be that God will change your speech, your attitude, and your disposition. To more fully explain the change, Isaiah said (as I paraphrase), "Woe is me, for I am unclean; woe is me, for I am undone; woe is me; even though I am surrounded with material things, my life is empty; woe is me, my life is confused, and I am unworthy to stand in the presence of a Holy God; woe is me, I am unclean and am in the midst of an unclean people."

Admission of guilt is against our basic nature. It's much easier to blame someone else. However, when God heard Isaiah's admission (as when He hears ours) He's willing to forgive and cleanse. In Isaiah's case, He dispatched the seraphim with a live (hot) coal in his hand taken from the altar, and when the coal touched his mouth, guilt was taken away. Imagine, standing before God, we now become guiltless. For God has commanded, "Be ye perfect, for I am perfect."

Perfection does not mean to look at your neighbor, nor does it mean compare your perfection with someone else; rather the perfection Jesus referred to can only be achieved by looking at him. The Bible relates many incidents where the perfection of Jesus was not realized by man. Mary had a difficult time understanding that when her brother, Lazarus, died. Jesus said, "You will see him in the resurrection." Of course, Mary knew that, but Jesus said, "Look at me—I am the resurrection and the life, and even though he is dead he shall live again." And so he is saying to us today (if I might paraphrase), "Even though your life is void, and raging with sin, look to the perfect One, pattern your life after Me."

Cleansed for Service

Once Isaiah had been purged, God had a job for him. We fail to understand in our churches today that when God saves you, it is for a purpose. First and foremost, He saves you to worship Him. And beyond that He saves you so you can be an instrument to help someone else. I think it is a sad commentary for a Christian who confesses to be a believer in the Lord Jesus Christ as Savior, and yet he/she has not been instrumental in helping someone else know the Lord. Instead of reaching the lost for Christ we make it a practice of inviting people to church—*do not* invite people to church. Instead invite them to know Jesus Christ as Lord and Savior, and then they will come to church. Our life-style plays an important part in winning the lost to Jesus Christ. You may be able to quote Scripture from Genesis to Revelation, but if you do not practice what you preach, you have no drawing power because people look at what you do and pay little attention to what you say. The best sermon is not the one that is preached, but the one that is lived. I have heard that some have said, "I am not a Christian, but I would become one if I ever saw one."

Will You Go?

God did not expect Isaiah to stay in the Temple, but God expects His people to be about action, to go about winning the lost, to impact people's lives. He said, "Whom shall I send, and who will go for us?" What will be your response? What is your response? Will you say (as Isaiah said), "Here am I, send me"? What is your response? Will you say, "Here am I, send me"? or will you allow people, situations, and attitudes to deter you from fulfilling God's purpose? Here am I, send me—I am supported by Your Word. Heaven and earth will pass away, but the Word of God stands forever.

Imagine how and what our lives would be if Jesus would have permitted anyone or anything to hinder God's purpose in His life. As he looked into time and realized that He would be pierced in the side; that a crown of thorns would be placed on His head; that those who followed Him would deny Him and curse Him; and that He would ultimately be separated from God—what would your life be if Jesus had decided in the Garden of Gethsemane not to go the way of Calvary?

In my mind this is commitment day—I am going; you may try to slow me down, or even try to stop me, but I am going. And as I follow Jesus, who will be willing to make a public declaration by saying, "Pastor, as you follow Jesus, I will follow you"?

Cecil E. Sherman

What Kind of a Church?— a Believing Church
John 8:18-19; Colossians 1:15-19

Introduction

Church shopping and church hopping are epidemic in the Christian community. I learned this exercise while a college student. The Baptist offerings in Waco in the mid-forties were varied. Seventh and James had Woodson Armes and a service aimed at the college student. First Baptist had a Christian statesman in J. M. Dawson; the service was designed for the larger community. And if I wished the wisdom of a sage, I could travel across town to Columbus Avenue and hear W. W. Melton. Since I was a young, impressionable ministerial student, I wanted to hear them all. And I did. I did a little church hopping.

Looking back on the variety offered me in the personalities and the worship style of the churches, I see there was a remarkable sameness in Columbus Avenue, First Baptist, and Seventh and James. Those pastors agreed on what the gospel was. They agreed on the mission of the Church. And all worked together in a web of mutual respect. What little church hopping I did afforded me but slight variety.

Today things have changed. Once I frowned on church hopping; now I see some kind of church shopping as a necessity. The differences are so great, the gospel is defined so peculiarly, the polity is so varied until nothing can be assumed. Once a denominational label was a guide. Not so anymore. The variations within the Presbyterian Church are from fundamentalism to liberalism. The same is true to a lesser extent in Methodism. Episcopalians have been a "broad church" for years. And now this variety has come to Baptists. No longer can a pastor counsel against church shopping. If the pastor is honest, he has to encourage a prospective member to study the church options.

Four years ago a retired school administrator moved to Asheville, North Carolina. Recently his wife had died. He was looking for friends, for he was lonely. As soon as he unpacked his boxes from moving he joined a neighborhood church. The people were friendly, but with the passing months the teacher realized the gospel he was hearing was not the gospel he knew over a lifetime as a Sunday School teacher and deacon. He was restless and a little bit embarrassed. He did not want to appear unstable, but he was very unhappy with his church choice. After visiting our church for a few Sundays, he made an appointment to see me. He wanted to change churches. He had not shopped enough before he made a commitment.

Sometimes I hear pastors lament that people do not just move to town and join a church anymore. Most people make commitments more slowly. While I like to welcome new members to our church as much as anyone, I think the laity are doing the right thing. If they do not church shop, they are likely to have the same sadness the retired school teacher had.

What makes churches different? Can it be analyzed? Ought it be analyzed? Is it irreverent to think about it? Who gets to decide? These are some of the questions I want you to think about today.

I. The Laity Have to Think About Church

The Christian community is divided into two parts on a basic question: What can the lay person think and do? Where does the laity stand inside the church? Let me line out for you two points of view:

1. One way to do church is by clergy. In this system the clergy do the preaching, the ordinances, the theology, and the programs of the church. There is some Bible sup-

port for this arrangement. Surely the apostles had an exalted position in the life of the Early Church. Paul appealed to the Galatian and Corinthian churches to obey him because he was an apostle. Out of this model the church of the Middle Ages was formed. The clergy stood in places the laity could not. They handled sacraments laity could not hold. They interpreted the Bible and declared what correct doctrine was. They sat in council and made pronouncements. The church was ordered by the bishops.

2. But out of the Reformation came another interpretation of the life of the Early Church and the way today's church ought to be designed. A larger place was given the laity. These judgments were not accidental or peripheral to the Reformation. They came out of the heart of it. Now the laity would stand before God without benefit of any high priest except Christ Himself. The Bible was put into the hands of the laity. The laity would call the pastor; the laity could dismiss the pastor. In some Protestant churches the responsibility for the life of the church would be divided evenly between clergy and laity. In others the laity would be the final and highest authority.

Now I have lined out the two classic positions on the laity. It would appear Roman Catholics are an illustration of the authoritarian model. There is theology to support this appearance. It would appear Baptists would be an example of the lay-ordered church. But in these days appearances can deceive.

Hear me carefully. Churches that have Catholic in their name now give large place to the layman. In fact, the drift of the Roman Church in the past twenty-five years has been toward a larger place for the layman in the life of the Church. Old clichés and "conventional wisdom" need to be reexamined. But now let's turn that idea around. Churches that have Baptist in the name on the sign ought to give large place to the laity, right? Yes. That is the classic position of Baptists. But don't bet the ranch on what you will find inside the doors of any Baptist church. You may find an authoritarian leader that would rival anyone you could find in a history book about the Medieval Church. Once again, classic positions have broken down. Labels mean little.

So, what does this mean to the layman? You have to examine. You have to think. You have to study the Bible and make up your mind about what a church ought to be— then you have to go out and find a church that measures up. Right at this point I feel sorry for some of you. You are unaccustomed to this kind of word from the pulpit. All your life you have been spoon fed. Now the pulpit is telling you to study and make up your mind. Quietly the people called Baptists have been dividing. One part has gone away from a lay-ordered church. Another group has held fast to the lay-ordered church. It may be that while you were inside a church with Baptist on the sign you have been practicing clergy-ordered religion. Your pastor may have been "ruling the church." If this is what you want, you can find it under the Baptist label, but it is not consistent with our history. It is out of sync with what we have always said we were. Baptists have to make decisions about what the gospel is and what the church ought to be. It has always been that way— it is that way today. In this church the laity have real power to order the life of the church. They seriously study and interpret the Bible. Laity do theology here. So, when I say, "The laity will decide," I am doing no more or less than a Baptist pastor ought to say. As you examine the churches I am asking you to do no more than Baptists have done for years. You have to decide. You have to make up your mind.

II. Appearances Are Not the Part That Matters

When you were doing your courtship, you were working hard to cut through style and get to substance, and with some people it is hard to separate style from substance. So it is at church. Style is so important until sometimes it seems style is substance.

The Apostle Paul laid down a principle we need to call to mind. He said, "I become all things to all men, that I may save some of them by any means possible" (1 Cor.

9:22*b*, GNB). In a contentious environment; in a time when Jews were insisting that all live like Jews; in a time when Gentiles were pressing hard for their full place in the life in the Church; in that explosive church setting Paul said style was not the part that matters.

In these days church style is a cafeteria before you.

You can attend a church that is classic in worship. God is transcendent, holy, high, and to be held in reverence. But three blocks away there is a church where God is imminent, nearby, close, personal.

Churches entertain, regale, and amuse. Other churches are severe or dull.

And there is the church that functions like an American business. The more the better, and whatever gets the people is the theology of the moment. But other churches are unbending and straight. They are what they are, whatever changing style would dictate.

Church is not style. Style surely has much to do with all I do. I like a certain kind of clothes; I will not wear some of the stuff on the rack these days. Some kinds of music turn me off; other music inspires me. I like some houses; other houses are unsightly to me. This same personal preference is a part of what happens at church. I do have a preference about our hymns. I like some preaching, and I don't like other kinds of preaching.

But style is not the mission of the church. No single organization has done more to the life and manners of Western man than the church. Church has shown us great architecture. The architecture is great because the people who designed the buildings had a vision of a great God. The same is true of art and music. These artistic creations were pulled from the artist when the artist pondered the kind of God we worship.

Privately I wonder about some of the worship style on display these days. If that style mirrors the kind of God those people worship, then maybe there is more substance in our style than I want to admit. But style simply ought not be a point of fellowship. Church is more than a quarrel about which song or whether the choir is in robes or not. People are different, and people do have different tastes. So long as we are speaking of style alone, style is open. Any style that pulls people to Christ is a style the church can and ought to use. Our church ought not define herself by style alone. Such classification is too narrow and open to a smug snobbery. We are not artists; we are Christians, and being Christian is our first work.

III. Belief Is About Essentials

What does a Christian have to believe? All sorts of answers would come from this preacher or that church. In fact, it seems to me one of the great sins of Christian people these days is the requirement that prospective Christians are asked to believe too much. Jesus had a lot of trouble with people who were into a religion of little rules. To be a good Jew in the time of Christ, a good Jew as measured by the Pharisees, one had to do too many little things and believe too many doctrines. Jesus simplified religion. He cut through the many rules and reduced the number. He got at the essence of the thing.

Pull away at the body of Christian doctrine. Tear away the loose and the little, the tangent and the peripheral, and what is essential? You know that I will be giving you an interpretation, but you check this interpretation against the New Testament and make up your own mind.

The core idea in the Christian religion is that in Jesus Christ we get a new and a clearer look at what God is like. It is the aim of all religions to tell us about God. So, when a Jew tells about God, the Jew tells about the God who was described to him by Moses and the prophets. Moses and the prophets are the glass through which the Jew sees God. When the Muhammadan tells you about God, he is telling you of the God he can see through the insights of the founder and the prophet of that religion, Muhammad. When the Christian tells you of God he is telling of the God he sees through the life and words, the death and resurrection of Jesus Christ. This is our core doctrine.

The author of the Hebrews said, "In the past God spoke to our ancestors many times and in many ways through the prophets, but in these last days he has spoken to us through his Son" (Heb. 1:1, GNB). That is the sum of it; that is the nut of it. That is the part which makes all the other parts fit into place. Jesus is a later and better revelation of what God is like. So, Paul wrote, "Christ is the visible likeness of the invisible God . . . and in union with him all things have their proper place" (Col. 1:15,17, GNB).

It is not the purpose of this church to force more belief than the Bible asks. It is not the purpose of this church to make following Christ a series of rules and regulations. The basic message is Christ. Look to Him and see God more clearly. Look to Him and see more clearly what God wants you to be.

We are a believing church. We want to agree on essential things. But we want to leave room for the believer to search and seek in those parts of the Christian life that are left open. Today I call you to believe in Him who said, "If you knew me, you would know my Father also" (John 8:19, GNB).

Theodore R. (Ted) Sisk

The Stance
of the "Immoral Majority"

I want to address you on the theme, "The Stance of the Immoral Majority." Before I go further, however, I want to make it clear that I am casting no aspersion toward Dr. Jerry Falwell and the Moral Majority organization; that is neither my style nor my intention.

Having said that, I must admit that I do question the *name* of the Moral Majority organization, for the name seems to imply that most persons in our country are good, law-abiding, moral, God-fearing, righteous people. But such is not the case. There are two reasons I make that statement.

First, the general tone of the Bible says otherwise. Psalm 53:3 states, "Every one of them is gone back: they are altogether become filthy; there is none that doeth good, no, not one." Genesis 6:5 tells us, "And God saw that the wickedness of man was great in the earth, and that every imagination of the thoughts of his heart was only evil continually." The prophet Isaiah confessed, "All we like sheep have gone astray; we have turned every one to his own way . . ." (53:6). And the Lord Jesus said toward the conclusion of the Sermon on the Mount, ". . . Strait is the gate, and narrow is the way, which leadeth unto life, and few there be that find it" (Matt. 7:14).

The second reason I cannot believe the majority of people are moral is this: all the studies I have seen indicate that most people in our beloved country see nothing wrong with taking home from the office a few gem clips, a supply of stationery, and a few stamps; but the moral law of God forbids it. The majority sees nothing particularly wrong

367

with falsifying income tax returns, cheating on tests, and lying when it is advantageous; but the law of God says all of these are wrong. This is why I call it the IM-moral majority.

There is something worse still. It is quite clear that the majority of persons in our land do not love the Lord God with all their hearts. They are either outright atheists, or else they are practical atheists, living as if God does not matter, as if He is optional.

That brings us to the primary emphasis in this message: *the stance of the immoral majority can be stated in two words: quite unconcerned!* Let us turn in the New Testament to the Book of Acts (chapter 18). The Apostle Paul was in Corinth, on his second missionary tour. As he always did on the sabbath, he went to the synagogue, and while there he testified to the Jews that Jesus was the Messiah (vv. 4-5).

Now let us read verses 6-17:

> And when they opposed themselves, and blasphemed, he shook his raiment, and said unto them, Your blood be upon your own heads; I am clean: from henceforth I will go unto the Gentiles.
>
> And he departed thence, and entered into a certain man's house, named Justus, one that worshiped God, whose house joined hard to the synagogue.
>
> And Crispus, the chief ruler of the synagogue, believed on the Lord with all his house; and many of the Corinthians hearing believed, and were baptized.
>
> Then spake the Lord to Paul in the night by a vision, Be not afraid, but speak, and hold not thy peace:
>
> For I am with thee, and no man shall set on thee to hurt thee: for I have much people in this city.
>
> And he continued there a year and six months, teaching the word of God among them.
>
> And when Gallio was the deputy of Achaia, the Jews made insurrection with one accord against Paul, and brought him to the judgment seat,
>
> Saying, This fellow persuadeth men to worship God contrary to the law.

> And when Paul was now about to open his mouth, Gallio said unto the Jews, If it were a matter of wrong or wicked lewdness, O ye Jews, reason would that I should bear with you:
> But if it be a question of words and names, and of your law, look ye to it; for I will be no judge of such matters.
> And he drave them from the judgment seat.
> Then all the Greeks took Sosthenes, the chief ruler of the synagogue, and beat him before the judgment seat. And Gallio cared for none of those things.

Tourists look forward to going to ancient Corinth, where the *Bema* still stands; that was the judgment seat of the Roman proconsul. My heart was stirred when I stood there and recalled this story. Secular records reveal that Gallio was the Roman proconsul in Achaia; he was the older brother of Seneca the philosopher and an uncle of the poet Lucan. One of his responsibilities as proconsul was to preside over a tribunal to hear complaints and to render judgments.

On this particular day, some angry Jews made a united attack on Paul and hauled him into court, charging, "This fellow persuadeth men to worship God contrary to the law" (v. 13). Gallio's ruling was this: "If it were a matter of wrong or wicked lewdness, O ye Jews, reason would that I should bear with you: But if it be a question of words and names, and of your law, look ye to it; for I will be no judge of such matters. And he drave them from the judgment seat."

Gallio had a point: he was not there to settle theological debates and religious disputes; he was there to judge in matters of civil and criminal law. His stance appeared to have been that of proper religious neutrality.

Such a neutrality today means a Christian judge will do everything in his power not to let his own religious convictions incline him to rule in favor of someone of his own church or denomination. He must be impartial and rule in harmony with the law, without fear or favor or reward or hope of reward.

Verse 17 says, "And Gallio cared for none of those things." He was like many in our day, quite unconcerned. There seems to be two levels of unconcern. One is the level of *easy, indifferent unconcern*. This is reflected in the apparent total disregard of God, morality, and justice by many people. They live as if there were no God, no authority, no moral absolutes, and no judgment. No wonder the Book of Hebrews asks the question: "How shall we escape if we neglect so great salvation?" The question in Hebrews 2:3 is introduced by this basic premise: ". . . We ought to give the more earnest heed to the things which we have heard, lest at any time we should let them slip." That addresses those who are the easy, indifferent unconcerned. They are just drifting past the eternal realities and claims of God.

When I was a student in Chicago, I walked frequently on Sunday mornings from Moody Bible Institute to the Moody Memorial Church for the worship service. On North Lasalle Street, I passed the Lutheran Church which has on its front a large statue of Jesus dying on the cross, His head crowned with thorns, His side opened up by the spear. And underneath was this stabbing question: "Is it nothing to you, all ye that pass by?" (Lam. 1:12). Millions of persons pass by that cross, who, if they are honest, must say, "No, it is nothing to us; we are too busy with our own concerns."

Beyond the level of easy, indifferent unconcern is the level of *callous unconcern*. To me, this is where Gallio fit in. Why? Because even though he stated his proper religious neutrality, he stood by as the Greeks took Sosthenes and beat him before the judgment seat; and verse 17 says, "Gallio cared for none of those things." That is callous unconcern. What did he care?

Pontius Pilate lived life on that level. Remember when Jesus was brought before him and Pilate ruled, "I find no fault in this man"? (Luke 23:4) Then, in a mocking act of neutrality, he called for a basin and washed his hands in full view of the people, saying, "I am innocent of the blood of this just person: see ye to it" (27:24). Then what did he do? He had Jesus flogged, and then delivered Him over to the soldiers to be crucified. Callous unconcern!

Every time we refuse to do something that is difficult but right, and then say, "I wash my hands of this matter," the spirit of Pilate is coming out in us.

Here is a word to all who think agnosticism is the only intelligent response to Jesus Christ, and to all who try to straddle the fence or play the game of neutrality. *This is the one crucial point of life where there is no neutrality; we either acknowledge Jesus as the Son of God and Lord of life, or we refuse to acknowledge Him as such. Refusing to believe is the same as denying Him.*

If you do not read the Bible to your children, and if you do not pray with them, and if you do not go to church, and take your children with you, and if you call for the removal of God from your children's education, *then you are teaching them there is no God, and that He is not important! And to me, that is the level of callous unconcern.*

Some years back, a father—a Christian and a Baptist— told me, "I don't intend to interfere in my sons' spiritual decisions; I want them to make up their own minds. When I was a lad my father was a pastor and I had to go." I told him he was wrong. After that, I watched as those sons grew up. Not a one of them made the right decisions about the Lord or the church. One died before he was thirty years old; the other two the last I heard were living outside the church, as if God does not truly matter.

It is irresponsible and unconscionable for parents to try to influence their children about where to go to school, what kind of company to keep, what they will do with their lives, and whom they will marry, but exert no influence when it comes to loving and serving God. After all, that is the only eternal consideration; all the others are temporal concerns.

Where did I get such an idea? From the Lord Jesus. He said, "He that is not with me is against me; and he that gathereth not with me scattereth abroad" (Matt. 12:30). He also said, "Whosoever therefore shall confess me before men, him will I confess also before my Father which is in heaven. But whosoever shall deny me before men, him will I also deny before My Father which is in heaven" (Matt. 10:32-33).

My firm conviction is that the stance of the immoral majority is that of basic unconcern about God, sin, righteousness, and judgment. Isn't that interesting in the light of what Jesus said the Holy Spirit would come to do? "And when he is come, he will reprove the world of sin, and of righteousness, and of judgment" (John 16:8). But most people are not listening to Him. They are callously unconcerned.

We might as well face it: we who follow Christ and try to walk in His ways are the minority—just a remnant. It has always been that way, and it will be that way until the "kingdoms of this world become the kingdom of our God and of his Christ."

Elijah had the question for the people of his day and for the people of ours: "How long halt ye between two opinions? If the Lord be God, follow him: but if Baal, then follow him . . ." (1 Kings 18:21).

Joshua had the right response for Israel long ago and for us all today: "Choose you this day whom ye will serve . . . but as for me and my house, we will serve the Lord" (24:15).

J. Alfred Smith

An Ageless Christ in an Aging World
Hebrews 13:8

Jesus Christ is the same, yesterday, and today and forever (NIV).

In his book *Who Is Jesus Christ?* theologian William L. Hendricks explains that Jesus is always ahead of us. Somehow Jesus never allows us to catch up with Him. Even in our age of speed, space travel, and scientific research, Jesus is out in front of us with His elusive presence, inviting us to follow Him. Every age has had to look forward in time in order to see Jesus. Therefore, in relationship to time, Jesus is the same yesterday, today, and forever, but He is always in front of us.

Yesterday's pilgrimage of Jesus through the first century makes possible our pilgrimage of following Jesus today. The pilgrimage of tomorrow will allow us to meet Jesus face to face. In this sense of historical transition, Jesus is the same yesterday, today, and forever.

Jesus remains the same in His essential nature which defines Him as preincarnate or prehistorical. This is why John's Gospel begins by saying: "In the beginning was The Word, and The Word was with God . . ." (NIV).

In His existential nature which reveals Him as incarnate or historical, His physical body knew the changes of infancy, childhood, youth, and adulthood. This is why John's Gospel said: "The Word became flesh and made His dwelling among us . . ." (NIV).

Before we can properly exegete or examine our text, we must pause long enough to allow Jesus and our text to ex-

373

amine us. Jesus, and not ourselves, is the subject. We are
the object. Jesus and the text have us on trial. We are not
research scholars or prosecuting attorneys addressing or
interrogating the text and Jesus. When we are scrutinized
by both the Living Word and the Written Word, we must
confess like the Apostle Paul: "Now we see but a poor reflection in a mirror: then we shall see face to face" (1 Cor.
13:12, NIV).

Our understanding of Jesus is changing always, if we
are growing as Christians. Our images, languages, and
pictures of Jesus change as we change, and grow as we
grow, but essentially Jesus is the same, yesterday, today,
and forever.

Not only does our perception of Jesus mature and enlarge with our own spiritual maturity and enlargement,
but our own human definitions of Jesus change with our
changing cultural symbols, and they differ with the equality of our personality diversity. To put it very simply both
the Living Word and the Written Word command us to look
at the diversity of Christological definitions in the four Gospels.

In the four Gospels we see four portraits of Jesus the
same yesterday, today, and tomorrow. Matthew, according
to W. H. Griffith-Thomas, demonstrates; Mark depicts;
Luke declares; and John describes the same Jesus. Matthew demonstrated Christ Jesus as the Jewish Messiah, the
Lion of the Tribe of Judah; Mark depicted Christ Jesus as
the servant, symbolized by the beast of burden, the ox;
Luke declared Jesus to be the Son of Man, symbolized by
the man; and John described Jesus as the Son of God, symbolized by the eagle. Matthew used his culture to associate
Jesus with the Priest, Luke used his culture to associate
Jesus with Savior, and John associated Jesus with The Divine Son.

But they were all writing theologically, historically, so-
ciologically, linguistically, and empirically about the same
Jesus. According to Griffith-Thomas, this same Jesus is

perfect inspiration for the young and perfect consolation for the old. He is present help and present companionship. This same Jesus may be opposed helplessly and hopelessly, or He may be accepted joyously and wholeheartedly. Sadly speaking, far too many have simply ignored this same Jesus as an irrelevant relic on the trash pile of history.

Let us pause long enough to make an analysis of the book context of our text.

I. The Book Context

Who wrote Hebrews? The scholars at Alexandria voted for Paul. Tertullian believed Barnabas wrote it. Martin Luther said Apollos wrote it. Harnack thought Priscilla did. Origen concluded that only God knows who wrote the Book of Hebrews. Because the Book of Hebrews was mentioned by Clement of Rome, scholars believe it must have been written before then. Hebrews refers to the Temple. So then scholars argue that it must have been written prior to AD 70 when the Roman army under Titus destroyed Jerusalem and the magnificent Temple erected by Herod.

Since there were Gentile and Jewish Christians who made up the first-century church, Hebrews was written primarily to warn the Hebrew Christians to steer clear of the ritual religion of Judaism. Secondarily, Hebrews was written to advise Gentile Christians to ignore the Grecian philosophy of Gnosticism. Both Gentile and Jewish Christians were advised to center their faith and ethics in Jesus Christ of Nazareth. In chapters 1—4 of Hebrews, Christ is the living and revealing Word of God. In chapters 5—8, Christ is the living High Priest, not after the line of Aaron but after the order of Melchizedek. In chapters 9—11 Christ is the perfect sacrifice for sin. In chapters 12—13 Christ is the example of sanctification. *As High Priest in chapters 5—8, Christ gives us access to God. As High Priest and Blood Sacrifice Christ gives us cleansing from sin chapters 9—10. In chapters 12—13 Christ is the Sanctifier who guides us in discipline and holiness toward God.*

Scholars often state that chapter 13 has the ethics of Jesus Christ that rest on the doctrinal foundation of chapters 1—12.

Some scholars argue that our text words in chapter 13, verse 8 are misplaced. They fail to see that Jesus Christ is the basis for both creed and deed. In our text Jesus is the basis for doctrine and doing. No situation ethics are allowed. No cultural norms are acceptable. No philosophical rule, "when you are in Rome, you must do as the Romans," is permitted. Jesus is the same yesterday, today, and tomorrow. Jesus is the way, the truth, and the life for every generation, for every culture, and for every age.

Look at the context. Because Jesus is Who He is, in verses 1-3 of chapter 13, Christians are to care for each other, especially for those in prison. Because Jesus is unchanging, in verses 4-6, marriage is sacred and value must be placed on persons and not things. Verse 7 says: "Remember your leaders, who spoke the Word of God to you. Consider the outcome of their way of life and imitate their faith" (NIV).

This verse precedes the text. Why is verse 7 in front of the text of my sermon? Why ask that we remember our leaders and then ask that we remember "Jesus is the same, yesterday, and today, and forever"? You see, under Judaism, Aaron was followed by Eliezar, and Eliezar was followed by Eli, but no one follows Jesus, our High Priest. Isaiah was followed by Jeremiah, and Jeremiah was followed by Ezekiel, but no one followed Jesus as a prophet. He is in a class by Himself. Hezekiah, the good king, was followed by Manasseh, the bad king. Manasseh was followed by Amon, the bad king, but no King of Judah or Israel followed Jesus, Who was, Who is, and Who will be King of kings and Lord of lords. Jesus is King Eternal. Jesus is the Author of our faith. Jesus is the object of our faith. Jesus is the Finisher of our faith. He is the same in all generations.

Lord, you have been our dwelling place throughout all generations. Before the mountains were born or you brought forth the earth and the world, from everlasting to everlasting, you are God (Ps. 90:1-2, NIV).

This text, "Jesus is the same yesterday, today, and forever," calls us away from a contextual analysis to an analysis of the text itself.

II. The Analysis of the Text

We know that earthly leaders pass on, but Jesus passes by. Earthly leaders stay for awhile. Jesus stays always. Earthly leaders serve their generation. Jesus serves all generations. Now, who is this Peerless Prince? Who is this Ageless Christ? Who is this Matchless Master?

The early church fathers answered these questions for us in the fourth and fifth centuries. Therefore let us look deeper at the questions that are impregnated in the text. Is Jesus really God for us? They answered yes in AD 325 at the Council of Nicaea. Is Jesus really man with us? They answered yes in AD 381 at the Council of Constantinople. Is Jesus really one person, or is He God Who seemed to have been man, as the Docetists said, or is He more man than God as Gnostics would argue, or was He made God at His baptism, as the Adoptionists said?

They answered, "Yes, Jesus is one person," at the Council of Ephesus in AD 431. Does Jesus have two dimensions? They answered yes in AD 451 at the Council of Chalcedon. Yes, Jesus is fully divine and fully human. It is too bad that some cults don't know this. They steal members from Baptist churches by telling our members that Jesus was not really God or man. They claim with Arius that Jesus was less than God and more than man. It is sad, terribly sad, that many cults don't know Jesus as the virgin-born One, nothing of Him as victim at the cross, nothing of Him as victor over the grave. Jesus is the wonderful Word, the Wonder of wonders, the Worthy of worthies. Speak, Thomas. Who is Jesus? He is "my Lord and my God." Who is Jesus, Isaiah? He is "wonderful, counselor, the mighty God, the everlasting Father, the Prince of peace."

Who is Jesus? Son of God and Son of man, Son of David and David's Lord, Ancient of Days, born of woman, yet older than His mother. He is God's mystery, God's revelation, Prince of Life, dying on Calvary, death's Conqueror transfixed on death's spear, Fountain of Life bursting from the grave of death. He is the Rose of Sharon, blooming in the garden of Sheol.

Who is Jesus? Heaven's love for earth's hate. Heaven's glory for earth's shame. Heaven's grace for earth's guilt. Heaven's gladness for earth's grief. Heaven's pity for earth's pain. He is God, our Redeemer. He is God, the Purchaser of our lost estate.

He is the same yesterday, today, and forever. This text *destroys* transubstantiation. This doctrine teaches that every time the Mass is stated by the priest, the bread and wine become the body and blood of Jesus. This is not necessary. The same Jesus that died for us once and for all on Calvary does not need to die every time we come to the communion table. He had to die only one time for our sins.

Our text *demolishes* a Unitarian Christology which says that each one of us can become a little Christ. No, there is only one Lord, one faith, and one baptism. Jesus is the same yesterday, today, and forever. There is nobody like my Jesus. There is nobody like my Lord.

This text *defeats* the teaching of process theology which talks about a growing God who is growing and maturing with His creation. Our Christ is not the creation. Our Christ does not grow with nor is limited by His creation. He is the timeless One, and in Him all things are held together. He is the Originator and the Consummation of human history. Our destiny is linked to Christ's destiny for glory or for shame, for heaven or for hell. This text *disposes* of the philosophy of Deism which says that the stage of history is Godless. Christ is Emmanuel.

Bishop Stephen Neill has written a theology of the New Testament entitled *Jesus Through Many Eyes*. He says that after the middle of the first century there are five great centers of Christological preaching. Each center emphasized a distinctive truth, but they all were preaching about the same Jesus. These centers were Jerusalem, Antioch, Ephesus, Alexandria, and Rome. No one center of preaching and no single theological emphasis could fully capture all that Jesus is.

Jesus is more than any pen can write or any tongue can tell. Orators, whose sentences are flights of golden arrows, express only a meager measure of the honor due Him. Writers, words falling from their pens like golden pollen from stems of shaken lilies, feel the inadequacy of all words to set Him forth in His beauty. Profound scholars, researching with angelic passion through mysterious realms of theology, fail in their quest to tell us all about Jesus. Musicians who create majestic hymns, matchless anthems, moving spirituals, and modern gospel songs feel inadequate in describing the Lamb of God who is also the Lion of the tribe of Judah. That is why musicians will sing a new song in the New Jerusalem. No architect can ever design a cathedral that will give full honor to Jesus. All that can be said or done was given to us by the writer of our text: "Jesus is the same yesterday, today, and forever."

This is why we call Jesus *Master*. Only the Master can say:

> Come unto me, all ye that labour and are heavy laden, and I will give you rest. Take my yoke upon you, and learn of me . . . for my yoke is easy, and my burden is light (Matt. 11:28,30).

The Master speaks three important verbs to us. They are all in the imperative mood. *"Come, Learn, Go."* Because Jesus is still the same yesterday, today, and tomorrow, we can still come to Him. We can still learn of Him. We can still go and serve Him.

He is the Master. When He speaks, nature obeys. The lightning ceases to play its glimmer game on the bosom of the clouds. *When He speaks* the thunder ceases to play the volcanic roar of bass drums in nature's symphony orchestra. And singing winds give up their melodic sounds that make mighty trees bend to their harmonic breezes. *When He speaks* the salty sea slaps rock-ribbed coast lines with misty sprays that fall to soak the sand and all nature behaves itself at the sound of His voice, so that the raging sea is transformed into a mirror of glass that reveals the silver reflections of the moon which presides as the queen of night. *When He speaks* demons vacate human lives, Sauls become Pauls, and Jezebels become Esthers. *When He spoke in creation,* the morning stars sang together, and the sons of God shouted for joy. *When He spoke* in the manger *at Bethlehem,* sleeping prophecy woke up to see the light shining in the darkness. *When He spoke at Calvary* justice cried out, "The old account is settled." *When He spoke at Pentecost* the prophet Joel said, "At last my prophecy is fulfilled."

When that same Jesus speaks in the eschatalogical future Isaiah will say to Joel: "Now my prophecy is fulfilled: 'The wolf will live with the lamb, the leopard will lie down with the goat, the calf and the lion and the yearling together, and a little child will lead them. The infant will play near the hole of the cobra, and the young child shall put his hand into the viper's nest. They will neither harm nor destroy on all my holy mountain, for the earth will be full of the knowledge of the Lord as the waters cover the sea" (Isa. 11:6-9, NIV).

Charles F. Stanley

The Seven Stages
of Spiritual Growth
1 Peter 2:2

When you were born into the world physically, you were born as a tiny baby, and the natural, normal response of your birth was to grow: mentally, physically, emotionally—until today, you are a fine young man, young woman, adult, or senior citizen. You have been maturing in all of these facets of your life all of these years. If your growth had been abnormal, you would be deficient in some area of your life.

The Bible says that when you and I become Christians, "born again," we are born into the kingdom of God. The Scriptures say: "as newborn babes desire the sincere milk of the Word that you may grow thereby" (1 Pet. 2:2, NASB).

As it is natural and normal for a little baby physically born to grow in every facet of his or her life, so it is in the spiritual realm. If you will think about all the references in the Bible that deal with spiritual growth, God brought you and me to birth in order to grow us and mature us in our spiritual lives. You and I were not born spiritually mature. We were born with many rough edges, many jagged edges, many thought patterns. Many ruts in our thinking, habits, ideas, and attitudes were pre-programmed into our thinking for years that you and I had nothing to do with. When we were "born again," God did not deal with all the facets of our lives, but primarily with our spiritual relationship.

In 2 Peter 3:18, the apostle says, We are to "grow in the grace and knowledge of our Lord Jesus Christ." Also, Paul writes to the Christians at Ephesus (4:15), "But speaking the truth in love, we are to grow up in all aspects into Him

who is the head, even Christ." Also in Colossians 2 he again
talks about our growing: "Being firmly rooted and now being built up in Him and established in your faith, overflowing with gratitude."

Then, he says that when we discover Who Christ is, in
Him we are made complete. In Philippians, the third chapter, Paul says, "What things were gain to me, those things I
count as loss for the sake of Christ." He also states, "I have
discovered as I have begun to grow in the life, I have
counted all things but loss and everything else as rubbish
in my life—just to know Him in the power of His resurrection."

Paul was a great saint of God, but he still knew what it
meant to grow in the Lord. The Apostle Paul is a good example of these "Seven Stages of Spiritual Growth."

As we examine these seven stages, it will not prove
that one person is "more spiritual" than anyone else. However, it will help you to determine whether you have become
"settled-in" (stagnant) in a given area, or it may help you to
understand why you are feeling frustration and inadequacy in your spiritual life when you are doing the very
best you know how at this given point in your life.

Unbelief

There was a time in your life when you did not trust
Jesus Christ as your Savior. You may have grown up in a
home where the Bible was taught or where at least it lay
around. You did not place your trust in Jesus Christ—you
were separated from God. You did not love God or have
faith in God. You did not follow God or attempt to obey God
or His commandments.

You were ruled, dominated, and dictated to by a fleshly
nature with which you were born. The old principle of sin
within you dominated, directed, and dictated to you. The
plans in your life and the bottom line of all the decision-
making in your life at that point was: What is it that meets
my needs?

So, a person who has never trusted Jesus Christ as their personal Savior was acting normal or "fleshly." They were doing "what comes naturally." The goal was to get their needs met, no matter if it meant stepping on other people, mistreating other people, taking advantage of other people, lying to other people. Also, there was immorality, impurity, whatever it took to get their needs met at any cost—that's the way we come into this world.

So, you live that way a pretty good while, and somebody shares the Gospel with you. Maybe you were not interested the first time you heard about it. Then, you turned on the television and heard it again. But you still were not quite interested. Somebody else shared the Gospel with you—you began to read the Bible and listen a little more attentively. Then, you began to think of all the things you would have to give up in order to become a Christian.

"No, I can't do that."

"It's not a matter of giving up things."

"But here are all the reasons I can't live a perfect life."

"You don't have to live a perfect life. In fact, you can't live the life. It's a life that God lives through you." At this point, the Spirit of God began to work in your life.

There came a specific point in your life where you were under conviction over your sin, your separated condition from Almighty God. You wanted to love Him, but you didn't know how. You wanted His acceptance, but you didn't know how to get it. You felt the guilt of your sin, the judgment of God, the wrath of God, the fear of God, and in a moment under conviction, you broke beneath the convicting power of the Holy Spirit, and you received Jesus Christ as your personal Savior. At that moment, you were "born again" (received salvation).

Salvation

The moment you received Jesus Christ as your Savior, the Holy Spirit sealed you for eternity with a seal of promise. Your name was written in the "Lamb's Book of Life."

Now you could pray and God would meet your needs. Now you could read the Bible, and the Holy Spirit would begin to show you the truth of God's Word. You felt a joy that you never felt before. You felt clean for the first time in your life. You wanted to go to church, prayer meeting, read the Bible, and understand something about the Scriptures.

In fact, you just had to tell somebody about it. You couldn't wait to talk about it. You didn't exactly know what to say or how to explain it. Sometimes you were embarrassed, and you stumbled, but you were saved (born again). Your life had been changed—something wonderful had happened to you, and you were excited about God.

After being saved for a while, you began to get a little restless and thought, *After all, the Lord has saved me and when I look back to see where I was and what God's done for me, it is about time I did something for Him.*

God moved you from the stage of unbelief to the stage of salvation. Now that you have been saved and understand something about salvation, the next stage is service.

Service

So, you begin with your motive as pure, but the method is wrong. Somehow, you had the idea that, after all God has done for you, you need to do something for Him. After all, you owe Him your whole life, so you need to get started "paying Him back."

So, you join a church. You are "shoved" into a Sunday School class, you are "shoved" into the choir—you've never even sung before. You are told that the least you can do is be an usher, or you could do this or do that! That's OK, you wanted to "serve the Lord." Somebody points out a Scripture to you in Ephesians 2. You had been reading the first part: "that you were dead in trespasses and sins." Well, you've come through that. "Saved by God's grace." You've come through that. Then verse 10 says, "We are His workmanship created in Christ Jesus for good works."

Therefore, you think, *I've got to get busy for God because after all, look what He has done for me.* So, you started serving God out of your experiences, knowledge, and understanding.

Well, you began to serve the Lord, and once in awhile, you realized you weren't doing so well. You'd share your faith, but it didn't seem to be very effective, and what you intended to say didn't come out exactly right, and you felt very inadequate in serving Him. Then you began to wonder: *Well, I know I'm saved by the grace of God, now I'm serving the Lord—what next?*

Frustrated Inadequacy

Here is how it happens. You are reading the Bible, going to church, praying, serving the Lord, but something's not right. Things just aren't working out exactly right, and you are trying to serve the Lord, and you get so weary serving God. Sometimes you just want to say, "God, I think I'll just quit."

Then, you begin to look at your failures, temptations, trials, and heartaches. Sometimes you say what you shouldn't have said, and you get to a point where you don't want to serve God. You begin to read the Bible, and you say, "Lord, is all this what it's cracked up to be? Either I have missed something somewhere in the Word of God, or there's something wrong with salvation. I know I'm saved and I'm serving you, trying to do the best I can. Reading the Bible. Praying. Why am I so tempted? Why am I so tired? Why am I so defeated? Why did I fail so many times when I am trying so hard to do the best I can?"

Then, one day, you thought, *Boy, oh boy, have I found it now!* Reading the Word of God you came across Romans 7, and all of a sudden out of the depths of your despair, you got so excited! You said, "Hallelujah! Here's somebody that feels just the way I feel."

You begin to read these verses: "That which I am doing I do not understand. For, I am not practicing what I would like to do, but I am doing the very thing I hate. But, if I do the very thing I do not wish to do, I agree with the law confessing that it's good. So now, no longer am I the one

doing it, but sin which dwells in me. For I know that nothing good dwells in me. [That's exactly the way you are feeling.] That is, in my flesh for the wishing is present in me,
but the doing of the good is not."

"God, that's exactly the way I feel! The Apostle Paul
felt the way I feel. Lord, is this it? Is this the Christian life?
One gets saved to serve God and stumbles, fumbles, falters,
and falls. I wish, want, hope, pray, dream, and somehow
things just don't work out. God, is that it?"

You find yourself in the state of Frustrated Inadequacy. You tried everything you know to be as good as you
know how to be, and you are not good enough. You write
down all the things that Jesus said and you pray, "God,
that's impossible. There's no way to do that. You are perfect,
I am imperfect. There's no way for me to be perfect. Lord,
there's something wrong with this whole Christian life.
You know I can't live that way!"

When you reach this stage, one of two things will happen to you: either you will be sensitive to the Spirit of God—
that He is within you, attempting to get your focus on
Him—or you will conclude there's something wrong with
the whole Christian life, it's not all it's cracked up to be.

If the Christian life is no more than being saved from
my sins and shut into Heaven eternally and securely with
God, then the Christian life is one of bondage. You see, it
isn't just being saved. God doesn't want you dependent on
anything or anybody in this world but Him.

God brings you to the stage of frustrated inadequacy
in order to lift you to the next stage, *Spiritual Dependency*.

Spiritual Dependency

At no point in your life did Jesus ever intend for *you* to
live the Christian life. Now, you begin to hear about "being
filled with the Holy Spirit." What does this mean?

The day you were saved, the Holy Spirit came into your
life, and what He intends to do is work in and through your
life so you are no longer working out of your resources,

your knowledge, and your experiences. Now, you are beginning to live and walk and talk and work out of the power of the Holy Spirit who is indwelling you. You have learned the wonderful lesson of total dependence upon God.

The most difficult lesson I have to deal with in my life is that one. So often, I feel like God keeps me living on a ledge. Right here on a ledge, thinking that at any moment I am going to fall off. Now, I know I'm not going to fall off unless I do something stupid by an act of my own will. But, you see, God keeps us dependent upon Him.

So, what does He do? He sends us through the stage of frustrated inadequacy in order to break us, to crush us, until we say, "God, I can't live the Christian life. I can't serve You. It won't work this way." And God says, "That's right."

Then He fills you with the Holy Spirit, and you begin to walk in the Spirit, serve in the Spirit, talk in the Spirit, love in the Spirit. The fruit of the Spirit is love, joy, peace, patience, goodness, kindness, gentleness, faithfulness, self-control—all of these begin to flow in your life, and you begin to enjoy the Christian life. Now, you say, "Whew! O, thank you, Lord, I thought I was confined to the stage of frustrated inadequacy for the rest of my life. Hallelujah! There's something better!"

Now, you can't wait to tell it! "Have you been filled with the Spirit? Let me tell you how to be filled with the Spirit. I used to be where you are. Let me tell you what God can do in your life." You are so excited! Now your service for the Lord becomes more effective, your walk becomes more pleasurable, and you begin to enjoy the Christian life for the first time.

Now, you are walking along and living in the Spirit, being obedient to God. God is blessing you, and then, suddenly there begins to grow in you a sense that God is up to something, but you can't put your finger on it.

The first thing you do is look around for sin. *Is it this sin? Have I done this? Have I done that or the other?* You can't find anything. So, you begin to pray, "Lord, what are You saying to me?"

You are serving the Lord, He's working in your life, you are effective in your walk, you are enjoying the Christian life—but deep down inside there is a little sense of discontent. The first thing you want to do is give the devil credit, "O, the devil's after me now!"

Has it ever occurred to you that sometimes God is after you? He isn't really "after you." He is with you and loving you up to the next stage.

Battle of Pre-programmed Bondage

The day you were saved (born again), God dealt with the sin problem in your life. He did not deal with your emotions. He did not deal with all the things you had been programmed or pre-programmed with as a child.

When you were born into your mother's arms and she began to hold you, you began to receive messages of acceptance or rejection—love and warmth or coldness. When you grew up in that home, you began to receive messages from your parents, from your school teachers, from your instructors, from your friends. You and I were programmed that we were either somebody or a nobody, that we were guilty or we were not guilty, either accepted or rejected.

But all of us came into the world and immediately began to be programmed by someone else into thought patterns that we never chose to think—because we were infants we just began to think as we were taught.

There are many people who are full of the Spirit of God, who are serving the Lord God, who are effective in their service, yet who do not like themselves. People who have yet to experience their emotional being—who are yet to experience the love of God. They know it in their minds, but they have not experienced it in their emotions! They do not understand fully the meaning of the love of Almighty God.

There are many people who are serving the Lord who do not "feel" God's acceptance; they "feel" rejection. They "feel" that they have to somehow please God. Deep inside of them there is something that keeps saying, "Work harder. Do more. Do a little bit more. You want to please God. You want to make Him happy with you." Somehow this is a part of the overflow of those old emotions with which they grew up as children. This is a pre-programmed attitude that has them in bondage.

Now you ask, "You mean to tell me that you can be full of the Spirit and not understand love?" That's right. As believers we berate ourselves. We criticize ourselves. We make ourselves feel like nobodies. Yet, we are not sinning against God. God must pull these things up by the roots and deal with them in order to maximize our potential as servants of God.

God isn't just interested in getting you saved, or just in your serving Him. He is interested in your reflecting the life of His Son, and in order for you to do that, God has to pull up all those old pre-programmed, imprisoning attitudes of bondage. He does not reject us. We are somebody special! We have the right to love ourselves in the Spirit and accept ourselves just the way we are.

We are not guilty. The blood of Jesus Christ has atoned for our guilt. The level of battling with pre-programmed bondage is God's level of release where He wants to liberate us and free us from an emotional past which every single one of us has.

Everybody's past isn't the same. So, we can't say that everybody goes through these stages exactly the way I am describing them. Some people were programmed beautifully when they grew up. They can accept themselves. Yet, for most people there is a crisis at that point in their life just the way there is at the stage of frustrated inadequacy.

Now, you think, "All right, then what? You mean to tell me that as God lifts me and raises me to this particular level, I am understanding that some of the things I do, some of the things I feel, are not things that I have decided, 'Yes, I choose to feel this,' but there are those old thoughts that just surface?" Sometimes they surface when you are not even thinking about them—then you have to deal with them. Then you feel guilty for thinking what you thought. "Oh, God, how could I think such things?" These are not the things we choose to think; they are patterns, habits, and roots.

We are not battling with things; we are battling within ourselves. We have to look at ourselves from an entirely different perspective—not just being a sinner, but I am a saint saved by the grace of God. I am indwelt by the Holy Spirit, and the Spirit has filled me.

We are to "grow in the grace and knowledge of the Lord Jesus Christ" and in the knowledge of ourselves—to know who we are in Christ Jesus. What are we really like on the inside? God wants us to grow balanced in our physical, mental, emotional, and spiritual life.

We need to be willing to deal with those things that He brings to the surface. We will always be plagued by those old feelings. They are not ours—they are pre-programmed. You may serve the Lord, and God will bless you and others, but you will miss the blessing unless you are willing to deal with those things that God surfaces in your life.

The Exchanged Life

God is not satisfied with your living in the flesh, in sin, serving out of the flesh, doing the best you can, just having the Holy Spirit in you. He has goals for you. His goal is what Paul said, "What I want to do I cannot do. What I hate doing, I find myself doing."

The Apostle Paul struggled and then said this: "I am crucified with Christ; nevertheless I live, yet, not I but Christ liveth in me, and the life which I now live in the flesh, I live by the faith of the Son of God, who loved me and gave himself for me" (Gal. 2:20, KJV).

I need to understand that I, myself, am totally inadequate and that the Holy Spirit didn't come in only to "help" me. Those old root patterns that still govern and dominate my life in ways that I am not even aware of, don't have to imprison me any longer—when I understand that a big exchange took place in my life, that I died, was buried, and now have a resurrected new life. All my needs are met by Christ, all my energy is supplied by Christ, everything is supplied by Jesus Christ who is within me. I need now to choose day-by-day to walk in total dependence upon Him.

God says, "I want you to walk on the edge every day. Just trust Me within you to be through you everything your heart could ever desire." This doesn't mean that you will be sinless. It does not mean that you have reached a pinnacle in your Christian life, but it means that you have grasped the truth of where release and liberty are to be found from every form of bondage and imprisonment. You have discovered the secret that Christ is your life. He will meet your needs. He will be everything you need Him to be. Just trust Him.

On the level of the exchanged life, here's what He'll do—He will keep on expanding and expanding your understanding of Him, your love for Him, your devotion to Him. What appears to be the contradiction is one of the great mysteries in the Christian life—it is an ever-expanding, unending, always continuous growing process.

As you begin to live the life of the exchanged life, here's what happens. There is a deeper hunger for Him than you have ever had before. But somehow there is a greater sense of satisfaction than you've ever experienced. There's a deeper desire for Him than you have ever had in all of your life. There's a greater sense of loving contentment that you cannot explain.

This is what seems to be the contradiction: *Desire*—but contentment. *Hunger*—but filled. How do you explain this? When Christ becomes your life, He is just continually creating within you a hunger and thirst and yearning for Him so your life is focused on Him, fed on Him, glories in Him, takes pleasure in Him. While He creates the hunger, the desire, the thirst, the yearning, the Christ within you is fulfilling every bit of that desire.

Are you where God wants all of His children? Have you given up and exchanged all for His life? You say, "How do you do that?" It's simple. Here are three words:

AWARENESS—You need to be aware of where you are. If you are going to grow in the spiritual life, you need an awareness of where you are already.

HUNGER—Do you have a hunger for a deeper walk with God? Do you really want to know Him better? Do you really want to know Him more? Do you really want to love Him? Do you really want to experience God's wonderful love reaching out to you?

WILLINGNESS—Do you have a willingness to be broken? I must be willing for God to break me. I must be willing for God to shatter my desires. I must be willing to open my hands and say, "God, You can take it all!"

I must be willing to abandon my total being to Him and say, "Lord, not my will, but Thy will be done."

T. G. (John) Sullivan

The Gift of a New Name

While reading a little book by Paul Tournier, *The Naming of Persons,* the idea for this sermon emerged. In the introduction, Tournier, that famous Swiss theologian-psychiatrist, states his thesis for the book: that a particular name means something to someone and that it may mean something different to another. I remember hearing Dr. James L. Sullivan say, "In a crowd like this revival meeting, if I say the name Paul, immediately there would come to mind missionary, Bible writer, Damascus Road, Rome, and other connotations about Paul. If in this same crowd I were to use the name Nero, just as immediately those with any background of Christianity would think persecutor, death, tribulation, anti-Christian. That's why we name our children Paul and our dogs Nero." Did you ever know a child named Nero? I never have. Did you ever know a dog named Paul? I never have. Names mean something.

John writes the Revelation of God to the churches of Asia and addresses the angel of the church in Pergamos:

> And to the angel [or the messenger] of the church in Pergamos write: These things saith he which hath the sharp sword with two edges;
> I know thy works, and where thou dwellest, even where Satan's seat is: and thou holdest fast my name, and hast not denied my faith, even in those days wherein Antipas was my faithful martyr, who was slain among you, where Satan dwelleth.
> But I have a few things against thee, because thou hast there them that hold the doctrine of Ba-

laam, who taught Balak to cast a stumbling block
before the children of Israel, to eat things sacrificed
unto idols, and to commit fornication.

So hast thou also them that hold the doctrine of
the Nicolaitans, which thing I hate.

Repent; or else I will come unto thee quickly, and
will fight against them with the sword of my mouth.

He that hath an ear, let him hear what the Spirit
saith unto the churches; To him that overcometh will
I give to eat of the hidden manna, and will give him a
white stone, and in the stone a new name written,
which no man knoweth saving he that receiveth it
(Rev. 2:12-17).

As John writes to the church at Pergamos, he uses the
analogy of the new name and the white stone in verse 17. I
take them to be synonymous. You cannot have one without
the other. To receive one, you must receive the other. In this
earthly life there are many names that can be given to individuals. In the Christian life, there are only two. Your spiritual name is either *saved* or *lost*. To be almost saved is to be
completely lost. By a personal relationship to the person of
Jesus Christ this eternal name comes.

You can have many names in the physical realm, but
in the Christian realm you can only have one or the other. I
am either saved or lost. You can get your name in the physical life by one of three ways: (1) you get your name by *family,* (2) you get your name by *fancy,* or (3) you get your name
by *fact.* Let me illustrate. Some of you have the same name
as your father. You are a junior. Some of you may even have
the same name as your father and your grandfather. I have
a young man in my church who goes by the name of Trey.
Since he is the third to have the same name, I suppose if he
and his wife have a little boy, they will name him the fourth
and call him Quad! There is something in certain names
that families want to perpetuate.

Some of you got your name by fancy. I keep a list of
names that have been given by fancy. Part of this is due to

the fact that my own name came by the fancy of my mother. In this list of names, I have the name of a man who was born on February 14. His last name is Card, C-A-R-D. Would you guess, by the fancy of his father, what his first name is? Valentine. His name is Valentine Card!

I was preaching at the Ford Park Baptist Church in Shreveport, and a man who worked at the Air Force Base in Leesville, Louisiana, came to me and said, "Preacher, let me add a name to your list. I was mustering a young man out of the military recently and I asked him, 'Son, what is your name?' He said, 'Sir, my name is Half-Acre Jones.' I said, 'Son, we cannot use nicknames on official documents.' He said, 'Sir, my name is Half-Acre Jones. When my daddy was a share-cropper in Mississippi, the only thing he ever wanted out of life was to own one-half acre of land. On the day he paid for that half acre of land, I was born, and in celebration my daddy named me Half-Acre Jones. That is my name.'"

I was preaching at the Westmoreland Baptist Church in Huntington, West Virginia, and the BSU Director at Marshall University said, "Let me add a name to your list." He declared, "My neighbors down the street just had a new baby girl. Their last name is Lear, L-E-A-R. They named their baby Crystal Shanda—Crystal Shanda Lear." I was preaching at the Calvary Baptist Church in Garland, Texas, and my good friend, Dr. Bob Campbell, said, "John, I know you are interested in names, and I have a name." I said, "Bob, it must be authentic." He said, "Oh, it is authentic. He was the treasurer of the first church that ever paid me a salary. His name was M. O. Outhouse, and everybody called him John!"

You might have gotten your name by fancy. I got my name by fancy. When I started school, I came in and said to my mother, "Mother, I have the strangest teacher. She keeps calling the name Travis Sullivan, and looking in my direction." And my mother, for the first time, said to me, "Son, that is your name."

I said, "Mother, my name is John."

She said, "No, Son, that's just what we call you. Your real name is Travis Gene."

I said, "Mother, that doesn't even sound like John!"

She replied, "No, it doesn't."

I asked, "How did I get the name Travis Gene and come to be called John?"

She explained, "All of my life I wanted a little girl. I had only one name picked out to name my little girl. The doctor said you would be the last child born into our family and the name I had picked out was June Travis. When you were born, and you were not a little girl, I simply changed the name a bit and named you Travis Gene."

I asked, "How did I get the name John?"

Her reply was, "When you were three days old I came to the bed where you were and said to your father, 'You know, he looks like a little boy who should be called John.'"

I am fifty years old and no one has ever called me Travis or Gene! Everyone has always called me John by the fancy of my mother.

Did you get your name by fancy? Did you get your name by family, or did you get your name by fact? These are usually nicknames. However, they are names that stick. While you are growing up, someone gives you a nickname you can't escape. Have you known someone who was called "Red," when his hair was no longer red? Or someone who was called "Slim" when that was no longer the character of his body?

Five of us first cousins ran together as we were growing up. We were all within two and one-half years of each other in age. We hunted together, fished together, camped together, went swimming together, and played ball together. Everything we did, we did together. We had one other first cousin who liked none of those things. He preferred to stay home and help his mother cook, make beds, run the vacuum cleaner, and wash dishes. Now there's nothing wrong with doing any of those things, except as five other boys watch you do it. So we nicknamed him "Sister." The last time I saw him was in 1954. He was with the telephone company in Baltimore, Maryland. He is 6 feet, 4 inches tall and weighs about 225 pounds. He is all man. Would you guess what I said to him as I hugged his neck? "Sister, how are you?" I suppose he will always be Sister for that was the characteristic of his life as I observed him growing up as a boy. Did you get your name by family, by fancy, or by fact? All of us get our name in one of these three ways.

How do you get a spiritual name? Did you get the spiritual name *saved* because of your family? There are some who believe that if you are born into a Christian family, you are automatically a Christian; that if you are born into a Christian family you are going to grow up to be a Christian.

My wife and I will be married thirty-two years in June. We got married at age 18. We have done everything we know to do to build a Christian home. There have been times when we have failed. There have been times when we have not done all we should have done; times when we have simply missed the mark. But we have done the best we could, even with our failures and our mistakes, to bring up our children in a Christian home.

We have three children, same mother, same father. They have lived the major portion of their lives in a parsonage, but hear me when I say that in the matter of their redemption, it doesn't matter that Daddy is a pastor, that Mother is active in WMU, that they both teach Sunday School. I applaud families that are active in the church. I thank God for Christian homes and Christian families! But you cannot receive the new name on the basis of your family. You receive the new name on the basis of the fact that Jesus Christ came into this world and died for your sins.

You cannot receive the new name and the white stone on the basis of fancy. Some fancy there is no heaven and no hell. They reason that once this life is over, it is over. They declare that God is incapable of punishment and eventu-

ally everyone will be redeemed. You cannot fancy yourself
into the kingdom of God. You can only be saved by the fact
of Jesus Christ.

John uses the analogy of the white stone to support
this concept. In the day of our Lord, the white stone was
used for at least three purposes. First, when a person was
put on trial for his life, a person in the jury was given a
white stone and a black stone. Once all the evidence was in,
the jurors would pass by to vote. If they considered the person to be guilty, they dropped in a black stone. If they considered the person to be innocent, they dropped in a white
stone.

When you and I stand at the judgment of God, the only
thing that will make any difference is Jesus. It is going to
be our innocence by the blood of the Lamb! It is our innocence as our names are written in the Lamb's Book of Life.
Man could stand before God and plead, "But, Lord, don't
you know how many times in the middle of the night I was
rousted out to go down to the hospital and hold someone's
hand who was dying? To hold someone's hand who was going through major surgery? Don't you know the number of
times I was called in the middle of the night when someone
was in jail? When I had to go down and stand with a mother
and father and weep with them? God, doesn't all of my good
work count for something? Don't you know the number of
times I have preached, prayed, studied? Doesn't this count
for anything? Can't I get into heaven on the basis of what I
have done?" The Heavenly Father will say, "No! You can
only enter into the glories of heaven by the blood of My Son
who died on the cross for you."

It is my innocence in the blood of Jesus Christ that
gives me entrance into eternal life. When Jesus meets us at
the gate and He says to us, "What right do I have, why
should I let you into My heaven?" we can answer anything
we want. "I was a good person. I came from a good family. I
never did anyone wrong to my knowledge. I never lied,
never cheated." The Lord will say, "Depart from me. I never
knew you." However, when we stand in the judgment of God

and can say, "I have Jesus Christ as my Savior," God welcomes us in.

The white stone was also used as a mark of identification. The earlier believers apparently had two marks to identify themselves to one another. One was the sign of the fish. The other sign was a white stone that they would show to each other.

An interesting thing about the word *Christian* in the New Testament; it is used only three times. All three times it is used not when a Christian identifies himself, but rather as the outside world observed his life. In the eleventh chapter of the Book of Acts, they were called Christians first at Antioch. How did it come to pass? Did they call a business meeting on Wednesday night and say, "Now, I'm tired of being called 'people of the way'? I'm tired of being called 'follower.' I am tired of being called 'disciple.' Someone make some suggestions about what we might be called. Think of some good names since we may be called by the name for the rest of time. The name may well go down in posterity. God is going to put it in his Book." Finally someone said, "Why don't we call ourselves 'Christians'?"

That's not how it happened at all. *They* called them Christians first at Antioch. The outside world pressed its nose against the window of the church and observed how they acted. On the basis of observance, they named them Christians because they earnestly sought to imitate the life of Christ.

The second time the name Christian is used, Paul stands before Agrippa (Acts 26:28) and gives a magnificent testimony. Agrippa says, "Almost thou persuadest me to be a Christian." This context is a confrontation seeking to persuade another to believe.

The third time "Christian" is used is in 1 Peter. Peter says, "You may suffer at the hands of the world because you are a Christian." Are you that identified with Christ? Is the recognizable characteristic of your life that of Jesus Christ? When I ask a question like this in my church, everybody starts looking at someone else as if saying, "I wonder who he's talking about." Is the most observable characteristic of your life that which characterizes Jesus Christ?

Did you ever stop to relate the fruit of the Holy Spirit in the Book of Galatians to the characteristics of Jesus while upon this earth? They are identical! The fruit of the Spirit is nothing more than the characteristics of the life of Jesus. When you and I are living in the Spirit, we will be characterized, motivated, and empowered by the Spirit of God. The outstanding characteristic of our life will be that we look distinctly like Jesus Christ, God's Son! The white stone was a mark of identification.

The white stone was also used as a mark of entry into significant events. It was used as a ticket into the great events of the city. We need to realize that God has prepared for us a great event. It is so wonderful that once you read it in the Bible, you constantly seek to comprehend it. In the Book of Revelation, chapters 21 and 22, the author comes to grips with a new heaven, a new earth, and the city of God. He describes streets that are gold, gates that are pearl, rivers of life, trees constantly bearing fruit, and eternal joy. Having tried to describe eternal life in the most flowing and beautiful terms, we still have to say with another writer, "Eye hath not seen, nor ear heard, neither have entered into the heart of man, the things which God hath prepared for them that love Him." It has been my challenge to try to get a grip on the concept. I want to try to understand as much as possible that which God has prepared for the redeemed. I have come to this conclusion. Heaven is not important for me as a *place*. It is important for me because of a *person*. I am going to a *person* when I go home!

My wife and I now live in the best house we've ever lived in in all of our lives. It is a red-brick house with white shutters and beautiful pine trees. We love it! It is a splendid house. Neither her parents nor my parents ever had the opportunity or privilege of living in a house as nice. It hasn't always been that way for us.

In September, 1957, we started to Grand Canyon College in Phoenix, Arizona. We left San Jose, California, with everything we owned packed in the backseat and trunk of a 1956 Ford. We were going to school—all three of us, me, Nancy, and three-month-old Johnny. We got to college and had to find a place to live. We scouted around and finally found a place. It was just off Maryland Avenue about thirty yards on a dirt road. The house was small. The front part of the house was a converted barn. It had a kitchen and a living room. The bedroom was a thirteen-foot trailer. These entities were hooked together by a hallway that was also the shower. We actually went through the shower to get to the bedroom. That was our house when we moved to college. On any given night when the moon was bright, you could see through the walls but it didn't matter because it was in Phoenix. Utilities, furnishings and all—$40 a month! Everything for $40 a month! We thought it was a bargain, and we jumped at it.

I worked for the Thom McCann Shoe Store. We had one car. Nancy took the car to work, and I hitchhiked from school to the shoe store. Every day I would "ride my thumb" up Camelback Highway, and every night I would "ride my thumb" after nine o'clock at night to Maryland Avenue. I would walk down Maryland and up that thirty yards of dirt road. I was home—not to a place but to a person. Now when I pull into my driveway at 618 Balmoral, Shreveport, geographically I am home. But I do not go into my house and hug my television and kiss my refrigerator. I go in and kiss my wife! I go home to a person! Nancy is there, just like she was when I went to that little house on Maryland Avenue where you could see through the walls, and the hallway was the shower.

One of these days when this life is over and God sees it in His divine sovereignty and plan to take me out of this life, I will know I am *home*—not because I stand on streets of gold, not because I stand under gates of pearl, and not because I relax by rivers that flow with endless water. I will know that I am home because I will stand face to face with the person of Jesus Christ, my Lord. I am home because of a *Person*, not because of a *place*. I will be with Him for all of eternity. I will show Him my white stone, my entry to eternity.

How about you? Do you have a new name? If you do, it is not because of your family, and it is not because of your fancy. It is because of the fact of Jesus Christ. Through him you have a white stone of identification, of innocence, and of eternity. It is yours because of Him!

Daniel Vestal

Religious Liberty
and Christian Citizenship
Micah 6:8

Freedom and responsibility are not mutually exclusive, but mutually complementary. Both are biblically true. Since our beginning Baptists have believed in both freedom and responsibility, particularly as they had to do with our relationship to government and politics. Baptist insistence on religious liberty is rooted in Scripture. At the same time our insistence on Christian citizenship is rooted in history. We have believed that Christians ought to be "in the world but not of the world."

My purpose is to see how we who have been champions for religious liberty can at the same time be champions of responsible Christian citizenship. The text that forms a partial answer to this dilemma is Micah 6:8. "He hath shewed thee, O man, what is good: and what doth the Lord require of thee, but to do justly, and to love mercy, and to walk humbly with thy God?" My method will be to seek understanding of religious liberty and then the practice of Christian citizenship from this prophetic message.

Religious Liberty

A Free Church: Religious liberty means a free church in a free state. A free church means that people enter the church freely, i.e., each person must accept Jesus Christ personally. Each person must confess that faith personally in the waters of baptism for themselves. That is a free act—done by a person who has reached the age of accountability. No one can enter the church for you, not by proxy or infant baptism. The privilege of individual initiative in salvation

403

must never be put in the hands of parents or sponsors. A regenerate church membership means that each person chooses to become regenerate. No one can choose for another.

A free church also means that people of the church are free to hear and respond to the Holy Spirit for themselves, i.e., no one can dictate doctrinal convictions or moral behavior to another person. Each one of us must arrive at convictions of conscience though prayer, study, and struggle. Each one of us is responsible to God for the formulations of our convictions.

A free church also means that the people of the church are free to determine the life and ministry of their church. We have a democratic polity that is born out of a conviction of soul freedom and soul competency. Each person in the church has access to God and should be a part of decision-making. Democratic polity is often cumbersome, inefficient, tedious, and sometimes borders on being unbearable. But it is a part of the price to be paid for liberty.

A free church also means that we reject the state church. State churches exist because of the assumption that man without the aid of the state is incompetent in matters of religion. In contrast to that, we believe that the individual is competent in himself to relate to God and doesn't need the state to dictate how that relationship should be. We believe that under Christ man has the capacity for self-government in the church and doesn't need the state to dictate its life and ministry.

Finally, a free church means our mission is fulfilled under the premise of freedom. We do not evangelize with manipulation or coercion. We cannot be deceptive or devious in any way. We must maintain integrity of motive and method so as to protect the liberty of the ones we would evangelize. Even if they refuse our Gospel, we must respect their right of refusal and never seek to evangelize in a way that would violate their freedom. Our mission is accomplished as we appeal to persons' consciences, and not as we coerce them with laws, intimidate them with culture, or combat them with rhetoric. We preach so as to persuade. We pray so as to influence. We live and minister to demonstrate our sincerity and validate our message. But we always leave the free choice to the individual.

A Free State: We as Baptists believe in a free church, but we also believe in a free state. To say we believe in a free state is to say that we reject the church state. The church state is one in which the government is no longer neutral in matters of faith but becomes an advocate for the church. In the church state Christ is elevated to rule on Caesar's throne and to use Caesar's power and position to extend the heavenly Kingdom. The problem with this is that while on earth Jesus refused Caesar's throne. He didn't want it. The extension of the heavenly Kingdom came in other ways—not through political power, coercion, or intimidation.

There have been several noble attempts to make the state the instrument of the church to bring about God's Kingdom on earth, but they have all failed. The story is told of the school teacher who asked her students, "Why did the Puritans come to this country on the *Mayflower?*" One little boy responded, "To worship in their own way and make other people do the same." The pilgrims came seeking freedom, but then they themselves practiced the same oppression from which they fled.

The Massachusetts Bay Colony was preceded by John Calvin's efforts in Geneva to create a theocracy. And this was preceded by the Holy Roman Empire where the marriage of church and state ended in divorce. If history has taught us anything, it has taught us that when a state ceases to be free and comes under the church's control, it isn't long before the church ceases to be free.

On the other hand, to say we believe in a free state is to say that the state should not discriminate against the church. The state is not to act hostile to the church, to rival the church, or to entangle itself in the church. Some Baptists believe that in recent years the state has moved away from being neutral about religion and has become increasingly hostile to religion, and in its place has endorsed another religion—secularism. Reinhold Niebuhr wrote a letter to Felix Frankfurter, a justice of the Supreme Court before he died: "The prevailing philosophy which is pumped into our public schools day after day is itself a religion . . . which preaches the redemption of men by historical development and scientific objectivity. It does not have to worry about the separation of church and state" (from *Reinhold Niebuhr, A Biography,* by Richard Fox).

A free state is one that recognizes a pluralistic society and seeks to protect that pluralism. It is not an advocate for the church, but neither is it antagonistic to the church. The rights and privileges of all are guaranteed. A free state treats believers and unbelievers alike. One is not to be preferred over the other, nor is one to be discriminated against. The liberty of each is to be guarded. The freedom of each is to be protected.

Christian Citizenship

We as Baptists have been champions of a free church in a free state. Liberty is our history and heritage. But there is another value just as precious to us as religious liberty—Christian citizenship. We as Baptists have also championed personal involvement in the affairs of state. We have believed and sought to practice the words of Jesus. "You are the salt of the earth and the light of the world." We have believed that the Gospel ought to affect and permeate every area of life, including politics, public policy, and government. We do not believe separation of church and state means separation of God from government, Christ from culture, or faith from life.

But how is the church to influence the state? How can Christians act as responsible citizens in a way that affects the actions of government without manipulation? How do we, who believe in a free church and a free state, act like salt, light, and leaven in a sinful world? How do we guard our freedom and the freedom of those with whom we disagree, and at the same time fulfill the mandate of our

Lord? How do we recognize the pluralism of our society and the necessary neutrality of the state, and at the same time refuse to be neutral about truth as we understand it, injustice as we see it, and the Gospel as we believe it?

At this point the words of the prophet Micah are important. We must hear them, understand them, and apply them in our political involvement as Christian citizens.

I. *Be careful not to engage in politics with the attitude that the end justifies the means.*

Our methods of influence and patterns of involvement in politics must always be consistent with the Gospel itself. We are to be faithful to our mission and message. Our goal is redemption and reconciliation, not just winning at any price. We are to be prophetic when necessary (which requires courage) and priestly when necessary (which requires mercy), and we are always to be honest in purpose. We are to promote individual and corporate responsibility at all levels of government among our members without any hint of manipulation. I have seen, as you have seen, Christians on different sides of a political/theological spectrum whose personal morality was inconsistent with their public profile, whose rhetoric stretched the truth, whose methods bordered on being deceptive.

In our Christian zeal to influence government, let's be very careful that we don't sacrifice character. Let's do all we can to make sure our motives are pure without judging the motives of others. Let's refrain from rancor or revenge. Let's subject our actions to the standards of justice, decency, and honesty. In other words, let's practice Christian integrity as we practice Christian zeal.

II. *Be careful not to reduce or identify Christianity with any particular political program.*

The political agendas of a party or group—however noble—are not identical with the Gospel of Jesus Christ. To be sure, certain issues that are political in nature have moral and even biblical implications. But be careful not to equate the social/political causes of the moment with the eternal Gospel of the Kingdom of God.

In the 60s if you didn't protest the Vietnam War, you were considered less than Christian in the eyes of some. In the 70s if you believed in gun control or the Panama Canal Treaty, you were considered less that Christian in the eyes of some. In the 80s if you don't subscribe to the political agenda of the Moral Majority, you're considered less than Christian in the eyes of some. The problem with all of those positions is the same—the eternal, unchanging Gospel is being too closely identified with current social, political, and moral agendas.

In our zeal to influence government as Christians, let's be very careful in equating our political convictions with the Gospel, and let's be careful that we not label those who disagree with us as non-Christians or non-biblical. In other words, let's practice Christian charity as we practice Christian zeal.

III. *Be careful not to be triumphal in assuming that God is on your side of the issues.*

Lincoln said in 1862: "The will of God prevails. In great contests each party claims to act in accordance with the will of God. Both may be, and one must be wrong. God cannot be for, and against, the same thing at the same time. In the present Civil War, it is quite possible the God's purpose is something different from the purpose of either party."

We must be careful in making God the champion of our cause, of assuming we alone understand His ways, of acting as though we alone have discovered divine providence. This is not to deny passion to political debate or moral consideration to political decisions. This is not to deny the reality or possibility of knowing and doing the truth, but it is to acknowledge that our understanding of the truth may be partial and influenced by our prejudices and presumptions.

In pursuit of right we need to add the words, "as we understand the right." Let's ask God to deliver us from triumphalism and self-righteousness. In other words, let's practice Christian humility as we practice Christian zeal.

The prophet Micah asked the question, "What is good and what doth the Lord require of thee?" That question, it seems to me, is not only appropriate for our personal lives, but for public lives as well, and the practice of politics in particular. He then answers that question. "Do justice, love mercy, and walk humbly with thy God." Integrity, charity, humility are the essence of biblical faith. And in this interaction between religious liberty and Christian citizenship these virtues need to be lovingly embraced, deeply believed, and doggedly practiced.

Of all the verses of Fosdick's hymn none is more poignant than the last one as we seek to be Christian in the practice of politics.

> Set our feet on lofty places;
> Gird our lives that they may be
> Armored with all Christlike graces
> In the fight to set men free.
> Grant us wisdom, Grant us courage,
> That we fail not man nor thee!
> That we fail not man nor thee!

Excuse Me

Luke 14:15-24

At the end of every sermon I invite people to receive Jesus Christ as their Lord and Savior. I do so on very good Bible precedent. The last page of the Bible has this marvelous invitation.

> And the Spirit and the bride say, Come. And let him that heareth say, Come. And let him that is athirst come. And whosoever will, let him take of the water of life freely (Rev. 22:17).

The Bible constantly invites people to come to Jesus for salvation. The parable of our Scripture passage is one of the reasons I am going to invite you to receive Jesus Christ into your life. The parable is about a very wealthy man who went to a great deal of trouble to prepare a feast. When the feast was prepared we are told: "And he sent his servant at supper time to say to them that were bidden, come: for all things are now ready" (Luke 14:17).

The application of this great supper is clear. This supper represents the feast of salvation which God has prepared for every one of us. I'm glad the Lord compared salvation to a lavishly-prepared supper. Salvation *is* a feast, not a funeral. Too many people have fallen for the devil's lie that when you come to Christ you forfeit all happiness and joy in life. Unfortunately, some Christians also convey to people the same idea. Some Christians go around with a tombstone under one arm and a coffin under the other. When you come to Christ you are not coming to a funeral—you are coming to a feast.

Recently, I saw a bumper sticker which said, "I like to party." I fear the driver intended the wrong party. I like to party at the great party of salvation which the Lord Jesus has prepared. I am inviting you, not to a concentration camp, but to a sumptious supper meal which has been prepared.

Further, I am so glad the Lord compared salvation to a *great* supper—a *great* banquet. When I read that, I thought about some of the tremendous suppers I have attended. By the way, I'm glad the Lord is orthodox in what He calls the meals. I'm suspicious of these folks who call dinner lunch and supper dinner! The Bible talks about suppertime. The old gospel song says, "Come home, it's supper time." I reflected on all the suppers I have attended. I recall the first banquet in our magnificent new dining room. We had our deacons' and wives' banquet. I never saw such a supper. Steak and lobster were served. The baked potatoes had been mashed up with butter and cheese added while still in the skins! What a tasty supper. But that banquet was like cotton candy at a carnival compared to the great supper feast of salvation.

Then I thought about an experience in Mississippi. A preacher friend asked, "How would you like to go with our group tonight to a fish camp for a catfish supper?"

I said, "Man, that sounds good to me."

We drove about an hour to the fish camp way back in the boonies. They had catfish, slaw, big onions, and all the trimmings. I ate and ate and ate. When it was over I was afraid to look in the mirror for fear I might have fins on my face and hushpuppies on my feet! As fantastic as that supper was, it was like watery soup in a jail compared to the great feast of salvation God invites us to attend.

When I was a boy I went to all-day singings with "dinner on the grounds." I would go through the line one time and eat all I could hold. Then, I would go through the line again and get another plate for later on. Sometime in the afternoon I would have another feast. Ah, but that was like bread and water at a pauper's table compared to the great

feast of salvation Jesus is talking about in this parable. We
have been invited by the Lord to attend this wonderful
feast. Everything you need is prepared on the plentiful table of salvation. Here are dishes of forgiveness. There are
trays of peace. Bowls of joy abound. All around are sweet
layers of love. This parable is about the invitation I am ex-
tending to you to come to Christ.

Let me share with you several aspects of the Gospel invitation. Think with me about how the invitation is . . .

I. Extended

Verse 17 says that the great man of the feast sent his
servant at suppertime to say to those who were bidden,
"Come, all things are now ready." That's how the invitation
is extended. There is . . .

A. *Simplicity* about this invitation

The Lord very simply says, "Come." God has taken the
initiative. He has done all the work. He has made every
provision. Plainly put, God says, "Come." Come! This is one
of the great words of the Bible. Noah uttered it when he
stood at the open door of the ark and said to come in. Isaiah
continued it when he said, "Come now, and let us reason
together . . ." (Isa. 1:18). The Lord Jesus fills the word with
heart-moving meaning when He says to sinful men, "Come
unto me all ye that labor and are heavyladen, and I will
give you rest" (Matt. 11:28).

What a word:

> C —let the *children* come.
> O —let the *older* people come.
> M—let the *middle-aged* folks come.
> E —That means let *everybody* come.

What a simple, yet magnificent, invitation God gives
us.

A few weeks ago I had the privilege to present the gospel to a 69-year-old man. After I had gone through God's

simple plan of salvation he said to me, "That's just too simple."

I replied, "Yes, it is simple, but let me explain. Suppose one of your grandchildren was at your house. You had a glass of milk in the kitchen for her. What would you do? Would you barricade the door of the kitchen? Would you hide the milk? Would you make it as hard as possible for the child?"

He answered, "Oh, no. I would just give the child the milk."

I continued, "That's exactly what God has done. He has made it very simple for anybody who wants to be to be saved."

When I said that, big tears welled up in his eyes, and he quietly said, "It's just too good to be true."

That's right—it is just too good to be true, but it is true. God gives the invitation to salvation in a very, very simple manner.

There is also . . .

B. *Availability* about this invitation

God's invitation is, "Come, for all things are now ready." Every provision necessary for salvation has been made. We do not have to devise or implement our salvation. God Himself has planned salvation and done everything necessary. Our salvation depends, not upon human merit or upon any deeds of goodness we can do, but solely upon the finished work of Jesus Christ at the cross. Take all the tears Jesus ever shed; they say, "Come, all things are now ready." Take every groan that ever escaped His lips and they say, "All things are now ready." Take all the pain that ever racked His body; it says, "All things are now ready." Take every drop of blood that ever flowed from His hands or His feet or His side; every drop says, "Come, all things are now ready." The difference between religion and salvation is right there. Religion says, "Go and do." Salvation says, "Come and be."

D. L. Moody was traveling by train. He engaged in conversation with a man who belonged to a religious group
which teaches you have to do something in order to achieve
your own salvation. As the journey ended Mr. Moody said,
"Sir, after listening to you I have come to the conclusion
that there are only two small letters' difference between
what you believe and what I believe. Your religion is
spelled d-o. My salvation is spelled d-o-n-e." "'Tis done, the
great transaction's done, I am my Lord's, and He is mine."
God has made all the provisions. He has made this great
salvation supper available to all who will come.

There is also . . .

C. *Punctuality* about it

Notice the little word in the middle of the invitation.
God says, "Come for all things are *now* ready." God has
done His part in providing salvation. You must now do
yours. I heard about a little boy who came forward to profess his faith in Christ. The strongly Calvinistic pastor required the little boy to give his salvation testimony.

He said, "I did my part, and God did His part."

The pastor responded skeptically, "Son, explain what
you are talking about."

"I did the sinning, and He did the saving." Amen!

That's what Revelation 1:5 says: ". . . and washed us
from our sins in His own blood" (Rev. 1:5).

Ours was the sin; His was the blood. He invites us to
come. God is ready. Are you? Will you come now and receive
God's provision? God furnishes the appetizers; you furnish
the appetite. God furnishes the meal; you furnish the
mouth. God furnishes the sweet tray; you furnish the sweet
tooth. God says, "Come, all things are now ready." Be punc-
tual about it. Don't put it off. The Bible says, ". . . Now is the
accepted time; behold, now is the day of salvation" (2 Cor.
6:2*b*).

Have you ever wondered why God puts the invitation
in terms of the now? Yesterday is gone forever. Broken
dreams and wasted years can never be retrieved. Tomorrow

may never come. The Bible says, "Boast not thyself of to-morrow; for thou knowest not what a day may bring forth" (Prov. 27:1).

The only time you really know you have to come to Christ is right now. So, in a few moments I am going to invite you to do the most wonderful thing you have ever done, to respond to the invitation which God has extended to you to be saved.

There is a second aspect about this invitation which comes from these verses. We learn how the invitation is . . .

II. Evaded

A wonderful meal has been provided. A loving Master invites people to come. Wouldn't you think people would be clamoring to get to this great, resplendent supper?

When God called me to preach I was so excited and thrilled about it. I still am enthusiastic about the opportunity to preach and tell people they could come and be saved. I envisioned that each time I preached every lost person in the building would rush to the front and be saved. They didn't. This has been one of life's enigmas to me. People hear the Word preached, apparently understand the invitation God has extended, and yet evade and excuse themselves for not coming. Jesus talks about it in this parable. Three people who were invited to come to the supper made excuses. I want us to examine these excuses.

They are . . .

A. Apparently Acceptable

The servant knocks on the door of the first house. A man in a three-piece business suit comes to the door. He has dollar signs for eyes and deposit boxes for hands. The invitation is extended to him to come to the supper. He says, "I'm sorry, I've bought a piece of land, I have to go check it out. I can't come, excuse me, please."

The servant then moves to the next house. He knocks. A cowboy with boots and a ten-gallon hat comes to the door.

"Come to the great supper."

He answers, "Howdy, partner, I'm sorry I can't come. I have bought some oxen, I have to check them out. Please excuse me."

Finally, the servant knocks at the third house. A young man in a tuxedo comes to the door. He has a flower in his lapel. His hair is combed back so straight he can't close his mouth. He has been to a wedding—his own. The invitation is extended to him.

He replies, "I'm sorry. I have married a wife." Poor fellow, he is already henpecked. Either she has tied his legs or love has paralyzed him.

All three excuses are apparently reasonable. I can almost see the look of satisfaction on their faces when they give their excuses. They look at the servant as if to say, "This is perfectly reasonable." On the surface it does sound reasonable, doesn't it? All have legitimate concerns. One has a real estate concern. Another has an animal concern. The last man has a domestic concern. My wealth! My work! My wife! We can't come. All appear to be apparently reasonable.

Something similar happens when people are invited to come to Jesus. When the invitation to come to Christ is extended perhaps the majority of the unsaved have an excuse on the tip of their tongues. If not, the devil provides one. People use all kinds of excuses to evade coming to Jesus Christ. They sound so very legitimate.

One says, "I would come, but there are too many hypocrites in the church. Excuse me." He is very self-satisfied with that excuse.

Another says, "I'm not going to come, I'm afraid I can't live the Christian life. Excuse me."

Still, another says, "I am not going to come, I don't feel like it. Excuse me."

Yet, another says, "I'm going to come, but not now. Excuse me."

People feel very comfortable with those kinds of excuses. Excuses are alibis which keep people from doing what they know in their hearts they ought to do. But alibis become lullabies which rock people to sleep and give them a false sense of security. Those excuses were apparently reasonable but they were . . .

B. Actually Unreasonable

Let's look at them again. One man says, "I have bought a piece of land."

Can you imagine a good businessman buying land he had never seen? Or would he survey the land at night? The land wasn't going anywhere. An unreasonable excuse.

The second man must test some oxen. Can you imagine a man buying animals without checking them before he has paid for them?

Then there is the man who married a wife. What wife wouldn't like to dress up and go to a banquet? By the way, this was in the early years of the marriage, evidently. He might like to miss one of those first meals she was preparing while she was learning to cook! It is totally, absolutely unreasonable for people to give excuses why they don't come to Jesus.

You say, "I would become a Christian, but there are too many hypocrites in the church." I know there are hypocrites in the church.

But the false merely proves the true. There are shyster lawyers, but there are honest ones. A few doctors are quacks, but that does not eliminate the competent ones. Some preachers are charlatans, but that does not mean there are no preachers who are the true servants of Christ. The false proves the true. Of course, there are hypocrities, but as the old preacher used to say, "I'd rather come to church and sit between two hypocrites than to die, go to hell, and live with all the hypocrites forever!"

Someone else says, "I'd like to become a Christian, but there is too much to give up." There is only one thing God ever asked anyone to give up to come to Christ. All you have to give up to be saved is your sin. That would be like a man in the hospital. His doctor says, "You have cancer. I must cut it out if you are to live."

The guy might say, "I know cancer is fatal, but I have grown attached to it. I hate to give it up." That doesn't make a bit of sense, does it?

Then, there is the other person who says, "I don't feel it. When I get saved I want to have a feeling. I want to get knocked in the floor and cry like a newborn baby. I want to have goose pimples run up and down my back."

I have been studying the Bible intensely since I was a sixteen-year-old boy. I have never found one single verse in the entire Bible which says God is obligated to give you any kind of feeling to be saved. If you know that you are lost and that Jesus died on the cross for your sins, that's all you need to be saved.

Another guy says, "I'd like to be saved, but I'm not sure I can live it." That is like saying, "I'm not getting into any water until I learn to swim."

Or it's like the person who says, "I'm going to get well before I dare go to see a doctor." You don't come to Christ because you don't think you are going to be able to live it. You come to Christ because you know you can't live it and must have Christ in your life to help you live it.

Then there is someone else who says, "I intend to be saved later." You are too busy right now. But you are not too busy to go to work in the morning. You are not too busy to sleep late on a Saturday. You are not too busy to watch hours of TV. You are not too busy to spend time and money and effort on pleasures and entertainment you enjoy. You are not too busy to die. Now is the time you ought to come to Jesus Christ. Away with these unreasonable excuses. Upon closer examination we discover they are . . .

C. Absolutely Inexcusable

". . . They are without excuse" (Rom. 1:20). Romans 2:1 says, "Thou art inexcusable, O man."

There is no rational reason why any person should reject Jesus. An excuse is the skin of a reason stuffed full with a lie. The reason these three made excuses is that they didn't want to come! Jesus said: "You will not come to me that you may have life."

Sinners are without excuse. When Elizabeth II was to be crowned Queen of England, selected invitations were sent to certain people. On the bottom each invitation read, "All excuses ceasing." When royalty invites you, it is a very serious matter to refuse. God has prepared the great supper of salvation. God has sent His servants to invite people to come. His invitation is framed in the terms of a command, "Come, all things are now ready." *All excuses ceasing.* In a few moments I am going to invite you to respond to the great call of the Lord—to the great salvation supper.

We observe also how the invitation is . . .

III. Expanded

When the servant came back and told the master of the house about the excuses, the master of the house was angry (v. 21). In those days to refuse such a request in the Middle East could result in war. Here is the picture of the wounded heart of God. But the master does a magnanimous thing. He expands the invitation. Verses 21-24 indicate he says to the servant to go out quickly into the streets and lanes of the city and bring in needy people. The servant went, came back, and reported, "I've done that, and there is still room."

"Go out again. This time go out into the highways and hedges and compel them to come in. I want my house to be full."

That's why I preach. The invitation to salvation was extended by God. First, it was sent to His own—the Jewish people. "The gospel is the power of God unto salvation to everyone that believeth, to the Jew first and also to the Greek" (Rom. 1:16b). God, in His wonderful love, has expanded this invitation. On the authority of the Lord Jesus Christ Himself I can say to you that God's invitation to salvation has been expanded.

God has expanded His invitation . . .

A. Lovingly

". . . Go out quickly into the streets and lanes of the city, and bring in hither the poor, and the maimed, and the halt, and the blind" (Luke 14:21).

Invite those who know they have a need. That's what God has done. People today normally invite the beautiful people to banquets, don't they? The prosperous, the acceptable are invited. But God says, invite those who know they have a need. Invite the poor, lost sinner to the table. Find the person who is maimed, scarred by sin. Bring him to the table. Get that man who has been crippled by sin and bring him. Bring the man blinded by sin. Have you ever looked around at the Lord's banquet table to see who the guests are? It's a glorious picture. There is an old drunkard, made sober. He is sitting at the table. There is a harlot, made pure. She is sitting at the table of salvation. There is the stingy man, made generous, at the table!

There is the infidel, made a believer. He is sitting at the table. There is Paul, the "chief of sinners." He is sitting at the table. Oh, what a loving God to invite poor, needy people like us to sit at the table of salvation!

God extended His invitation . . .

B. Generously

God wants his table full. He wants a full heaven. Two thousand years ago the disciples sat down at the table of salvation. They thought they were going to enjoy a meal just for themselves. Then the Lord Jesus said, "Put a leaf on the table to the north. Put one to the south. Put another to the east; put one to the west. Invite the whole world! Invite whosoever will to come and sit down at the table of salvation." What a God we have! God is saying, "I don't want to have this feast in heaven and you not be there. I want My table filled. I will go to your hell so you can go to My heaven." That's what happened at Calvary. When Jesus cried, "My God, my God, why hast thou forsaken me?" He endured hell's miseries so we could enjoy heaven's glories.

That's how generous God is with His invitation.
God expands this invitation . . .

C. Urgently

Look at verse 23: "And the lord said unto the servant,
Go out into the highways and hedges, and compel them to
come in, that my house may be filled."

The word, *compel,* is a strong word. Not that you bang
sinners on the head with a big family Bible. Loving persua-
sion is what is intended. There is a sense of urgency about
the invitation. I am amazed at how a sense of urgency and
compulsion is so acceptable in many realms, yet unacceptable in the spiritual realm. Let a man get real enthusiastic
about sports, and we call him a fan. Get enthusiastic about
Jesus, and you are called a fanatic.

At the 1986 Southern Baptist Convention in Atlanta,
one night, my wife Janet and I decided to take a ride in a
horse-drawn buggy. The time was about midnight. Janet is
from Atlanta. We dated all over Atlanta, up and down
Peachtree Street. So, there we were, about midnight, in a
horse and buggy. I said, "Sugar, twenty-five years ago when
you married me, did you ever dream the night would come
you would be riding down the middle of Peachtree Street in
a buggy with me?"

She said, "I never dreamed it."

As we rode on Peachtree Street I saw the place where
the old Winecoff Hotel used to be. I recalled when I was a
nine-year-old boy. One Sunday morning, as I looked for the
sports pages and comics in the paper, on the front page I
saw a picture of a man leaping out a window of the Winecoff Hotel. The hotel had burned and many people lost their
lives. People were trapped in the hotel.

Women took babies to the windows and dropped them
to certain death below. Why? They were trying to get them
out of the fire. Grown, intelligent people leaped to their
deaths from those windows. Why? They were trying to get
out of the fire. People cried and screamed; the alarms
sounded, the sirens whined. They were trying to get people

out of the fire! The Bible says we are to snatch others from the fire.

Men, outside of Jesus Christ, die and go to a terrible place called hell. I cannot bear to let you go. I would be derelict in my duty today if I stayed calm and refined and restricted my concern. No. I must not let you go. I must not let you walk out of this building undisturbed, with your little excuses in your mind, and die and go to hell. "Compel them to come in." Decision time has come. Jesus said in verse 24: ". . . That none of those men which were bidden shall taste of my supper."

To be invited will not suffice. You have to taste. Just being invited doesn't save you. You have to taste of the supper. You have to respond to the invitation. Take the meal.

What will be your response? If you have an acceptable excuse, hold on to it. Take it all the way to the grave with you. Carry your excuse to the judgment and throw it into the face of God. But be sure your excuse is acceptable to you.

Take an imaginary piece of paper and write, "Jesus Christ." Then write down the date and where you are. Then write, "A preacher named Jerry Vines passed on to me Your invitation to be saved. But, Jesus, I refuse your invitation to be saved because . . . . ." Put down your reason. At the end of your reason, sign your name to the paper. Are you willing to do that? If not, chances are your reason is unacceptable.

Take another sheet of paper and write, "Dear Lord Jesus." Write down the date and place. Then continue: "I heard the invitation to be saved. Dear Jesus, I am so thankful you made it possible for me to be saved. I am so honored you would invite me to sit down at your great table of salvation. At this time, I humbly and gladly accept your invitation."

Come to the supper. Come right now.

David Walker

Daybreak at Midnight
Deuteronomy 8:1-10

All the commandments that I am commanding
you today you shall be careful to do, that you may live
and multiply, and go in and possess the land which
the Lord swore to give your forefathers.

And you shall remember all the way which the
Lord your God has led you in the wilderness these
forty years, that He might humble you, testing you,
to know what was in your heart, whether you would
keep His commandments or not.

And He humbled you and let you be hungry, and
fed you with manna which you did not know, nor did
your fathers know, that He might make you understand that man does not live by bread alone, but man
lives by everything that proceeds out of the mouth of
the Lord.

Your clothing did not wear out on you, nor did
your foot swell these forty years.

Thus you are to know in your heart that the Lord
your God was disciplining you just as a man disciplines his son.

Therefore, you shall keep the commandments of
the Lord your God to walk in His ways and to fear
Him.

For the Lord your God is bringing you into a
good land, a land of brooks of water, of fountains and
springs, flowing forth in valleys and hills.

a land of wheat and barley, of vines and fig trees
and pomegranates, a land of olive oil and honey;

a land where you shall eat food without scarcity,
in which you shall not lack anything; a land whose

stones are iron, and out of whose hills you can dig
copper.

When you have eaten and are satisfied, you
shall bless the Lord your God for the good land which
He has given you (Deut. 8:1-10, NASB).

Have your feet ever trod the rocky and lonely path of a
personal wilderness that seemed unending? How did you
survive it? How *are* you surviving it?

Hetty Wesley was the most outstanding of all of Samuel and Susannah Wesley's daughters. Overshadowed in
history by her two brothers, John and Charles, she was nevertheless physically beautiful, exceptionally intelligent,
high-spirited, and deeply sensitive.

At twenty-seven, though expressly forbidden by her
father to have anything to do with a certain "beau," she
lived with her lover in the belief that he would soon marry
her—a not-so-unusual matter today, but a highly unusual
one for an Anglican pastor's daughter in early eighteenth-
century England. His pledges, however, proved empty, and
Hetty returned home, brokenhearted and pregnant with
her suitor's child.

She wanted to fall at her father's feet, begging his forgiveness, but Samuel Wesley treated his daughter as something practically untouchable. His name had been shamed,
and his commands disobeyed, and now he would virtually
banish Hetty from the family. He forced her to marry a
man equal, in his opinion, to her deplorable act, one who
drank heavily and was given to physical abuse.

Hetty bore up nobly amid a life of many sorrows, and
her pleas to her father for reconciliation, especially at the
birth and early death of her child, were met only by heartless and even sarcastic rebuke. Samuel Wesley went to his
grave without ever having softened or having shown his
daughter the slightest mercy.[1]

Hetty Wesley walked a rocky and lonely path in a
wilderness brought on by her sin. But poor Hetty is not the
only one. Because of sin too delicious to deny, some of the
choicest among *us* have been placed on the shelf marked

"Disqualified" and have stumbled into a wilderness from which they may never return.

But there is another wilderness that may befall a minister. It is the wilderness, not of sin but of stupidity! Some of what damages the peace in our pastorates can be blamed on no one but ourselves.

Take for example the pastor who convinced his church that the problems in the fellowship over his preaching could be solved if he just had more study time. Marriage counseling was consuming his energies, he analyzed, and if the church were to hire a full-time counselor to allow him more hours for sermon preparation, his messages would have the power the people were wanting, and tensions would be eased in the church.

The church was willing to try anything, and the counselor was hired. Amazingly, on the first day of his duties, the counselor was surprised to find that the first knock on his door came from the pastor and his wife. As the three of them visited, the chief reasons behind the problems in the home emerged with striking clarity to the counselor.

At last, the counselor stood up, walked across the room, raised the pastor's wife to her feet, passionately embraced and kissed her, turned to the pastor, and said, "Brother, she needs that at least three times a week." To which the pastor replied, "All right, Doc, I'll bring her by Monday, Wednesday, and Friday!"

Blindly stupid or stupidly blind, our problems are sometimes brought on by our own insensitivities and inconsistencies. The wilderness of stupidity—may the God who called us save us from ourselves!

One other wilderness remains. It is not the wilderness of sin or of stupidity, but it is the wilderness of full surrender.

It is the wilderness that sometimes engulfs a pastor and his family when he is attempting to do nothing other than follow explicitly the Word of God in his preaching and in his leading.

The pastor's assumption is that God will bless His

Word eventually, in every situation, all the time, but suddenly he finds himself opposed by those he is desiring to bless. He refuses to soften the standards of a totally reliable Bible to meet with the acceptable norms of the worldly ones in his congregation. Trouble breaks out and he is loathe to leave, and eventually dampens enthusiasm everywhere in the church.

That plight, known to practically every preacher at one time or another, to one degree or another, may describe the wilderness of full surrender. Flagrant sin did not cause it; blind stupidity did not evoke it.

Trouble came because God's man was following as best he knew exactly what the Word of God said for him to do, and because he was surrendered with his whole heart to the pursuing of God's plan for his ministry.

It is to just such a dilemma that Moses' words are addressed in Deuteronomy 8:1-10. The children of Israel were on the brink of the land of promise. They had wandered forty years, waiting for God to take them in, and up until then He had denied them their dream.

But notice which group of Israelites this was. This was not the same congregation that heard the report of the spies at Kadesh Barnea and turned away in fear. This was not the group that fatally doubted the Father.

This was the *second generation,* made up of those who were either born in the wilderness or born in Egypt but were too young to be held responsible for the failure at Kadesh Barnea. They were not in the wilderness because of their own sin nor were they trapped in the wilderness because of some foolish act.

They were in the wilderness because they were following God! His schedule called for them to be in the wilderness— at that time, for that length of time! He had a plan for their lives in being there that could be accomplished in no other place.

Pastor friend, perhaps there is a word of encouragement here for us. Could it be that trouble is breaking out around us—unsolvable, lingering problems in the church are weighing heavily upon us; dreams and plans are being sorely tried—and yet, could it be that we are exactly at this moment in our lives *precisely* where God wants us to be?

It is the wilderness of full surrender.

But how do we *cope?* Moreover, how do we *conquer* in the wilderness midnight of full surrender?

Two matters must be settled in order to survive the wilderness.

First, to survive the wilderness I must be convinced that it was God's plan and not my manipulations that put me where I am. Moses reminded the young people, "And you shall remember all the way which the Lord your God has led you in the wilderness these forty years." Without the assurance that we are where we are by the sovereign design and certain intervention of Almighty God, we could eventually become casualties in the wilderness.

Second, it most assuredly helps in surviving the wilderness not only to be assured of God's plan, but also to be standing on God's promises. Moses in verse 1 of chapter 8 refers to the "land which the Lord swore to give to your forefathers."

At some point it must have dawned on this second generation that the promises to their fathers and forefathers were meant for *them!* Waves of joy must have swept across their souls when they realized that God had marvelously predetermined the promises to include *them! They* were the children of promise, being prepared to enjoy the land of promise!

For the pastor today, walking the wilderness way, it is essential for his survival that he have a set of promises upon which to stand. Moses declared in verse 3 that the Israelites were allowed to be deprived of all else save the Word of God in order that they might learn "man does not live by bread alone, but by everything that proceeds out of the mouth of the Lord."

The saintly C. H. MacIntosh of the last century wrote of this verse:

"It is not merely going to the Bible to find doctrines

there, or to have our opinions or views confirmed . . . it is going to the Bible for . . . food, for light, for guidance, for comfort, for authority, for strength. . . . We may not perhaps have specially noticed the Scripture before, but when the difficulty arises, if we are in a right condition of soul . . . the Spirit of God will furnish us with the needed Scripture, and we shall see a force, beauty, depth, and moral adaptation in the passage which we had never seen before."[2]

The same emphasis appears in Romans 15:4, "For whatever was written in earlier times was written for our instruction, that through perseverance and the encouragement of the Scriptures we might have hope."

What an amazing thought—that a personal promise could be given from the Heavenly Father out of His Word and could be driven with such force into our hearts that the promise would bring daybreak to the midnight of our desperation and weariness!

To bring "Daybreak at Midnight" is therefore one goal of the giving of promises. Notice the progression of thought in Deuteronomy 8:

I. The Promise of Daybreak Often Comes at Dusk (8:1)

Where were the children of Israel when the promise to the fathers and the forefathers became *their* promise! They were in the wilderness. The Hebrew word for "wilderness," *midbar,* may also be rendered "desert" and is derived from the root verb *dabar.* The verb may be translated to speak, to declare, to command, or to promise.

Isn't it interesting that if God is going to speak to us, to declare something to us with abiding impact, He will often take us into the wilderness of suffering or loneliness or deprivation to deliver His truth?

Is it not equally as significant that *the unveiling of His promises* to us *often comes in the wilderness?* The connection between the verb, *dabar,* to speak or to promise, and the noun, *midbar,* wilderness or desert, appears more than accidental.

In the wilderness the promises of God were written across the Israelites' hearts. Perhaps it is in your wilderness that the Father intends to make His promises known to you!

Notice also that the receiving of the promise in the wilderness marked the beginning of a long period of unchanged circumstances during which time God was at work in other areas. The promise did not mean immediate fulfillment. Their journey was just beginning in a sense when the promise became real to them. Decades of Darkness were to follow. Days and months and years on end of waiting and wandering were to fall around them and to obscure them from the world's view.

Are you in that predicament today? You know you were given a promise from the heart of God a long time ago. It evidently came at Dusk because you have been in the Darkness of waiting ever since.

Take heart from the dealings of the Father with His Old Covenant children. Time passes between the promise and its fulfillment. The passage of time or the unchanging nature of the circumstances do not mean that the promise has failed.

But how we do wonder! Notice the second step in the progression of the promise.

II. The Promise of Daybreak Is Often Debated in the Darkness (8:2-6)

As time passes and circumstances do not improve, even the boldest among us may begin to doubt. In the darkness of waiting for the promise to be fulfilled we are put to the greatest spiritual tests.

It has been said that the Father can ask a no more difficult duty of His children than to ask them to wait solely and indefinitely upon Him. Questions arise, debates occur. Sometimes they are spoken; sometimes they are hidden. But if we are honest, we must admit that in the wilderness midnight questions arise.

Questions Arise as to Outlook (v. 2).

"And you shall remember all the way which the Lord your God led you in the wilderness these forty years" (v. 2). Who led me here? Was it Satan, Sin, or the Savior? In spite of what some would teach, God does lead his dear children along, "some through the fire, some through the flood, some through great sorrow, but all through the blood!" The assurance that the Father has *led* us is to remind us of His presence, and where we are reminded of His presence, there we must also be reminded of His power! And where we are reminded of His power, there we must also be assured of His provision for our every need! The outlook is never dim if we were led here by Him!

Questions Arise as to Obscurity (v. 2).

Often when *we* are led into the wilderness, but *others* are allowed to tend the popular cities, we question our God. As evangelist Junior Hill has said, "I wonder what the Father is up to when all the invitations I get come from churches like New Hope Baptist Church, No Hope Baptist Church, Lost Hope Baptist Church, New Ebenezer #9 Baptist Church, First Church—Toadsuck!"

The lesson from the Father for His children at this point must be that of faithfulness. The concern must not be on achieving success as the church world measures success, but on achieving faithfulness as the Master measures it.

Alan Redpath has said, "When God wants to do an impossible task he takes an impossible man and crushes him." Sometimes the crushing takes place in the wilderness of obscurity.

Questions, Debates May Arise Concerning the Threat of Old Age (v. 2).

They had been in the wilderness forty years. They must have had to deal with the emotional conflict between the passing of time and the unfulfilled promises of God. They knew they were not getting any younger, and so much time had passed, had they really heard Him after all?

Abraham's classic response is one to be remembered during the midnight hours of waiting: "And without becoming weak in faith he contemplated his own body, now as good as dead since he was about a hundred years old, and the deadness of Sarah's womb; yet with respect to the promise of God, he did not waver in unbelief, but grew strong in faith giving glory to God, and being fully assured that what God had promised, he was able also to perform" (Rom. 4:20,21).

Questions May Also Arise as to Our Opinions of Ourselves (vv. 2-3).

Verses 2 and 3 deal with God's process of humbling His people. The verb for humble here means literally "to depress," "to deal sternly with," "to weaken," or "to find oneself in a stunted, humble, or lowly position." It expresses the intended outcome of affliction—humility connected with gentleness.

God has set Himself to resist the proud, but to give grace to the humble. The blessings of the promises are forfeited if the wilderness fails to produce brokenness and humility.

Evidently, the Jewish nation had a latent ego problem, which perhaps was unknown to them but obvious to God. Consequently, they were sent on a journey that was tailor-fitted to deal with that weakness: They were unable to feed themselves; yet *God* provided manna (v. 3).

They were unable to maintain their clothing; yet *God* preserved their garments (v. 4). They were unable to guarantee medical care; yet *God* prevented their injury (v. 4). They were unable to guide themselves; yet *God* produced the cloud by day and the pillar of fire by night.

God took away their sense of accomplishment in every facet of living, except one—leaning upon Him! Even in the way that He fed them, there was no glory in achievement. They did not prepare the ground, plant the seed, cultivate the plant, or harvest the crop—it was instead sovereignly dropped from heaven!

The Father's provision for us in the wilderness may be designed in just such a fashion—to strip away all self-confidence and place us totally in His care. Programs that have worked in other places may not work now. Sermons that drew visible results elsewhere may have gotten nowhere here. In the Darkness of the wilderness we often get the feeling that we "can't do anything anymore," as we find ourselves deprived of visible results.

The thrust of the humbling process is always away from self and toward the Savior.

The wilderness Midnight of waiting and wanting will do that to us.

The Darkness of the night helps to center our attention around the only source of Light we have—the *promises* of God and what we will do with them.

What will we do with them? That leads to another area of midnight debate.

Debate Often Arises at Midnight as to the Outcome (vv. 3,6).

The thought here has not so much to do with the outcome of the *trial* as with the outcome of the *tried*.

The Scripture records that the Israelites were led into the wilderness to be humbled, to be tested, and to know what was in their hearts, whether or not they would keep His commandments.

The verb for testing here means to prove the quality of something, often through hardship or adversity. The testing is suited to the individual and will often touch the "apple of his eye." It is intended to break open his heart and determine the depth of his loyalty.

A test implies at least two options: the right one and the wrong one. "Whether you would keep my commandments or not" is the goal of testing. It is true that we will not obey a God Whom we do not trust. If His promises are doubted, then the obedience so integral to them is in jeopardy.

"When the going is tough, when there are few visible proofs of My love, to what or to whom are you going to turn?" the Father asks. "Will you turn to what you can't see or to what you can see? Will it be to what I have promised or to what you can produce? I will wait for the wilderness to determine what is in your heart," the Father seems to say.

An anonymous poet records the journey of the tested one:

> When God wants to drill a man
> And thrill a man,
> And skill a man,
> When God wants to mold a man
> To play the noblest part;
>
> When He yearns with all His heart
> To create so great and bold a man
> That all the world shall be amazed,
> Watch His methods, watch His ways!
> How He ruthlessly perfects
> Whom He royally elects!
>
> How He hammers him and hurts him,
> And with mighty blows converts him
> Into trial shapes of clay which only God
>   understands;
> While his tortured heart is crying
> And he lifts beseeching hands!
>
> How He bends but never breaks
> When His good He undertakes,
> How He uses whom He chooses,
> And with every purpose fuses him;
> By every act induces him
> To try His splendor out—
>
> God knows what he's about!

Indeed, the promise of daybreak may be debated in the darkness. But here is a happy resolution for those who will dare to go one step further.

III. The Promise of Daybreak Is to Be Delighted in Before Dawn (8:7-10)

Notice in particular verse 7. It divides easily into three aspects, each of which declares a secret of how to enjoy "Daybreak at Midnight."

First, the verse reports, *"for the Lord your God* is

bringing you into a good land. . . ." In other words, "Delight in the Promise-Giver!" The God of all the earth has chosen to limit His sovereignty to the fulfillment of those words of promise spoken to your heart! His very nature prevents Him from ever being able to violate His pledge!

"God's promises are thus bound up with His character and rest on four of His divine attributes: (1) His truths, which make lying impossible; (2) His omniscience, which makes His being deceived or mistaken impossible; (3) His power, which makes everything possible; (4) His unchangeableness which precludes vacillation or change."[3]

The focus, therefore, in the wilderness Midnight of loneliness and waiting must not be on my ability to *believe,* but on *His inability to fail!* It is "the Lord your God" who is bringing you in! Delight in the Promise-Giver!

But also, Delight in the Progress Made. Moses reminded the Israelites, who were at the time of this speech still waiting in the wilderness, that an amazing thing was happening: "For the Lord your God *is bringing you* into a good land . . ." Though great chunks of time had passed, and they had seen nothing by which to chart their advance, progress was nonetheless being made! They were closer that day than they were yesterday? One less day in the wilderness, one day closer to the Promised Land!

As it was with the Israelites, so may it be with us. We must gladly acknowledge that we are even now being brought nearer to the promises; we are on the way out! The promise is nearer now than it was then! Daybreak at Midnight begins to dawn when we are by God's gracious Spirit able to delight in the progress made!

Last of all, this verse teaches that not only are we, who are longing for Daybreak at Midnight, to delight in the Promise-Giver, and to delight in the Progress made, but we are also, while still in the wilderness, to Delight in the Promised Result!

"For the Lord your God is bringing you *into a good land* . . ." Moses then uses the next several verses to describe the tremendous bounty of that oft-dreamed-of land.

This aged servant of the Lord desired for his listeners to gather a heart full of the riches of God's promised blessings—before they ever crossed the Jordan! He wanted the Promised Land to be so wonderfully vivid in their imagination that they would taste the lush grapes and sweet honey of that place and feel against their faces the cool spray of the crystal-clear fountains and rushing springs!

To survive the wilderness, to find Daybreak at Midnight, there is no greater aid than to Delight in the Promised Result! To fill the mind with dreams of how it is going to be one day is perfectly biblical and thoroughly helpful for the disciple who is seeking to order his life according to the promises of God!

A five-year-old black boy lay dying of lung cancer in a Southern California hospital. His mother, a large woman, a sweet Christian, came faithfully to comfort her child day after day. She, unlike the majority of parents of terminally ill children, refused to let her boy suffer alone.

One night as the child's condition worsened, the nurses began to hear cries coming from his room. The sounds continued throughout the night unabated. The next morning the mother arrived and in her typical fashion asked how her son was doing. The nurses replied by saying that he had begun hallucinating and talking in his sleep. They said that he kept saying something about bells ringing.

The mother abruptly halted her departure from the nurses' desk, turned, and spoke in an emphatic tone, "Now you listen to me. My little boy isn't hallucinating; he isn't out of his head. 'Cause you see, I told him when he gets to hurtin' real bad, so bad he can't stand it—if he'll look up toward the sky and listen real hard, he'll hear the bells of heaven ringin' for him. It'll be Jesus ringin' those bells, ready to welcome him home!"

And with those words, the mother spun on her heels, and calmly walked down the hall and into her baby's room. There she lifted the child up, cradled him in her large arms, settled back in a rocking chair, and gently began to stroke his small face. They rocked and talked, and rocked and talked about the bells of heaven, until the child gave a whisper-soft gasp and went to be with Jesus.

Do *you* hear the bells ringing?

Oh, they may not be the bells of heaven, but they may be the bells, heard through the ears of faith, signaling to your weary heart that the wilderness of Midnight of waiting on the promises of God is closer to a conclusion now than it ever has been! The Promise-Giver is faithful! The progress being made is steady! And the promised result is certain and is certainly wonderful!

Look up! Take heart! Lay hold of Daybreak at Midnight!

NOTES

1. Arnold A. Dallimore, *George Whitefield, Vol. II,* (Westchester, IL: Cornerstone Books, 1979), p. 12.

2. C. H. McIntosh, *Notes on the Book of Deuteronomy* (New York: Revell Co., 1879), pp. 43,44.

3. J. Oswald Sanders, *Prayer Power Unlimited* (Chicago: Moody Bible Institute, 1977), p. 33.

Bill Weber

Rejoice

The Book of Philippians is the "Joy Book" of the Bible. It is the "How to Be Happy" instruction manual. It is for those of us who find ourselves discouraged, despondent, lonely, or dejected. Paul, the author, was a man under pressure. He was not in a bed of ease, not on the Florida coast enjoying a vacation, not drinking an ice-cold glass of lemonade, not enjoying the luxuries of life, but rather he was writing while in prison.

Logic says that if a man wrote a letter while he was in prison, he could complain about all of the difficulties he would be experiencing and would be angry at God for permitting them. You would think he would complain about the soldiers, the guards, the food, or the treatment. However, this man had a spirit of gratitude, joy, peace, praise, and spiritual anticipation in the midst of a situation that seemed unbearable. This great spirit was a result of his deep, abiding faith in Jesus Christ.

The average Christian is more circumstance-centered than Christ-centered. We have the idea that if we could just have all of our problems removed we would have a lot more to be thankful for and be forever happy. Some feel that if all of our taxes were lowered, and all of our troops were brought home from different corners of the world, and all of the poor people had plenty of food and sufficient clothing to wear, and no one was sick any longer, and everyone would have a good job, *then* our nation would be happy! And yet, we know that real joy, real peace is much deeper than that. All of these things could take place today, and there would still be an absence of gratitude and meaningful joy. As we read the Book of Philippians, we are encouraged to *rejoice* rather than complain.

> Therefore my brethren, dearly beloved and longed for, my joy and crown, so stand fast in the Lord, my dearly beloved (Phil. 4:1).
>
> Rejoice in the Lord always, and again [I repeat it] I say rejoice. Let your moderation be known unto all men, the Lord is at hand. Be careful for nothing, but in everything, by prayer, and supplication with thanksgiving, let your requests be made known unto God, and the peace of God which passeth all understanding shall keep your hearts and minds through Christ Jesus (Phil. 4:4).

One cold, rainy morning a teenager awakened on a farm and walked out to the back of the barn where she kept her favorite pet—her animal friend, the mule. The mule was standing outside in the rain, and as the drops of water rolled off the end of the long nose of that ugly animal, the mule seemed discouraged and depressed. She looked at her favorite friend and then said, "You know, Betsy, you would make a wonderful Christian because you look like so many Christians I know! You look like you have lost your last friend. You look like the world is coming to an end."

It is sad to think the world could have a picture of the average Christian like that depressed mule. He is a member of a church, has his name on a roll, but he really can't enjoy the world very much, because he feels guilty when he does. He really doesn't enjoy his faith very much because he always has his eye on something outside of the will of God.

The average Christian, all too often, leaves the impression that the Christian life is something to be *endured* rather than *enjoyed*. With many people, their Christian life is like a person who has a broken arm. They carry their broken arm around in a sling, hoping everyone notices, hoping someone will ask them how their arm is feeling because they like to talk about the arm. It draws a lot of personal attention as they grit their teeth and endure it. They are certainly not *enjoying* it! Many feel that if we can just hold on until Christ comes again, or God calls us home through disease or some other premature death, we will have a wonderful experience in the life beyond and really be happy *someday*.

But, whether you recognize it or not, the Christian life and the joy that God has for us is not something we have to wait for until we die. The joy we have in Christ is a present-tense experience as well. It would be a tragedy to go through another day not being grateful and not being able to experience the real spiritual joy that God intends—*in spite of our circumstances*.

When Paul is writing this group of Christians at the church of Philippi in Philippians 4:4, he gives them three words of admonition. He first of all places stress on *rejoicing*. He says, "Rejoice in the Lord always, and again I say rejoice." He recognized the importance of a continual attitude of praise, gratitude, and thanksgiving.

Then, secondly, he speaks of his *source of rejoicing*. Paul says, "Rejoice *in the Lord*." The reason many of us are not as joyful as we could be is because we only grow to the point that we can thank God for the good things that happen to us. Frankly, you don't have to be a Christian to be grateful for something good that happens to you. When someone does something nice for you, such as giving you a gift or a compliment that boosts your ego, it doesn't take much of a spiritual person to be grateful for that. But Paul says that we are to rejoice in the Lord. Only that person who knows the Lord personally can have an attitude of gratitude and thanksgiving in times of trial and tribulation. Paul said, "Rejoice in the Lord."

Finally, Paul speaks of the *season for our rejoicing*. How often are we to rejoice? Once a year when Thanksgiving season rolls round? Just when the church is growing? No! Paul says, "Rejoice in the Lord *always,* and again I say rejoice." He recognized something very important. Gratitude should not be spasmodic for the mature Christian *but* rather should be a daily experience of appreciation and thankfulness toward God for what He has done for us in Christ Jesus. If daily joy is the standard and the objective that God has for every Christian, why are many who have been Christians for a long period of time miserable in their daily spiritual life? Why is there a lack of joyful vitality and praiseful enthusiasm that the Bible commands for every Christian? Is this quality absent in your life?

There are a number of obstacles to experiencing this joy. One obstacle is *secret sins in your life.* Some of you are harboring sins that no one knows about but you and God. They haunt you when you get up in the morning and when you go to bed at night. You say to yourself, "They are so insignificant and only affect me." And yet, the so called "little sins" are like grit in the eye. It's something that irritates, annoys, and stands in between our love and fellowship with the Lord. *Any sin* in your life, whether it is a large sin or small sin in the eyes of society, is a barrier to the joy that God would like to bring into your life. There is no way for you to have the spiritual peace God wants you to experience as long as you are harboring these little attitudes. Maybe it is an attitude or a deed, but none the less, secret sins between you and God block His joy.

Another reason why many Christians are not experiencing the joy that God would like them to experience is because *they are constantly questioning and doubting God.* A Christian breaks the heart of God when he doubts Him. God grieves when He sees a lack of faith in our lives. In fact, the Bible says, "without faith it is impossible to please God" (Heb. 11:6).

Imagine your child breaking something and then apologizing and asking your forgiveness as a parent. You forgive the child for what he has done. However, repeatedly, that child comes running to you begging for your forgiveness for the same ill deed. You continue to assure him that you have forgiven him, and you say, "I know that you didn't do it on purpose, I have forgiven you." Yet the repeated return of the child asking, "Please, Daddy, please forgive me," indicates that he really has faith in you and your word. God has forgiven us as His children, and we do not have to beg for His forgiveness. We do not have to chant or yell. God is not hard of hearing. When a sin is confessed it is already forgiven, but there are many Christians today who have given evidence of lack of trust, faith, and dependence on God's Word. Such allows Satan to rob us of our spiritual joy. Trust rather than doubt.

Some are not experiencing the joy God wants you to experience because there is an *attitude of presumptuousness or lack of gratitude.* You feel it is God's responsibility to bless you and to meet your needs. *He is obligated to do it,* you think. Young people have that attitude toward their parents. Parents feel that way toward their children. We presume on our loved ones, our friends, and our co-workers. Don't you like to hear a child pray at the table? They may take a long time doing it, but they cover everything. They thank God for the mustard and the mayonnaise, the plates, the ice tea, the chair, and then they mention everyone in the neighborhood! But there is something about their spirit I think is good. They are thinking about specific things to be thankful for. So many of us are so routine in our prayers. We say the words and go through the motions without being conscious of anything that we have really said, and then we wonder why we don't have a more meaningful prayer life. Let me encourage you to let your prayers permeate with an attitude of gratitude and thankfulness. In fact, practice praying without asking for one single thing. Bow down before God and enumerate with thanksgiving the wonderful blessings he has bestowed upon you.

Some are not experiencing the joy God wants you to have because you have been *neglecting the spiritual disciplines* that are so vital to spiritual joy. You have been neglecting your Bible study, you have been neglecting your prayer time, you have been neglecting regular fellowship with God's people in a local New Testament church, you have been neglecting these vital essentials to doing the

will of God, and then you wonder why you don't have the joy
that other Christians seem to have.

Some of you are not experiencing the joy because *there
are broken relationships between you and other people.*
Maybe there is a Christian somewhere, maybe a member of
your family somewhere, a loved one somewhere, a son somewhere, a daughter somewhere, a neighbor somewhere, a
past acquaintance somewhere, a boss somewhere—with
whom you have had a conflict. Perhaps there was a misunderstanding, a serious argument, and things were said that
should never have been said. You parted ways, and yet, you
know you were wrong. Maybe you weren't wrong in what
you did, but you were wrong in your attitude. A spirit of
irritation crept in between you and someone else; and, my
friend, this is a violation of a vital principle in God's Word.
In fact, Jesus taught us that in the Lord's Prayer. "Forgive
us our trespasses, as we forgive those who trespass against
us." The principle is this: As long as there are unresolved
conflicts with someone else, as long as there are poor attitudes, as long as there are unresolved arguments, you will
never have the joy in your life that you desire to have.

I remember that some time ago a man invited Jesus
Christ into his life; and after about a week, he came back
and said, "You know, there is still something missing. I am
really not having the joy you said I would have." I replied,
"I'd like to ask you a personal question: Is there anybody in
your family or anyone at work with whom you have had a
conflict? Has there been a conflict which has resulted in a
severed friendship?" He looked at me as if someone had
shocked him and said, "How did you know? There is a man
at my office with whom I had a disagreement several years
ago. To this day, we don't speak—we just avoid each other."
And I said, "It could be that God is waiting for you to be
reconciled with that man before you are going to have the
real joy He wants you to have." The next evening he called
me and told me that he had gone home and prayed about
the broken relationship. He then felt led to go tell the man
that he was wrong and ask for his forgiveness. This re-

sulted in a renewed friendship and an attitude of joy in this man's life.

Now there are *several occasions in which God's people are commanded to rejoice* and be grateful and to praise God. The first one is *rejoicing in the problems of life*. "Count it all joy when you fall into divers temptations" (James 1:2). The word *temptation* when it is used in God's Word has several different meanings. In one instance, it is used as an enticement to sin—an inducement to evil. However, in another instance the word *temptation* is used as a difficulty or a persecution that the believer faces. In this instance, this is the reference. The writer is saying, "Rejoice when the problems of life come." Now wait a minute! This sounds strange that God would ask us to rejoice when something bad happens to us. If you read about the lives of the early Christians, much of their lives were lived under persecution. They were constantly running for their lives. They were constantly in and out of jails; they were continually being martyred; and yet in spite of all of the difficulties they faced, there is not any evidence of pessimism. There is not any evidence of complaining or griping or fussing or doubting God's Will. In the midst of bad circumstances, there was a peace on the inside. There was a joy on the inside because they had learned to thank God for the problems that came.

I love testimonial services. People give one account after another of how God has seen them through their individual struggles and trials. They tell of answered prayer regarding restored health, a newly found job, a long-awaited restoration of a relationship, or a special someone who has come to know the Lord—all wonderful answers to prayer. Yet, how long has it been since you have been in such a service, and someone stands up and says, "I have just come from the doctor, and he tells me I am going to have to have surgery, and I want to stand tonight to thank God because I know that in all things I can give thanks"? How long has it been since you heard, "I just lost my job this past week, and yet because I know God loves me and is interested in me, I am thanking Him for the loss of my job"? The book of 1 John says one of the tests that we are abiding with Christ and that we are maintaining fellowship with God is that we learn how to rejoice and be thankful, even under adversities.

Then there is a second occasion in which we are taught to rejoice, "Rejoice with them that rejoice and weep with them that weep" (Rom. 12:15). We are to rejoice when great things happen to other people. I have discovered in my life that it is a lot easier to weep with people, from the human standpoint, than it is to rejoice with people. It is often easier to share peoples' burdens, heartaches, and sorrows than it is to share the good things that happen to them. However, the mark of maturity is that Christian people will know how to rejoice when good things happen to other folks. Let me illustrate it.

Let's imagine that while I am standing up here someone walks in from the side, interrupts the service, and says, "Are you Bill Weber?" And I say, "Yes." And they say, "We hate to tell you this, but a tragedy has come into your family, and some of your dear loved ones have been killed in an automobile accident." My heart would be broken—and when you heard about it your heart would be broken along with me. You might want to send a telegram or send flowers; you would give words of sympathy and condolence because you would be interested in bearing my sorrow with me.

Now let me give you another example. Someone walks in and says, "Are you Bill Weber?" And I say, "Yes." And the man says, "I have a message to deliver to you. You had a long lost uncle that lived in Canada, an uncle you have never even met. He was a multi-millionaire, and he died several weeks ago. His will has just been probated, and he has left his entire inheritance—his multi-million dollar inheritance—to you! I have come to deliver this to you in your brand-new gold Cadillac convertible that he left you as well!" How many of the people around would say, "You know, that's wonderful! I just can't think of anybody that

I'd like to see get *that* kind of good fortune more than you!'"? Often we hear the opposite kind of remark. It irritates people when wonderful things happen to those about them. There is a tendency to be jealous and fault-finding. God discourages that attitude! Learn to be glad when something good happens to someone else rather than to be envious.

We are also to *rejoice in the preaching of the gospel.* In Philippians 1, Paul wrote the church at Philippi stating that while he was in prison, he was hearing about a lot of people preaching with different motives. He didn't particularly like that. Yet, he reasoned, "If they are preaching Christ, and Christ is being exalted, I am not going to be angry about it. I am going to be glad." "What then, not withstanding every way, whether in pretense or in truth, Christ is preached and I therein do rejoice, yea, and will rejoice" (1:15-18).

I guess one of the finest things that ever happened to me was when I came to the place in my spiritual life that I learned to receive a spiritual blessing from anyone who was preaching Jesus Christ—even some ministers with whom I did not agree 100 percent. I am grateful that in my library I have a lot of books and tapes by men and women from all kinds of denominations. I am grateful that God has taught us to receive a blessing and inspiration from people of different walks of life. Aren't you? Some people have the idea that "only my favorite preacher can speak to me and my needs." That is not what God teaches. We are to glean truth whenever Christ is preached or taught—no matter who is delivering the message.

A long time ago, I was listening to a preacher on the radio shouting his message. Pretty soon his voice became raspy, and it was irritating to listen to. My first inclination was just to reach over and turn the knob to another station. But about that time, I just felt an impulse from God. "Wait a minute, Bill. Here is a guy who doesn't sound like maybe you like to hear a preacher preach, but it just could be that he might have something to say that would be a blessing to your life. Leave it on!" And so I sat back and started listening. In his message that day, there was something he said that was a great blessing to my life! Have you learned how to *rejoice in the preaching of the gospel* whether or not it is someone you like personally?

What is the outcome of rejoicing? What would happen if just the members of our church would rejoice and have a spirit of praise and thanksgiving to God? One thing that would happen is that you would be *healthier physically*. Often doctors say that many of our illnesses are psychosomatic; they have to do with our attitude. If you have a bad attitude toward yourself, if you have a bad attitude toward God, or a bad attitude toward other people, that, my friend, can adversely affect your health, whether you want it to or not. But, if there is a spirit of rejoicing and gratitude to God, you will be amazed how your physical health will improve.

Another outcome of rejoicing is that *you will be a blessing to other people*. We all want to be around people who are wholesome, who have a healthy relationship with Christ, who have a healthy attitude toward themselves, and who have a spirit of joyfulness. You may wonder why people don't seem to seek you out for friendship, advice, or mere conversation. It could be because you are known for being a "complainer." You have just won that wonderful distinction of always seeing the black side of any issue. Let me encourage you to practice being more joyful. Learn to be grateful; learn to praise God, and then you will be a true blessing to other people. God will be pleased with your spirit of rejoicing.

Often, our prayers selfishly say, "Lord, bless my life; Lord, bless my family; bless me for this; and bless me for that." Have you ever wondered where God gets His blessings? I think it brings joy to the heart of God when he looks down and sees His children with an *attitude of gratitude for everything* that happens. As the Bible says, "*In all* things give thanks." It doesn't say give thanks *for* all things, but it says give thanks *in* all things. And although your circumstances may be bad today, there is much to be thankful for if Christ is your Savior.

Now if you are not a Christian, then your life has every reason to be full of discouragement. You have every reason to be despondent. You have every reason to feel like there is no point in living another day. I would encourage you to recognize that Jesus Christ is God's Son. You will not understand it; there is no way to understand it. But *by faith* say, "Lord Jesus, I recognize that I am a sinner; I have disobeyed you; and I want Jesus Christ to come into my life. I want His joy to come into my life. I want His peace to come into my life." When you invite Jesus Christ into your life, *He will come in.* He is not a liar. When you invite Him, He will keep His promise.

Fred H. Wolfe

The Call to Humilty
Luke 18:9-14; James 4:6-7; Isaiah 57:15

Recently, I was in a revival meeting in Enterprise, Alabama. There were some things happening in that meeting which I couldn't understand. It was evident that the Spirit of God was present and at work, but I was not seeing a visible expression in the response of the people to what God was doing.

I kept telling the Lord, "I don't understand this. I know your Spirit is working. I have been preaching long enough to realize when the Spirit of God is present, but I don't understand what is happening in this meeting."

It was Wednesday that God revealed to me the situation. During that time of God speaking to me He gave me this message. God revealed to me that the hindrance in that meeting was the spirit of pride—that because of the pride in people's hearts they were not willing to do what God wanted them to do. I thought that I had understood pride before; I thought I had understood humility; but to be honest with you, the understanding God gave me of humility and of pride, I had never, never had before. The Lord showed me that one of the greatest hindrances of the church of Jesus Christ today is pride. If one of the greatest hindrances is pride, then one of the greatest needs is humility.

Oh, I had an idea of what it meant to be proud. I had a concept of what it meant to be humble, but being able to grasp and to express what real humility and what real pride are, I had been unable to do. This message is a call to humility! There are two introductory ideas I want to share before I launch into the definition of pride and humility. What is God's *attitude* toward pride and humility? How does the living God respond to pride and humility?

First of all, let's review what the Bible says about pride. The first verse is found in Psalm 138:6. "Though the Lord be high, he has respect unto the lowly, but the proud he knows afar off." This Psalm says God knows the proud afar off. Next, Proverbs 6:16: "These six things doth the Lord hate: Yea, seven are an abomination unto him: a proud look, a lying tongue," and the like.

It says here that a proud look is an abomination to God himself. Proverbs 8:13: "The fear of the Lord is to hate evil, but pride and arrogancy and the evil way and the froward mouth do I hate." This says God hates pride and arrogance. Proverbs 16:5: "Everyone that is proud in heart is an abomination to the Lord." You know, when God exposes this kind of attitude toward pride, I say, "Lord, I have to take this seriously." Everyone that is proud in heart is an abomination to the Lord. Proverbs 16:18: "Pride goeth before destruction and a haughty spirit before a fall." The Old Testament clearly reveals God's attitude and response toward pride.

Well, what about the New Testament? Notice what it says in James 4:6; "But he giveth more grace. Wherefore he saith, God resisteth the proud, but giveth grace to the humble." Then in 1 Peter 5:5 we further see God's attitude toward pride. "Likewise, ye younger, submit yourselves unto the elder. Yea, all of you be subject one to another, and be clothed with humility: for God resisteth the proud and giveth grace to the humble." This is God's attitude and response toward pride.

But at the same time, what is God's attitude and response toward humility? In the Old Testament, God tells us in 2 Chronicles 7:14: "If my people which are called by my name shall humble themselves and pray . . ." There God puts a premium on humility. We read in Isaiah 57:15, "For thus saith the high and lofty One that inhabiteth eternity, whose name is Holy; I dwell in the high and holy place, with him also that is of a contrite and humble spirit, to revive the spirit of the humble, and to revive the heart of the contrite ones." So, we see in the Old Testament that God puts a premium on humility.

What about the New Testament? In Matthew 18:1-4, you will see exactly how God feels about humility. Notice what Jesus said about humility. "At the same time came the disciples unto Jesus, saying, Who is the greatest in the kingdom of heaven? And Jesus called a little child unto him and set him in the midst of them and said, Verily, verily, I say unto you, except ye be converted and become as little children, ye shall not enter into the kingdom of heaven. Whosoever therefore shall *humble* himself as this little child, the same is the greatest in the kingdom of heaven." How does God feel about humility? Whosoever will humble himself as this little child is the greatest in the kingdom of heaven.

As you look through the New Testament you see over and over again God's attitude about humility. In Luke 18:14, where the *Pharisee* and the publican went to the Temple to pray, Jesus said the publican who humbled himself went home exalted. In James 4:6 it says God gives grace to the humble. In 1 Peter 5:5, it says that God gives grace to the humble. You and I can quickly see God's attitude toward pride and humility.

I make another point. How does God respond to pride and humility? Concerning pride, God hates it. How does God respond to a person who is proud? God loves that person, but God hates his pride. Go on to the New Testament, and you find something that has always alarmed me, something I know to be absolutely true. In the Book of James and in the Book of 1 Peter, twice, it says this: "God resists the proud." My picture of God has always been that of God with open arms, saying, "I want to forgive you, I want to save you, I want to help you, I am inviting you to come to Me." And that is the picture of God we have in the Bible. But I also want you to know the Bible says that God resists the proud.

When a lost person is proud, when a Christian is proud, when the church is proud, God doesn't bless them. God resists them. It is one matter for you to resist me and for me to resist you. It is one thing to be resisted by man, but can you imagine the seriousness of being resisted by God? The God Who created this world, the God Who spoke it into being out of nothing, the God Who is all-powerful, all-knowing, all-seeing, and ever-present, the God who created us and Who holds us in the very palms of his hands. It is dreadfully serious to be resisted by God.

What, then, is God's attitude toward humility? The Bible says that God esteems humility. Jesus declared, "Whosoever shall humble himself as a little child, the same is the greatest in the kingdom of heaven." The Bible also teaches, "God gives grace to the humble." Grace is God's undeserved love; grace is God's undeserved mercy; grace is God doing for us what we could never do for ourselves. Grace is God meeting us at our point of need. What a contrast! On one hand, God is resisting the proud, but on the other hand God is giving grace to the humble. If you want to live a proud life, you can live your life resisted by God, but on the other hand, if you live a life of humility, the Bible promises that God will pour out His grace—undeserved love, undeserved mercy—upon you!

Let me share with you the understanding God gave me of pride and of humility. How do you really define pride? We have thought that pride is when a person is struck on himself, haughty and bragging a lot. Pride goes much, much deeper than that. What is pride? Pride refuses to admit its need! Look with me at Luke 18:11-12. You will see how a proud person won't admit that he really has a need before God.

"The Pharisee stood and prayed thus with himself, God, I thank thee that I am not as other men are, extortioners, unjust, adulterers, or even as this publican. I fast twice in the week, I give tithes of all that I possess." This man never admitted that he had a need. As I was preaching at Enterprise, the Spirit of God spoke to me and said, "Fred, the people in that congregation are refusing to admit that they have a need before God. They feel that what you are saying is for everybody else, but it is not personally for them. They are not at the place where they are willing to admit before God their own personal need."

The very root of pride manifests itself when a person fails to admit his need before God and will not admit he is poor and needy. This Pharisee had no idea about his real needs. He was thanking God that he was not like other men, and not one time did he say, "God, I have a need in my life." Are you honestly willing to admit your need before God? All of us are desperately needy before God today. You have a need in your life, and if you refuse to admit your need, you are guilty of the sin of pride. Take a person who won't admit his need. Look at pride in a lost person. Listen to him or her speak, "I don't need Jesus, I don't need Christian people." That person is proud, and the Bible reminds us that God resists the proud.

A proud Christian also refuses to admit his need. Many Christians can say, "Well, Lord, You know, I know that the other people in my church have a need. They need revival. If they get right, we'll have revival." Listen, if you don't see your needs as a Christian, you are guilty of the sin of pride. Pride is a refusal to admit your need before God.

Humility humbly lays its needs out before God, unashamedly confessing its needs. Want to see a picture of humility? Look right there in Luke 18:13. "And the publican, standing afar off, would not so much as lift his eyes unto heaven, but smote upon his breast, saying, God be merciful to me a sinner." Here was a man who recognized his need. He was not afraid to admit his need. Listen to how humility sounds in a lost person. Humility confesses, "I am a sinner, I need Jesus Christ, I need to be forgiven, I need the Word of God, I need the body of Christ." When a lost person becomes humble before God, that person is going to be saved. The Bible says, "God gives grace to the humble."

Humility in a Christian is when that Christian realizes he is the one with the greatest need. Humility in a

Christian says, "God, I am the one who needs mercy. I am the one who needs forgiveness. I am the one who needs forgiveness. I am the one who needs to grow spiritually. So, the first idea I want you to nail down about pride is this: Pride refuses to admit its needs before God.

Pride refuses to admit that it cannot meet its own needs! You see, that's the core of pride. Not only does it have trouble admitting its need, but it won't admit it can't meet its own needs. In other words, the heart of pride is a feeling of self-sufficiency. Not one time did this Pharisee in Luke 18 imply that he couldn't meet his own needs. He proclaimed, "I fast twice a week, I give tithes of all that I possess." That Pharisee thought he was meeting every need he himself had.

It did not occur to him that he had needs only God could meet. Do you know what has happened today, not only in the lives of lost people, but also in the lives of Christians? Not only do we have trouble admitting our needs, but we won't admit we can't meet our own needs! "I can straighten out my own life, I don't need any outside help!" That's pride. Pride is refusing to admit that you can't meet your own needs! The root of it is self-sufficiency. I will solve my own problems, I will work out my own difficulties, I will fight my own battles, and I will accomplish my own goals with the exclusion of the supernatural God Who wants to come to my aid.

As I look at the church of Jesus Christ today, I see the visible church, the organized church, and I see it struggling. The world is more intensely lost than it ever has been. The world is on a jet plane speeding into hell. Immorality and pornography and drunkenness and dope addiction are eating this country alive. But the church will not admit its needs and, if it does confess a need, it believes it can meet its own needs. We will get a new program, a new plan, a new organization, and we will meet our own needs. All God is waiting for the church to say is, "God, we have got a need, and we can't meet it ourselves." There is no program, plan, organization that can meet the needs of the church—nothing short of divine intervention will ever suffice for the church of the living God. When will the church admit its great needs and cry out to God to meet them?

But humility is just the opposite! Humility constantly admits, "I can't meet my own needs." Humility falls on its face before God and cries, "My needs will never be met unless you, the living God, meet them." The difference between pride and humility is that pride looks to itself to meet its needs. Humility looks to God to meet its needs. And the church today is guilty of pride, for the church is looking to itself to meet its own needs. The idea is if we could get more money, more buildings, new programs, we could meet our own needs. Humility confesses, "God, only you can meet my needs, no one else, nothing else." When we begin to believe that only God can meet our needs, we will watch God meet our needs. This is the attitude of the publican—"God, be merciful to me." He was looking to God, not to himself. He was humble before God.

A third truth the Lord showed me about pride was: Pride is more concerned with what man thinks than what God thinks! I am convinced that many people would really humble themselves before God, but they refuse because they have an image they must hold up before people—"I have got to be respectable, I have got to hold up the image of 'Mr. Spiritual.' I can't dare let them know I have a serious need." In Luke 18 the Pharisee knew there was going to be a crowd of people there. He walked in, stood up, and thought to himself, *They are listening and looking.* "God, I thank You that I am not like other men." And he went on to describe his goodness. He was more concerned about what those around him thought about him than what God thought.

But what about the publican? The Bible says he stood afar off, and he wouldn't even lift his eyes toward heaven, but he smote upon his breast! He wasn't concerned about his image; he wasn't concerned about being respectable. He called out, "God, be merciful to me a sinner." I want to ask you, my friend, when will the church of Jesus Christ not only admit our needs, and not only admit we can't meet those needs, but also come to the place where we are more concerned about what God thinks than what man thinks? That will be humility.

Jesus spoke to this issue in John 5:44. "How can ye believe, which receive honour one of another, and seek not the honour that cometh from God only?" Jesus was saying as long as you are more concerned about what people think than what God thinks, you are guilty of the sin of pride, and God resists the proud.

The fourth truth about pride is: Pride always sees the faults of others! Did you notice how the Pharisee prayed in Luke 18:11? "I thank you that I am not as other men are—extortioners, unjust, adulterers." A proud person always sees the faults of others. I am often around people who are extremely critical of everybody else; they are finding fault with everybody and everything. It is clear that such persons are headed for a spiritual fall, because they see the sins of others, and they are not even seeing their own sins. Pride always sees the faults of others! This Pharisee kept saying, "Lord, look at their faults," and not one time did he ever consider that he had a sin in his heart before God. Humility always sees its own faults and sins. The publican in this story cried, "God, be merciful to me!" He saw his own sins and asked God for mercy. Humility sees its own sins and confesses and forsakes them. Paul testified, "Christ Jesus came into the world to save sinners; of whom I am chief" (1 Tim. 1:15). Humility sees its own sins and its own needs rather than the sins of others.

Another truth about pride is: Pride always claims to be right! Pride will go to any and every extent to justify itself and to defend itself. Show me a person who is always right—it never occurs to him that he could ever be wrong—and I will show you a proud person. Humility readily admits when it is wrong.

I want to ask you a question. How can God help a person who won't admit his need? How can God help a person who won't admit that only God can meet his needs? How can God really help a person who is more concerned about what man thinks than what God thinks? How can God help a person who is always seeing the faults of others, and how can God help a person who is never wrong? That is pride. God resists the proud. However, you let a person walk in humility, admitting his needs, confessing that only God can meet his needs; becoming more concerned about what God thinks than what man thinks; dealing with his own sins before he looks for the sins of others; let him readily admit when he is wrong, that is humility. Then the grace of God is poured out on that humble person. He abundantly pours out his grace on a humble church. The blessings of God flow to the humble.

Will you answer God's call to humility? The Bible says, "Humble yourselves under the mighty hand of God that he may exalt you in due time."

"If my people, which are called by my name, will humble themselves and pray . . ."

God gives grace to the humble. Humble yourself before God right now, and he will give you superabundant grace.

H. Edwin Young

Building Blocks
1 Corinthians 3:1-15

Carl Wallenda was one of the greatest tightrope aerialists who ever lived. He once wrote, "For me, to live is being on a tightrope. All the rest is waiting." In 1968, he commented that the most important thing about walking a tightrope is to be confident you can do it and never to think about failure.

In 1978, Wallenda fell to his death from a tightrope that was seventy-five feet up in the air above the city of San Juan, Puerto Rico. His wife, who is also an aerialist, reported that, for three months prior to attempting the most dangerous feat he'd ever tried, all he talked about was falling. She said never before in all their career together had Carl ever given a thought to falling. She said he spent all of his time prior to that fatal walk putting up the wire (which he had never bothered with before). He worried about the guidewires and spent endless hours calculating the wind, which he had also never done before. After his death, she said, "I believe the reason Carl fell was because he spent all of his time preparing not to fall, instead of spending time preparing to walk the rope."

In his first letter to the Christians in Corinth, Paul was diligently encouraging them to think positively about their growth as believers, to recognize the potential that was available to them in Christ, and not to be deterred by all the negative obstacles that could stunt their spiritual growth. The first word Paul has for the church at Corinth in 1 Corinthians 3 is *that they are a living body, and that their goal, both corporately and individually, should be maturity. Secondly, he compares them to a field, the goal of which is productivity. The third comparison in 1 Corinthians 3:1-15 is that of a building with a goal of quality construction.*

> And I, brethren, could not speak to you as to spiritual men, but as to men of flesh, as to babes in Christ (v. 1, NASB).

The fact that Paul refers to the Corinthians as "brethren" is significant. He is identifying with them before he speaks a hard word. "I am in this with you. I am not above you. I am your brother and a part of your family."

The word Paul uses in verse 1, for "flesh," is *sarkinos,* which simply means "flesh and blood." It is not the same word that is used in verse 3. There the word is *sarkikos,* which is translated "carnal" or "fleshly." *Sarkikos* is used twice in verse 3 and carries with it the connotation of one dominated by the world. The use of the word, *sarkinos,* in verse 1, shows us that Paul is simply saying, "You're human."

> . . . I, brethren, could not speak to you as spiritual men . . .

When Paul speaks of spiritual men, he is describing those who are controlled by the Spirit. Every Christian is controlled by the Spirit. You might say, "Wait a minute, that doesn't make sense. Sometimes I'm not controlled by the Spirit and I'm a Christian." That's not what Paul is talking about. There are only two types of people in the world: there is the "natural" person and there is the "spiritual" person. A "natural" person is one who is outside of Christ. A "spiritual" person is one who is a Christian and has a "control mechanism" built inside of him. The spiritual man can be disobedient to his "mechanism," but positionally, from God's perspective, he is still controlled by the Spirit. Practically, because of disobedience, we may be away from God and His plan. But from His perspective, we are right with

Him because we are covered by the blood of Jesus Christ. We are positionally "A-OK."

Paul is saying, "When I came to you five years ago and spent two-and-a-half years with you, I spoke to you not as spiritual men, not as Christians who had been Christians for a while but . . ." he said, "I had to deal with you as if you were babies."

Now there's nothing wrong with being a baby. Everybody has been a baby. Babies are little bundles of ego. You won't find anything on this earth as egotistical as a newborn baby. Someone said, "A baby is a digestive tract with a loud noise on one end and no responsibility on the other!"

> I gave you milk to drink, not solid food; for you were
> not yet able to receive it. Indeed, even now you are not
> yet able (v. 2, NASB).

Paul is saying that all this time had gone by, and the Corinthians were still on pablum. It was no wonder there were problems and divisions in the church—strife, jealousy, exploitation, and misuse of the gifts. First Peter 2:2-4 deals with this same immaturity:

> Like newborn babes, long for the pure milk of the
> word, that by it you may grow in respect to salvation,
> if you have tasted the kindness of the Lord (NASB).

As newborns, we long for milk. A baby cannot consume solid food. How long, however, does one stay on milk? A child must move on to solid food if there is to be growth. Paul is telling the Corinthians that they have been surviving on milk for too long. They fell prey to what so many of us today are still falling prey to. James 1:25 tells us: "We have lost our hearing of the Word." When one receives Jesus Christ he reads the Bible, and the Holy Spirit gives real unction to that Word. Then, if that unction is not there in one's life, and he's not really growing in his Christian life, he often looks around for someone to blame—the preacher, a teacher, a group—because it *has to be someone else's fault that growth has not occurred*. Peter declares in verse 1 of chapter 2: *"Therefore, putting aside all malice and guile and hypocrisy and envy and all slander, . . ."* (NASB).

Do you see what Peter is saying? We want to grow while there is still sin in our lives. We want to grow, even though pride, self-righteousness, malice, slander, and all sorts of immorality are alive and well in our personalities. Then we wonder why we are not growing. Peter sets us straight. He says we are to put aside all sin and then go to the milk of the Word. Soon we will begin to be nourished, teeth (discernment and understanding) will appear, and we can begin to enjoy "solid" spiritual food.

It is interesting to see the "diet" the Bible prescribes for Christians. In 1 Peter 2, the Word is compared to milk; in Matthew 4, to bread; in Hebrews 5, to meat; and in Psalm 119, to honey. Just as a mature person recognizes the importance of a nutritionally balanced diet, one who is spiritually mature will see to it that his spiritual food is appropriately balanced. Those who are content to remain spiritual infants will be content to stay on "milk" and never progress.

For example, if I declare, "Jesus Christ died on the cross for your sin," some would state, "I understand that He took my sin and my place when He died on the cross for me, and that is a wonderful comfort to me." That's an example of surface or "milk" understanding. Others would consider the deeper implications of the cross: the propitiation, justification, sanctification, glorification. They would think about all the complex ramifications of that simple statement. The result would be awe and humility—something far more than simple comfort.

Hebrews 5 tells us that the *facts* of Jesus' life constitute the "milk" of the Word. At a deeper level, the "meat" of the Word is *understanding the significance of and reason behind* those same facts about His earthly ministry. Certainly, every message that is true preaching must end up at the cross and give an invitation for people to come to Christ. Yet, in so many churches, there is a steady diet every Sunday of "salvationitis." Those people who have already been saved are not growing because they are not being nourished with the whole counsel of the Word. They are not being fed the "meat," the "bread," and the "honey," which is the whole Word of God.

Prophecy, milk; eschatology, milk. Even the knowledge and use of the gifts of the Spirit were "milk" to Paul. He reminded the church at Corinth that they possessed every imaginable gift and still behaved like spiritual infants. Because they were not being nourished by "meat," they were not producing the fruit of the Spirit. And the common ingredient of all the fruits of the Spirit is *love*. He acknowledged their expertise in all the prophetic gifts, but he did not see in them the primary evidence of the fruit of the Spirit: the evidence of love. That, affirmed Paul, was the very essence of the Gospel, and the best evidence that the "meat" had been "digested."

In verse 3:

> . . . for you are still fleshly . . .

Paul uses a different word. Some translations read "worldly" and others "carnal." The Greek here is *sarkikos,* and it means that a person is not only alive, and flesh and blood, but dominated by the spirit of the world. In other words, the world is calling the shots in such a life.

> . . . you are . . . fleshly. For since there is jealousy and strife among you, are you not fleshly, and are you not walking like mere men? For when one says, "I am of Paul," and another, "I am of Apollos," are you not mere men? (vv. 3-4, NASB).

It is important to notice the order of the two words, "strife" and "jealousy." When jealousy enters a relationship or comes into a business or into a church, strife always follows. The world had so thoroughly saturated the church at Corinth that fleshly thinking and philosophy were permeating its entire agenda. They were divided into cultic sects and cliques on the basis of individual personalities and emotion, rather than on the basis of sound doctrine. The church was totally without meaning and unity. This is why Paul says they are dominated by the spirit of the world.

So Paul has shown us that there are various criteria for assessing a person's level of maturity. Even his diet, what he eats, says something about him. The way a person handles interpersonal relationships also says something about his maturity. Paul repeatedly reminds the Corinthians—three times in three chapters—that they have the finest pastor-teachers to be found anywhere, and still they are consuming pablum. Any church that's built around the pastor or another staff member, around a particular doctrine or program, is one not built upon the Word of God.

> What then is Apollos? And what is Paul? Servants through whom you believed, even as the Lord gave opportunity to each one (NASB).

Have you ever seen a statue erected to a bus boy? Statues and portraits usually honor "bigwigs" and not the folks behind the scenes. Paul emphasizes that he and Apollos are mere men who are no more than servants. He is pointing out that God is the One who deserves the "statue." Paul is giving a clear call to humility, and he is reminding us that we are always to acknowledge God as the Author of everything worthwhile.

He reiterates this principle in Romans 12:3. Every time we begin to think we are indispensable, we need to remember we are to be only a conduit or an instrument of the Word of God. Paul affirmed that both he and Apollos were nothing more than clear channels through which the Word of God could easily flow. Pride has no place in the life of a servant of God.

The author is chastising the church at Corinth for their spiritual immaturity. He reminds them that milk is certainly acceptable, but they need to progress and to include some of the other "staples" (bread, honey, meat) of God's Word. He wanted them to move out of the "pablum" stage to a more mature stage of depth and understanding of the Word of God. As Paul moves from the emphasis on the gifts possessed by the Corinthian Christians, he begins to emphasize the fruit produced by the use of the gifts.

In verses 1 through 5, Paul employs the analogy of a growing body. In verses 6-9, a field and its productivity are used to illustrate the quantity and quality of life to which God is calling the Corinthians.

> I planted, Apollos watered, but God was causing the growth. So then neither the one who plants nor the one who waters is anything, but God who causes the growth. Now he who plants and he who waters are one [See it? There's unity. They are one.]; but each will receive his own reward according to his own labor. For we are God's fellow workers; you are God's field . . . (NASB).

A field does not just appear ready for planting. Land, in its untouched "wilderness condition," is usually covered with wild, tangled undergrowth, and the soil is full of rocks, roots, and trash. The first job of the planter is to clear the land of all visible wild growth in order to prepare it for the plow. Then, as land is repeatedly plowed and cultivated, it becomes increasingly easy to cultivate.

First of all, in his agricultural metaphor, Paul stresses the fact that his and Apollos's work were complementary and should be evaluated only from that perspective. One of the characteristics of immaturity (that Paul addresses in verse 4) manifested by the Corinthian Christians was their partisan spirit within the church. Some aligned themselves with Paul and wrongly inferred "license," when he actually preached "liberty." Others favored the Hellenistic politics and rhetoric of Apollos. Still others who were faithful to "Cephas" wanted to "hang on" to the Hebrew rituals and laws in addition to the Gospel of Jesus Christ.

Paul compares the establishment of the church at Corinth to the planting of a tree or vine. Because he had established the church, he called himself the "planter." Apollos, on the other hand, came to Corinth after Paul had left, for the purpose of directing and cultivating the work of the established church. He did the "watering." But Paul quickly comes to the point that only God's work in the process is indispensable. It is He, and He alone, who causes the growth.

In verse 7, the apostle established even further the relative significance of the various "workers." Neither the planter nor the "waterer" is anything—in *comparison* to God. This is but an echo of Jesus' words in John 15:5: ". . . apart from Me, you can do nothing" (NASB).

Think about one of the main characteristics of fruit. Every piece of fruit contains seeds that can produce more fruit of its kind. If the gifts of the Spirit are properly used, they will inevitably produce fruit which is the real goal of every Christian. The gift of evangelism has to be effectively used—planted and watered—before it will be manifested in love. If we stop at a knowledge of prophecy and do not move on to the truth about Jesus Christ that is revealed in that prophecy, then we have only "stored" the gift without allowing it to produce the fruit.

Paul further states that unity is necessary to achieve this productivity. He explains that he and Apollos are "in the same business" and that harmony should always be the goal of Christians working together. He is, in fact, explaining why the cliques and "inside" factions he decried in verse 4 were not viable. Christians corporately using their individual gifts for the upbuilding of the body were encouraged. But Christians who gave their loyalities to personalities instead of principles, because of personal preferences or idiosyncracies, were not contributing to the growth of the church or to their own individual growth.

The ninth verse describes the relationships conducive to spiritual productivity. As fellow workers, we are to live and work in harmony, but everything we do is to be under the possessive supervision of God alone. We are *His* "fellow workers."

Paul not only knew about spiritual requisites for the growth of individual Christians but also knew about the mechanics of building a church. He was a master strategist. As soon as Paul entered a community for the first time, he would head straight for the local synagogue and start his preaching with the reading from the Law. When enough of the local Jews had come to know Jesus Christ, he would then go with that small band of converts and begin to preach to the Gentiles outside the synagogue. Because of Paul's strategy—first preaching within the synagogue and then outside it—the foundation of the church which he would subsequently build in that particular community would include both Jews and Gentiles. At one point in Acts, Paul alludes to a town into which he would not go because the church was already started, and he believed that the foundation of that church was unstable. He refused to build on any foundation other than the Lord Jesus Christ.

His refusal to build on someone else's base had nothing to do with pride. He knew the foundation of any structure predetermined the quality of the structure. The foundation determines how high a building can be. It determines the length and width, and dimensions, the function, the purpose—all of those things are dependent upon the foundation of any building.

The Greek word for "master builder," *architekton,* is also the word from which we derive our English word, "architect." This is not just a draftsman who draws some plans. He is a person who "lives" and works with a structure from conception to completion. He does indeed draw plans, but even before this happens there is a concept and a dream. He has a clear understanding of what the building will be used for, and that understanding is the base from which he designs and plans the entire structure. And because he has a considerable time and interest investment in the structure from the drawing board forward—when the actual construction begins, he will be directly involved in the entire process.

In the New Testament, there was not much necessity for "home office" folks—those who merely direct and promote from far away without ever getting down in the trenches where the work is actually being done. Similarly, I have a problem with "establishment" people—ministerial and denominational types—who spend all their time in bureaucratic ivory towers, planning, overseeing (literally), and strategizing, and they never get down where real people live who desperately need to be introduced to Jesus Christ. Paul, in stark contrast, *stayed* in the ditch. He was constantly utilizing his spiritual and human gifts to promote the Gospel of His Lord and Savior. Those folks who think they cannot knock on doors, because they are too busy "teaching the Bible," need to understand they first must practice what it teaches before they have any right to share those teachings with anyone else.

Having established his own credibility as a "foundation man"—a master builder—Paul moves on to the foundation itself. He had stated precisely what that foundation was back in verse 2 of chapter 1, when he told them:

> For I determined to know nothing among you except
> Jesus Christ, and Him crucified (NASB).

Jesus was the whole and the only foundation of all the churches Paul started on his missionary journeys. The Gospels tell us the story of the life, death, and resurrection of Jesus. Acts begins with the story of His ascension and continues with the coming of the Holy Spirit and the activities within the early church. The Epistles comment on how we are to implement the teachings of Jesus that He enunciated during His earthly ministry, and Revelation reaffirms that He will, indeed, come again and rule over the earth.

There is a very simple reson for the ineffectiveness of liberal churches across our land today. They have built upon the weak and fragile foundation of the humanness of Jesus Christ, and they have rejected the supernatural aspect of His person and His ministry. Although the very Deity and infiniteness of Jesus are what human beings need so desperately, these are the characteristics which are often "played down," so human beings can "relate" or "understand" better. The inherent problem with that premise, however, is that anything or anyone we can humanly comprehend cannot possibly be adequate to meet all our human needs and inadequacies. Instead of building on the omniscience and omnipotence of our Lord and Savior, these churches build on personalities or certain palatable doctrines (to the exclusion of others), rather than on the full counsel of God as it is revealed in the Person of His only Son. Paul knew that such a foundation was not viable. It could not stand any weight or pressure.

Because Paul was *confident* of the foundation he had laid, he could be *comfortable* when others built upon it:

> . . . and another is building upon it. But let each man be careful how he builds upon it.

Apollos, Peter, Barnabas, Silas, Timothy, John Mark—all these made contributions to the "buildings" for which Paul had provided the foundation of the Gospel of the Lord Jesus Christ. The reason for Paul's consternation with the Corinthians was that he had provided a foundation on which they could have placed a magnificent superstructure—a skyscraper, even—and because of infighting, jealousy, and spiritual immaturity, they had settled for not much more than a "chicken coop."

That same embarrassing situation occurs in so many churches. God blesses a foundation that is based on His Son, and subsequently a controlling group of members decide they will be content to be an exclusive clique, content just "to hold our own," and no more. They can become so paranoid about not doing anything wrong, that they don't do anything creative or courageous either.

In verse 11, Paul explains that there is not even the possibility of laying a genuine foundation without Jesus Christ. Do you remember the story in Acts 3 and 4, in which Peter and John went to the Temple for prayer, and were confronted by a lame beggar? They told the man that although they had no money, they would heal his affliction. Of course, this action only further alienated Peter and John from the Sadducees, Pharisees, and scribes, causing the disciples to be questioned in court to explain their actions. Peter's response to the Jewish leaders in verses 10 and 11 told them more than they really wanted to hear:

> Let it be known to all of you, and to all the people of Israel, that by the name of Jesus Christ the Nazarene, whom you crucified, whom God raised from the dead—by this name this man stands here before you in good health. He is the stone which was rejected by you, the builders, but which became the very cornerstone (NASB).

Peter told the Jewish leaders that their rejection, and even their laws, ethics, and rituals, could not prevent Jesus from becoming *the* Cornerstone. From this same Peter, Jesus had earlier elicited that unequivocal declaration of faith: *"Thou art the Christ, the Son of the living God."* And it was because of the faith expressed—not because of the person who expressed it—that Jesus said, *"Upon this rock I will build my church."*

Having established the necessity for, and the nature of, the foundation, Paul goes on to talk about the materials that will be used to erect the building. He lists the options that are available: gold, silver, precious stones, wood, hay, and straw, and states that the durability of the buildings to be built will speak most loudly about the wisdom of the respective builders and their choices of materials. Not much needs to be said about the worth or value of gold and silver, but the implication of the phrase, "precious stones," is especially interesting. Paul is not referring to gems for ornamental purposes, but he is talking about expensive marble or granite building stones that were very costly because they were difficult to find and to mine from the ground.

In contrast, the other "optional" materials are far more common and more easily acquired. Wood, hay, and straw or "stubble" are readily available, but they are just as readily destroyed. At first glance, the choice seems clear: Anyone would choose gold, silver, and marble over wood and straw—or would he? What kind of materials have you chosen to build the life that God has planned for you? Even Christians who already have the foundation of Jesus Christ, will settle for cheap and temporary "materials" because they do not have the discipline or discernment to hold out for the very best. Still others who know they have chosen inferior building materials rationalize that these "makeshift" items are only temporary, and the "real stuff" will be put in place eventually.

Marriages are in trouble in our society because of the materials that have been used to construct and equip our homes. First of all, the two people who are thinking about getting married must *both* have a personal relationship with Jesus Christ. Second, each must know and be willing to practice God's biblical plan for the family. Instead, so many marriages are being built on the "wood" of social status and materialism, and the "straw" of physical gratification and the "me-syndrome." Then, when the wind of financial adversity or the fire of physical illness or infidelity strike, the home is an emotional and spiritual disaster. There is no stability because the marriage has neither the foundation nor the materials to withstand the onslaught.

Wanting the durable materials is not an issue. *Being willing to pay for and to go after them* is another matter. It costs something to see that your family is centered on Christ and His church. It can be expensive to forego some of the things the world says should accompany corporate success. It is sometimes far more difficult to love and work and cry through a family problem than it is to blame another person and ignore one's own responsiblity in the matter. Without the supernatural enabling of the Holy Spirit, most of us would never be able to survive such experiences. But with the promises of His Word in 1 Corinthians 10:13, 2 Corinthians 5:17, 2 Corinthians 12:9, and John 14:16, we know we have an Advocate and a Comforter. A home based on none other than Jesus Christ and the principles of His Word will stand any test this world can offer.

Verses 13 through 15 promise and describe the day

that will come when the structure we have chosen to build and the materials we have used to build with will be examined by the Lord Himself. In 2 Corinthians 5:10, Paul calls this "day" the Judgment Seat of Christ. This is the time when the work of all believers will be revealed and tested in the fire of His presence.

> Each man's work will become evident for the day will show it; because it is to be revealed with fire; and the fire itself will test the quality of each man's work. If any man's work which he has built upon it remains, he shall receive a reward. If any man's work is burned up, he shall suffer loss; but he himself shall be saved, yet so as through fire (NASB).

The fire of His judgment when He returns will not only be a revealing fire, it will be a refining and purifying one. The Greek verb for "declare" is *delosei,* and it means to show in its true character or to reveal for what it is.

If a believer's work is found to be worthy of the foundation on which it is built—the foundation of Jesus Christ— then it will not only survive, but it will be purified by the fire. That workman will be rewarded with the wages he has earned. But if a man's work is "burned up" (v. 15), then he will receive no reward, although his salvation remains intact. The distinction Paul is making is not between the saved and unsaved but between those who have built wisely and those who have built foolishly. The imagery is that of a structure which can either withstand fire (because it is built with gold, silver, and precious stones—non-combustible materials) or one that will be consumed by the same fire (because it built with combustible materials like wood, hay, and straw). Because of God's grace, even foolish builders will make it to heaven, but there will be the pain of realizing how much more could have been accomplished for His purposes if the right materials had been used.

In these fifteen verses, Paul's emphatic word to the Corinthians was not about their relationship to Christ but about their service to Him. While he lovingly identified with them and called them "brethren," he sternly admonished them to "grow up." He pointed out that their spiritual "diet" was a clear indication of their immaturity. Then he used two other analogies to show them their options. As God's "field," they could preoccupy themselves with the petty concerns of who would "water" and who would "plant," or they could appropriate God's priority and be concerned with the productivity of the field that symbolized each life. As God's "building," each individual Christian could choose to build either a dilapidated hovel with inferior materials or a durable, lasting, "fire-proof" structure on the foundation of Jesus Christ.

Because Paul cared deeply for his Corinthian "children," he wanted to be sure they understood the potential consequences of their choices. He reminded them that the results of their decisions would be judged by Jesus Christ when He returns. The eternal fruit that is harvested because of their individual efforts would be acknowledged and rewarded. Similarly the "buildings" that have been constructed out of durable and worthy materials will be rewarded and refined. Sadly, and just as surely, the unproductive field and the shoddily thrown-together building will be justly attributed to those who have misappropriated God's equipping power and blessing.

How They Prepare

R. Earl Allen

Preparation begins with planning for the coming church year. Special seasons of the year, as well as special days, are noted. Some topical, textual, and mainly expository messages are used in preparation for these seasons such as Easter, Christmas, and revivals. In a broad sense, these are worked on during summer vacation time or special study time between Christmas and early in the new year.

Planning ties you to preparation, and the subject is usually set. I preach in series. These may or may not be announced. I try to prepare one or two New Testament books and one or parts of one (Psalms, etc.) Old Testament book. Theme preaching is used, such as parables, Sermon on the Mount, Ten Commandments, biblical characters, and the like.

When the text is selected, I use several translations and word studies. Then I use my commentaries and seek my outline which is often alliterative in style.

Then I seek other sermons on that text, as well as quotations. I find many illustrations from books, as well as from life.

I write prayerfully on legal pads as I read. Later I fill in my outline which I write down. I am careful to make notations in case I might later want to publish the sermon.

Saturdays are limited to visitation, study, and prayer. I like to spend some time in the auditorium late that afternoon. People usually sit in about the same sections. I think of them as I look out at the pews and pray for them. This reminds me of their needs. I try not to accept invitations out on Saturday evening. I ask the Holy Spirit to use my preparation and to give me freedom in delivery.

I love the ecstasy of preaching and the discipline of preparation. As a pastor, I do things all week for the sheer joy of preaching on the Lord's Day. I have always told my people they don't pay me to preach; they pay me in order that I can give full-time to pastoring and preaching.

John R. Bisagno

In 1 Peter 5, the sainted apostle challenges preachers with several admonitions regarding their motives. *Why* they do what they do is to be under constant scrutiny. But as to precisely *What* to do, only two directives are in view: feed the flock of God; take oversight thereof. I take this to mean that my primary responsibility is preparing to teach and preach the Word of God and give general direction to the work of the church. Virtually every other need in the church can be met by someone else, but no one can study, pray, and preach for you, and no one else can make the big decisions.

A preacher's preaching must be his priority. My people will forgive a missed hospital call or an unaccepted social invitation, but there is no forgiveness, there is no excuse for a poorly prepared or ineptly delivered sermon. My personal sermon preparation style is my own. I do not recommend it to everyone, but it works for me. I preach the same sermon to two Sunday morning services, a second sermon to the evening service, and a third Wednesday night sermon weekly. These three messages are normally through books of the Bible. At this writing, I am preaching through 1 Corinthians Sunday mornings, James on Sunday nights, and Ezekiel on Wednesday nights. Brief, topical series are normally inserted between each book series. Most of the books take from six months to a year. The Gospel of John took three.

For ten years, I have been preaching verse by verse through the Old Testament beginning with Genesis 1:1. I am presently in Ezekiel 38—a little over halfway through the Bible.

The morning hours of 8 to 12 are normally the best for study. My first step is to spend fifteen minutes in devotional prayer and another fifteen-thirty minutes praying over the text I am preparing to study. After reading over the text three or four times, I begin to pray and meditate on it with two or three thoughts in mind.

First, of all the things Jesus, the prophets, and the apostles ever said and did, why did the Holy Spirit choose to preserve this portion for the biblical canon? Second, what is the one simple, central truth of this passage of Scripture? Until you reduce the passage to one simple propositional statement, you are not ready to outline the passage. Third, how does this relate to my people? I put myself in the pew and sit in the place of the laymen and laywomen who will be my hearers. I imagine them on Monday morning back at work, home, or school and ask myself the question: What am I going to say that will translate into practical help for them tomorrow?

After prayer, my first step is to take the King James Version of the Bible, a legal pad, and a pen. I do not use any commentaries, study books, or helps of any kind until I have pored over the text with only the help of the Holy Spirit, arrived at the central truth, and determined the basic application. Occasionally, my study will reveal a misunderstanding of the basic interpretation of the text, and I will start all over again. But the great majority of the time, the single, central message of the text is obvious.

Every passage of Scripture has only one correct interpretation. The charismatics have done us a great disservice, in interpreting Scripture with a "that's what it means to me" mentality. No Scripture is of private interpretation. A

Scripture doesn't mean what it means to *you*—it means what it *means.*

Once you determine the correct interpretation, each Scripture may have a hundred applications. Commentaries can help you understand the meaning of a text, but no human being can help you apply the text to the needs of your people on Sunday or Wednesday. Only the Holy Spirit can do that. The great need in the pulpit is for preachers to be able to think like laymen to the degree that Ezekiel did when he said, "I sat where they sat," and apply God's truth to their lives.

I use the King James Version of the Bible because I was raised that way. I "think" in King James. You should use the version that is most comfortable for you. After prayer, I begin to read where I left off preaching in the book series the previous week. I read very carefully, poring over every word and trying to pick up the propositional statement—the one truth I will try to put across next Sunday. Once that is determined, I continue to read until the subject changes. That is where I stop. The message then will be based on the text bound by the parameters of the two verses which, like brackets, introduce and conclude the passage and surround the central truth. That will normally be ten-fifteen verses. Having found the central truth, I find supporting truths in the passage.

The next step, still without commentaries or study books, is to expand an outline from the text, with only the resources of my own knowledge as my mind is offered up to the Holy Spirit for ideas and insights. Good preaching contains good logic, and I never assume my hearers agree with what I say, so I am attempting to prove my point, argue my case, prove my thesis. It is one matter to say, "Jesus is the only Way"; it is quite another to anticipate that some of your hearers are thinking, *But I don't believe that!* It is incumbent upon the communicator of eternal truth that he defend his thesis. Every good sermon includes a central theme, an outline, illustrations, supporting Scripture, applications, and the like, but the great missing ingredient is often logic—or argument.

Having used my own creative resources under the guidance of the Holy Spirit, I then turn to the commentaries, Greek lexicon, word study books, and illustration books for help. Most of the time, preachers preach only a bouquet of truth from someone else's thoughts—a rose here, a carnation there, and perhaps a sprinkling of a few of their own thoughts overall. My style is the opposite. The central truth, the outline, the logic, the application, and as much supporting information as possible are my own. Then I sprinkle in background word meanings, thoughts, and illustrations of others. The finished product is now 90 percent mine, 10 percent others.

Having prepared my sermon in this manner, the last step—memorizing the sermon—is easy. I always preach without notes. Having given birth to the material, it is easy to deliver what I already know; to memorize what I have created. There are two important ingredients in preaching: the content of the message and its delivery. In my judgment, far too little emphasis has been made on the importance of delivery, and nothing will improve delivery like memorizing the material. I reduce each sermon to twenty-five—fifty key words, each of which means an argument, fact, verse, quote, illustration, etc., and preach off of that visualized mental outline. Preaching without notes adds unspeakably to the effectiveness of preaching. It gives authority, confidence, liberty, and allows the Holy Spirit room for the spontaneity required to make each sermon a unique experience personally fitted to the needs of that particular congregation. I have preached some of my "sugar stick" sermons two or three hundred times, but while they have always been without notes, they have never been without variety. My most important preaching time is Sunday morning. That is to the masses and is on television and radio. Three or four hours are spent every Saturday night praying over the material, praying for myself, praying for my hearers, and praying for my memory as I repreach that sermon dozens of times before I fall asleep.

Weak preaching builds weak sheep that necessitate hours and hours of counseling and personal ministry. I prefer to put the emphasis on preaching and teaching and build strong sheep that can more easily stand alone, rather than emphasize propping up weak sheep created by poor preparation, inept delivery, and powerless preaching. To me, preaching is as Vince Lombardi said of winning in football—"not just everything . . . it's the only thing!"

Morris H. Chapman

Through the years I have come to the strong conviction that expository preaching is essential to the spiritual growth of God's people. The prophets of old thundered, "Thus saith the Lord." God is looking for men who preach His Word with a sense of urgency and a spirit of authority. People are desperate to hear a Word from God. They are inundated with words from the world—thus the God-called and Spirit-anointed preacher must first seek and then speak the whole counsel of God.

Isaiah declared, "The Spirit of the Lord God is upon me; because the Lord hath anointed me to preach good tidings unto the meek; he hath sent me to bind up the brokenhearted, to proclaim liberty to the captives, and the opening of the prison to them that are bound; To proclaim the acceptable year of the Lord, and the day of vengeance of our God; to comfort all that mourn" (61:1-2).

Preparation must be a priority for preaching. My study is at home where I spend three to four mornings a week. The entire day of Thursday is set aside for study. Monday particularly is given to administrative matters, including program staff meetings. I have discovered if I do not discipline my time, preparation for preaching easily can take a back seat to other demands and duties which are part and parcel of a pastor's life. Solutions are not easy to the time crunch which we face. The choices are often difficult. Yet our primary calling is to "preach the word; be instant in season, out of season; reprove, rebuke, exhort with all longsuffering and doctrine" (2 Tim. 4:2). Preparation is a priority!

For us to redeem the time we must bathe our preparation in prayer, asking for God's power in preaching. Not only do we need to pray for God's anointing upon us, we need to focus our spiritual eyes of faith upon Jesus so that when we preach, we are preaching out of the overflow of our devotional lives. Then we must surely remember to pray for those who shall hear so they might perceive they have heard a word from God.

The people whom we have been called to pastor need to hear our convictions drawn from hours, even years, of preparation and prayer. To preach a dozen theories of men is confusing and disconcerting to a congregation. A person comes to hear what "my" pastor believes. Our expressed conviction will always create a response, whether it be agreement or disagreement. Nevertheless, when we stand with the courage of our convictions, our people will grow spiritually.

I often develop alliterative outlines for the convenience of those in the congregation who take notes. But I am not bound to alliteration. In other words, alliteration does not take precedence over the meat of the message.

I preach most often in series, either preaching through an entire book of the Bible or preaching through the development of a theme. In either instance, I develop the text expositionally so that teaching God's Word is consistently the foremost ingredient of my preaching. I believe a text must be set in context, but I do not permit historical awareness to supercede spiritual application. People are crying for help. God's people are seeking spiritual maturity and the unsaved world is searching for a Savior.

Expositional, even exegetical, preaching does not have to be dull. In fact, careful and prayerful preparation will cause a sermon to be fresh and exciting to all who come to drink from the "fountain of living waters." I make frequent references to the text itself and to supportive Scriptures. Therefore, people keep an open Bible before them throughout the sermon. The rustling pages of God's Word is a welcome sound not only to the pastor and his people, but also to our Lord Jesus Christ. Discovering the nuggets of Truth is more precious than panning for silver and gold.

My heart's desire in preaching is stated eloquently by Paul, "My speech and my preaching was not with enticing words of man's wisdom, but in demonstration of the Spirit and of power: that your faith should not stand in the wisdom of men, but in the power of God" (1 Cor. 2:4-5).

W. A. Criswell

In preparing the sermon, bring to bear in the message all of your understanding and knowledge. If you can read the text in Hebrew or in Greek, that ought to be first. Then study the text through the eyes of great commentators. When you have done this, you will have a thorough understanding of what God is saying.

With a complete and absolute knowledge of the passage, read all of the things that you can find that might be pertinent to it. Use encyclopedias, Bible dictionaries, other sermons, other homiletical material. Find it, read it, and make notes on it. Remember, everything is grist for the preacher's mill. Draw on anything in history, in literature, or in life to make the passage God has inspired meaningful and pertinent to the people.

After you have studied the passage prayerfully and earnestly, and after you have read all you can, ask God to form in your soul the message that ought to be delivered. God will not fail you in this. The message will form in your heart as you study. Outline the sermon under two, three, four, or five main headings. Drive toward a final appeal as you write down the main points and the subpoints that follow each heading.

Always have some great, godly direction and purpose. Drive it home with all your force. Stand on the Word of God and on the basis of the Lord's authority and His holy revelations in the Scriptures. Make your appeal. It may be for consecration. It may be for prayer. It may be for salvation. It may be for ministry commitment, but always drive toward that final appeal. The Holy Spirit will work with you, and the power of God will rest upon you if you do. The Lord has a marvelous reward for us if we will thus give ourselves to the expounding of the Word of God.

Earl C. Davis

I feel my approach to preaching is both Bible-centered and people-centered. I try to deal with the everyday problems and spiritual needs of my people and try to do that by biblical preaching. By that I mean I seek to apply the Gospel in definite texts to the contemporary situation. Most of my preaching is exegetical in the sense that I try to see what God was saying in the biblical situation, and translate that spiritual truth into application to current situations.

To illustrate, last year's preaching brochure shows a seven-sermon series on "Light on Dark Scriptures," dealing with problem texts. A series of four sermons presented "Essentials for Understanding [Jesus, Salvation, Prayer, Bible]." I also preached a four-sermon series at Christmastime entitled "Christ and . . . [Buddha, Hinduism, Muhammad, Judaism]." There was also a three-sermon series which explored healing for inner hurts such as "Loneliness: That Twilight Feeling," "Worry *Can* Change Things," "Common Sense About Forgiveness," and a current-issues series giving biblical guidance on such issues as abortion, hunger, and peacemaking.

My approach is to determine the subject and text and do the exegetical work as early in the week as possible. I have kept up with my Greek and use the Greek New Testament in study and often in exegetical series. Sometimes the subject comes first, as in a current-issues series, while the text may come first if I am preaching through a Bible book or on a character such as Moses. Then, I let the sermon rest in my subconscious until Thursday or Friday, when I begin to put pencil to paper. I am constantly on the hunt for good illustrations and have found that people can see a lot of light through homey, personal stories.

As I think and pray about the sermon, I have a host of helpers—that is, I can hear in my mind various members of my church saying the major points of the sermon, and it gives me some objective idea of how this sermon and these ideas sound coming from someone else. Friday or Saturday is computer time. My library is indexed by subject and Scripture, and there is another file of illustrations collected from my reading. All this is on the computer at home—the best thing that ever happened to my preaching! I do the actual writing of the sermon at the computer keyboard.

I take this manuscript to church very early on Sunday morning for study, then preach without any notes. While I do not memorize the sermon, I can see in my mind the pages of the sermon as I preach. I always keep in mind that God may give me a fresh thought or sharper illustration, but I seldom, if ever, say more than is already on the sermon pages. Sunday afternoon or Monday, I make any corrections to the manuscript, and it is then printed for distribution to the congregation the following Sunday.

Cristobal Doña

While attending GGBTS, a layman showed me the hidden treasure in Acts 5:42. I learned that preaching is limited to giving the Gospel for the salvation of people, but that teaching is for instruction in the ways of the Lord and for growth in the Christian life. In other words, the Gospel is "unto salvation," not unto growth. Since then, I have changed my method of preparation both to preach and to teach. For the most part, I stand at the pulpit to teach, to instruct my church, and to equip them to do the work of the ministry. So, my sermons are mostly didactic. But from time to time I also preach, and my preferred kind is the expository sermon.

Deciding what I should preach is not that difficult; I select a theme directly aimed at meeting spiritual needs of people. I pick the theme early in the week as I relate to my people with the assistance of my associate pastor and staff. The process of selection of the theme is a sort of "taking of the pulse" of the constituency through records, reports, casual conversation, and direct observation at the time of visitation in the homes; then I do research that will produce a homily that will be practical, timely, and simple.

The kind of constituency in my church permits me to deliver the discourse in an informal, casual, instructional way. Sometimes I engage in dialogue with the congregation. Their participation is most rewarding and illuminating. From time to time I ask the church to come prepared to take notes about the message, the messenger, and the delivery. Those notes are then brought back to the evening service and used to discuss together the morning preaching.

The use of that method has resulted in a healthy habit: the audience has learned to bring their notebooks, take notes, and after the service, buy the cassette of the sermon. I suggest that they listen to the sermon all week long. My purpose is to provide for them material that will facilitate their sharing their faith with others (preaching), which results in life-style evangelism, something they do joyfully. Doing it this way, we have *one pastor and many preachers*.

James T. Draper, Jr.

I view my first calling to be that of a preacher of the Word of God. For every one person I will personally minister to or counsel with, there are hundreds who will only know me from my preaching. For that reason I approach preaching as my primary responsibility as a minister. It must occupy the center of my concentration, prayers, and preparation. I must maintain a discipline in study and preparation that allows me to give the proper attention to this vital part of my ministry.

I endeavor to reserve the mornings for spiritual renewal and preparation. I am an early riser, usually getting up and jogging or beginning the day no later than 6 AM. I am usually in the office by 7:30 AM. This allows me several hours of uninterrupted study time before the day begins to clamor for attention. Unless it is an emergency, I do not answer or return phone calls or have appointments before 11:30 AM. Of course, when there is a true emergency, I am always available. However, it is extremely important for me to hold these morning hours. This is the greatest challenge in my ministry. Truthfully, very few, if any, individuals really believe I need time to study. Close associates will infringe on the time if I allow it. No one but the preacher will fight to protect this time. Without a doubt, it is the hardest part of my ministry, protecting the time for spiritual preparation. However, the morning is my time for spiritual preparation.

My preaching is basically expository. Currently I am preaching through Psalms on Sunday mornings and Daniel on Sunday evenings. The sermon included here is one of my most recent sermons from Psalms. It is typical of the expositions I do week by week.

My pattern of preparation is simple. I study four to eight basic sources on each passage. I use a yellow marker to highlight the portions I want to use for reference. Then my secretary types what I have highlighted in yellow so I have all of the study reference notes in concise form, usually eight to twelve pages. Then I go back to the text and outline the sermon from the text. I endeavor to use alliteration for the main points and sub-points of the sermon. This is primarily a help to remembering the material, both for me and for the listeners. After completing the outline, I then go back to the reference notes and add the "meat" on the "bones" of the outline. I usually go into the pulpit with an outline of the sermon to be sure that I keep on target. I do not manuscript the sermon ahead of time but have an extensive outline. I usually take into the pulpit with me a half sheet of typing paper with notes on the front and back.

The presentation of the sermon is spontaneous for me. I do not rehearse my sermons in advance. I try to be well prepared for the presentation, so that I have more material than I need for the sermon. The preaching then becomes an overflow of the preparation. It is exciting to me to see how God brings certain things out as I preach, many times things I had not really planned to say. I am spontaneous in my preaching within the context of good preparation. I try to be perfectly natural. I am an enthusiastic person by nature, so my preaching has that element in it. The biggest thing to me for the preacher is to be himself!

Paul D. Duke

Preparing a sermon is a systematic affair, but not necessarily a controlled one. The preacher will set aside blocks of time and will undergo a disciplined regimen of reflection, reading, and writing toward the preparation of a sermon. But this weekly discipline is only the outer form of an inner process that is more profound and less predictable.

In my experience, at least, the process of sermon preparation is ultimately less like *building* something and more like *giving birth* to something. There is a gestation, an interior stirring and kicking, a feeding and growing. And all the preacher's unborn "children" are different. To be pregnant with some sermons is to glow; with others it is to feel mostly sick. In the actual birthing, some arrive rather easily while others require considerable pushing; some are breech, some don't want to come forth at all by Sunday but must be seized by force, arriving at the pulpit like Paul at his apostleship, "untimely born." Most good sermons take the preacher down to the gates of pain. All of them bear the most notable—sometimes the most ludicrous—resemblance to the preacher. But by some wonder they will often not only live and breathe, but cry out with a sound that is eerily or beautifully the voice of Another.

So when I address the subject of "How I Prepare My Sermons," my answer can only be provisional. Whatever one's prescribed method may be, the method will not be static, it will shift in shape and color week by week, depending on the peculiar struggle of each sermon to be born.

My own method, like that of many preachers, comes in two phases: the long, low-heat phase, and the short, high-heat phase. The long phase goes on for months, if possible. In the summer I try to project a preaching plan for the coming year. I choose texts and sketch a paragraph summary of each sermon's trajectory. These tentative projections are shared with others who will lead in worship. For myself I make individual files for each sermon and as time passes will drop into the files various reading notes, observations, and ideas which seem to relate. This gives the unconscious mind a crucial headstart. It also means that when a new week dawns, I am rarely faced with the horror of having to be like God and create something out of nothing. Mondays, of their own accord, are sufficiently "without form and void" to carry that high-handed burden.

The intensive phase of preparation then begins. I start again with the text and only the text: to learn it, to question it, to let it question me. This dialogue is *private;* that is, without benefit yet of commentaries or someone else's sermon. But it is also *priestly;* my conversation with the text is in behalf of particular people in a particular place and time. From such dialogue I may attempt a tentative strategy for structuring the sermon. Then come the commentaries, theologians, preachers, and friends to give deeper meanings or new directions. Then the structure is finalized, and the writing begins. I write the sermon word for word. For me, the writing is a labor of love and part of my worship. I do it in order to find the most worthy language—the clearest, most evocative, most *functional* language. I work hard to write in *oral* language, for I will not read to the people but speak with them. I work hard to write in *worthy* language, for my speaking—to my unceasing awe—will be in behalf of the Christ of God.

Another commitment I make is that, insofar as possible, I will not preach *about* biblical texts but will *let* biblical texts preach. For this reason, I seldom structure my sermons in listed "points," for fear of objectifying the Word of God, setting the people at distance from it and abstracting distilled principles from it. I seek more often to preach in "movements" of thought congruent with the movement of thought within the text. My aim is to let the Word unfold its own life, to release itself among us and do its work among us. Scripture itself *is* preaching, and the more I appropriate its own images and metaphors, structures and forms, the more powerfully it preaches.

Peter James Flamming

Preaching has both divine and human dimensions. The power of preaching comes not from the words of the preacher but from the Holy Spirit who uses these words to convict, save, nurture, comfort, call, challenge, bless, and motivate. The Holy Scriptures suggest those areas for which the Holy Spirit has an affinity. In my judgment, preaching should center on these five areas.

1. Christ-centered

Jesus said that the Holy Spirit was to teach us all things and to bring to remembrance all that He said (John 14:26). In addition, Jesus said, "He will glorify me, for he will take what is mine and declare it unto you" (John 16:14 RSV). Any preaching that does not eventually involve the centrality of Christ can hardly be called Christian preaching. Paul said, "Him we proclaim, warning every man and teaching every man in all wisdom, that we may present every man mature in Christ" (Col. 1:28, RSV).

2. Biblical

Inasmuch as the Scripture is God-breathed (2 Tim. 3:16), the Bible is the textbook of the Spirit. Biblical preaching is most effective when the preacher has "crawled" into the text and explored the inner situation from which it has come. The preacher is something of a biblical detective, searching for that which has been so easily overlooked and misplaced. The Spirit seems to use the effort of one who has spent the time and has an empathy with the text to see what is going on within the text itself.

3. Personal

The Scripture is a personal book. When the Holy Spirit ministers, He does it through people. Even the Word was fleshed out in personal dimensions (John 1:14). Preaching that is abstract and impersonal is apt not only to miss the listener but to be devoid of the Spirit.

4. Full of the Gospel

Jesus did not bring a new set of rules, doctrines, and rituals. He brought the Gospel, good news. Gospel is good news, not new judgment. It is hope, not condemnation. Christ came "not to condemn the world, but that the world might be saved through him" (John 3:17). The Gospel is the good news that God cares about us and has, in Christ, done something for us that we cannot do for ourselves. In Christ we are not chained with new directives, but redeemed.

5. Related to the Chaos and Emptiness of Modern Life

The first work of the Spirit recorded in Scripture is His moving across the face of the deep (Gen. 1:2). The world was described as chaos, without form, and empty. The moving of the Spirit is to overcome chaos and emptiness. This work of the Spirit has not changed through the ages. He is still about the business of bringing freedom from personal chaos and fullness in the midst of personal emptiness.

The Present Age

Every age has its own peculiar ways of responding. Ours is an age directly affected by television and by advertisements. This means that any effective communication must be more image- and picture-oriented than in former times. Verbal communication is no exception.

The good fortune of the preacher is that the Scripture is full of vivid imagery, textured with vibrant verbal pictures, and alive with stories that live. Jesus Himself taught with metaphors (images) and with parables. Preaching must brace itself against the temptation to be theologically abstract.

An implication of the "picture bentness" of our age also relates to the number and use of illustrations. Our age thinks in story-book fashion. Even thirty-second commercials sometimes have a plot to them. The modern listener is ill-equipped to hear a sermon that has no plot, no story, and few illustrations. After all, the Bible has a giant plot that runs from first to last and all sorts of stories and plots in between. The good fortune of the modern preacher is that the mind-set of the age in which he lives matches his basic text, the Bible.

Methodology in Preparation

Scriptural materials should be studied first. My own practice is to follow a three-step procedure. First, the body of material used should be outlined in what Joel Gregory calls "syntactical analysis" (*Southwestern Journal of Theology,* Spring 1985, pp. 16-17). This has also been called a "block diagram" and "sentence-flow schematic." This is particularly helpful in the letters of the New Testament. Second, the words must be studied. If the text is from the New Testament, Kittel's multivolume *Theological Dictionary of the New Testament* is of great value in the study of the words, as are the word studies of Vincent, Robertson, and Wuest. Commentaries are of greater value when they deal with the original languages. Third, the preacher should try to "crawl into" the text, trying to sense what is involved, what is at stake. When the preacher has done this he is ready to relate it to the world in which we live.

Outlining is the easiest part. It should be tentatively set early but changed without hesitation as the manner in which the text is to be communicated develops.

The most difficult challenge the preacher faces is the finding and using of appropriate illustrations. Like a recruiter who never ceases looking for talent, the preacher can never cease looking for illustrations. Quotes and anecdotes are helpful if they do one of two things: either say what is needed in a beautiful way or the person who said them has clout in the view of the listener.

When it is time to put the sermon together the ways are as varied as the preacher. My own preference is to manuscript them, but to manuscript them as I speak, not as I write. I take the manuscript in the pulpit but seldom refer to it.

Delivery

The acid test of a preacher's delivery is whether it reflects the way he talks when he is out of the pulpit, but with more energy and force. This means no "preacher's tone." Also, the delivery must reflect who he is. Copying someone else wears thin and has a hollow ring to it.

The best aids to catching flaws in delivery are listening to cassette recordings of the sermon and preaching in front of a mirror. The goal is to avoid making the listener overcome visual and auditory barriers while listening to what the sermon is trying to proclaim.

A final word. Since our age is biblically illiterate, it helps if the preacher turns to his related texts in the sermon rather than just quoting them. The congregation is not going to use the Bible if the preacher doesn't. Such a practice takes time but it is, in itself, a teaching method.

Alfonso Flores

The method I have been using in the preparation of my
sermons is one I have formed in studying other preachers
whose sermons have been a blessing to me, along with
some things I have learned from my own experience.

I am of the opinion that the first element of sermon
preparation is the man himself. I have prepared sermons
which I thought were good and which I anticipated would
be well-received and produce good results. But when I came
to preach them they fell as flat as a pancake. What went
wrong? Reflecting upon those times I believe the reason
was an inadequate spiritual preparation on my part.

On the other hand, I can remember many times when I
didn't think the sermon was very well-prepared, but when I
came to preach it, the simple message was used of the
Spirit of God, and the results were evident and abundant.
The reason again was the spiritual preparation. I believe
what a great preacher of another generation said in that
respect: every sermon ought to be saturated in prayer before the Lord. The Spirit of God is not limited by sermons
that don't have all the elements of good sermon preparation, but He is limited by preachers that are not properly
prepared spiritually.

In my actual preparation of the sermon I begin with
the passage that I want to preach upon. I frequently preach
through the different books in the Bible. When I do that I
just follow the chapters and the verses one by one. At other
times, I locate the passage that suits the idea or the topic I
want to preach upon. Those topics or ideas are ones impressed upon my heart by the Spirit of God as I visit in my
people's homes, a problem or challenge which the church
may be facing, and so forth. I have on several occasions
preached a sermon to one individual and was amazed to

learn how many others were blessed by the message. All that, the selecting of the passage and the topic, is done on Tuesday morning. On Tuesday I also start to make some rough outlines of the passage and gather other materials related to the subject.

The sources I gather my materials from are multiple and varied. I use several encyclopedias which are very valuable in providing precise information that I may want to use. I also use several religious dictionaries and commentaries. In addition, I go through my library which includes several thousand volumes and consult other men who have spoken on the same subject.

The first thing on Wednesday morning I work on the introduction. I believe the introduction is of great importance. From the first sentence the congregation should see their interest in the subject before them. When a preacher loses their attention at the start, it requires a heroic effort to draw it back and sustain it.

After I have the introduction pretty well set, I start thinking directly on the passage. I go over the final outline selected of the passage and start filling it with my own ideas and thoughts, as well as the ideas and thoughts of others. At this point I may also change the outline if my careful study of the text dictates it. Or I may eliminate a point or add another if I deem it necessary to make the message more effective and clear. It used to be that most of my sermons had three points. Now I just try to let the Word of God speak for itself with clarity to the congregation.

Finally, on Thursday morning I start to type the manuscript. Since my seminary days I formed the habit of writing my sermons out in full, and it has proven to be beneficial to me. That's not to say I am enslaved by the manuscript. I seldom glance at the manuscript during the preaching of the sermon. Many times in the preaching of the message large chunks of the sermon as written in the manuscript are omitted, while at other times as the Spirit of God impresses and moves me, I incorporate things that were not written.

Usually by Friday noon the manuscript is finished. On Saturday night I read and review the sermon several times in my preparation for the pulpit the following day. I read the message out loud, putting the emphasis where it is due, the way I will do in my preaching the following morning. Finally, I preach the sermon. As I said, although I take the manuscript with me to the pulpit, I never read it and seldom even glance upon it. Such is my method. By the grace of God it has proven very effective for me.

Charles G. Fuller

My basic approach to preaching, in recent years, has been by way of various sermon series. More often than not, the series are based upon a certain book of the Bible or a sequence of books. Sometimes, the series will follow a subject theme or a doctrinal sequence. The sermon series will vary in length and are always subject to appropriate interruptions, due to seasonal emphases or special occasions.

Recent sermon series used have been on the books of Acts, Romans, and the Psalms. During the Psalms series, preached on Sunday mornings, I incorporated a companion series for Sunday evenings on the life of David. One of the most meaningful sermon series used was one wherein I preached through the Bible, a book a Sunday, requiring nearly a year and a half.

Though I do preach topical and textual sermons, the vast majority of my preaching is expository in approach. Making repeated references to the biblical text encourages Bible-bringing by the congregation and enhances both memory and application.

A brief introduction and outline to the sermon is

printed each Sunday in the bulletin, making it easier for the congregation to follow the message and to take personal notes.

Most of my week-by-week preaching focuses upon the Christian life, discipleship, and spiritual growth. There is always, however, some evangelistic content, and there is always an appeal to accept Jesus Christ as Savior.

During my sermon study, I make numerous notes, often writing out whole sections, in the interest of my own thoroughness and discipline. I do not use extensive notes in the pulpit and often prefer to use no notes at all.

As to sermon delivery, I believe a combination of evangelistic and didactic styles would best describe my style. A degree of the confessional approach is involved in my preaching, and I make extensive use of illustrations.

Having been in the same pastorate for the past twenty-five years (since 1961) perhaps accounts for one of, what I consider to be, the more important elements in my preaching. That is an attempt to stay fresh. I attempt to stay fresh in my study and by sharing my own spiritual growth from the pulpit.

Jack Graham

The purpose of preaching is not simply to discuss a subject but to achieve a specific object. Therefore, in all sermon preparation, it is my desire first to determine in my own mind the personal and pressing purpose of the message God has laid on my heart. This involves actually writing a thesis or subject sentence to crystallize in my own mind what the biblical text is saying in its contemporary application to our people.

Once the specific object is clear, I can proceed in the exegesis of Scripture. With great joy I study the text, finding the meanings of words, phrases, and ideas. Before consulting commentaries and the writings of others, I ask God to speak to me through His Word and interpret the passage as I understand it. After completing this personal, inductive study, I consult my books and Bible study helps to add the rich resources of the great men of God who have written before me. My library contains works from the Puritans through contemporary authors.

By now an outline for the sermon is developed, and I am ready to organize the sermon. I often alliterate the outline for the sake of clarity and style but always seek to avoid straining the text or overwhelming the sermon with cleverness. The outline is simply scaffolding upon which to build the message.

With the outline now complete, the sermon is written. I do not write a manuscript but make copious sentence notes that contain the essence of what I plan to say. During the writing of the notes I search for illustrations and applications of the text. This is the most exciting adventure of all. It is the time God speaks to me and lays the burden of the message upon my heart. Once the body of the sermon is complete, the introduction and conclusion are formulated with a strong emphasis on the public invitation and the appeal for decision. It is always my desire to exalt the Lord Jesus, to accurately explain the Scriptures, and to persuade people to act upon the truth delivered. For this reason, I am absolutely dependent upon the power of prayer and the ministry of the Holy Spirit.

Joel Gregory

A biblical sermon may move from text to congregation or from congregation to text. That is, the idea for the message may begin with the text or begin with a need in the congregation. Almost all of my preaching begins with the text and moves to the congregation.

The first task of the expositor is the choice of an appropriate and manageable amount of text. The paragraph divisions in different translations or the outlines of a book by exegetes can help here. Nothing can substitute for the careful outlining of the book or chapter by the preacher himself in order to decide the unit of Scripture treated in a sermon.

My next step is the examination of the passage's context, both remote and immediate. Most biblical preaching that misses the mark begins to err at the point of ignoring context. Careful and repeated reading of the context always enlarges insight into the text itself.

Next I prepare an intensive exegesis of the passage. My method has been the same for years. I type or write a single verse from the text at the top of a blank page. My goal is to fill that page with notes and impressions about that verse. I begin with a study of comparative translations of the passage. I move from there to my own best thinking about the passage in an attitude of prayer. From that, I turn always to the analytical, exegetical language commentaries that treat the passage word by word. I garner insights into the grammar, syntax, definition, and historical background of the words in the text. Finally, I read some of the lighter, popular commentaries and expositions to learn better how to popularize the technical exegesis of the text.

Throughout the above process I am prayerfully seeking the single sentence that states in the present tense the timeless truth of that passage. I cannot preach until I have captured that sentence, the sermon in a sentence. That emerges at various points in the process, but it must emerge. Following that, I divide the thesis of the message into several divisions of the sermon. In those I attempt to popularize the exegesis, find contemporary illustrative material, and make narrow, particular application to that congregation at that time.

I write a full manuscript on a word processor for the Sunday morning message. For Sunday evening a very full sermon brief is prepared. I feel this helps keep an extemporaneous quality in preaching. About two hours are spent early Sunday morning in mastering the manuscript for pulpit delivery. I also place a three-hundred-word synopsis of the message in the Sunday bulletin. This enables the congregation better to follow the message and to have a permanent help for devotional use.

In my own approach to sermon preparation, I cannot overstate the significance of the exegetical task. Wrestling all week with every word, phrase, and clause of the text is the very center of the act of preparation.

Brian L. Harbour

Of all the tasks confronting me as a pastor, I have always considered the preaching responsibility my top priority. When I am in the pulpit, I touch the lives of more people in a significant way than at any other time. Therefore, doing a good job of communicating the Gospel on Sunday has always received my primary attention.

What kind of preacher am I? Descriptive labels about

a preacher mean different things to different people. I consider myself a biblical preacher. By that I mean I always seek to preach in such a way that the authentic Word of God is communicated to those who listen.

With the Word of God as my source, I like to use different styles in communicating that Word. At times I preach through a book of the Bible, developing each succeeding text. A series on the Gospel of John, for instance, included thirty-six sermons on this incomparable Gospel. On other occasions I try to capsule a truth communicated in a verse and then develop that biblical truth along several lines. I enjoy biographical preaching, taking a character from the Bible and using him or her as a model for our lives today. My three books on the family, *Famous Couples of the Bible, Famous Singles of the Bible,* and *Famous Parents of the Bible,* all follow this approach. On other occasions I will focus on a particular message and simply walk through the text verse by verse. The challenge Paul issued to young Timothy is still our mandate today when we enter the pulpit: "Preach the Word" (2 Tim. 4:2). Creativity and variety should mark the methods by which we carrying out that mandate.

In preparing a message I begin with the text. After studying the text and discerning the meaning of it, I try to develop the points I will use in preaching the message. With these points written at the top of separate columns on a piece of paper, I will then go through my illustration file and jot down several possibilities under each point. In such a way, I develop some meat for the outline. When adequate research has been done, I then type the message in full manuscript form. I am up at 5 on Sunday morning with my manuscript before me. By 7 I have the message memorized and ready to present. I carry the manuscript into the pulpit with me for an occasional glance. During the delivery of the sermon I maintain as much eye contact with the congregation as I can.

With the gifts that God has given me, this approach has been most effective. Prayerful preparation, a well-developed illustration file, an intense study of the text, a careful typing of the manuscript, and the ability to memorize are the tools I use in preparing each week to proclaim God's Word.

O. S. Hawkins

I still consider my Saturday soul-winning visitation some of the most important time spent in sermon preparation. My pastor, Dr. W. Fred Swank, now in heaven, taught me that we were to equip the saints to the "work" of the ministry. He instilled within me the importance of not stepping into the pulpit to preach without sharing the good news of the Gospel with someone during the course of the week. Consequently, Saturday is a work day for our entire ministerial staff and is spent in soul-winning visitation.

A preacher's heart is an important part of sermon preparation. We should never use our people to build our ministry but always use our ministry to build our people. As our own church has continued to grow across the years I have found one of the best ways of "staying in touch" with my people is through my own personal prayer ministry. I pray for five different families in our church every day and two weeks previous to this they receive a card from me encouraging them to write me concerning any prayer request their family may have. While the primary purpose for this is to pray for my people, it also enables me to know where they are and what they need in their spiritual, mental, and emotional growth.

In order to be effective the sermon must come out of a burning heart. There are a lot of great orators who have no fruit in their ministries and little power. There is a very real sense in which it is more important what we are when we preach than it is what we preach. The only way we receive a burning heart is like the disciples on the Emmaus Road—"when He speaks to us along the way." The pastor who does not have an effective personal Bible study and prayer life will not be effective in the pulpit for an extended period of time.

For many preachers, determining the text to be preached is one of the most difficult matters in sermon preparation. For me it is easy because I preach through books of the Bible. Therefore, I do not have to spend the first half of the week looking for a text. It is always before me. I always know where I am going because I pick up with the verse I have just concluded. Ninety-nine point nine percent of my own preaching is expository in nature. We journeyed through the Book of Ephesians over the course of two years in our fellowship. For the last twenty messages I have been preaching through the Epistle of Jude. God honors His Word! The one common characteristic of all growing churches is an insistence upon the absolute authority and inerrancy of Scripture. I have found that people in this modern day and age want to know "what saith the Lord?"

Once my text is settled upon, I begin to "live with it" for a time, letting it speak to me. I have found that reading it scores of times and putting the inflection upon a different word each time helps me to see its meaning, and an outline begins to immerge. I am fortunate in that innately I have always thought in an analytical sort of way. I often say that one of the greatest helps in sermonizing came from my high school English teacher, Miss Alva White, who taught me how to outline. After I have "lived with the text" and done the exegesis to see what it says, I then move to the commentaries. I read many of the Puritans and Arthur Pink in particular. While he sometimes goes to the extreme in typology, I find many nuggets in what he has to say. Of course, I read all of the classics such as Maclaren, Spurgeon, and the like. In our generation I find the writings of R. T. Kendall of Westminster Chapel in London particularly stimulating.

I am careful not to read the outlines of others until I have formulated my own. This keeps me from using from what God has given someone else and forces me to "search out" my own outline. While I am sermonizing to meet particular needs in my own congregation at the present time, I keep in the back of my mind the fact that someday the sermon will be in print. This forces me to have a manuscript on file and causes me to make sure it is my own.

While I use alliteration in order to help my people in note-taking and enable them to follow the text, I am also aware of the danger of letting alliteration get in the way of the text. We have to be careful we do not seek to try and improve upon what God has said in His Word. One layman remarked that his preacher's sermons were like a "dirty old wrench." When asked to explain, he replied, "They are not very pretty, but they always fix something." Certainly, this should be the end of our preaching to glorify God—that is, that we "fix something" in someone's life by our message.

No discussion about preparing to preach would be complete without a final word about the invitation for people to respond to the sermon. After the great sermon preached at Pentecost, the Bible says of Peter that "with many other words he did exhort them." I believe the invitation should be as thought-through and prayed-over as the body of the sermon. It should be given positively and expectantly. I never preach without expecting someone to be saved and many to be built up in this "most holy faith."

Jim Henry

As I surveyed my views of preaching during the last quarter century, I found I had made a gradual change in my approach to it. In the beginning, it was more of an addendum to the many things I found myself responsible for as pastor of a small church. As time passed, and I observed the impact of the Word of God in the lives of people, I deepened my commitment to making preaching the priority of my public ministry. That is not always easy. I once heard J. Oswald Sanders, the great preacher and writer, say to a small group of preachers that a successful ministry didn't just happen—it is paid for, and not in one lump sum. It's on the installment plan. The more it costs, the more effective we become.

There is a certain amount of pain in preaching. It takes something out of you. While you're giving life, a piece of you dies. The pulpit, like marriage, is not "to be entered into unadvisedly or lightly; but reverently, discreetly, advisedly, and in the fear of God." That sense of awe and commitment, I trust is the hallmark of my approach to the privilege of preaching the Good News.

My method of preparing sermons has settled into a pattern in recent years, although I don't think it's routine. I believe all preaching preparation begins with the preacher. Several things prepare me for the study. First and most important is my quiet time with the Lord. I guard this jealously. It is the first order of the day and varies anywhere from thirty minutes to an hour or more. I study a portion of Scripture that has nothing to do with current sermon preparation and spend the concluding part of this time in praise, confession, thanksgiving, intercession, and petition.

I do quite a lot of reading. Books, papers, and periodicals serve as fertile fields for me to scavenge illustrations, anecdotes, and insights. I clip out, tear out, cut out, and photo copy hundreds of pieces of material each year and file them under a series of titles such as "Issues of the Day," "The Church," "Evangelism," "Missions," "The Holy Spirit." I always have a fresh supply of interesting material to flesh out my sermons.

I seek to spend about twenty to twenty-five hours a week studying and preparing my major sermons for Sunday. My study is located away from the busy area of our church so I have quiet for concentration and writing. My secretary screens my calls, and I've found that for the most part, our people understand the primacy of this time in my ministry.

I have a wraparound desk on which I lay out my materials for the morning message on one side, and the evening message on the other. In the middle of my desk, I keep the majority of my study helps which makes them easily accessible to both preparations. My administration and counseling office is in another area. This allows me to leave my desk in "organized clutter," enabling me to walk away from it and return to it with a sense of picking up where I left off.

In order to keep my preaching where people are hurting, facing challenges, and looking for encouragement, I block off one afternoon every week for counseling. I visit the hospitals, bury the saints and the sinners, marry the young, and share fellowship luncheons with members and prospects. This allows me to keep a healthy tension between the study and the people. I think it was Philip Brooks who said something like, "I never go to the study that I don't see my people's faces; and I never get among my people, that I don't hear the summons from the study."

I usually write out my sermons in manuscript form, coming out with six to eight pages for each sermon. I sometimes use alliteration for my major points, which vary from three to five at the most. At other times I use sentences as major points, ask questions, or state principles, usually letting the text dictate my outline form.

My basic form of preaching is expository. It gives preaching power and authority. In my earlier pastorates it was topical and textual, but I found a growing hunger for preaching from and through the text, and found that same desire on the part of our people. I preach through one book of the Bible in the morning, another in the evening, most often a New Testament book and an Old Testament book. I interrupt these from time to time to preach a brief series on a subject like the family, or for special occasions such as Christmas, Easter, cataclysmic local or international events, missions, etc. I preach primarily to the church but always close with an evangelistic appeal and weave the urgency of the Gospel and the gentle appeal of Jesus throughout the message. Whatever I'm preaching, like Spurgeon who said that wherever he was "he cut across country to Jesus," I seek to do the same.

Sermon delivery has also varied through the years. I found myself imitating everyone from Billy Graham to W. A. Criswell and finally discovered my most satisfying delivery came through letting the Holy Spirit work through the man He was making in His image. When I realized this, it took a lot of pressure off my mind, and I found the Lord using me more effectively. I suppose you would classify my communication style as intensely conversational, with occasional outbursts of thunder! I use gestures freely, but I trust not obtrusively. Humor and personal experiences usually find a place in most of my messages, but I try not to do an overkill in those areas.

I use very few notes in the pulpit. Free delivery gives a dynamic that I would never exchange for the bondage of a manuscript or extensive notes. I spend Saturday night and early Sunday morning praying and studying my sermons and hopefully exhaust the riches of my pilgrimage in life and the study into the needy minds and hearts of my fellow pilgrims. The focus of my preaching is found in Jesus' priestly prayer in John 17:3: "that they might know thee the only true God, and Jesus Christ, whom thou hast sent."

William E. Hull

Preaching is an act by which the living God asserts His claim in the lives of those who hear His word. As such it has two foci: the ancient Scriptures and the contemporary situation. My sermons always attempt to build a bridge between these two realities now separated by two thousand years. At times, as in the case of the sermon chosen for this volume, I major on clarifying the biblical text so the relevance of its life-situation for today will become obvious. At other times, I concentrate on interpreting a current need so the congregation will grasp how it is addressed by the Gospel of Christ.

This general approach determines my specific methodology. I continually study Scripture, not just as an historical document, but in terms of its intentionality, i.e. the life-changes it seeks to effect. At the same time, I am a perpetual student of my congregation and of the complex influences in modern American culture to which it is constantly exposed. I am always looking for creative "points of contact" between the deepest insights of Scripture and the manifold needs of my people. A sermon idea is born when I realize how a biblical truth and a human need can so address each other in a message as to foster authentic dialogue between God and those who hear it.

Once an idea is born, my next task is to search for the optimum setting in which it may be shared with the congregation. That timing may be determined by some special emphasis within the church, by celebrations on the church and civil calendars, or by pressing private and public concerns. As the time for delivery approaches, I seek to make a careful study of all relevant Scriptures and to analyze the precise needs which the sermon can best address. Whether the format of the message is topical, textual, or expository depends largely on the type of Scripture chosen as the text. Words and phrases lend themselves to topical sermons, sentences to textual sermons, and paragraphs to expository sermons. If the primary need is to explain an obscure text, I will usually begin with Scripture, then move forward in time to the modern scene (as in the sermon here in this volume). However, if the greater need is to clarify a complex modern problem, I will begin there and then move backward in time to a pertinent passage of Scripture.

What this means is that the shape of almost every sermon is dialogical. It may have only two parts, as when the biblical proclamation and the contemporary predicament are set in the sharpest juxtaposition. Or it may have several parts, as in a narrative sermon when each stage of the biblical story is used to engage the unfolding story of the listening congregation. Notice how the sermon included here moves back and forth between a first-century church grappling with cultural pluralism in a way that opened its horizons to world mission and a twentieth-century church/ denomination needing to grapple with the same kind of diversity in modern form if it is to move in united fashion on a Bold Mission Thrust. If the divine/human dialogue is built into the sermon itself, then its proclamation becomes a living dialogue between God and the congregation in which the Gospel can address our deepest dilemmas.

Warren C. Hultgren

There are many books written about preaching and preparation of sermons. Everyone develops his own style. Whatever type of sermon is being prepared requires the same basic process, be it topical, textual, expositional, or extemporaneous running commentary.

Assuming one has chosen the text, passage, topic, or chapter of Scripture, the first question to ask is: "What is this saying?" It will be read through several times and the structure either falls into place quickly or one prayerfully struggles with it. It has been my experience that unless I let the Scriptures speak to me personally, I will become mentally paralyzed by the wealth of material in my library and filing cabinets.

The next step is to study the language of the passage and know what the words really mean. One does not need to be a language scholar to refer to dictionaries and exegetical commentaries. Different translations throw different shades of meaning that are enlightening. A regular dictionary is usually the most neglected and can often be the most helpful.

At this point, I try to develop some kind of outline in words or sequential ideas. I begin to write as much as I can; illustrations and other ideas come from previous reading and experiences. Given a rough outline or series of developing ideas, I turn to available resources: commentaries, books of sermons, material that has been filed—all are helpful. With a rough outline in front of me and books on my desk, I write on legal-sized pages. When I have squeezed as much as I can from my reading, I take a red pencil and mark in the margin of my notes Roman numerals which point out under which heading they belong. By this time, a fuller outline takes shape. Often it becomes altogether different. One's thoughts are changed several times in the process until it flows from subject to developing thoughts that start the progression of ideas.

Aside from the regular Sunday sermons, I have three different Bible studies and a television devotional that are regular responsibilities. At present I usually work with eight or ten pages of notes. Next, the outline is put into one or two basic words which I memorize. It is then easy to get the key ideas in order. At this point, I keep thinking it through and praying it in. Before preaching (preferably the night before), I will write the outline several times and wait for it to get out of my head and into my heart. One must feel it to preach it. Even at this time, various point rearrange themselves and fall into more logical places. I take the Bible into the pulpit and let the spirit of the occasion and the encouragement of the Holy Spirit clothe and inspire the preaching.

As the years have unfolded, I am increasingly convinced that it is the preaching of the Word of God which is blessed. It has long been my practice to read widely in secular and religious areas. One must always begin with people where they are. You cannot lead them where you have not been.

Richard A. Jackson

While the preparation to preach is as personal as each God-called proclaimer, the steps to skilled use of content are probably quite consistent. In preparing sermonic content, I begin with the text. My normal pattern is to preach expositionally verse by verse through complete Bible books. When not preaching through a book, the exposition follows the same textual treatment. The Scripture passage is read devotionally until it grips my heart. It is then read analytically until a clear direction surfaces. At that point, attention is given to homiletic techniques that will allow for accurate recall in the preaching experience and for the hearers' continued enlightenment.

The next step is to study the text, exegeting each word, phrase, or sentence with attention given to language word study and other interpretive tools. The expositional material is then arranged to follow the homiletic form previously chosen.

I add illustrations and applications to the manuscripted paragraphs as they naturally fit the flow.

When all of this is done, the most important preparation begins. The preparation of the messenger is Holy Spirit inspired. The last step of predelivery preparation is prayer. The final stage of preparation is the Spirit-guided, inspired delivery of the sermon. Preaching is never done until truth is imparted to the hearers, and change is affected in the lives of the preacher and the congregation.

Peter Rhea Jones

When I came out of seminary teaching, I had a gracious backlog of expository material but a short ration of good illustrations. Saturday panic was punishing. Long-term preparation became the key.

I organized a real minister's workshop. In my workshop are filing cabinets devoted to future and former sermons and illustrations. Two drawers are set aside for sermons wanting to be preached. One drawer is expository, my preferred form of preaching, and the other is topical. In the topical drawer subjects are related to coping with life. From the expository drawer have come series on the Ten Commandments, the Seven Sayings from the Cross, great texts and great chapters, the Beatitudes, and the parables. Sermon illustrations are filed by topic alphabetically. One of the most helpful things is a card file on texts and references that my secretary does.

I immediately record anything of sermonic potential. I write down or dictate with my portable dictaphone any ideas I come across anywhere. When I read a book I mark illustrations, quotable remarks, and stimulating paragraphs, and put them into written form. After pastoral conversation I write down meaningful aspects. After a sermon I jot down significant personal application made by members. I am learning to prepare sermons as I visit and talk with people during the week.

I find a strong temptation to prepare only for the next sermon. In recent years I read more biography and scan newspapers and magazines. Occasionally I read a great sermon by James Stewart or A. J. Gossip. I find the stories of F. W. Boreham an absolute delight. In reading the Bible devotionally I write down compelling passages in complete form. Incidentally, I find three or four scraps of good material that just did not fit into the sermon. I now carefully save them.

I generally plan my preaching program ahead a quarter. I feel free to make changes. I am not worried on Wednesday about what I am going to preach. I put down the major denominational and national dates. I follow the Christian year to a limited degree. That is, I begin the first Sunday in December and preach throughout the Christmas season on the great topics of Old Testament prophecy, the preaching of John the Baptizer, the second advent, and then the birth of Christ or the incarnation. I often do a series on preparing for Easter. During the Easter season I preach two to four times on the resurrection and the appearances. Departing from the Christian year I turn to an annual family series for May. I prepare my sermon files in advance for these future sermons. It is encouraging to open a folder on Tuesday and find several lively possibilities.

The short-term preparation begins Tuesday. I set aside Monday morning for administration and encourage the staff to do likewise. Tuesday morning I start with free association in dialogue with the text. I love the Greek New Testament. I find this to be a creative time, and often the application comes during the very first preparation. Then I read the heavier commentaries. I put fresh sheets of paper in a notebook and mark the first page *introduction* and the second page *outline*. The next several pages are for exegetical comments and applications. Toward the end of the week I look at sermons or expositions by people like Maclaren and A. M. Hunter. I write a rather full manuscript, but I am not a manuscript preacher. Preferably I tape to the pulpit three small pages of outline marked up with red ink.

A good Saturday night's rest is imperative. On Sunday morning I warm up my voice at home. I go over my sermon several times before Sunday School to recapture the excitement. At the outset of Sunday School I visit around, speaking to folks in the halls but soon settle into my office. In the privacy of my office I pace up and down with my sermon notes in hand. I have a final personal prayer and then go into the worship expectantly.

Phil Lineberger

My approach to preaching has been guided by Phillips Brooks's definition of preaching in his *Lectures On Preaching* (p. 5), "Preaching is the communication of truth by man to men. It has in it two essential elements, truth and personality. Neither of those can it spare and still be preaching."

Planning is an essential part of my approach to preaching. Sermons are planned six months to a year ahead according to a preaching calendar. Special occasions such as Easter, Christmas, Thanksgiving, etc., are marked on the preaching calendar. The rest of the calendar is put together according to a series or on books of the Bible being addressed. My usual method is to preach a series or through a book of the Bible. Very rarely will I preach a topical or textual sermon. The calendar can be adjusted when needed to address a crucial issue, such as a recent tragedy, a world-shattering event, and the like.

The morning hours from 8:30 until noon are best for my study. The first thing I do is read the passage of Scripture from several translations. Second comes the outline. Third is a study of the historical context. Fourth is a study in the original languages, looking for key words or phrases. Fifth is a search for appropriate illustrations. Sixth is making the proper application. Finally, the sermon is put together with an introduction and conclusion.

My sermons are delivered in an expositional and extemporaneous manner. I carry with me to the pulpit a full outline in case I need to refer to it during delivery of the sermon. Most of the time I will rarely consult my notes, but since beginning as a preacher, I have kept my notes near. They provide an element of security.

I preach forcefully, clearly and with moderate to strong gestures. Humor is used periodically. After all, preaching is truth through personality.

Kenneth L. Mahanes

My preaching style is relaxed and informal. My father, who was an effective Baptist pastor for nearly half a century, was a forceful and animated preacher of the Gospel. His sermons were strong in evangelistic fervor and zeal. In many ways, the difference in style between me and my father, who served as my model, is a study in contrasts. I seldom raise my voice or move around the pulpit—traits that were characteristic of my father's preaching.

I try to create a warm, personable relationship with the congregation when I preach. In my opinion, communication is enhanced when the congregation, regardless of its size, believes the preacher is speaking to each one personally as opposed to addressing a crowd. My goal in communication is to be perceived as talking *to* rather than talking *at* the people.

I generally preach expository messages, preaching through books of the Bible. But I vary my preaching by using topical or thematic messages on occasion. The message I have included for publication was preached at a state convention and is, therefore, not typical of the expository preaching done week by week from my pulpit.

Only a handful of times in twenty years of preaching have I preached from a manuscript. Normally, I take with me to the pulpit only a broad outline of the message. I fill in the gaps from memory. Thorough familiarity with the Scripture passage helps me retain, without the necessity of extensive notes, the salient points I want to present in the message.

I firmly believe good preaching includes good teaching. Hence, I strive to be a preacher-teacher. My preaching is an attempt to teach the Bible and to apply biblical truths to life. When my schedule permits, I stay about two or three months ahead in my sermon planning.

Wayne McDill

I try to take an inductive approach to my handling of the biblical text. I look carefully for what it actually says: the words, phrases, grammar. I bombard the passage with questions to get at its central idea. During this process I write random paragraphs of sermon material as the text opens up ideas and illustrations.

Once the idea of the text is clear I plan the sermon structure around it. I have found the use of a "key word" to be most helpful in keeping the divisions of the sermon parallel and balanced. This is vital to clear thinking. For this simple method, see James Braga, *How to Prepare Bible Messages*.

For the sake of effective communication I attempt in the introduction to get attention to the subject and demonstrate the need for the biblical answers so the audience will be eager to look with me at the text.

Overall I aim to preach for faith, to help the hearers to be confident they can trust God in the area being discussed. This calls for the use of faith language like "can" instead of duty language like "ought," "must," and "should." It keeps the focus on the adequacy of Christ for every need.

Alton H. McEachern

A young preacher was impressed with a sermon delivered by an experienced pastor. The young man asked, "How long did it take you to prepare that sermon?" The older man answered, "A lifetime!"

My preparation begins from six months to a year in advance as I plan my preaching. A quarter of our planning is already done for us by Christian seasonal themes. There are four Sundays in Advent, beginning the last Sunday of November. I preach on the Bible, John the Baptist, missions, the promise of the Messiah and His birth. We also have special services such as Christmas Eve communion, Palm Sunday, Maundy Thursday communion, and Easter.

The secular calendar also contributes to my planning: Mother's Day, Father's Day, July 4th, Labor Day, and Thanksgiving. Special worship services and preaching take on the tone of these seasonal themes.

I also plan sermon series such as: the Ten Commandments, Jesus' Beatitudes, and the Sermon on the Mount, selected psalms, Bible personalities, great doctrines, and the like. It is also good in the winter to have a series of sermons from the book of the Bible used in January Bible Study. Denominational themes shape both my preaching and worship plans: Baptist World Alliance Sunday, Race Relations Sunday, Layman's Sunday, and emphasis on state, home, and foreign missions.

I select sermon topics and Scripture passages at least six months in advance. These are shared with our minister of music. She builds the choral music, litanies, and congregational singing around these themes and Scripture passages. I evaluate the orders of worship and make suggestions, returning them to the minister of music for publication in the church newsletter. We communicate frequently in staff meetings about how we can improve the worship services.

Variety is the spice of preaching and worship, as well as life. Many services tend to have a dull sameness. It is deadly to worship if you can always anticipate what comes next. The services should not be radically different each Sunday. That would be jarring. There needs to be the familiar, such as the use of the Lord's Prayer, the doxology, the Gloria Patri; but don't have all the services identical. We tend to use a particular worship feature for four to six weeks, and then vary the service. I also strive for variety in preaching. While I most often do expository preaching (60 percent), I also intersperse textual and topical sermons as well as an occasional dramatic monologue sermon (two or three times a year). On occasion, I strive to achieve the element of surprise in the sermon so my conclusion is not a foregone one.

We have two or three Parent Dedication services each year. The parents of newly-born children participate in a litany of commitment, and the church presents each child with a New Testament. These are highly meaningful services which afford me an opportunity to speak on some facet of Christian home life and parenting.

Our church observes the Lord's Supper twelve times a year, including a Thanksgiving Eve banquet, Christmas Eve candlelight service, and Maundy Thursday communion. This gives me ample opportunity to preach on various facets of the Lord's Supper in my table devotionals.

My preparation for preaching begins in a spirit of prayer and searching the meaning of the Scriptures. Worship of God is the most important thing we do and deserves our very best effort. Preaching is my primary task as a pastor. My method of delivery is extemporaneous, though I do carry two small note cards into the pulpit. Sermons are transcribed after delivery, and those which appeared most helpful are reproduced for distribution to the congregation and to those on the sermon mailing list.

No task is more demanding, nor more rewarding, than the pulpit.

Calvin Miller

Sermon preparation, for me, has always been three-fold, like the outlines of most sermons themselves, I suppose.

First of all, life itself is the relational matrix which provides me with a sense of need, as well as the substance and illustration of a sermon. The relational world of the parish is one in which I visit, pray, minister, and lead people to Christ. Out of these kinds of activities, I discover what needs to be said for the equipping of the Body with all its various members.

But in our world of relationships, many things happen which provide the meat of the sermon as well. From these relationships, one gleans and records in a notebook or diary what can be profitably used for the instruction of the flock as a whole. Of course, discretion and professional confidence must never be violated. The names and circumstances may need to be altered to keep any specific person from being hurt or made uncomfortable.

The second part of sermon preparation is the long-range general reading and/or cultural enlightenment. Every journal or magazine article, each new book, and plays and movies all furnish a great deal of information and illustration for the sermon. From television, video, and audio cassettes, I make notes which can be tabulated, footnoted, and made a part of the sermon.

This long-range preparation crystallizes into "footnote sheets." These sheets are 5½ by 8½ (half a sheet of typing paper), which include the reference and citation (publisher, page number, etc.) and are filed in twenty-eight file folders under broad categories like "Jesus," "Leadership," "Prayer and Positivism," "Writing and Speaking," etc. Then this material can be quickly drawn out of file folders and used in whatever sermon may require them.

The third and final step of my preparation is the actual mechanics of getting a sermon down on paper. For more formal occasions, I prepare a complete manuscript, usually twelve to fourteen 8½ by-11 pages, double-spaced. For the regular Sunday morning presentation, I prepare a full outline, including phraseology I may want to use to give the sermon some sense of literary excellence, even as a spoken document. If I am going to read or quote from a book, I will have the quote properly underlined and near at hand. I prepare most quotes from a book or journal article on 5 by 7 cards which easily slip into my pocket or my Bible. Since I do not use a lectern when I speak, this allows me to be free of the need to carry a lot of books or Bibles with me into the pulpit area.

Following the presentation of the sermon in the Sunday morning service, it is transcribed from a cassette recording, then heavily edited as a manuscript the first of the next week. This process enables me to keep a complete manuscript file of sermons now numbering well in excess of 600 manuscripts. When I want to preach this series again, the outline and the manuscript both furnish me a thorough picture of the sermon as it was last presented.

Jess Moody

Preparing a sermon is not preparing a talk. It is the overflow of a committed life—years of experience talking to other followers on the quest for spiritual reality.

It is a conception, a gestation, and a birthing.

It is the joy following labor that brings into the world something beautiful and hitherto unknown, something akin to pure creation: the Word is spoken—the truth is transferred from soul to soul.

It is the first soul praying that the light will be transferred to the next soul—and the Light breaks.

Yet, there can be no light to come through if the communicator is clogged with carnality. One must be a continually filled channel for the transfer to be made.

Seventy-five percent of sermon preparation is soul preparation.

It is a method of imparting life, encouragement, and hope. It is defeating sin, fear, and a poor self-image.

A sermon is searching for the basic needs of human beings, isolating those needs, and applying the Scriptural cure upon those needs.

The first thing I do is write the conclusion. Only by defining where I want to go, am I able to chart the course I wish to take. You must know that you are going to Sacramento before you can choose what road to take.

It is then extremely important to try to discover a deeply-felt need, focus upon it, and search the Scriptures for every application to that need.

At this time, I try to exegete the texts chosen, looking for the nuances and purposes of the original language, and to make certain that the particular text is applicable to the need addressed.

I then concentrate on all the practical applications I can imagine. Then I try to break it into the most impactful points, and reduce them down to bite size by removing from the writings every difficult word.

After this, I do what I call "street-ify" the message. That is, I put it in semantics of audience identification which let the listeners know I understand their pain.

The next thing I do is seek "street parables" which are stories that let the light shine upon the truth I am trying to impress upon the hearers.

I strongly recommend avoiding illustration books. They are the cookery of fast-food fad-preaching, giving psychic indigestion. These books are brain paralyzers, encouraging the Saturday night late, late show all honest ministers have experienced.

Finally, I write the introduction and the title. I do not name the baby until it is born.

After I have written the message and have it down on paper, I start tuning up my soul to transfer the message and the spirit of the sermon.

I ask, "Could this be a song?"

A sermon has the element of song and poetry to it. Keep a diary of the spiritual and aesthetic journey of this particular message.

Charles D. Page

My philosophy of preaching is a very simple one. I love expository preaching, allowing the text itself to formulate the outline for the message. I usually preach in series, working through the different books of the Bible, trying to give a broad range of Old Testament and New Testament books to my congregation. I will often break in on a series for special occasions with messages to match those special occasions.

My study habits also are very simple. I always do an in-depth background study of every book I preach from and then a background study of every passage, doing an in-depth key word study, which I think is vitally important for understanding the passage. I try to absorb the passage in my mind and heart by repeated reading and meditation. Once the passage is securely in my mind and the outline has been formulated, I will then check several commentaries on the passage to make sure the direction I am taking has credibility with others who have studied it.

My preaching style could be expressed as enthusiastic and simple. I have a great love for preaching and have felt the call to preach since I was sixteen years of age. God has wonderfully blessed me with opportunities to exercise what gifts and skills He has given.

Franklin D. Pollard

Gordon Clinard, my preaching professor at Southwestern Baptist Theological Seminary, said: "Can you imagine our Lord standing on the mountains saying, 'Blessed are the ah . . .' and having to look at his notes?"

That statement prompted a promise to our Lord that I would never read from anything other than the Bible while preaching. This means at least four extra hours of learning (not memorizing) the completed sermon. It means for me writing a full word-for-word manuscript.

The preparation begins with a choice of text. This Scripture must be selected on Monday. The text and context are read over and over. Before any word studies or commentary work is done, I write down every thought the Scripture brings to mind. Then comes the mechanical effort: the word studies, commentary reading, and other sermons on the same text.

After this comes an imagination process. I try to image the Scripture, to be there, to see, feel, smell, experience the biblical episode. Then a mental effort is made to bring the incident into today's world. Questions are asked like: "How would we react to that today?" "What people are living today who are like the biblical characters?"

On Thursday the manuscript is written. I prepare it first verbally, talking it out paragraph by paragraph. As this is done, I write it down as I have spoken it. This manuscript is then read into a tape recorder, and the sermon is played on my automobile cassette for the rest of the week. Of course, all of this is bathed in prayer. There is the constant prayer that our Lord will help me bring the Scripture alive for the people.

I preach one sermon each week. The other two preparations are Bible studies.

Paul W. Powell

The most difficult step in my sermon preparation is deciding what to preach. Some preachers plan their sermons well in advance. I have never been able to do that. I seldom have more than a subject and text in mind by the Monday morning. Two things help me decide what to preach. First, generally I preach expositorily, going through books of the Bible section by section. I like this approach because it gives continuity to my preaching. It forces me to deal with subjects I would otherwise pass over, and it keeps me from a frantic Monday-morning search for a subject for the next Sunday. I just preach on what comes next in the Book.

I'm not a slave to this approach, however, and I deviate from it readily when I feel impressed. I am continually collecting sermon ideas, titles, texts, and outlines for future use. I find these in my own devotional time, in general reading, in listening to or talking to other preachers, and in personal experiences. I place them in a folder marked "sermon ideas," and they become a seed bed for future messages.

My title and text are picked on Monday. Next I exegete my text. I feel divinely obligated to know its full and correct meaning. This is usually done in the morning hours in the study I maintain in my home.

By the time I complete my exegesis, a thesis and a tentative outline have usually emerged. Both are very important to me. The thesis is a one-sentence statement of what I want to say to my audience. It is the nail I want to drive home. Each point of my outline is like a blow of a hammer that drives the thesis deeper and deeper into the hearts and minds of my hearers. I try to make the points of the sermon very definite and repeat them often so they will be remembered easily.

I want each point of the sermon to include three things: exegesis, illustration, and application. So once I have my outline I go to my files for illustrations. Illustrations are like windows that let in both light and fresh air. They help to make the sermon understandable and interesting.

I'm often asked where I find my illustrations. Everywhere! From all kinds of reading, from talking to others, from listening to other speakers, from television, and as I go about my pastoral duties. You can train yourself to see and hear illustrations everywhere. I copy or clip and file these away by subject. I carry a pen and paper with me at all times for this purpose.

The conclusion usually emerges naturally as the sermon develops. In it I try to reach a spiritual climax with an evangelistic appeal and an invitation to accept Christ.

The last thing I decide is what comes first. I like to introduce my messages with a current event, a story, a quote, or a personal experience that will capture the attention and hold the interest of the audience.

I seldom manuscript my sermons, but I outline them fully and then preach from scant notes.

When I stand to preach I have the outline and illustrations well in mind, so I am able to speak freely. I have full eye contact with my audience, using only an occasional glance for key words or for an exact quote. I believe that people want to hear a man who will stand up, look them in the eyes, and speak as if he believes what he is saying.

Some preachers have their sermons completed by Friday. I seldom do. I am continually working on my outline until the very moment of delivery. Each sermon is taped and then typed in manuscript form after it is preached.

Naturally, I bathe the whole process in prayer. I earnestly desire that God will lead me in my preparation and bring the sermon alive in the hearts of the hearers.

Even then I seldom preach without wishing that I had just one more week, one more day, or even one more hour to work on my sermon. As I walk to the pulpit I usually breathe the prayer, "Lord, Thou who canst make something out of nothing, do it again." And, miracle of miracles, He usually does it!

Nelson L. Price

Preaching is speech on fire fueled by human personality and oxygenated by the Holy Spirit. In order to communicate with conviction, one must be saturated with truth-consumed compassion.

In order to be prepared to preach I endeavor to spend an average of twenty hours a week in the study. People will forgive their pastor of almost anything other than not being prepared in the pulpit. Nothing is so important as allowing a preacher to step into the pulpit at his best.

Being privileged to preach in an auditorium that seats 4,000, I find it necessary to animate. Studies in sensory perception reveal that 82 percent of what we remember comes from what we see and 14 percent from what we hear. Therefore, there must be some sanctified dramatics in our declaration.

Sunday morning messages tend to be inspirational and motivational. Sunday night messages are more informational and mobilizational. The AM messages are topical/textual, and the PM ones expository.

I preach through a book on Sunday nights each year. I write out all the messages in the last quarter of the previous year before preaching the first one. Thus I know from the beginning the total theme.

Morning messages are frequently short series consisting of from four to eight messages. These are frequently exhortations. Heavy reliance on Scripture is a hallmark.

Application is a must in all preaching. The hearer must be led to understand how to apply what is heard and how to relate it to life.

Joe Samuel Ratliff

One of the greatest joys of my life is the preaching event. Coupled with that joy is the awesomeness of the responsibility that falls my lot each time I mount the sacred desk.

The personal preparation for this moment involves private devotion and reflection seeking divine direction. This is needed and anxiously pursued to insure that the medium of the message is ready for the preaching moment.

This preparation also includes private reading. I read everything: newspapers, comics, digests, magazines, children's stories, Westerns, etc. One would be surprised at the wealth of illustrations found in sources other than commentaries.

The texts are selected normally to reflect the thrust, program, season, or emphasis of the church community. The social Gospel becomes a hallmark theme because we have led our church in this path of ministry. To keep my preaching fresh, balanced, and useful, I've relied on a rich Black tradition—the use of imagination. The creativity which springs from this ally extends beyond just recreating Bible scenes. I've tried to commune and interact with people, allowing me to observe and listen to what is going on in the "real world."

Children and children's stories by their very nature spur one's imagination. Humor and wit are gifts that God have given me, so I use them skillfully and prayerfully.

I also leave a lot to the imagination of the listeners by leaving some things unsaid.

There is seldom a manuscript taken to the pulpit even though there is one (normally in outline form) to support it in my files.

I enjoy the Spirit's introduction of illustrations or moods during the worship. So the delivery style may appear to be extemporaneous to the casual observer.

The tone, fervor, or mood of preaching is normally gauged by the setting or occasion. Prethought is given to such items to insure the audience's involvement.

Timeliness is a concern in delivery. My sermons normally will last thirty minutes from start to finish, invitation included.

We've implemented preaching clinics involving our staff and assistant preachers. This in-house activity permits us to critique and instruct one another on how to improve our preaching. This healthy exchange permits us to learn from one another's mistakes.

Because of our church's mission statement, I've tried to enhance my preaching by challenging our people to world visions, global perspectives, and Kingdom views. There is that ongoing challenge to keep the congregation thoroughly aware of the bigger world, noting social, political, and economic signals of concern.

Overall, I feel my preaching is evangelical in that I am always seeking and hoping, if not demanding, a decision or action. Such response is critical in my thinking. It becomes the object of my preaching, not the measure.

Darrell Robinson

My approach to preaching if from a pastor's perspective. I have a threefold goal to exalt our Lord Jesus Christ, to equip the people of God, and to evangelize the lost. My attempt is to, through preaching, equip the people of God for their work of ministry so the Body of Christ will be built up in maturity and in number.

My methodology is not centered in one particular type of preaching. While my preaching is biblical, I vary the approach to include expository, exegetical, topical, textual, biographical, and other types of sermons.

My delivery will depend to some extent on the type of message I am preaching and the type of congregation. Generally, it is my goal to deliver sermons under the anointing of the Holy Spirit of God with divine enthusiasm, allowing my sermon to so grip me that I preach with spontaneity out of the overflow. If the sermon does anything for others, it surely must do something to and for the one who preaches it.

Perry R. Sanders

I consider preaching the greatest calling in the world. Because of that, I magnify my pulpit ministry. Many things are important in a pastor's life, but he absolutely must be at his best when time comes to preach the Word of God.

In preparing sermons, I frequently do a series such as the Ten Commandments, which I have recently done, or a book of the Bible, or relevant subjects. A recent one included sermons on "Is Homosexuality Really Wrong?"; "Is Abortion Really Wrong?"; "Are Alcohol and Drugs Really Wrong?"; and so forth.

After twenty-eight years in one pastorate, it is absolutely mandatory that I read extensively and stay on a "sermon search" at all times. My previous longest pastorate was about five years. I had not been here long before I had "hit the bottom of the barrel."

My preaching style is declamatory, and I use several

pages of notes. I never preach from a manuscript, though I have carefully thought through almost all of the phraseology, particularly of the major points and the transitional sentences.

Without exception, I always have one overarching purpose for every sermon. There may be several minor emphases, but all eventuate in and lead up to a forceful conclusion to drive home the major theme of the sermon. The exception to this would be when delivering expository sermons that cannot always be gathered together under one main topic.

I deliver my sermons with a very direct style, including eye contact at all times, except when glancing at my notes for reference. I do not hesitate to use great volume, but never sustain any one style of delivery for a long period.

I am never reluctant to confront moral issues and generally try to do so with hard facts, as well as spiritual and moralistic pronouncements. For example, I delivered to two capacity morning audiences and to live television audience a declamation against the evils of gambling, specifically proposed statewide lottery.

I always preach for decisions. This is true, even if it is in a civic club setting or some other such outside-of-the-church function. Of course, no invitation is given in those kinds of meetings, but I still want the Truth proclaimed to produce a result in the hearts and minds of the hearers. I never fail to magnify Jesus, even in secular settings, such as a United Givers Fund Drive or a National Communication Worker's Convention. My rationale is that they would know I am thoroughly committed to the lordship of Christ when they ask me to speak, so without apology I magnify Him.

My philosophy is: heaven is too wonderful; hell is too awful; Christ is too good; the Gospel too great, and time too short to do anything less than talk about the Savior at every opportunity! The effectiveness of this philosophy of preaching would have to be measured by those who have patiently endured across more than a quarter of a century in this one church.

William L. Self

I have a strong conviction, like Luther, that the preaching of the Word of God *is* the Word of God, and I believe it is the primary tool for the leadership of the church. My friends in the business community tell me they envy the preacher the opportunity to address his constituency every week. No other profession has this privilege.

In a real sense there is no time when a pastor isn't thinking about his sermons. Sunday always comes, ready or not. If you are prepared, it never gets here; if you are not prepared, it seems to come every other day. There are seasons when the mind and heart are more open to the preaching ministry. These times of openness and the flow of creative adrenalin do not always arrive at eleven o'clock on Sunday morning week after week. In order to deal with this, I try to play a year's preaching in the summertime and announce it to the church immediately after my vacation. This focuses the direction for both the church and the pastor and prevents a capriciousness from occurring directly or indirectly in the preaching ministry.

It is generally acknowledged that the pastor spends his morning in study and his afternoon doing other things related to his church. This schedule for the week will not fit my particular emotional pattern. I spend Sunday morning through Wednesday night doing the public things relating to the ministry of our church, but Thursday, Friday, and Saturday is the quiet time when the soul, heart, and mind are prepared for Sunday. Also, I am convinced that, regardless of how good the preparation is, if the pastor walks into the pulpit on Sunday morning tired or depressed or hassled by a full work week, that emotional disposition will be communicated to his church. And so, a part of my preparation is the preparation of the man, as well as the preparation of the material.

I strongly believe that sermons are oral documents—not written essays—and so after a very detailed outline, I then preach that sermon over and over until I feel as though I have it thoroughly prepared. This is the preparation of an oral manuscript. Sunday morning I get up at five o'clock for one last period of emotional/spiritual preparation and to make sure that when I arrive for the eight-thirty service, I am thoroughly awake. The old preacher, when asked how he prepared his sermons, may have been correct when he said, "I read myself full, I think myself straight, and I pray myself hot."

Don Sharp

Sermon preparation basically involves an understanding of needs. God must be seen and felt as real, not some abstract entity. Not only is He real, but He has feelings and emotions. He is also concerned about everyone, not simply as groups of people but also as individuals.

James Earl Massey in his book, *Designing the Sermon,* states, "The ultimate goal in preaching is to connect the hearer with the grace of God, and nurture that hearer in the life that grace makes possible when it is accepted and regarded in full. Nothing less than this basic objective is worthy of any pulpit, and nothing other than this concern can rightly qualify as Christian preaching. Christian preaching is always rooted in the purpose Jesus announced for His coming: 'I came that they may have life, and have it abundantly' (John 10:10). A preaching ministry maintains focus and balance when that purpose of Christ is kept central in all sermon planning."

All sermon preparation must begin with prayer. There have been times when I have been so concerned about the sermon that I did not take the time to consult the Sermon Giver. All channels must be open and clear in order for the Holy Spirit to illuminate the Word for and to us.

The next issue is what is God saying to His people. As we look at the Scriptures, what is the message that the people should leave with? Not only should they leave with a message, but the message should have some impact and effect on their lives. The basic premise is that there is no way that anyone who is confronted with the Gospel can remain the same. The Gospel confronts, convicts, and conforms.

Another trap to avoid is to remember the KISS principle (Keep It Simple, Stupid). Jesus always communicated with people on their level. He had the capacity to be profound; He had the capacity to communicate with the most learned. We find, however, that He always kept His conversation at a level where people came away with a sense of direction and an understanding of what He was talking about. The reason some did not respond is because they understood too clearly what Jesus was saying, as in the case of the rich young ruler. This is why on Sunday mornings I try to use the shotgun approach. That is, I try to use the Gospel to hit as many people as possible.

Sermon preparation should not be objective. In many instances it should not be "you people" but "us." In the preparation, I must constantly ask, "What does this mean to me? as I deal with who I am and how I am letting God use me. The congregation in many instances will not hear the sermon as much as they see the sermon being acted out in my life-style. The sermon must be more than rhetoric, but the effectiveness of the sermon will be measured by how the individual is employing the principles in his lifestyle.

Perhaps the greatest weakness in my sermon preparation is that I am not always cognizant of the technical aspects of sermon preparation. Many times, when after I have finished, I have repreached the sermon to myself and torn it apart. I have seen areas where I did not do as thorough a job as I should have researching and exegeting the Scripture, and I wasn't too clear as to whether the sermon was topical, narrative, or expository. At times I wasn't sure if I had defined all of my three points clearly (I never use poems); I am not by any means implying that this isn't useful in sermon preparation. I am reminded of Dr. D. E. King's response, when asked how he goes about sermon preparation, "After the Holy Spirit has revealed to me what I need to know, *then* I consult the commentaries to see if they are correct."

In summation, sermon preparation is wholly dictated by the direction and leadership of the Holy Spirit. He will lead, direct, and guide us to all truths, according to Massey's book.

Donald E. Demaray closes his illuminating book, *Pulpit Grants,* with some summary statements about the major characteristics held in common by the twenty-six master preachers he has discussed. Among those characteristics Demaray listed were these:

(a) An utter seriousness about the call to preach.
(b) A passion to communicate.
(c) A readiness to be individual.
(d) An eagerness to study, learn, and use the learning.
(e) A sensitive concern for persons.
(f) An ability to concentrate meaningfully and faithfully on their given task.
(g) A healthy discontent with their own spiritual progress and ministeral success.
(h) An honorable view of preaching as the most important activity in which they could be involved.

Ted Sisk

Pastor Sisk endeavors to plan his pulpit ministry by taking into account the Christian year, the denominational calendar, the great doctrines of the faith, and the needs of his congregation. He seeks to give his flock a balance of expository, textual, and subject sermons.

He writes out every sermon word for word, and he takes a manuscript into the pulpit with him; however, he tries to maintain eye contact with his congregation and to be free from his notes.

Daniel Vestal

Someone once commented to a pastor about his being paid to preach, to which he responded, "You don't pay me to preach. You pay me for what I must do during the week so I can preach on Sunday." For me preaching is a joy and privilege. Nothing in the ministry brings me greater exhilaration than preparing and delivering a message from God's Word to the people I love and shepherd.

My preparation process is a continuous one, involving regular study of Scripture, wide reading of theology and other disciplines, and developing manuscripts from which I do oral preparation.

Ninety percent of my preaching is systematic and expository. I study a biblical book and share the results of that study with my congregation. Those sermons which are topical or thematic seek to uncover a biblica text or truth for specific application. My sermon in this book is such an example. This sermon was delivered October 6, 1986, in the First Baptist Church, Washington, D.C., at a national conference on religious liberty sponsored by the Baptist Joint Committee on Public Affairs. It is a topical sermon that addresses a particular problem from a biblical text.

My homiletical style involves a constant tension between the exposition of the ancient text and an application to the modern context. I seek illustrations from literature and everyday life, from history and experience, from biography and personal struggles.

My call to preach is something I have never doubted. It is the most determinative factor in my ministry, and it has sustained and motivated me through the years. Preaching to me is more of a passion than anything else. I wouldn't trade places with anybody in the world.

Jerry Vines

My personal approach to preaching is the expository method. I preach consecutively through books of the Bible. I follow this pattern on Sunday morning and on Sunday night.

I preach paragraph by paragraph through Bible books. My methodology is to study the passages of Scripture grammatically, contextually, historically, comparatively, theologically, and practically. I make every effort to preach without notes based on a total saturation of my mind and heart with the substance of the message.

I place great emphasis upon turning my expository

messages toward an evangelistic emphasis. My goal is two-fold; to edify believers and to evangelize the lost.

David Walker

Amidst the components of any great church, in my judgment, the heart of the *people* is a vital ingredient, but the heart of the *preaching* is an equally strategic determinant. I use the term "heart of the preaching," because it is the heart, and not the head alone, that gives preaching its force and raises its significance above the level of a common lecture. A lecture informs; preaching motivates. Certainly, proper spiritual motivation includes proper spiritual information; but without a thorough dose of both, either not enough of the right thing or too much of the wrong thing will be the result of the preaching.

Assuredly, proper spiritual *information* is gained directly from the *Scripture,* and proper spiritual *motivation* is gained directly from the *Spirit.* The conclusion then, is that the best preaching is that which has the Bible for its content and the Spirit for its energy.

I have become convinced that the Spirit must be the energizer throughout the preaching process—from disciplined preparation to dynamic presentation. Therefore, He must be allowed the leadership role in the selection of which books or passages from Scripture to preach.

Once the text is selected, I am convicted that a careful word-by-word investigation should be launched, entailing the best historical and grammatical tools available in an effort to determine what originally was intended. It is important to see the text as far as possible *through the eyes of the Author.* I term this phase *examination.*

Next, the text must be prayerfully considered for relevant truths that will impact the lives of twentieth-century people in general, and men and women hearing the message in San Antonio, Texas, in particular. What does the text say to young adults with children, older single adults, career military men, professional women, financially troubled entrepreneurs, the new rich, the long-term poor? I sincerely ask the Holy Spirit to help me see *the text through the eyes of my people*.

It has been remarkable to discover that when I have spent as much time praying over the *application section* as I have the *examination section,* the results have been striking. It has also seemed apparent that the better I know my people, the more precise will be the application. Distance from the flock as a shepherd also means distance from the shepherd as a sheep. I speak more clearly, and they hear more attentively when the gap between pulpit and pew is small. This endeavor I call *"application."*

Finally, there is *exhortation.* Herein lies what may be the central expression of the energy of the Spirit at work in the art of preaching. At this point the preacher seeks to follow the leadership of the Spirit into the hearts of his listeners, aiming to touch their feelings strongly enough to motivate them to action.

Is it not true that humanity behaves not so much according to *cerebral* impulses as to *emotional* ones? It does appear that we most often move because our *hearts* stir us and not because our *heads* reason with us.

Preaching that fears the shadowy land of human emotion can expect little for its effort. For the conquest of that land determines the boundaries of the lordship of Christ in His church.

A preacher who is moved to song, to tears, or even to shouts from a burning, overlowing heart will assuredly go much farther in applying biblical truth and motivating to action than one who is boringly one-dimensional in his preaching. Often, but not often enough, the cry of my soul as I prepare to preach is, "Lord stir *me,* break *me,* move *me* that I may move others by Your Spirit and for Your glory."

Accounts of modern-day victories and tragedies, the touching words of songs, powerful historical illustrations, stirring devotional insights from other men's sermons, majestic progressions of Scripture pursuing a grand theme, are all examples of means I am led regularly to employ in exhorting the congregations to whom I speak. Though it is not an absolute principle, it is a fairly consistant one, that those illustrations which *move me* generally move my people, and I relate them with vigor.

Whether it is in teaching through a book of the Bible or in calling men and women to Christ in an evangelistic crusade, I have come to believe that preaching is motivation—motivation to change, motivation to start, motivation to finish, motivation to act for Christ's sake. Cotton Mather, the American Puritan of the early eighteenth century, summed up the phenomenon in this way in his book, *Student and Preacher:*

> The great design and intention of the office of a Christian preacher are to restore the throne and dominion of God in the souls of men; to display in the most lively colors, and proclaim in the clearest language, the wonderful perfections, offices and grace of the Son of God; and to attract the souls of men into a state of everlasting friendship with Him . . . It is a work which an angel might wish for . . . It is such an honorable, important and useful office, that if a man be put into it by God, and made faithful and successful through life, He may look down with disdain upon a crown and shed a tear of pity on the brightest monarch on earth.

Bill Weber

Bill Weber's sensitive style of preaching goes to the heart of hurting people. His aim is to reach the unchurched and nurture the believer through practical applications of God's Word for daily living. His insight into the problems of our age, coupled with his ability to apply the Scriptures dynamically, enable him to deliver an applicable message to his hearers across the nation.

He plans for messages that give people encouragement and hope about the daily problems of life. He preaches to affirm his congregations as valuable human beings God loves and wants to redeem and use in a special, significant way. His goal is to share the abundant life in Jesus Christ.

Fred H. Wolfe

My approach to preaching is that of doing expository preaching. I study the Scriptures to find out their original meaning to the people to whom they were spoken and interpret those Scriptures in light of present application today. While I do topical preaching, as well as expository preaching, I would say that 80 percent of my preaching is expository.

I deliver my sermons, basically, without the use of notes, and seek to use a clear, simple approach of the presentation of the Gospel. Many people describe me as a teacher who makes the Scriptures easily understood.

I have great confidence in the authority of the Word of God and the power of the Holy Spirit to anoint that Word. With this approach I preach the Word of God after much prayer and preparation. Normally, I preach from thirty to thirty-five minutes.

H. Edwin Young

As I prepare a sermon, I begin by reading the text to see what it says to me. I then read and reread the text (in the original language, if time permits) in an effort to understand it. My next step is to note the natural outline of the passage I am studying. I then consult various commentaries to learn what other theologians and homileticians have to say about it. Most importantly, I finally ask the question: "So what? What difference will these principles make in the lives of those who are listening to this particular sermon?"

About the Preachers

R. Earl Allen

R. Earl Allen has been pastor of Rosen Heights Baptist Church, Fort Worth, Texas, since October 1, 1956. It is located across the street from the elementary school that he attended, as later did his children. This church has had only one pulpit committee in over sixty years.

He was born in Fort Worth, Texas, May 26, 1922. He and his wife, the former Norma Joyce Lovelace, have three children, Norma (deceased), James Todd, and Joy Earline. They rejoice in their four grandchildren.

Dr. Allen was licensed to preach at age twelve and ordained at age eighteen. He has been pastoring since that time. He pastored rural churches while in college. He pastored First Baptist Church, Archer City, Texas, 1945-1947; First Baptist Church, Seagraves, Texas, 1947-1950; and First Baptist Church, Floydada, Texas, 1950-1956.

He holds the Bachelor of Arts, Bachelor of Science, and Master of Arts degrees from Howard Payne University, Linda Vista Baptist College, and Midwestern University. He attended Southwestern Baptist Theological Seminary where he serves as adjunct professor.

He holds five honorary degrees: Doctor of Divinity from Howard Payne University, Doctor of Laws from Atlanta Law School, Doctor of Literature from John Brown University, Doctor of Humane Letters from Linda Vista College, and Doctor of Sacred Theology from Southwest Baptist University.

Howard Payne gave him the Doctor of Divinity Degree at the youngest age given to a minister. They also recognized him with a Distinguished Alumnus Award in 1967.

He is the author of twenty-three books, as well as other writing contributions. He is the recipient of three George

Washington Freedom Foundations awards. Allen is widely known for his books, including these from Broadman— *Memorial Messages, Christian Comfort, Strength from Shadows, Sign of the Star, The Personal Jesus, Persons of the Passion, Prayers That Changed History, For Those Who Grieve, Jesus Loves Me, Let It Begin in Me,* and *Southern Baptist Preaching Today* (Co-compiler with Joel Gregory).

He has served in denominational life in the association, state, and Southern Baptist Convention. He is serving as a trustee at Howard Payne University and is a past trustee at Valley Baptist Academy and Wayland Baptist University. Allen served for twenty four years as a member of the Southern Baptist Sunday School Board, Home Mission Board, and SBC Executive Committee.

John R. Bisagno

Dr. John R. Bisagno is pastor of the 20,000-member First Baptist Church of Houston, Texas. He is author of twenty books and has served as the President of the Southern Baptist Pastors' Conference.

Dr. Bisagno was born on April 5, 1934, in Augusta, Kansas. He has a BA in Music from Oklahoma Baptist University and holds the Litt. D. from Missouri Baptist University and the D.D. from Houston Baptist University, where an endowed chair of evangelism is named in his honor.

Dr. Bisagno began his ministry in evangelism, traveling extensively conducting crusades for twelve years. He pastored the First Southern Baptist Church of Del City, Oklahoma from 1965 to 1970. In February 1970, Dr. Bisagno began his pastorate at First Baptist Church of Houston.

The First Baptist Church facility is one of the most modern in the world, with a sanctuary seating more than 4,000 persons. Dr. Bisagno conducts services twice on Sunday mornings, again on Sunday evenings, and on Wednesday evenings. He preaches three times weekly on the nationwide Acts television network.

Dr. Bisagno has spoken at the Southern Baptist Convention, the World Congress on Evangelism, and every major state convention and state evangelism conference. He has lectured at five of the six Southern Baptist seminaries. He has conducted major overseas crusades in Brazil, Taiwan, Nigeria, the Philippines, Hong Kong, Guyana, Zimbabwe, South Africa, Malawi, and Mexico.

Morris H. Chapman

Dr. Morris Chapman has been pastor of the historic 7,700-member First Baptist Church of Wichita Falls, Texas, since February, 1979. He previously served as pastor of the First Baptist Church, Rogers, Texas; First Baptist Church of Woodway (Waco, Texas), and First Baptist Church of Albuquerque, New Mexico.

He served as President of the SBC Pastors' Conference (1986) and is a member of the Board of Trustees of Hardin-Simmons University. He served as chairman of the Committee on Order of Business of the Southern Baptist Convention (Dallas, 1985). Dr. Chapman served two terms as president of the Baptist Convention of New Mexico, 1976-78. He is the author of *Youth Affirm: The Doctrine of Christ,* Convention Press, 1984, and the contributor—compiled of *Jesus: Author and Finisher,* Broadman Press, 1987. He preaches on radio and television weekly. The Freedom Foundation has honored him for his sermon, "Hear This Word, America."

During the time Dr. Chapman has been pastor in Wichita Falls, the church budget has increased 2½ times (1.3 million to 3.2 million), total mission giving has tripled ($219,000 to $692,000) and gifts through the Cooperative Program have more than tripled ($151,000 to $486,000). Dr. Chapman has led the church to raise the Cooperative Program from 12 percent to 15 percent of the annual budget and to launch direct mission initiatives to the Northwest United States and Haiti.

Dr. Chapman is a native of Kosciusko, Mississippi, and a graduate of Mississippi College, Clinton. He received the Master of Divinity and Doctor of Ministry degrees from Southwestern Baptist Theological Seminary, Fort Worth. In 1985 Southwest Baptist University, Bolivar, Missouri, conferred an honorary Doctor of Sacred Theology Degree upon Dr. Chapman.

He is married to the former Jodi Francis of Memphis, Tennessee. She is a trustee of the Sunday School Board of the Southern Baptist Convention and a member of the SBC Peace Committee. They have two children, Christopher, age 22, a graduate of Baylor University, and Stephanie, age 18, a student at Hardin-Simmons University.

W. A. Criswell

Dr. W. A. Criswell was born in Eldorado, Oklahoma, on December 19, 1909. On February 14, 1935, he married Bessie Marie Harris. They have one child, Ann Criswell Jackson (Mrs. Kenneth).

He was educated at Baylor University (B.A., 1931)

with a major in English and minors in psychology, philosophy, and Greek. He received his Th.M. from Southern Baptist Theological Seminary in 1934 and his Ph.D. from the same institution in 1937. Baylor University awarded him the D.D. in 1945.

His pastorates have been First Baptist Church of Chickasha, Oklahoma (1937-1941), First Baptist Church of Muskogee, Oklahoma (1941-1944), and First Baptist Church of Dallas, Texas (1944—).

He has authored thirty-six books with several companies, including Broadman's *The Gospel According to Moses, The Scarlet Thread Through the Bible, Why I Preach That the Bible Is Literally True, Look Up, Brother!, What to Do Until Jesus Comes Back, Welcome Back, Jesus, What a Savior!,* and *Criswell's Guidebook for Pastors.*

Among his many positions have been former trustee of Baylor University, past member of the Southern Baptist Annuity Board, past president of the Sunday School Board of the SBC, former member of the State Executive Board of the Baptist General Convention of Texas, past director of *The Baptist Standard,* former trustee of Baylor University Medical Center, president of the Southern Baptist Convention (1968-1970), chairman of the Development Committee of Friends of Baptist World Alliance, appointee to Committee by Governor of Texas for the Handicapped, chancellor of Criswell Center for Biblical Studies, chairman of the Board of Trustees of Dallas Baptist College, member of the Board of World Evangelism Foundation, and editor of *The Criswell Study Bible* (Thomas Nelson Publishers).

Dr. Criswell followed the world-famed George W. Truett, who was pastor of First Baptist Church, Dallas, for forty-seven years. Dr. Criswell is now pastor in his forty-third year, meaning that the church has had only two pastors in the last ninety years. During the years he has been undershepherd, the First Baptist Church has grown to over 22,000 members, with an annual budget in excess of eight million dollars. The Sunday School enrollment exceeds ten thousand members with fully graded departments. The church supports seventeen missions and two Sunday Schools outside the church complex. These missions have full-time pastors. The church staff (including maintenance, nursery, and First Baptist Academy) numbers well in excess of 300.

Earl C. Davis

Dr. Earl C. Davis is pastor of the First Baptist Church of Memphis, Tennessee, where he has ministered since 1976. Born in Madison, Florida, Dr. Davis is a graduate of Stetson University, B.A., 1960; Southeastern Baptist Theological Seminary, B.D., 1963; and Southern Baptist Theological Seminary, Ph.D., 1967.

He has served as pastor of Ekron Baptist Church, Ekron, Kentucky; First Baptist Church, Marianna, Florida; First Baptist Church, Dalton, Georgia; and First Baptist Church, Memphis, Tennessee.

He has served as President of the Georgia Pastors' Conference; member of the Committee on Committees of the SBC; trustee of the Sunday School Board; and as a member of the Baptist World Alliance Pastoral Care Commission. He has traveled extensively in Europe and the Middle East, and has preached at SBC mission points in Thailand, Taiwan, Indonesia, Germany, and Upper Volta.

Dr. Davis is a popular conference speaker and author of four books: *Forever, Amen; Somebody Cares; Christ at the Door;* and *Life in the Spirit,* all Broadman. His sermons, televised weekly, reach a large Mid-south audience.

He and his wife, Pegeen, have two children—Deryl, a graduate of Wake Forest University and the University of Virginia and presently studying in England, and Dawn, a student at Memphis State University.

Cristobal Doña

Cristobal Doña is pastor of Iglesia Bautista White Road, San Jose, CA, since 1976.

Born in Managua, Nicaragua, April 6, 1927. Married Dec. 20, 1947, to the former Eugenia Moreno; have eleven children from 21 to 38 years of age. Arrived in U.S.A. Feb. 10, 1953; Called to the Ministry in Aug., 1959. Graduated from San Jose State College, B.A. 1969; Golden Gate Baptist Theological Seminary, M.R.E. 1972.

Served as pastor of Primera Iglesia Bautista, Wilmington, CA, 1959-1967. Moved to San Jose in 1967 and served as pastor of Calvary Spanish Baptist Mission which evolved to the present church.

Has served: second vice-president of Southern Baptist General Convention of California, 1973; trustee, Golden Gate Baptist Theological Seminary, 1975-1984, Mill Valley, CA; trustee, Baptist Spanish Publishing House, El Paso, TX, 1980-1984; president, Pastors' Conference, San Jose Baptist Association, 1979-1980; moderator, San Jose Baptist Association, 1982-1983; writer of Adult Spanish Sunday School material for teachers, BSSB; speaker, local and worldwide radio program "Wonderful Words of Life" since 1972. Served: Resolutions Committee, SBC 1984; Credentials Committee, SBGCC 1985; Trustee, California Baptist College, 1986.

While none of my children is a preacher, every one of them is faithfully serving the Lord in their respective churches. Four of them are police officers. Eight of the children are married; these have produced fifteen grandchildren so far.

James T. Draper, Jr.

Dr. Draper, known by all as "Jimmy," is the son and grandson of Southern Baptist pastors. His grandfather, L. M. Keeling, preached for fifty-four years, mostly in the state of Arkansas. He was a graduate of Southwestern Baptist Theological Seminary. Jimmy's father, James T. Draper, graduated from Ouachita Baptist University in Arkansas and Southwestern Baptist Theological Seminary. He preached for thirty-six years before dying at the age of fifty-two. Both of Jimmy Draper's brothers, George and Charles, are Southern Baptist preachers.

Dr. Draper graduated from Milby High School in Houston, Texas. He went on to graduate from Baylor University and Southwestern Baptist Theological Seminary. He has been awarded honorary doctorates from Howard Payne University and Dallas Baptist University in Texas, and from Campbell University in North Carolina.

Dr. Draper has authored sixteen books and has written extensively for the Sunday School Board and Holman Bible Publishers. Most recently he wrote the annotations on Proclamation and Worship, as well as the outline and introduction to 1 Corinthians for a new study Bible soon to be released by Holman.

He has served in many capacities within the denomination including: associational committeeman, Administrative Committee and Executive Board of the Baptist General Convention of Texas, Board of Trustees of Baylor University, Board of Trustees of the SBC Annuity Board, Board of Trustees of Southwestern Baptist Theological Seminary, president of SBC Pastors' Conference and president of the SBC, 1982-84.

Paul D. Duke

Paul D. Duke is pastor of the Kirkwood Baptist Church, St. Louis, Missouri.

Born in Montgomery, Alabama, in 1953. Son of Dr. G. Nelson Duke and Wilma Awbry Duke. Raised in Montgomery, Alabama, and Jefferson City, Missouri. Graduated from Samford University, B.A., 1975; Southern Baptist Theological Seminary, M.Div., 1978; Ph.D., 1982. Served as pastor of Burks Branch Baptist Church, Shelbyville, Kentucky, 1977-1980; Highland Baptist Church, Louisville, Kentucky, 1982-1986; Kirkwood Baptist Church, St. Louis, Missouri, 1986—. Adjunct Professor of Preaching, Southern Baptist Theological Seminary, 1985-1986. Author of *Irony in the Fourth Gospel* (John Knox, 1985). Married to Cathy Chandler Duke, with two children, Stephanie and Christopher.

Peter James Flamming

The Baptist Hour preacher during 1986-87, Dr. Peter James Flamming is senior pastor of the historic First Baptist Church in Richmond, Virginia. He is in frequent demand as a preacher on seminary and university campuses. These ministries have included the Northcutt Lectures on Preaching at Southwestern Baptist Theological Seminary and the Hester Lectures on Preaching at Golden Gate Baptist Theological Seminary. In addition, he has served as the speaker for preaching weeks at Midwestern Baptist Theological Seminary, Stetson University, and Hardin-Simmons University. He also speaks frequently at conventions and Bible conferences.

A native of Colorado, he grew up in Arizona and California before attending Hardin-Simmons University in Abilene, Texas. His M.Div. and Th.D. are from Southwestern Baptist Theological Seminary in Fort Worth, Texas. Early pastorates were in Eastland and Dallas, Texas. He served the First Baptist Church of Abilene, Texas, for seventeen years before coming to the First Baptist Church in Richmond, Virginia, in 1983.

In addition to his interest in preaching, Dr. Flamming has a keen interest in pastoral leadership. He has led seminars in pastoral leadership at Southwestern Baptist Theological Seminary in Fort Worth and at New Orleans Baptist Theological Seminary at New Orleans. His writing has included numerous articles and periodicals. He has written two books, *The New You* and *God and Creation*.

Dr. Flamming is married to the former Shirley Northcutt. They have three sons, J. D., Peter Dave, and James Douglas.

Alfonso Flores, Jr.

Alfonso Flores, Jr., pastor of the First Mexican Baptist Church of Dallas, Texas, was born in San Marcos, Texas. He was the only child of Alfonso Flores and his wife, Guadalupe. He attended school there and after graduating from High School, attended the University of Corpus Christ, Texas.

By the time he attended the University of Corpus Christi, brother Flores had already responded to the call to the ministry. Being saved at the age of fourteen, soon thereafter in a youth camp he heard the call of the Lord and responded to it.

He finished at the University of Corpus Christi, obtaining a B.A. degree. He then enrolled at Southwestern Baptist Theological Seminary in Fort Worth, Texas. There he obtained the M.R.E. degree.

Brother Flores has pastored several prominent churches in Texas. Just out of seminary he accepted the pastorate of the First Mexican Baptist Church in Corpus Christi, Texas. At that time, it was the largest Spanish-speaking Baptist church in the state and one of the largest in the nation. There he succeeded I. E. Gonzales, whom Flores considers one of the giants among the Mexican Baptist Convention of Texas. Flores served for six months as Gonzales's associate before assuming the pastorate in full and learned much from the great pastor.

From there, brother Flores went to pastor the First Hispanic Baptist Church of Manhattan, New York. The other churches he has pastored include Iglesia Bautista Antioquia in San Antonio and Trinity Baptist Church in Houston, Texas.

Brother Flores often serves as an evangelist and has traveled throughout the world proclaiming the gospel of Christ. He has preached throughout the states of Texas, California, Arizona, Illinois, New York, and New Mexico. He has also preached in Mexico, Central America, Argentina, Peru, and Nigeria.

As a writer, brother Flores has contributed to several evangelical periodicals. Brother Flores is married, and he and his wife, Susan, have four children.

Charles G. Fuller

Charles G. Fuller has been pastor of the First Baptist Church of Roanoke, Virginia, since October, 1961. This is only his second full-time pastorate, the first one having been at Pine Street Baptist in Richmond, Virginia, from 1957 to 1961.

Educational background includes public schools in Florida; graduation from Fork Union Military Academy, Fork Union, Virginia (1950); University of Richmond (B.A., 1954); Southwestern Baptist Theological Seminary, Fort Worth, TX (B.D., 1957); D.D. degrees from University of Richmond, Virginia (1970), and Campbell University, Buies Creek, North Carolina (1984).

Since June 1985 Dr. Fuller has served as chairman of the Southern Baptist Convention's Peace Committee. Dr. Fuller has also served as president of the Virginia Baptist State Convention; president, VA Baptist Pastor's Conference; chairman, SBC Radio-TV Commission; chairman, SBC Committee on Order of Business; chairman, SBC Committee on Boards; *Baptist Hour* preacher several times; host of Radio-TV Commission's *Listen* TV series. He is host for the "God's Half-Hour" radio program and writer, preacher, producer for "God's Minute" radio and TV segments (60-seconds of evangelistic, biblical truths capsulated and aired daily). He is also one of the Distinguished Alumni of Fork Union Military Academy (1975).

Charles Fuller was the Southern Baptist Convention preacher in 1985. He has been a speaker for the Southern Baptist Pastors' Conference on several occasions; makes regular appearances at both Ridgecrest and Glorietta Baptist conference centers; has preached throughout the United States at state conventions and evangelism conferences; has been the evangelist/preacher on several overseas crusades.

Dr. Fuller was born in 1931 in Andalusia, Alabama, but grew up in West Palm Beach, Florida. He is married to Pat Huff Fuller of West Palm Beach. They have three grown sons and one grandson (grandson Ryan's father, Mark, is a part of the Roanoke County Sheriff's Department; middle son, David, enrolled at Southwestern Baptist Seminary; youngest son, Michael, student, Medical College of Virginia). Charles Fuller played seven years high school and college football, making Virginia All-State Football Team in 1949. He is a racquetball enthusiast and is an avid armchair sports fan.

Jack Graham

Dr. Jack Graham was born on June 30, 1948, in Conway, Arkansas. He was saved and baptized at the First Baptist Church in Conway in 1958 and was called to preach at the Sagamore Hill Baptist Church in Fort Worth, Texas, where he was ordained to the Gospel ministry in 1970. He is married to Deborah Sue Graham of Mineral Wells, Texas, and they have three children: Jason, Kelly, and Joshua.

Graham graduated with honors from Hardin-Simmons University, where he received his B.S. in 1972, and Southwestern Baptist Theological Seminary, where he earned both his M.Div. (1976) and D.Min. (1980). Upon graduation from Southwestern, he was awarded the H. C. Brown Memorial Award for Outstanding Achievement in the Study and Practice of Preaching. He earned his doctorate with a major focus on the church and proclamation. He has served as evangelism chairman and moderator and on the Administrative Committee for the Palm-Lake Baptist Association. On the state level, he has served on the Board of Trustees for Oklahoma Baptist University and presently serves on the Board of Trustees for Palm Beach Atlantic College, the Florida State Board of Missions, and the Administrative Committee for the Florida Board of Missions. Areas of service in the Southern Baptist Convention have included serving on the Committee on Committees, Chairman of the Tellers Committee, and presently as a director of the Home Mission Board.

He has pastored in churches in Texas and Oklahoma and is presently pastor of the First Baptist Church of West Palm Beach, Florida. First Baptist of West Palm Beach has witnessed and experienced dynamic growth since Dr. Graham assumed the pastorate in 1981. Membership has increased to over 8,000, making the congregation one of the nation's largest. The church is noted for its aggressive evangelistic outreach and a balanced ministry of biblical exposition and teaching. Pastor Graham preaches weekly on the NBC affiliate of one of the largest media markets in America and on national television with the Liberty Broadcasting Network. First Baptist has recently launched an $8 million building program to accommodate the growth that has become a weekly experience. "Catch the Spirit" has truly become the watchword of this exciting fellowship and is a reality in every area of the church's ministry.

Joel C. Gregory

Dr. Joel C. Gregory is pastor of the Travis Avenue Baptist Church, Fort Worth, Texas. He is a "hometown boy," born in Fort Worth on April 9, 1948.

He came to Travis Avenue from his tenure as assistant professor of preaching at Southwestern Baptist Theological Seminary, Fort Worth. He taught there from 1982 to 1985. Prior to that he was pastor of Gambrell Street Baptist Church, also in Fort Worth (1977-1982).

He was married to the former Linda Mulvihill on January 22, 1968. They have two children, Grant and Garrett.

Dr. Gregory is a graduate of Baylor University (B.A., 1970, Summa cum Laude, with majors in religion and Greek); Southwestern Baptist Theological Seminary (M.Div., 1973); and Baylor University (Ph.D., 1983).

He writes extensively for magazines and journals and recently authored the study book for Southern Baptists' January Bible Study emphasis, *James: Faith Works!* With R. Earl Allen he is the co-compiler of *Southern Baptist Preaching Today* (Broadman).

Dr. Gregory is in constant demand for revivals, Bible conferences, special studies, and preaching tours.

Brian L. Harbour

Brian Harbour, born in Texas, has pastored in five states: Texas, Georgia, Mississippi, Florida, and Arkansas. Since November, 1985, he has served as pastor of the Immanuel Baptist Church in Little Rock, Arkansas.

He received his B.A. (1966) and his Ph.D. (1973) from Baylor University.

After four years of courtship on the Baylor campus, Brian married Jan Sportsman from Kansas City. They have four children ranging in age from ten to seventeen.

His special interest in writing has led to several books published by Broadman Press: *Famous Couples of the Bible* (1979), *Famous Singles of the Bible* (1980), *Famous Parents of the Bible* (1983), *From Cover to Cover* (1982), and *A New Look at the Book* (1985). He has also contributed to *Award Winning Sermons, Vol. 1* (1977), *Sermons and Services for Special Days* (1980), *Illustrating the Gospel of Matthew* (1982), *Illustrating the Book of Romans* (1985), *Single Adult: Resource and Recipient for Revival* (1985), and *Preach the Word in Love and Power* (1986). Convention Press also published a commentary he wrote on 2 Corinthians and Philemon. He is a regular contributor to *Proclaim* and *Biblical Illustrator*, both published by the Southern Baptist Sunday School Board.

Dr. Harbour has provided help for Sunday School teachers for several years with his video Sunday School lesson previews produced by Video Dynamics. In addition, he publishes a monthly newsletter for pastors entitled *Brian's Lines* which includes sermons, outlines, illustrations, and stories to be used by the busy pastor in preparation for his preaching task each week.

O. S. Hawkins

Dr. O. S. Hawkins is pastor of the First Baptist Church, Fort Lauderdale, FL, where he has served since 1978. His church is known internationally for its evangelism and ministry to human needs. The church baptizes between 500 and 1,000 persons each year and ministers to people from all walks of life. Each year at Thanksgiving the church has a feast for 3,000 or more.

Dr. Hawkins is a native of Fort Worth, Texas. He married the former Susan Kay Cavness of Austin on July 24, 1970. They have two daughters, Wendy and Holly. The Hawkins family enjoys travel and outdoor recreation together, including golf and fishing.

Hawkins graduated from Polytechnic High School, Texas Christian University (B.B.A.), and Southwestern Baptist Theological Seminary (M.Div.), all in Fort Worth. He was honored with the S.T.D. from Southwest Baptist University at Bolivar, Missouri, and with the D.D. from Dallas Baptist University, Dallas, Texas.

Before coming to Fort Lauderdale, Hawkins was pastor of First Baptist Church, Ada, Oklahoma (1974-1978), First Baptist Church, Hobart, OK (1972-1974), and assistant pastor at Sagamore Hill Baptist Church, Fort Worth (1969-1972).

He is on television across the nation and has published five books with Broadman—*Tracing the Rainbow Through the Rain, When Revival Comes* (with Jack R. Taylor), *After Revival Comes, Clues to a Successful Life,* and *Where Angels Fear to Tread.* Hawkins is seen on the television program, *Lifeline,* in 450 outlets of the Trinity Broadcasting Network. He exchanges pulpits annually with Dr. R. T.

Kendall of Westminster Chapel in London. He has served on the Home Mission Board of the SBC and on the SBC Committee on Boards.

Jim Henry

Dr. Jim Henry is pastor of the First Baptist Church, Orlando, FL. He was born in Nashville, Tennessee, in 1937.

He received his B.A. from Georgetown College (KY) in 1957; and his M.Div. from New Orleans Baptist Theological Seminary in 1963.

He has pastored, in addition to First Baptist Church of Orlando, Two Rivers Baptist Church, Nashville, TN (1965-1977), Hollywood Baptist Church, Sledge, MS (1963-1965), and Mt. Pisgah Baptist Church, Melvin, Alabama (1960-1963).

He has served as president of the SBC Pastors' Conference, 1981, and the Florida Baptist Pastors' Conference, 1979. He was chairman of the SBC Committee on Committees, 1983-1984.

He has been a trustee of Belmont College, of Palm Beach Atlantic College, of the Baptist Sunday School Board, of the Tennessee Baptist Convention, and the Foreign Mission Board. He is a member of the SBC Peace Committee (1985-1987).

He has honorary degrees from Georgetown College (D.D.) and Southwest Baptist University (S.T.D.). He is the author of two Broadman books, *Heartwarmers* and *The Pastor's Wedding Manual*.

William E. Hull

William E. Hull was born on May 28, 1930, in Birmingham, Alabama, where he attended public schools, 1936-1948. He was graduated from Samford University in 1951 with a B.A. in religion and from The Southern Baptist Theological Seminary in 1954 with a M.Div. and in 1960 with a Ph.D. in New Testament. He has done post-doctoral study at the University of Goettingen in Germany and at Harvard University.

After three student pastorates in Alabama and Kentucky, he joined the faculty of The Southern Baptist Theological Seminary in 1958, where he served as professor of New Testament Interpretation until 1975. During this time he also served in a number of administrative positions, including director of Graduate Studies, dean of the School of Theology, and provost of the seminary.

In 1975 he became pastor of the First Baptist Church, Shreveport, Louisiana. In addition to pastoral duties, he has been deeply involved in civic affairs, currently serving on the Futureshape Shreveport Commission, charged with planning goals for the city to the end of this century. He is also active in denominational life, having served for many years as a trustee of Louisiana College, as a member of the SBC Peace Committee, and as chairman of various study commissions in the Study and Research Division of the Baptist World Alliance.

Hull is a frequent contributor to religious periodicals and theological journals. He is the author of several books, including *The Broadman Bible Commentary* on John, *Beyond the Barriers, Love in Four Dimensions,* and *The Christian Experience of Salvation,* all Broadman.

He is married to the former Wylodine Hester of Wedo-
wee, Alabama, and they have two children, David and
Susan. *As this book was prepared for the press Dr. Hull
accepted the position of provost at Samford University.

Warren C. Hultgren

Warren Curtis Hultgren was born in Minneapolis,
Minnesota. He married Wanda Lee Wadsworth of Lubbock,
Texas, and they have three children. His education includes
graduation from Northwestern Bible School, Minneapolis,
Minnesota, Hardin-Simmons University, and Southwestern Baptist Theological Seminary. He holds six honorary
doctor's degrees. His pastoral experience includes a student
pastorate during college days at Swenson, Texas. After
seminary, he went to the Downtown Baptist Church in Corpus Christi, Texas; from there to the Trinity Baptist
Church, Lake Charles, Louisiana. Since 1957, he has pastored the First Baptist Church of Tulsa.

His denominational service includes board and committee assignments with the Baptist World Alliance. He
was on three Program Committees for BWA Congresses.
He is a past vice-president of the Southern Baptist Convention and vice-president of the Southern Baptist Convention
Pastors' Conference. For two years he was chairman of the
"Missions Challenge Committee," which became Bold Mission Thrust. He has been past president of the Baptist General Convention of Oklahoma, acting dean, University of
Corpus Christi Night School, and advisor for the *Broadman Bible Commentary* and the *Baptist Hymnal.* He was
speaker on the *Baptist Hour,* 1971-72. He is heard regularly
on KTUL-TV, the ABC affiliate in Tulsa.

His community service includes the Board of Trustees,

Hillcrest Medical Center, and the Advisory Council of St. Francis Hospital, both of Tulsa. He is chairman of the Board, Dillon International, which includes adoption programs, drug rehabilitation, residential treatment programs, and an acute adolescent psychiatric hospital. He is a board member of the National Conference of Christians and Jews, chaplain of the Navy League, Tulsa Division, and member of the Air Force Association. He is past president of the Downtown Rotary Club of Tulsa.

Professionally, he is a member of the American Association of Marriage and Family Therapists, fellow of the Royal Geographical Society of Great Britain, and has been voted as Distinguished Alumni of both Hardin-Simmons University and Southwestern Seminary.

Richard Jackson

Dr. Richard Jackson, pastor of North Phoenix Baptist Church, Phoenix, AZ, is a native of Grapevine, TX (b.-August 3, 1938). He is the son of a Baptist preacher, Carroll Jackson. Jackson met his wife Wanda (Alexander) at Grapevine High School. They have three children, Don, Doug, and Tena, and one grandchild, Jay Don.

He attended Howard Payne College (now University) on a football scholarship and graduated with his B.A. in 1960. He received his M.Div. from Southwestern Baptist Theological Seminary. He has been honored with the Inaugural Award from Grapevine High School and the Distinguished Alumni award from both Howard Payne University and Southwestern Baptist Theological Seminary. He has been honored with the D.D. degree from Grand Canyon College and Howard Payne University.

He has served as pastor of local churches for over twenty-nine years and has now baptized over 15,000 persons. He has been president of the Arizona Southern Baptist Convention and has served his denomination in many capacities.

His pastorates have been: Concord Baptist Church, Bangs; Calvary, May; Bluffdale, Bluffdale; Henderson Street, Cleburne; First, Sulphur Springs; all in Texas. Since 1967 he has pastored the North Phoenix Baptist Church. Membership has grown under his leadership from less than 1,000 to over 17,000. Dr. Jackson preaches regularly on the "Acts" Network and on radio. He has published many articles and sermons and a Broadman book, *Freedom Is Never Free.*

Peter Rhea Jones

Peter Rhea Jones was born in Dyersburg, Tennessee, on April 17, 1937, the second of four sons of Judge and Mrs. Robert Jones. The family was active in church with both father and mother teaching Sunday School. He made an early profession of faith after recovery from a year of very serious illness. Peter was extensively involved in Boy Scouting and was selected "Most Outstanding Scout in West Tennessee." He was called to the ministry through the wooing of the hymn "Wherever He Leads I'll Go."

Jones attended Union University where he served as president of Student Government and pastored half-time churches in West Tennessee. He married his classmate Ellen Miles in 1959 and went on for an M.A. at the University of Mississippi, while continuing a pastorate in Saulsbury, Tennessee.

Jones attended Southern Seminary and received the M.Div. (1964) and Ph.D. (1968) and served as president of Student Government and student pastor of the Cash Creek Baptist Church near Henderson, Kentucky. He then did a Th.M at Princeton with Paul Scherer (1964) and was interim pastor of Manhattan Baptist Church in New York City. He pastored the Woodland Baptist Church in Middletown, Kentucky, 1965-1968.

Peter Rhea taught at Southern in the New Testament Department from 1968-1979 and served many interim pastorates. He often spoke at Ridgecrest and in BSU meetings and did Bible studies in local churches. He wrote numerous articles for *The Review and Expositor* and for denominational publications.

Since 1979 Jones has been pastor of the First Baptist Church of Decatur, Georgia. He published *The Teaching of the Parables* in 1982 (Broadman). He has been active in the Georgia Baptist Convention and on the Pastoral Leadership Commission of the Baptist World Alliance.

Ellen and Peter Rhea have three children: Peter Rhea, Jr., Heather, and Ramsey.

Don M. Kim

Dr. Don M. Kim is pastor of the Berendo Street Baptist Church, Los Angeles, CA, which he founded in 1957. He has served as second vice-president of the SBC (1981-1982) and as second vice-president of the Southern Baptist General Convention of California (1964-1965).

He is known as a founder of churches, among them being the Korean Baptist Church, Buenos Aires, Argentina (1980); the Korean Baptist Church, Caracas, Venezuela

(1981); the Korean Baptist Mission, Asuncion, Paraguay (1981); and the Korean Baptist Church, Sao Paulo, Brazil (1982).

Berendo Street Baptist Church has built a church building for Indian Baptist Church (Make Tribe), Asuncion, Paraguay. Dr. Kim has assisted in starting more than fifteen Korean Baptist missions and churches in the U.S. He is presently assisting twenty Baptist churches in Korea.

Born in Korea in 1922, he married Esther An Kim in 1949. Dr. Kim received the Bachelor of Engineering from Seoul National University, College of Engineering (1948); the M.Div. from Southwestern Baptist Seminary; and he did his residence work toward a Th.D. at Southwestern. California Baptist College conferred the D.D. on him in 1979.

He was the first Southern Baptist home missionary to the Koreans in the U.S.A. (1957). He has been a member of the Board of Christian Higher Education, Southern Baptist General Convention in California (1978-1980) and a member of the Executive Committee of the Southern Baptist General Convention of California (1978-1980). He has preached throughout the world—Korea, Japan, Greece, Italy, Spain, France, West Germany, West Berlin, Canada, Australia, the People's Republic of China, and the USSR.

Phil Lineberger

Dr. Phil Lineberger is the pastor of Richardson Heights Baptist Church, Richardson, Texas. He and his wife, Brenda, grew up in Texarkana, Texas. They have three teenage daughters, Becky, Amy, and Kathy. He has pastored the Calvary Baptist Church in Huntsville,

Arkansas; Calvary Baptist, Little Rock, Arkansas; and Metropolitan Baptist, Wichita, Kansas. He is a graduate of the University of Arkansas and Southwestern Baptist Theological Seminary (M.Div and D.Min). Academic honors include the H. C. Brown Preaching Award (Outstanding Senior Preacher, SWBTS) and "Who's Who in American Colleges and Universities," 1974-1978.

Dr. Lineberger was one of twenty-three North American pastors who represented the Baptist World Alliance in the Soviet Union in 1982. He preached at the Arkansas Baptist Evangelism conference in 1978 and the Texas Baptist Evangelism Conference in 1985. Dr. Lineberger has preached in Rio de Janeiro, Brazil, and Sydney and Newcastle, Australia, in connection with Texas Baptist Partnership Missions. He has lectured at William Jewell College, Southwestern Baptist Theological Seminary, and Midwestern Baptist Theological Seminary. He delivered the 1985 commencement address at Golden Gate Baptist Theological Seminary.

Dr. Lineberger served as president of the Arkansas Baptist Pastor's Conference in 1980 and the Kansas-Nebraska Pastor's Conference in 1982. He is currently serving on the Dallas Baptist Association Executive Board, the Baptist General Convention of Texas Executive Board, and the Baptist World Alliance Education and Evangelism Committee. He is a Trustee of William Jewell College and Dallas Baptist University. He has written Bible lessons for the *Baptist Standard*, Youth Commentary for the Sunday School Board, and recently completed a series of Youth Commentaries on the Baptist Telecommunication Network.

Kenneth L. Mahanes

Dr. Kenneth L. Mahanes is pastor of the Far Hills Baptist Church, Dayton, OH, where he has served since 1979. He is currently president of the Convention of Baptists in Ohio.

He and his wife, Evelyn, have two children, Mark Kenneth and Michael David.

He was educated at Georgetown College, KY (B.A.), Southern Baptist Theological Seminary (M.R.E., Ed.D.), and has done further study at Asbury Theological Seminary and Miami University, Oxford, OH.

He has served his denomination and community in numerous capacities, including the Executive Board, Convention of Baptists in Ohio; Executive Committee, Southern Baptist Convention; Refugee Resettlement Committee for Dayton Community; Board of Directors of Youth for Christ, Dayton, Ohio; Canada Study Committee, SBC; vice-chairman, Business and Finance Committee, Executive Committee, SBC; Resolutions Committee, SBC; Tellers Committee, SBC; Long-Range Planning Committee, Convention of Baptists in Ohio.

He has spoken to a number of pastors' conferences and evangelistic meetings across the Convention.

In college he was Mr. Georgetonian, B.S.U. president, and listed in "Who's Who in American Colleges and Universities," among other honors.

His other pastorates have been Friendship Baptist Church, Irvine, KY; First Baptist Church of Dent, Cinncinnati, OH. His present pastorate, Far Hills, is the largest Southern Baptist Church in Ohio.

Wayne McDill

Wayne McDill has served as pastor of Metropolitan Baptist Church in Portland, Oregon, since August of 1979. The family moved to Portland in response to a missionary call to the Northwest, the most unchurched area of the country. Dr. McDill also serves as an adjunct professor in Preaching and Christian Ethics at the Portland center of Golden Gate Baptist Theological Seminary of Mill Valley, California.

Born and reared in Beaumont, Texas, he met his wife, Sharon, while they were students at East Texas Baptist College in Marshall. They have four children. Michael Wayne (24) is a student at the Portland center of Golden Gate Seminary. Mark Stephen (23) is a student at Portland State University and also plans to continue with seminary. The two younger children are Matthew David (13) and Anna Elizabeth (11).

McDill served as a staff associate in evangelism with the Baptist General Convention of Texas from 1972 through 1979. For four years he was crusade coordinator, after that serving in a newly-designed position for helping churches in church growth and leadership strategy. He served earlier in pastorates and other staff positions in Texas, Louisiana, and Arkansas.

After graduating from East Texas Baptist college in 1963, he received M.Div. and Th.D. degrees from Southwestern Baptist Theological Seminary in Fort Worth. He is author of three books, including *Evangelism in a Tangled World* and *Making Friends for Christ,* published by Broadman Press.

Alton H. McEachern

Alton Howard McEachern was born in Thomaston, Georgia, September 3, 1932, and grew up in Atlanta. He married Betty Coleman of Rabun Gap, Georgia, in 1952, and they are the parents of five children: Mrs. Suzanne Case, Michael, Kathryn, Mrs. Bonnie Haun, and Andrew. Mrs. McEachern is a graduate of Tift College and attended the Southern Baptist Theological Seminary. The couple have two grandsons.

His educational background includes Truett McConnell College (A.A.), Mercer University (A.B. and D.D.), and The Southern Baptist Theological Seminary (M.Div., Th.M., D.Min.), with graduate work at the University of Glasgow and Oxford University.

Pastor for thirty-five years, he has served churches in Georgia, Indiana, Kentucky, and West Virginia. He has been pastor of the First Baptist Church of Greensboro, North Carolina, since 1974.

An author, McEachern has written Sunday School curriculum and journal articles. He has published eleven books with Broadman and Convention Press, including the January Bible Study Guide for 1989 on the Gospel of John. His books on the Lord's Supper, *Here at Thy Table, Lord* and *The Lord's Presence,* have been popular.

He has been adjunct professor in preaching at Southern, Southeastern, and Midwestern Baptist Seminaries, as well as in the Nigerian Baptist Seminary. He has lectured at Liberia and Golden Gate Seminaries.

Denominational service has included serving as trustee and chairman of the Sunday School Board, National Alumni president for Southern Seminary, Trustee at Wake Forest University, and on a commission of the Baptist

World Alliance. He has preached at mission meetings in Nigeria and Chile.

McEachern is a Rotarian, and his hobbies include rose gardening and travel.

The First Baptist Church of Greensboro, largest Southern Baptist church in North Carolina, has led in mission giving since 1910.

Calvin Miller

Dr. Calvin Miller was born in Enid, OK. He graduated from Enid High School and attended Oklahoma Baptist University, graduating with a B.S. in 1958. He attended Midwestern Baptist Theological Seminary in Kansas City, graduating with an M.Div. in 1961 and a D.Min. in 1975.

In 1959 he married Barbara Joyce Harmon. They are the parents of Melanie Dawn and Timothy Grant.

His first full-time pastorate was Plattsmouth Baptist Church, Plattsmouth, NE, 1961-1966. He came to Westside Baptist Church, Omaha, NE, in January, 1966, where he still serves as pastor.

He is widely known for his writing and speaking. He has had twenty-two books published, including *The Singer, The Song, That Elusive Thing Called Joy, The Table of Inwardness, When the Aardvark Parked on the Ark, Fred 'n' Erma,* and *The Brotherstone.* He has written for many magazines and journals, including *Campus Life, Christianity Today, The Student, Young Life, His,* and *Leadership.* Several of his books have been translated into other languages besides English.

He has been used as an inspirational speaker in various assemblies and religious convocations, both among Southern Baptists and other Christian bodies.

Dr. Miller believes in the primacy of evangelism for the church in every age. In his own ministry he has sought to be both a contemporary apologist, helping the church provide answers for a secular culture, and an equipper of the contemporary church for the task of missions and evangelism. He sums up his primary rule for life in four words: "Time is a gift."

Jess C. Moody

Dr. Jess C. Moody has been senior minister of the First Baptist Church of Van Nuys, CA, since October of 1976. The church now has close to 12,000 members.

He came to Van Nuys from the First Baptist Church, West Palm Beach, FL, where he served several years. Before that he was pastor of the First Baptist Church of Owensboro, Kentucky. From 1950 to 1955 he was an evangelist.

Moody was born in Texas on August 19, 1925. He is married to the former Doris Cummins. They have two children, Patrick and Martha.

Dr. Moody is a graduate of Baylor University (B.A.) and The Southern Baptist Theological Seminary, Louisville, (M.Div.). Campbellsville College (KY) bestowed on him the D.D. He also participated in a seminar at Oxford University (with C. S. Lewis) in 1947.

He is the founder and first president of Palm Beach Atlantic College, West Palm Beach, FL (correlated with his pastorate at First Baptist Church there).

His denominational service has included: Kentucky Baptist Education Committee; Baptist Education Study Task (B.E.S.T.) Committee; Home Mission Board; president, SBC Pastors' Conference, 1955; and the Board of Trustees, The Southern Baptist Theological Seminary (current).

Dr. Moody has a vast background in television production and hosting. He has hosted "Louisville Tonight" on WJAS-TV, Louisville; "Your Town" on WFIE, Evansville, IN; "Jess Moody Presents" on a network of twenty-five stations coast to coast; "Lifestyle," a two-hour daily talk show on TV; and "Livin'" (daily TV show in Los Angeles, San Jose, and San Diego, with more stations planned). He was the narrator for "Take Me Home Again," the life story of Burt Reynolds, NBC, 1974.

Moody received the "International Clergyman of the Year in Media" award from Religion in Media, Ambassador Hotel, Hollywood (1986); and the "Golden Circle Award'" from the Southern California Motion Picture Council, Sportsman's Lodge, Sherman Oaks, CA (1985).

W. Winfred Moore

Dr. W. Winfred Moore, a native Tennessean, has been pastor of the First Baptist Church in Amarillo, TX, since 1959. He received his education at Lambuth College and Union University in Jackson, TN. Wayland Baptist University and Baylor University honored him with doctor of divinity and doctor of laws degrees, respectively.

Prior to assuming his present pastorate, he served the Central Park Baptist Church, Birmingham, AL; First Baptist Church, Borger, TX; and Harrisburg Baptist Church, Tupelo, MS.

Dr. Moore and his wife, Elizabeth, have three

children—Elizabeth Anne (Preston), William Winfred II ("Fred"), and Maria Elena (Patterson).

First Baptist, Amarillo, with a membership of over 10,000, and an annual budget of over $4 million, has for many years been a leader in mission giving and was among the first to have lay people participating in evangelistic crusades in the United States and in foreign countries. In 1961 the church sponsored the pastor and a group of laymen to Orange County, CA, where, in cooperation with a local church and the associational director of missions, they established a new Baptist church in Orange, CA. From that time until the present, First Baptist, Amarillo, has been participating in evangelistic crusades and establishment of new churches at home and around the world.

During Dr. Moore's ministry, there have been almost 16,000 additions to the church. Mission giving has amounted to almost $18 million. The church voted goals for the decade of the 80s to increase Cooperative Program giving by 10 percent per year, and to increase each of the Week of Prayer offerings by 10 percent per year. Goals have already been reached and exceeded.

Dr. Moore is past president of the Baptist General Convention of Texas and has served as first vice-president of the Southern Baptist Convention. He has been nominated for president of the Convention for two years, 1985 and 1986. He has served on the Executive Committee of the Baptist General Convention of Texas, on the Program Coordinating Committee, and on the Boards of Blue Mountain College in Mississippi, Wayland Baptist University, Howard Payne University, and the High Plains Baptist Hospital, all in Texas.

He is currently on the Board of Trustees, Baylor University. He has also served as campaign chairman and president of the United Way of Amarillo and as president of the Amarillo Area Foundation. He is a Rotarian and was elected as Amarillo's "Man of the Year" in 1978. He has also served as campaign chairman of the Ronald McDonald

House Campaign and as chairman of the Hospice Campaign at St. Anthony's Hospital.

Dr. Moore is the author of *Faith for the Second Mile* (Broadman). He speaks widely around the nation and overseas, often addressing Southern Baptist Convention meetings, evangelistic conferences, and other civic and church meetings.

Charles D. Page

I was born on August 28, 1939, in Roanoke, Virginia to Reverend and Mrs. W. M. Page. My father was a pastor for forty-five years before his death in 1961. I was married to Sandra Groff Page in July of 1960, and we have two boys, David, who was born in 1963, and Robbie, who was born in 1971.

I was educated at Wake Forest University with a B.A. degree and Southeastern Seminary with an M.Div. and a D.Min. (1974). Between college and seminary, I served as a physical education teacher and coached football and basketball for seven years. I had a number of student pastorates while in the seminary. My first full-time pastorate out of seminary was the Lawndale Baptist Church, Greensboro, North Carolina. From there I moved to the First Baptist Church, North Augusta, South Carolina, and from there to the First Baptist Church of Charlotte, North Carolina. Presently I serve as pastor of the First Baptist Church of Nashville, Tennessee.

Franklin D. Pollard

Dr. Frank Pollard became pastor for the second time of First Baptist Church of Jackson, Mississippi, on March 1, 1986. He came to First Baptist Church from the Golden Gate Baptist Theological Seminary where he was president from 1983-1986.

Dr. Pollard has been host and Bible teacher for "At Home With the Bible," a television program sponsored by the Southern Baptist Convention Sunday School Board and the Convention's Radio and Television Commission. He has been the preacher for the worldwide *Baptist Hour* radio program from 1976-1986.

Dr. Pollard served as pastor of the First Baptist Church of San Antonio, Texas, from 1980-1983. He was pastor of First Baptist Church, Jackson, Mississippi, from 1974-1980. Prior to that, he was pastor of the Shiloh Terrace Baptist Church in Dallas, Texas.

He holds the B.B.A. degree from Texas A & M University and the B.D. degree from Southwestern Baptist Theological Seminary. He has the D.Min. from the New Orleans Baptist Theological Seminary and the L.H.D. from California Baptist College. He also received the D.D. from Mississippi College.

He is the author of three books: *How You Know When You're a Success,* recently reprinted as *The Bible in Your Life; After You've Said I'm Sorry,* and *Keeping Free,* all Broadman.

In 1979, he was elected by *Time* magazine as one of the "seven most outstanding Protestant preachers in America."

He was born in Olney, Texas, February 25, 1934. He and his wife, the former Jane Shepherd, have two children, Brent and Suzanne.

Paul W. Powell

Pastor of Green Acres Baptist Church, Tyler, Texas.

Born in Brookeland, Texas, in 1933. Graduated from Baylor University, B.A., 1956; received his B.D. from Southwestern Baptist Theological Seminary, 1960; Honorary D.D., East Texas Baptist University, 1978.

Pastor of Belfalls Baptist Church, Belfalls, Texas, 1955-56; First Baptist Church, Troy, Texas, 1956-61; First Baptist Church, Taylor, Texas, 1961-66; First Baptist Church, San Marcos, Texas, 1966-72; Green Acres Baptist Church, Tyler, Texas, 1972—.

President of Baptist General Convention of Texas, 1986-88; trustee of the Annuity Board of Southern Baptist Convention, 1984—, first vice-president of the Baptist General Convention of Texas, 1979-80; member of Board of Trustees, Baylor University, East Texas Baptist University, Mary-Hardin Baylor University, Texas Baptist Children's Home.

Author of *How to Make Your Church Hum* (Broadman Press 1977); *Beyond Conversion* (Broadman, 1977); *Why Me, Lord?* (Victor, 1982); *The Nuts and Bolts of Church Growth* (Broadman, 1982); *The Saint Peter Principle* (Broadman, 1982); *I Like Being a Christian* (Broadman, 1983); *Dynamic Discipleship* (Broadman, 1984); *The Complete Disciple* (Victor, 1984); *Jesus Is For Now* (Broadman Press, 1985); *When the Hurt Won't Go Away* (Victor, 1986); *Go-Givers in a Go-Getter World* (Broadman Press, 1986).

Nelson L. Price

Dr. Nelson Lynn Price is pastor of the 7,000-member Roswell Street Baptist Church in Marietta, Georgia, and current president of the Pastors' Conference of the Southern Baptist Convention. The broadcast ministry of the church, "Come Alive," reaches some two million viewers weekly through local airing on WXIA, Channel 11, in Atlanta, WFOM radio, and various satellite cable stations throughout the country.

Dr. Price is a graduate of Southeastern Louisiana University and New Orleans Baptist Theological Seminary where his specialization was homiletics. He has been awarded doctorates from Emmanuel School of Theology and Mercer University. He has served as trustee of NOBTS. for the past sixteen years.

In addition to academic honors, Dr. Price is a member of "National Who's Who in Religion." He received the Cobb County "Citizen of the Year Award" by *The Marietta Daily Journal,* the "Liberty Bell Award" by the Cobb County Bar Association, and the Cobb County "Public Service Award" by the Chamber of Commerce. He is on the National Board of Directors of the Fellowship of Christian Athletes and served two years as president of the Georgia Baptist Convention (1982-1984).

Dr. Price has been privileged to conduct the chapel services for most of the NFL teams. He preached the Inaugural message before the Congress of the United States for President Jimmy Carter in 1977.

In addition to being a distinguished preacher and motivational speaker, he is a renowned author. His books include *How to Find Out Who You Are, I've Got to Play on Their Court, Shadows We Run From, The Occult Is Lion*

Country, Supreme Happiness, Only the Beginning, The Destruction of Death, Farewell to Fear, Called to Splendor, and most recently, *Tenderness and 24 Other Ways to Make A Marriage Work.*

Dr. Price is married to the former Trudy Knight. They have two daughters and one grandchild.

Joe Samuel Ratliff

Joe Samuel Ratliff was born July 24, 1950, in Lumberton, North Carolina, to the proud parents, Mary Armwood and Lawrence Thompson. Because of their youthfulness, Joe was raised from infancy by his grandparents, Ellie and Rosa Bell Ratliff. In their home he was nurtured in the fear of God and appreciation for his culture and folklore.

This early exposure to Christian training led him to confess Christ as his Savior at ten years of age. He grew up in the church, becoming a leader and graduate from high school as salutatorian in 1968. This was the same year of the death of Martin Luther King, Jr. This became a pivotal year in his life in that he followed in the steps of his slain hero by enrolling at Morehouse College in Atlanta, Georgia.

While at Morehouse, Joe assumed the minister of music position of a local church and supported himself through college. During the summer of 1971, the Lord called, and Joe entered the ministry. The B.A. in history came in 1972. Then Joe entered the Interdenominational Theological Center in Atlanta, where the M.Div. and D.Min. were earned in 1975 and 1976, respectively.

While serving a local church, Cobb Memorial, for seven years (1971-78), Joe also taught at Morehouse College as an assistant professor of religion and philosophy and as acting dean of the chapel for four years.

Leaving Atlanta in 1978, he moved to Houston where he enrolled at Texas Southern University's Thurgood Marshall Law School. Legal pursuits were interrupted when the Brentwood Baptist Church extended the invitation for him to become their fourth pastor. Brentwood has experienced phenomenal growth in recent years. The church has grown from a membership of 400 in 1980 to a 5000+ present count. Of the 4500 additions, 692 have been baptisms of new converts. Four mission churches have been planted by this church in the last three years.

Joe is involved in many civic and political organizations, serving on boards ranging from the local Urban League to his leadership given to the Anti-Defamation League fostering dialogue between Blacks and Jews in Houston.

He serves as National Alumni president of the Interdenominational Theological Center of Atlanta and serves on the Executive Committee of the Board of Trustees of the same institution.

Denominationally, he serves the Union Baptist Association and the Baptist General Convention of Texas in many capacities. He has served as a member of the Southern Baptist Convention's Credentials Committee twice.

Joe is married to the former Doris Ernestine Gardner, a St. Louis, Missouri, native and a sales manager at AT & T.

Darrell Robinson

Dr. Darrell Robinson and his wife, Kathy, have four children. Their oldest son, Duane, is a banker in Bryan, Texas. Duane and his wife, Connie, have two children, Matthew and Blakely. Daughter, Lori, is married to Read Langford, banker in Waco, Texas. Lori is also a Baylor graduate. Sons, Robin and Loren, are both ministerial students attending Mobile Baptist College.

Dr. Robinson surrendered to preach at 17, began pastoring at 18. He held several pastorates in Texas and one in Liberal, Kansas. Each church experienced rapid growth.

He is a graduate of Baylor University and attended Southwestern Seminary. He received an honorary doctorate from Houston Baptist University and an earned doctorate from Luther Rice Seminary.

He has conducted meetings and conferences in numerous states and foreign countries, including Guyana, Korea, and Brazil. He was invited by the Brazilian Baptist Convention to teach the Total Church Life Conference in six major population centers, including Rio, Recife, Salvador, Belem, Brasilia, and Porta Alegra, to instruct pastors and church leaders in principles of church growth.

He has authored and published three books: *The Total Church Life, How to Be a Growing Christian,* and *People Sharing Jesus.* He is involved in many areas as a Christian and denominational leader, including being secretary to the Executive Committee of the SBC and serving on the Executive Committee of the Alabama Baptist Convention.

He is involved in, and speaker at, many social and civic organizations. He is a member of the Springhill Hospital Advisory Board and the Alabama Mental Health/ Mental Retardation Board. He is and has been strongly involved in mission programs in numerous states and foreign countries.

He wrote monthly articles for *Sunday School Leadership Magazine,* 1983-84, and numerous articles for other periodicals.

Adrian P. Rogers

Dr. Adrian P. Rogers has been pastor of the Bellevue Baptist Church, Memphis, Tennessee, since 1972. He has served two terms as president of the Southern Baptist Convention.

A native of West Palm Beach, FL, he is a graduate of Stetson University (B.A.) and New Orleans Baptist Theological Seminary (Th.M.). He has been awarded honorary doctorates from five educational institutions.

He has served his denomination in many capacities, including president of the Southern Baptist Convention's Pastors' Conference. At present he is a member of the SBC Peace Committee. He has been a trustee of Union University, Jackson, TN, and Luther Rice Seminary, Jacksonville, FL. In addition, he has been on the advisory council or board of reference for several other seminaries and institutions of higher learning.

Dr. Rogers is married to the former Joyce Gentry of West Palm Beach, FL. They have four grown children—Steve, Gayle, David, and Janice.

Under his leadership Bellevue has grown to over 17,000 members—and is still growing. Dr. Rogers's greatest joy centers in his relationship to Jesus Christ, his family, and the church he pastors.

He is the author of two books, *God's Way to Health,*

Wealth, and Wisdom (Broadman) and *The Secret of Super-natural Living.* His preaching ministry is spread widely through radio, television, and tapes.

Perry R. Sanders

Dr. Perry R. Sanders has pastored the First Baptist Church of Lafayette, LA, since 1959. A native of Allendale, SC, he began preaching at the age of 16. He is a graduate of Bob Jones College of Cleveland, TN (now Bob Jones University of Greenville, SC) with a B.A. and New Orleans Baptist Theological Seminary (Th.M.). He has received D.D. degrees from Louisiana College and United Theological Seminary.

Before coming to Lafayette twenty-eight years ago, he pastored the First Baptist Church of Jennings, LA. Before that he was the pastor of Florida Boulevard Baptist Church, Baton Rouge, LA; French Corner Baptist Church, Ponchatoula, LA; First Baptist Church of Springfield, LA; and First Baptist Church of Hillsboro, AL.

He has served his state Convention as president of the Louisiana Baptist Convention (two terms), president of the Louisiana Baptist Convention Executive Board (two terms), president of District Seven Baptist Convention, pastor advisor to Louisiana Baptist Student Union and Louisiana Baptist Music Conference, trustee of Louisiana College, chairman of Public Affairs Committee of the Louisiana Baptist Convention, and chairman of the Administrative Committee of the Executive Board, LBC.

He has served the Southern Baptist Convention in the following capacities: member of Foreign Mission Board (1966-1973) and chairman of the Middle America and Caribbean Committee; member of the SBC Committee on Committees (1966), chairman of the SBC Committee on Committees (1976), and member of the Home Mission Board of the SBC. Sanders preached the closing message at the Southern Baptist Convention in 1981 at Los Angeles.

He is a frequent speaker at conventions, conference centers, and evangelistic conferences. He is a Kiwanian and a division chairman of United Givers Fund. He is on the Board of Directors of Greater Lafayette Chamber of Commerce, a member of National Council of Americans United for Separation of Church and State, a member of the Fellowship of Christian Athletes, and on the Board of Directors of Acadiana Arts Council. His hobbies are golf, hunting, fishing, and snow skiing.

He married Gloria Hilda McMorris of Denham Springs, LA, in 1953. They had one son, Perry R. Sanders, Jr., born in 1954. Gloria passed away in 1983. Dr. Sanders married Kae Hollifield Chism in 1984. She has three children, Tiffanie, Brent, and Cliff.

William L. Self

Dr. William L. Self is a native of Delray Beach, Florida. He is a graduate of Stetson University, B.A., Southeastern Baptist Theological Seminary, B.D., and Emory University (Candler School of Theology), S.T.D. Dr. Self also holds honorary degrees from Stetson University, Mercer University, and Han Yang University in Seoul, Korea.

Since 1964 he has been pastor of the Wieuca Road Baptist Church in Atlanta, Georgia. He has served as president of the Georgia Baptist Convention, vice-president of the Southern Baptist Convention and president of the Foreign Mission Board of the Southern Baptist Convention.

In 1976 he was appointed special ambassador by President Gerald Ford to the inauguration of Dr. William Tolbert as president of Liberia. In 1977 he preached the annual sermon for the Southern Baptist Convention.

Dr. Self not only serves as pastor, but he also carries a full schedule speaking to the business and professional community. Together, he and his wife, Carolyn, have authored seven books. Dr. and Mrs. Self have two sons, William Lee, Jr., and Bryan.

Don Sharp

I was born on August 10, 1937, at Cook County Hospital in Chicago, Illinois. I am the youngest of five children. However, I am the only child born to the union of Pheobe Sharp and Lee Carr. Since my other brothers and sister were older than I, I grew up in many respects as an only child of a single parent. Through this experience I learned a great deal about myself.

My mother proved to be a great source of inspiration to me. For a considerable period of time, she was ostracized by many in the church where I grew up, but she never let that deter her from walking with her God. Her favorite passage of Scripture can be found in Psalm 51.

Growing up in the streets of Chicago was a multifaceted experience. Something was always taking place; very little was routine; we were poor but proud. Through my mother and my pastor, Rev. S. A. Grayson, I had much good moral character instilled within me. My Sunday School teacher, Henry Torrey, made the Bible come alive to me.

Through the St. Luke Baptist Church where I grew up

I begin to understand and see the church as an extended family. I had many surrogate mothers, grandmothers, and aunts, each making a significant contribution in molding me. This was indeed a positive experience for me. In 1958, I surrendered to preach. This came as no surprise to those in the congregation who knew me. Insofar as my extended family was concerned, it was merely an affirmation of what they had seen in me while growing up.

Soon after announcing my call, I was drafted into the United States Army. Upon completion of my military service, I enrolled in the college version of the Northern Baptist Theological Seminary which later became Judson College. While in college, I met and married Verdell McNairy. To this union two daughters were born. At the same time in 1964 the Lord gave me the vision of organizing the Faith Tabernacle Baptist Church. In the first five years, the church was not affiliated with any association.

The year of 1969 was a very memorable one. My first wife and my mother died about two months apart. This was the same year we joined the Chicago Metropolitan Baptist Association and also moved in and shared a building with the Cornell Avenue Baptist Church. After a period of five years we bought the building from them.

In 1972, I married again to a very lovely woman, Lurlie Heard; she is a constant source of inspiration to me. Also during this period of time my involvement in Southern Baptist life began to increase. In 1975 I was elected to the Board of Directors of the Illinois Baptist State Association. Upon completion of two three-year terms, I was elected vice-president of the State Association and in 1983 elected the first Black president of the State Association.

More recently, through involvement with the Foreign Mission Board, my travels have included revivals in Antigua, Finland, St. Thomas, and the historic Baptist World Alliance meeting in Nanking, China.

Cecil E. Sherman

Dr. Cecil E. Sherman is pastor of the Broadway Baptist Church, Fort Worth, Texas. He came to Broadway from a pastorate of over two decades at The First Baptist Church, Asheville, NC.

A native of Fort Worth, TX, Sherman graduated from Polytechnic High School there, Baylor University (B.A. in history and English), Southwestern Baptist Theological Seminary (B.D.), Princeton Theological Seminary (Th.M. in preaching), and Southwestern Baptist Theological Seminary (Th.D. in preaching). He was presented the Albert Venting Award as the outstanding theological student at Southwestern in the class of 1953.

He has served as a trustee of Meredith College, as a member of the Christian Life Commission, SBC; as chairman of the Christian Life Commission, SBC; and as member of the Church Growth Commission of the North Carolina Baptist Convention. In Asheville he was active in the Rotary Club, the Asheville YMCA Board, and the Human Relations Council.

In addition to his service in Asheville and Fort Worth, he worked with the Baptist General Convention of Texas, was pastor of the First Baptist Church of College Station, TX, and pastor of the First Baptist Church of Chamblee, GA.

He and his wife have a daughter, Genie.

He has written extensively for magazines, journals, and periodicals. He has done three books with Broadman, *Modern Myths, Preaching with Integrity,* and *A Kingdom of Surprises.* He gardens and jogs for hobbies and calls himself "a lousy golfer."

Theodore R. (Ted) Sisk, Jr.

Ted was born in Toccoa, Georgia, in 1928 to Theodore and Lena Smith Sisk. He received Christ as a junior-age boy and was baptized into the First Baptist Church of Toccoa.

Ted and Ginny Dalton were married in 1947 and have four sons: Lawrence Theodore, Jonathan Robert, Paul Bryan, and Mark Dalton; they also have two grandsons and one granddaughter.

Sisk's formal education included studies at Moody Bible Institute, Furman University, Piedmont College (B.A.), Emory University, the University of Georgia, and The Southern Baptist Theological Seminary (M.Div., D.Min.). He has honorary doctorates from Alderson-Broaddus College and Georgetown College.

Since 1970, Ted has been the pastor of Immanuel Baptist Church, Lexington, Kentucky. Before that he served the Highlawn Baptist Church, Huntington, West Virginia; the First Baptist Church, Hogansville, Georgia; and the Harmony Baptist Church, Baldwin, Georgia.

His denominational assignments have included: chairman of Trustees of the Baptist Sunday School Board, chairman of Trustees of Georgetown College, president of the West Virginia Baptist Convention, and president of the Kentucky Baptist Convention.

J. Alfred Smith

Dr. J. Alfred Smith, Sr., is pastor of the Allen Temple Baptist Church, Oakland, CA. Allen Temple has been the subject of a Broadman book, *Effective Urban Ministry* by G. Willis Bennett.

Dr. "Jim" was born in Kansas City, MO, on May 19, 1931. He was married on September 9, 1951. He and Mrs. Smith have five children and nine grandchildren.

He is a graduate of American Baptist Seminary of the West (master's) and Golden Gate Baptist Theological Seminary (doctorate). He has served in many capacities related to pastoral ministries and preaching, including assistant dean, American Baptist Seminary of the West and adjunct professor of worship and preaching, Golden Gate Baptist Theological Seminary.

Dr. Smith is currently president of the Progressive National Baptist Convention. He has previously served a term as vice-president of the same convention. He is a member of the School Board, Oakland Unified School District.

He has written and spoken extensively for revivals, conventions, evangelistic conferences, and preaching missions. He has contributed to theological journals of Golden Gate and Southern Baptist seminaries.

His books are *Preach On!* and *The Overflowing Heart* (Broadman), *Outstanding Black Sermons, For the Facing of the Hours,* and *Deacons Holding Up the Pastor's Arms.*

Charles F. Stanley

Charles Stanley's desire to make Christ known started early for him who, as a fourteen-year-old in Danville, Virginia, committed himself to the pastoral ministry. Subsequent years saw him pursue that calling, earning a B.A. from the University of Richmond, a B.D. from Southwestern Baptist Theological Seminary, and Th.M. and Th.D. degrees from Luther Rice Seminary, Jacksonville, FL.

He consecutively pastored First Baptist Church in Fruitland, NC; First Baptist Church in Fairborn, OH; First Baptist Church of Miami, FL; and First Baptist Church, Bartow, FL.

In 1971 Dr. Stanley accepted the pastorate of the now 9,000-member First Baptist Church of Atlanta from which his Scripturally based ministry has multiplied to a national outreach. Dr. Stanley has served two terms as the president of the Southern Baptist Convention.

His radio and television program, IN TOUCH, can be viewed or heard by a potential audience of an estimated 70 million households through six nationwide cable satellite systems and more than 100 UHF and VHF outlets. His IN TOUCH radio broadcast can be heard on 350 AM and FM stations.

A lifelong dedication to personal discipleship and the priority of prayer is reflected in his popular books, *Handle with Prayer, A Man's Touch, Confronting Casual Christianity, How to Listen to God,* and *How to Keep Your Kids on Your Team.*

Dr. Stanley's stirring patriotic sermon, "Stand Up, America," earned him the 1980 Freedoms Foundation of Valley Forge Award.

Dr. Stanley serves on the Board of Directors of the National Religious Broadcasters and on the Board of Trustees of Toccoa Falls Bible College in Toccoa, GA. Dr. Stanley and his wife, Anna, have two children, Andy and Rebecca.

T. G. (John) Sullivan

Dr. John Sullivan is pastor of the Broadmoor Baptist Church, where he has served since 1975.

He is a native of Ansted, West Virginia (b.—12-1-33). He accepted Christ as Savior at the Congress Heights Baptist Church of Washington, D.C., while in Washington working with the FBI. He was called to preach in the same church. He was licensed and ordained by the First Baptist Church of Cupertino, CA.

In June, 1955, he married Nancy Hinson of Jonesboro, AR. They have three children, John Michael, married to the former Jennifer Kennedy; Cheryl Ann, married to John Kirk Anderson; and Armena Jeanine who is a student at the University of Arkansas, Fayetteville.

Sullivan is a graduate of Ansted High School, Ansted, WV; Grand Canyon Baptist College (B.A. with double major in English literature and religion, 1961); and Southwestern Baptist Theological Seminary—B.D. (1963), M.Div. (1965), D.Min. (1973). He has done additional study at North Texas State University, Southwestern Baptist Theological Seminary Extended Education Program. He served as a grader for Dr. C. W. Scudder while in seminary; He is presently an adjunct professor for New Orleans Baptist Theological Seminary Center in Shreveport, LA.

His earlier pastorates have been Rainbow Valley Baptist Church, Buckeye, AZ (1958-1959), 27th Avenue Baptist Church, Phoenix, AZ (1959-1962), First Baptist Church, Aledo, TX (1962-1967), Ridglea West Baptist Church, Fort

Worth, TX (1967-1971), and First Baptist Church Sulphur Springs, TX (1971-1975).

Under Dr. Sullivan's leadership Broadmoor's average SS attendance has increased from 1,400 to 2,250. The budget has increased from $700,000 to $2,900,000. Mission giving has increased to over a million dollars, and many new social and spiritual ministries have been launched.

His denominational service on the state and national levels has been significant. He has served in the following capacities, among many others: Board of Trustees, Louisiana College; Executive Board, Louisiana Baptist Convention; Executive Board, Baptist General Convention of Texas; president of Louisiana Baptist Convention; executive director, Search Committee (Administrative Committee of the Executive Board) LBC; Executive Committee of SBC; Committee on Committees; Resolutions Committee; first vice-president of SBC (1983), Peace Committee; one of the parliamentarians, SBC (1986); SBC Legal Affairs Committee; and SBC National Task Force, Planned Growth in Giving.

He has preached or taught in thirty of the thirty-seven state conventions. He has conducted numerous revivals and has preached at Sunday School and Bible Preaching weeks at Ridgecrest and Glorieta a total of nine times. He has helped with seminars at the Baptist Sunday School Board (Shared Ministry).

Broadmoor has established the Broadmoor Chair of Discipleship at New Orleans Baptist Theological Seminary with an endowment of approximately $385,000. During Sullivan's ministry at Broadmoor twenty-five young people/adults have surrendered to full-time vocational ministry.

Broadmoor has averaged over one hundred baptisms per year since 1975. The church has established an extensive media ministry, including radio, network affiliate TV, and cable TV. The church has its own TV production studios and engages in spot announcements, billboards, and newspaper ads.

Daniel Vestal

Daniel Vestal was born in the home of a Southern Baptist evangelist in 1944. He graduated from Baylor University with a B.A. and an M.A. in religion, and then earned the M.Div. from Southwestern Baptist Theological Seminary, where he received the W. T. Conner award as the outstanding student in theology. In 1974 he received his Ph.D. from Southwestern with a major in philosophy of religion.

His pastorates have included the Meadow Lane Baptist Church, Arlington, Texas (1970-72), the Southcliff Baptist Church, Fort Worth, Texas (1972-76), and the First Baptist Church of Midland, Texas (1976 to the present). He is active in Southern Baptist life at the associational, state, and national level and is also very involved in the civic and community activities of Midland. His Sunday morning sermons are televised in much of West Texas, and more than 800 copies are printed for distribution and mailing each week.

Daniel and his wife, Earlene, have three children—Philip Thomas, Joel Keith, and Anne Elizabeth.

Jerry Vines

Since 1982 Dr. Vines has been pastor of First Baptist Church, Jacksonville, Florida. He has also served West Rome Baptist Church, Rome, Georgia, and Dauphin Way Baptist Church, Mobile, Alabama.

He is a native of Carrollton, Georgia. His wife is the former Janet Denney. They have four children: Mrs. Joy Williams, Jodi Vines, Jim Vines, and Jon Vines. He received his B.S. Degree from Mercer University, Macon, Georgia; the B.D. Degree from New Orleans Baptist Theological Seminary, New Orleans, Louisiana; and the Th.D. Degree from Luther Rice Seminary, Jacksonville, Florida.

He has authored several books: *Family Fellowship* (an exposition of 1 John); *God Speaks Today* (an exposition of 1 Corinthians); *Fire in the Pulpit; Interviews with Jesus; I Shall Return—Jesus; Great Events in the Life of Christ; A Practical Guide to Sermon Preparation;* and *Effective Guide to Sermon Delivery.*

David Walker

The thought of becoming a third-generation Baptist preacher never appealed to me during my high school years. I remembered with vividness the emergencies that cut short family outings and the long hours with limited pay that had marked my father's ministry.

My grandfather, Barney Walker, Sr., had also endured his share of rough times as a pastor and evangelist in rural Mississippi, and as a child, I had overheard occasional discussions between my father and grandfather dealing with various heartaches the ministry had brought their way.

I could not understand at that time how the call of God upon a life would provide vision enough to endure with resolve the hardships of the journey. What was foreign to me then, however, has in recent years become a cherished friend.

When the Fall of 1970 dawned, the preacher's son was a high-school senior, restless, frustrated, and hesitant about his future. The Spirit of God was moving steadily to disturb me, but for many weeks I was unable to recognize His voice. Eventually, tired of the battle and ready for a treaty, I began to open myself up to the probing of the Lord in a way I had never done before.

The Heavenly Father responded by raising up an awareness deep within my soul that there was a reason, a foreordained purpose for my life. There were not many things I could do with my life and please Him. There was only one: I must preach the Gospel of Jesus Christ.

Undergraduate preparation at Houston Baptist University followed the call; then came master's and doctoral work at Southwestern Seminary in Fort Worth. In the meantime, during the college and seminary years, God graciously allowed me to serve on the staffs of three wonderful churches whose influence remains in effect today. They are the Garden Oaks Baptist Church and the First Baptist Church, both of Houston, and the Sagamore Hill Baptist Church of Fort Worth.

Following the completion of a M.Div. degree from Southwestern, my wife, Shirley, and I moved in June 1978 to pastor the First Baptist Church of Hobart, a delightful little county seat town in Southwestern Oklahoma. No untried 24-year-old pastor and his new bride were ever trusted more or treated better than we were during those two brief years.

From Oklahoma we were led in 1980 back into Texas and to the San Jacinto Baptist Church in Amarillo, where we found a growing, warmhearted, aggressively evangelistic body of believers who taught us much about the joys of worship and the priority of personal soul-winning.

After four years in Amarillo, the Father shifted us from the Panhandle of Texas further south to San Antonio and the historic First Baptist Church of the Alamo City. It is here that we now are blessed to serve, and it is here we believe a great church is being built whose vision for discipleship and evangelism will someday encompass the globe.

Bill Weber

Dr. Bill Weber received the B.A. degree from Baylor University in 1964, the M.Div. degree from The Southwestern Baptist Theological Seminary in Fort Worth in 1967, and the honorary D.D. from Dallas Baptist University and Southwest Baptist University in Bolivar, Missouri.

Prior to founding and establishing Prestonwood Baptist Church in 1979, he pastored churches in Valley Mills, Mound, Alvarado, and Dallas, Texas.

Under his leadership, Prestonwood has grown to 7,200 members and over 10,000 Sunday School members. Prestonwood has been recognized as the fastest-growing Sunday School by the Baptist General Convention of Texas and the Southern Baptist Convention out of 34,000 churches for five years, 1981-1985. In 1984, Dr. Weber founded Discovery Broadcasting Network which broadcasts special programs live via satellite to over 160 churches across America.

He has served as moderator of the Dallas Baptist Association, a member of the nominating committee for the Executive Board of the Baptist General Convention of Texas and vice-president of the Pastors' Conference of the Southern Baptist Convention. He is presently on the Board of Trustees of Baylor University and Baylor Medical Center in Dallas.

Dr. Weber was selected one of the "Outstanding Young Men of America" in 1974, appeared in the 1978-79 edition of "Personalities of the South," and is the recipient of the Freedom Foundation Award of Excellence. He is the author of numerous articles and publications, including his book *Conquering the Kill-Joys: Positive Living in a Negative World.*

He is the son of the late well-known Baptist minister, Jaroy Weber, former president of the Southern Baptist Convention. He and his wife, Robin, have four children: Suzanne, Kathryn, Truett, and Jeannie.

Fred H. Wolfe

Fred H. Wolfe is a native of Rock Hill, South Carolina. He graduated from the University of South Carolina and received his M.Div. from Southwestern Seminary in 1967. He received an honorary doctorate from Mobile College in 1982. He has pastored Southern Baptist churches for the past twenty-nine years. Dr. Wolfe is pastor of the Cottage Hill Baptist Church in Mobile, Alabama, where he has pastored since 1972. This 8500-member church has been greatly used of God to reach the city of Mobile for Christ.

Dr. Wolfe has served on various committees and organizations of the Southern Baptist Convention and served as president of the Southern Baptist Pastors' Conference in

1983. Dr. Wolfe has held revivals and conferences in over forty states and a number of foreign countries. He is married to the former Patricia Anne Heath, and they have two sons, Mark and Jeffery.

H. Edwin Young

Dr. H. Edwin (Ed) Young is pastor of the Second Baptist Church, Houston, TX. A native of Laurel, MS, he was born on August 11, 1936.

He is married to the former Jo Beth Landrum, also of Laurel. She is a graduate of Blue Mountain College, Blue Mountain, MS, where she was listed in "Who's Who in American Colleges and Universities." The Youngs have three sons, Ed, Ben, and Cliff.

After attending the University of Alabama, Dr. Young earned a B.A. from Mississippi College in 1958 and a B.D. from Southwestern Baptist Theological Seminary in 1962. He was awarded a D.D. by Furman University in 1973.

On the Southern Baptist Convention level, he has served on the Peace Committee, on the Executive Committee, on the Sunday School Board, and on the Order of Business Committee. He has been president of the SBC Pastors' Conference and has addressed that conference several times. He has preached the annual Convention Sermon of the SBC twice. Dr. Young has spoken on *The Baptist Hour* and has also preached to many of the state conventions and evangelistic conferences across the SBC. He has preached at Ridgecrest and Glorieta Conference centers several times.

He has been a trustee of Southeastern Baptist Theological Seminary and of Houston Baptist University.

Before coming to Houston in 1979, he pastored First Baptist Church of Columbia, SC; First Baptist Church, Taylors, SC; First Baptist Church, Canton, NC; and First Baptist Church, Erwin, NC.

Among the books he has authored are: *The Lord Is...*, *A Winning Walk,* and *David: After God's Own Heart* (all Broadman).